THE DISCOURSE
OF CHARACTER EDUCATION

Culture Wars in the Classroom

THE DISCOURSE
OF CHARACTER EDUCATION

Culture Wars in the Classroom

Peter Smagorinsky
Joel Taxel
University of Georgia

LAWRENCE ERLBAUM ASSOCIATES, PUBLISHERS
2005   Mahwah, New Jersey   London

Lawrence Erlbaum Associates, Inc., Publishers
10 Industrial Avenue
Mahwah, New Jersey 07430
www.erlbaum.com

Cover design by Kathryn Houghtaling Lacey

Library of Congress Cataloging-in-Publication Data

Smagorinsky, Peter.
The discourse of character eduction : culture wars in the classroom / Peter Smagorinsky, Joel Taxel.
p. cm.
Includes bibliographical references and index.
ISBN 0-8058-5126-7 (cloth : alk. paper)
ISBN 0-8058-5127-5 (pbk. : alk. paper)
1. Moral education—Social aspects—United States. 2. Moral education—Curricula—United States. 3. Moral education—Government policy—United States. I. Taxel, Joel. II. Title.

LC311.S549 2005
370.11'4—dc22   2004056420
                                                      CIP

Books published by Lawrence Erlbaum Associates are printed on acid-free paper, and their bindings are chosen for strength and durability.

Printed in the United States of America
10 9 8 7 6 5 4 3 2 1

This book reports a study of proposals submitted to OERI for character education funding. We have taken direct quotes from that material, and cited some sources but have not provided references in order to protect the anonymity of the source.

Dedicated to our parents

Contents

Foreword   xi
    Nel Noddings

Preface   xv

Author Biographies   xix

PART I: FRAMEWORK FOR THE STUDY

1   Introduction to the Project   3

2   The Study   11

3   Historical Framework   19

4   The Current State of Affairs   33

5   Theoretical Framework   61

PART II: THE DISCOURSES OF CHARACTER EDUCATION

6   Discourses Shared in Both Regions   73

7   Discourses in Proposals From the Deep South   89

8   Discourses in Proposals From the Upper Midwest   103

9   Discourses of the OERI Request for Proposals   125
          Appendix   *135*

**PART III: THE DEEP SOUTH: DIDACTIC,
INDIVIDUALISTIC, AUTHORITARIAN APPROACHES
TO CHARACTER EDUCATION**

10   Cultural Context of the Deep South   149
          Appendix   *161*

11   Ancillary Curricula of the Deep South   167
          Appendix   *179*

12   The Discourses of the Deep South's Conception   189
          of Character Education
          Appendix   *202*

13   The Deep South's Character Curriculum   207
          and Assessment of Character Growth

**PART IV: THE UPPER MIDWEST: COMMUNITY-BASED,
REFLECTIVE APPROACHES
TO CHARACTER EDUCATION**

14   Cultural Context of the Upper Midwest   245

15   Ancillary Curricula of the Upper Midwest   259

16   The Discourses of the Upper Midwest's Conception   269
          of Character Education

17   The Upper Midwest's Character Curriculum   295
          and Assessment of Character Growth
          Appendix   308

PART V: CONCLUSION

18 Discussion 313

19 Toward a Reconsideration of the Character Curriculum 343

References 361

Author Index 381

Subject Index 387

"What the world today needs is character," says Vivekānanda. A man without character is like a wild bull let loose in a cornfield. Every fool may become a hero at one time or another, but the people of good character are heroes all the time. Establishing good character means acquiring established wisdom (pratishthita prajna). Nothing great can be achieved in life without a good character.

—Hindu Dharma

Foreword

Moral education has always been a basic function of education. In the past two decades, however, *character education* has become almost synonymous with moral education, and the growing emphasis on the direct instruction of virtues has eclipsed other valuable approaches to moral education. Kohlbergian cognitive developmentalism, caring, and values clarification all have important contributions to make to moral education.

Smagorinsky and Taxel draw our attention to the strongly conservative nature of the program advocated by the federal government. One need not condemn the entire enterprise out of hand. Even liberals can find points to praise, and we should work together to do the best possible job for our children. However, the authors of this book are right to question the language and assumptions in the federal call for proposals on moral education.

The stated assumption that six core values—trustworthiness, respect, responsibility, fairness, caring, and citizenship—*transcend cultural, religious,* and *socioeconomic differences* is highly questionable. Even if the labels were universal (and this is doubtful), every one of these values is subject to interpretation through various cultural and religious frameworks. *Citizenship,* for example, is notoriously difficult to define even at the national level. Those of us working on the concept and practice of global citizenship recognize that our project faces huge difficulties. This is not a reason for abandoning efforts to improve the teaching of citizenship, but it is a reason for educating in a way that encourages critical thinking, a tolerance for ambiguity, understanding of complexity, and openness to views that may collide with our own. It suggests, also, the rejection of dogmatic methods.

Smagorinsky and Taxel show convincingly that moral language differs across cultural/regional settings. Readers will not be surprised to learn that the language used by educators in the Deep South is more consonant with federal language than is that of educators in the upper Midwest, but both are heavily influenced by the federal language, a language that ignores the need for analysis and interpretation.

Consider the juxtaposition of precepts such as "respect authority" and "protect the environment." Suppose the "authorities" advocate policies that are demonstrably harmful to the environment. How should one's respect be shown to those authorities? I am not arguing that respect should be entirely withdrawn in such circumstances. Rather, I'm arguing that students need to learn how to think, criticize, evaluate, and argue for the commitments they can defend. Respect for authority does not preclude questioning it. The language of the Office of Educational Research and Improvement (OERI) suggests a blind obedience that its authors might not intend.

We might well question, too, the close linking of character education to academic achievement. Must a good person meet all of the standards specified by federal and state agencies? Why? What makes this "good"? Take, for example, the problematic advice given under *responsibility:* "Always do your best." Why in the world would anyone follow this very bad advice? It is a sure road to mediocrity, and yet teachers all over the country are advising children as early as first grade to do their "best in everything." At the same time, schools begin to grade children's work. What happens to a child who does his or her best for 4 years and regularly gets C's or worse? Small wonder that so many children are turned off by school somewhere between fourth and sixth grades. This situation is an example of the complexity too often ignored by character educators. I have long advised my graduate students to do an adequate job on all we force upon them but to save their best for the subjects and problems about which they are passionate. Do your best in *something,* not in everything.

Readers of this book need not agree with me or with the books' authors on specific point such as the aforementioned one to recognize that a genuinely moral education requires attention to complexity, subtlety, and ambiguity. We should present traditional virtues for analysis and discussion. Even young children can understand that meanness and cruelty sometimes masquerade as honesty. Older children should be invited to analyze all of the virtues and see how they are interpreted by different people in different situations.

In the previous paragraph, I alluded to a "genuinely moral education." John Dewey gave us important advice on this. He reminded us that there are two meanings of *moral education.* By one, we refer to an educational effort to produce moral people. That is what character educators are trying to do. By the other, we refer to a program of education that is itself morally defensible. If we focus on the latter, we may feel ill at ease with the character education movement. Is there something wrong with our kids, as many character educators claim? Or is there something fundamentally wrong with the system of present schooling? How can we morally justify a system of schooling that pits child against child, teacher against teacher, and school against school, one that penalizes those who can't quite make it although they may be doing their "best"? How do we reconcile such a system with the teaching of trustworthiness, respect, responsibility, and caring?

Smagorinsky and Taxel have done a real service in conducting and reporting this study. It will surely encourage readers to think about what we are doing to our children and, perhaps, to seek a better, morally defensible way to educate.

—Nel Noddings

Preface

Recent dramatic instances of school violence have fueled the perception that American youth are suffering from a crisis of character. This perception has helped motivate efforts to improve the ethics of students and make schools safer, healthier sites for learning. Generally falling under the label of *character education*, these initiatives are designed to create, in the words of one state Department of Education document, "a school environment where civic virtues are expected, modeled, taught, celebrated, and continually practiced."

In response to the perceived need for schools to address problems with students' character, the U.S. Department of Education's Office of Educational Research and Improvement (OERI) funded character initiatives in the latter half of the 1990s. In this book we analyze how character education is grounded, framed, implemented, and assessed, focusing on the discourse of the proposals submitted to OERI for character education funding. By *discourse* we mean the ways in which language embodies a way of being in the world, particularly a political and ideological way that implies a world view. We found that in proposals submitted to OERI, proposals fell along a continuum that suggests two distinct conceptions of character and character education. At one end of the continuum is a view of character that we characterize as orthodox or conservative, and most clearly articulated by two adjacent states from the Deep South. At the other end is a perspective best described as progressive or liberal, and central to the conception of two adjacent states from the Upper Midwest.

Our study identifies the ways in which the concept of character is culturally constructed, emerging from the belief systems historically developed in communities of practice. In making this claim we contest the doctrine that character consists of a set of culture-free, universal traits and dispositions.

The discourses presently employed to discuss character education are a continuation of discourse streams through which character education and the national purpose have been debated for hundreds of years, most recently in what are known as the *Culture Wars*. By focusing on these two distinct regions and their conceptions of character, we situate the character education movement at the turn of the twenty-first century in the context of historical notions about the nature of character and regional conceptions regarding the nature of societal organization. We also place the documents from particular states in dialogue with the OERI Request for Proposals, which we find to be infused with a conservative ideology that states must accommodate regardless of the conception of character that they propose.

Our study sought to answer the following research questions:

1. Discourse: In what ways are the curricula in dialogue with the call for proposals? More broadly, in what discourses are the curricula situated? Within these discourses, what assumptions are embedded? Within these assumptions, on what issues are the proposals silent?
2. Curriculum: What does the educational program look like? What is their conception of character? What is the rationale for a character education curriculum? What tensions or conflicts are exhibited in the curricula?
3. Assessment: What are the anticipated effects of the program? How do the programs determine that character has been educated or that other program goals have been achieved?

OVERVIEW

The book is organized into five parts. Part I includes five chapters that introduce the project. We begin by introducing ourselves and our interest in character education. We then describe, in chapter 2, how we went about our study of the OERI-funded character education proposals. Chapters 3, 4, and 5 frame the study, first in terms of the history of character education in the U.S., then in terms of the current perceived crisis, and finally by articulating the theories that inform our understanding of character education.

Part II is comprised of four chapters, each centered on elaborating the various discourses that we found in the proposals and illustrated with examples from a variety of sources in U.S. society. Chapter 6 defines and illustrates the discourses found in the proposals from both the Deep South and Upper Midwest. Chapter 7 focuses on those discourses exhibited only in the proposals from the Deep South. Chapter 8 attends to the discourses exclusively from the Upper Midwest. Chapter 9 looks at the OERI Request for Proposals to identify its ideological basis as revealed through the discourses that it incorporates.

Part III focuses on the discourses of the Deep South. We begin in chapter 10 by providing what we understand to be the cultural context of these two states and the region that they represent. In the chapter 11 we identify the ancillary curricula that these states drew on to generate their character curriculum. We then identify, in chapter 12, the discourses of the proposals from the states in the Deep South. In chapter 13 we examine the curriculum itself and the assessments used to determine the extent to which character has been educated.

Part IV has a four-chapter structure parallel to that of Part III, with a focus this time on the Upper Midwest. Again, we first identify the cultural context of the region (chapter 14), then review the ancillary curricula drawn on to inform their work (chapter 15), next review the discourses of the proposals from this region (chapter 16), and finally examine the curriculum and assessments from these two states (chapter 17).

Part V concludes the study with two chapters. Chapter 18 is a discussion emerging from the analysis, chapter 19 a more personal chapter in which we outline issues that we find important in the development of a character curriculum.

ACKNOWLEDGMENTS

A project of this scope is not possible without considerable help. We wish to thank all of the states that provided us with their character education documents, including those that we do not profile in this study; our reading of all of the material we received helped us to think about the questions we explore in our analysis. Thanks, of course, to Naomi Silverman and Erica Kica at Lawrence Erlbaum Associates, who guided this manuscript through review and on to publication. Thanks as well to everyone at Erlbaum involved with the review and production process. The book benefited greatly from critical readings provided by Jane Farrell, John Hoge, Nel Noddings, and Michelle Zoss. We thank them for taking time from their busy schedules to help us shape up the manuscript prior to publication. Finally, thanks to our families for allowing us the time to work on this project.

This book reports a study of proposals submitted to OERI for character education funding. We have taken direct quotes from that material but have not provided references in order to protect the anonymity of the source.

> *I believe that education is the ultimate poverty eradication tool of the 21st century. If we believe in our youth and their future, we have to give them something more than our love and best wishes. We must provide them with the information and knowledge they need to prepare for the economic realities of personal finance. Being poor is a state of mind.... [Operation HOPE's Banking on Our Future] is not just about dollars and cents. It's about building hope, character and belief in oneself, from the perspective of something we all understand and relate to: money!*
>
> *—John Bryant*

Author Biographies

Peter Smagorinsky is professor of English Education at The University of Georgia. He taught high school English in the Chicago area from 1976 to 1990 while earning his MAT and PhD from the University of Chicago. He has served as coeditor of *Research in the Teaching of English,* trustee and chair of the Research Foundation of the National Council of Teachers of English (NCTE), president of the National Conference on Research in Language and Literacy, cochair of NCTE's Assembly for Research, chair of NCTE's Research Forum, and chair of NCTE's Standing Committee on Research. Awards and distinctions include the Steve Cahir Award for Research on Writing from the Writing SIG of the American Educational Research Association (AERA), The Edwin M. Hopkins *English Journal* Award from NCTE, the Janet Emig Award from NCTE's Conference on English Education, and, in 1999, the Raymond B. Cattell Early Career Award for Programmatic Research presented by AERA to the scholar who has conducted the most distinguished program of cumulative educational research in any field of educational inquiry within the first decade following receipt of his or her doctoral degree.

Joel Taxel is Professor and Department Head of the Department of Language and Literacy Education at the University of Georgia. He taught elementary school in Brooklyn, New York, before receiving his PhD from the Department of Curriculum and Instruction at the University of Wisconsin, Madison. The focus of Joel's scholarship has been on the sociocultural, political, and economic dimensions of children's literature. His articles have appeared in such journals as *Curriculum Inquiry, Interchange,* and

Teachers College Record. His most recent article, "Children's literature at the turn of the century: Toward a political economy of the publishing industry," appeared in the November 2002 issue of *Research in the Teaching of English*. He was founding editor of *The New Advocate*, a journal devoted to the discussion of issues related to the writing, publication, and teaching of children's literature.

PART I

INTRODUCTION
TO FRAMEWORK FOR THE STUDY

In this part of the book, we introduce the study and review the key constructs that inform our thinking about character education. In chapter 1 we introduce ourselves and our interest in the topic of character education. Chapter 2 then presents the purpose of our study and explains how we conducted it. In brief, we became interested in the national character education movement when our own state began seeking federal funds to begin pilot programs. We then requested the character education initiatives from a variety of states and became intrigued by the ways in which both character and character education were construed. Our readings of the proposals for character education funding yielded a number of questions, which we refined and consolidated into questions that inquired into (1) the discourses and attendant ideologies through which character education is proposed, (2) the content and process of character education, and (3) the ways in which the interventions are assessed.

We then introduce the study in three chapters. First, we provide a historical overview of character education in the United States Next, we review the current state of character education, particularly with respect to how character education is constructed by various stakeholders and which assumptions undergird each perspective. Finally, we review the theoretical approach we take to our project, particularly with respect to the notion of discourse and its ideological nature.

> *Character builds slowly, but it can be torn down with incredible swiftness.*
> *—Faith Baldwin*

1

Introduction to the Project

This project began in part to extend a friendship that began in 1998 when we became colleagues at The University of Georgia. Our many conversations since then—about character education and much else—have helped clarify who we are and why we believe and act as we do. We hope that our work on this study has contributed to our understanding of how to be better people in our relationships with others and to be the kind of citizen a nation needs to keep a democratic society vital.

Our friendship undoubtedly has both a personal and cultural basis. Both of us are in our fifties, born at the beginning of the post-World War II baby boom to parents who grew up in New York City. Both of us claim a Jewish heritage, Joel through both parents and Peter through his father's family (Peter's mother comes from a German-Irish Catholic family). Our Jewish ancestors originate in Eastern Europe, where the pogroms—government-supported massacres of Jews—and conscription into the Russian army forced their families' immigration to the United States. Similarly, on Peter's mother's side, immigration was forced by the Irish potato famine of 1845 to 1850, which many current Irish historians now regard as both an act of nature and an act of genocide, given that food exports from Ireland actually increased for Protestant merchants during the great famine (e.g., Metress & Rajner, 1996). We recount this heritage not to begin by claiming status as victims, but because we are proud of these heritages and the courage and perseverance it took to escape from these hostile circumstances. We imagine that our forebears would fare well in just about any conception of good character, having maintained their beliefs and families despite vigorous efforts to suppress and eradicate them and having overcome tremendous obstacles to emigrate to a nation that provided them with new opportunities

3

for freedom of expression and belief and opportunities to provide good lives for their children.

For this reason and others, we are also proud to be U.S. citizens. We have often tried to imagine the experience of our grandparents and their families escaping their desperate circumstances, traveling across Europe with all their belongings in their hands and finally arriving at the seaports and doing what was necessary to board the ships heading west to the United States. These boats were crammed with other refugees seeking a better, more secure life. We wonder what it must have been to have finally seen, at the end of an arduous journey across the Atlantic, the Statue of Liberty slowly appear on the horizon as they approached New York City. What a magnificent sight that must have been! But the trip was not yet over. They had to endure the uncertainty of the immigration inspection, which could reject them for any number of reasons. Finally, however, they were admitted and, along with the other fortunate refugees, they dispersed to try to find and be reunited with their families in this strange foreign city, a different world altogether from the rural villages in which they had always lived.

Our pride in this heritage—both of our families and of the nation that took them in—acknowledges our disagreements with many of our fellow citizens on the purpose, substance, and structure of U.S. life. This sense of pride also recognizes that the people of our country, both those who share and those who oppose our perspective, have often fallen short of our nation's ideals, articulated in our Declaration of Independence and codified in our Constitution and Bill of Rights. We have disagreed with U.S. foreign and domestic policy on more than a few occasions and have engaged in critiques of our leaders. We view this dissent more as an objection to the political agendas and policies of politicians and opinion leaders than as a rejection of the fundamentals of the political system that insures our right to hold dissident views and speak them in public and, should we choose, run for office and replace those with whom we disagree. We are well aware that this cherished freedom has been defended on many occasions through military power. For their sacrifices—including those made by members of our families—we are grateful, even if we have not supported every cause for which our military has been called to action.

Like many urban immigrants and have-nots during the 1930s and 1940s, our parents became FDR New Dealers, an influence that we acknowledge has shaped our views of U.S. society and provided the common value system that has contributed to our friendship. Roosevelt still serves as the lightning rod for the disputes we review in our study of character education: hero to the marginalized working class for whom he provided opportunities for work by expanding government (e.g., Freidel, 1990), defender of the status quo to those on the left who view with suspicion the New Deal's preservation of capitalism during its greatest crisis (e.g., Davis, 1986), and scourge to those who believe that he undermined the United States' competitive capitalist economy and society through a more interventionist approach to governance (e.g., Powell, 2003). As members now of the relatively comfortable middle class, we see merit in contributing some of our resources to the national financial pool to provide the opportunities that enabled our own families to succeed, even if we are often horrified by some expenditures of our taxed income.

Roosevelt's introduction of the income tax to address the Great Depression remains a topic of debate today, serving as the great equalizer to those for whom taxation provides services and opportunities and as the slippery slope to socialism to those whose incomes are taxed most heavily to provide the social safety net that mitigates the extremes of business cycles. We see ourselves as products of our families' value systems and origins in the bottom rungs of the U.S. social ladder as immigrant urban Jews and Catholics. In that regard, we are in full agreement with those who argue that culture is transmitted from generation to generation, if not wholly and without alteration.

We are both also parents, each with two children and Joel with a stepson as well. In our role as husbands and parents we have faced issues of character development up close and personal. Our interest in this topic is hardly incidental. As parents we have sought to instill values in our children, values that often need negotiation with our wives. We have no illusions about our motives in doing so. We want our kids to become good people, or at least good people as we understand humanity. We hope that they adopt what we consider to be our better qualities, just as we have ended up embracing many if not all values of our own parents.

Yet in our reading about character education, we have come across criticisms of people like ourselves (i.e., political progressives) that presume that we have no interest in raising our children to share our values. By *progressive*, a term we use throughout this book to describe people of a generally liberal political orientation, we mean that we have a fundamental dedication to democracy, peace, social justice, civil rights, civil liberties, and environmental awareness. *Progressive* magazine, founded by Robert La Follett in 1909, defines its mission as striving "to put forward ideas that will help bring about a more just society and a more peaceful, humane world" (http://www.progressive.org/history.html). We recognize that these values must be compromised during extraordinary circumstances. We both, for instance, supported the retaliatory strikes against the Taliban following the September 11, 2001 attack on the World Trade Center and Pentagon, if not the subsequent unprovoked invasion of Iraq.

Conservative critics have, we believe, often misrepresented the views of progressives as a way to justify their own beliefs. We have read, for instance, that progressives or liberals want to cut the moral umbilical cord between parents and children so that morals can be constructed anew by each generation. We see this caricature of beliefs as extremely destructive in the national effort to educate for character, or for anything else for that matter. Like just about every parent we know across the political spectrum, we hope that our kids turn out okay (as we define it), all the while assuming that our kids will modify some of values that we have tried to impress upon them as they engage with the world on their own terms.

Although we see parental influence on children as being inevitable and within each parent's prerogative, we consider some parental transmission of values to be, at the very least, problematic. For many generations, for instance, racism has been transmitted from parents to children throughout the United States. Bringing up young children in an environment of hatred cannot possibly sustain healthy, moral civilizations. Although we seek to avoid making negative judgments about people whose values depart from ours, we are quite certain that value systems built on hatred violate what we understand to be principles of morality. We are especially grieved that so much conflict bred from hatred emanates from faith communities, which many people assert provide the origins for all moral thinking. We are certainly sensitive on this issue given the ways in which our ancestors were persecuted throughout Europe, both before and after the rise of Hitler and throughout much of the history of Ireland. Yet this accumulated cultural experience, accompanied by the New Deal's institutional compassion for ordinary people, has helped shape our perspective on human relationships, economics, and society.

Readers should not be surprised to learn that we are both registered Democrats and hold what most would regard as generally progressive or liberal views, although not always in accord with one another's or the policies of the Democratic party and its office holders. Our publications and presentations on the topic of character education have argued in favor of what we later characterize as a progressive or liberal orientation (e.g., Smagorinsky, 1999, 2000, 2001a, 2002a, 2002b, 2004; Smagorinsky & Taxel, 2002a, 2002b), and other publications have critiqued society from a progressive perspective (e.g., Taxel, 1997, 2002). It would be disingenuous for us to present our study as an impartial analysis of character education when we are well aware that we embrace certain positions and question others. Our biases aside, we have tried to present both conservative and liberal approaches to character education as faithfully as we can, and have used conservative critiques of liberal education as a way to sharpen our thinking on these issues.

Our study profiles character education initiatives from two distinct regions of the United States, the Upper Midwest and the Deep South. Perhaps some readers might find us guilty of regional bias in our presentation. Yet both of us have lived in the two parts of the country that we profile and have found much to appreciate in each. Joel earned his PhD at the University of Wisconsin-Madison, studying there from 1972 to 1979, and has lived in Georgia since 1980. Peter grew up in Virginia, where he lived for 15 years; lived in the Chicago area from 1976 to 1990; and has lived south of the Mason-Dixon line since 1990, first in Oklahoma (which allowed slavery as a territory and enforced racial segregation until the 1960s) and since 1998 in Georgia. Our experiences of living in these distinct regions ring true with the accounts of regional culture we provide to contextualize the character education programs. Although we acknowledge that we personally prefer the perspective offered in the Upper Midwest to that of the Deep South, we should stress that we are not trying to make value judgments about the qualities of the people in either region. Rather, we are attempting to situate different perspectives on character education in local history, culture, and ideology.

Our outline of our backgrounds and biases is designed to contextualize our presentation. As we will argue, situating any social issue in its cultural context helps to understand how it came to be and how it is socially sustained. We will call on our readers to decide how well we have done our job.

ORGANIZATION FOR OUR STUDY

We have organized our presentation into five parts. First, we introduce the study. This introductory section includes four chapters. We begin by stating the problem that motivates and focuses our inquiry, and by outlining our method of investigation. Simply stated, we have analyzed proposals submitted to the U.S. Office of Educational Research and Improvement (OERI) for character education funding. From these proposals we identify two regions that provide consistent conceptions of character and character education that sit on opposite ends of a philosophical continuum, and describe

---

Ten Commandments: Take a stand for moral character

Cherokee County should be commended for taking a stand on the Ten Commandments issue. All other counties in the country should follow suit. This isn't about the separation of church and state; it's about the constant degradation of the moral character of our society. The argument over separation of church and state would be no argument at all if liberals realized what our Founding Fathers meant: It wasn't that the government should never speak of God or any religion; it was that the church, of whatever religion, should not be the government.

—Ryan Gunnin, Fayetteville, GA, letter to the Atlanta Journal-Constitution

them in detail. This analysis and presentation are designed to highlight the ideological nature of any conception of character and to locate the origins of any belief system in cultural practice. We next review the history of character education in the United States as a way to establish that the character education movement, while justified with great urgency, represents a recurring pattern of concern that has persistently affected the European American society established on this continent. We then outline the terms of the debate as currently enacted in the United States, situating the present movement historically and identifying its main terms. Finally, we review the theoretical approach that we take to our analysis, focusing in particular on the ways in which discourse is ideological and a part of historical streams of belief about the nature of human relationships and economy.

In the second part of the book, we review in general terms the discourses of character education. First, we outline discourses shared in each of the two regions that we profile, the Upper Midwest and the Deep South. At this point in the presentation, we illustrate how these discourses are employed in broader discussions about character and other aspects of what are known as the Culture Wars—that is, a disagreement over the purpose and process of U.S. society, generally conducted in liberal or conservative terms. We then review the discourses specific to the Deep South, again giving examples of how this discourse is part of an intertext of ideas that tends to adopt a conservative or orthodox view of the structure and process of U.S. society. Following this review, we provide a similar account of the discourses specific to the proposals submitted by states from the Upper Midwest, again situating it in an ideological perspective on U.S. society, this time from a more liberal or progressive perspective. Finally, we look at the OERI Request for Proposals (RFP) itself and see how it was developed, who contributed to its vision, and how its ideology affected the conceptions of character embedded in the different states' proposals for character education.

In the third part of the book, we focus on the proposals from the Deep South. We again divide this section into four chapters. First, we provide the cultural context of the region itself, identifying cultural values and practices that we believe informed the conception of character included in the proposal for character education funding. Following this effort to situate the character education movement, we review the ancillary curricula that the proposals identify as informing and abetting their character education effort. These ancillary curricula, we find, provide both an ideology and a set of practices that shape the notion of character emphasized by these states. We then identify the discourses that run throughout the proposals, including both those shared in both profiles and those specific to the Deep South. Finally, we analyze the actual character curriculum and how character development will be assessed to evaluate the effects of the program.

The fourth part of the book has a parallel structure to that of the third, focusing instead on the proposals from the Upper Midwest. In similar fashion, here we review the cultural context of the region, the ancillary curricula drawn on by these two states, the discourses common to both regions and specific to this one, and the curriculum and assessments used to teach and evaluate character development.

The fifth part of the book includes two chapters. In the first we discuss our study and draw conclusions about the current character education movement as revealed through proposals to OERI for funding. Here we both review our findings and extend them to broader considerations of education and ideology. Finally, we try to rethink how character education might be redefined and re-envisioned, drawing both on our analysis and on our other experiences as educators to inform out consideration.

We hope that our project enlightens those who find these topics important and interesting. We have surely learned a great deal ourselves from our inquiry.

Trials, temptations, disappointments—all these help instead of hinder, if one uses them rightly. They not only test the fiber of a character, but strengthen it. Every conquered temptation represents a new fund of moral energy. Every trial endured and weathered in the right spirit makes a soul nobler and stronger than it was before.

—James Buckham

Chapter 2

The Study

I think we ought to have character education in our schools. I know that doesn't directly talk about Hollywood, but it does reinforce the values you're teaching. Greatly expand character education funding so that public schools will teach children values, values which have stood the test of time.

—George W. Bush (2000)

Presidential candidate George W. Bush offered this view during the third debate of the 2000 presidential campaign (Commission on Presidential Debates Transcripts, 2000). Bush's belief in the need for character education is based not only on the perceived immorality of Hollywood but on what he and many contend to be problems throughout U.S. society. Indeed, his remarks echo ideas expressed in President Bill Clinton's 1996 State of the Union address when he said, "I challenge all our schools to teach character education, to teach good values and good citizenship."

Those who believe in the need for character education typically recite a litany of vices committed by today's youth to justify the intervention. In a survey released during the 2000 presidential campaign, the Josephson Institute of Ethics (2000) described "shocking levels of moral illiteracy" and "a hole in the moral ozone." Institute director Michael Josephson added: "Being sure children can read is certainly essential, but it is no less important that we deal with the alarming rate of cheating, lying and violence that threatens the very fabric of our society." His nationwide survey of 8,600 high school students revealed that 71% of all high school students admitted they had cheated on an exam at least once in the past 12 months, 92% lied to their parents in the past 12 months, 78% lied to a teacher, 27% said they would lie to get a job, 40% of males and 30% of females said they had stolen something from a store in the past 12 months, 16% said they had been drunk in school during the past year, 68% said they had hit someone because they were angry in the past year, and 47% said they could get a gun if they wanted to.

The findings by the Josephson Institute and the belief that character education can be a curricular remedy are part of a recent, although not historically unique, movement for using schools as an instrument of moral improvement. On February 12, 1998, the U.S. Senate instituted Character Week, a dedication that we traced in the Congressional Record to the Aspen Declaration of 1992 at a conference hosted by the Josephson Institute of Ethics. The interest in the U.S. Congress in character education has resulted in federal funding initiatives through the Office of Educational Research and Improvement (OERI), with awards going to 3 states in 1995, 4 states in 1996, 4 states in 1997, 10 states in 1998, and 9 states in 1999, with awards of up to $375,000 though typically about $250,000 per year.

In this book we analyze the current character education movement as revealed through the discourses found in proposals submitted to OERI to fund character curricula. We elaborate our understanding of *discourse* in chapter 5. For the present, we will briefly define it as the ways in which language embodies a way of being in the world, particularly a political and ideological way that implies a world view. Although language is typically the focus of studies of discourse, it includes a whole range of symbols, both those constructed (e. g., the images on Web sites) and those enacted (e. g., body positioning and adornment) through which an ideology is represented.

We focus in particular on discourses that suggest two distinct conceptions of character and character education, one articulated by two states from the Deep South and one by two states from the Upper Midwest. Our study suggests the ways in which the concept of character is culturally constructed, emerging from the belief systems historically developed in communities of practice. Furthermore, the discourses presently employed to discuss character education are a continuation of rhetoric through which character education and the national purpose have been debated for hundreds of years. By focusing on these two distinct regions and their conceptions of character, we hope to place the character education movement at the turn of the twenty-first century in the context of historical notions about the nature of character and regional conceptions regarding the nature of societal organization.

Fame is a vapor, popularity an accident, riches take wing, and only character endures.

—*Horace Greeley*

METHOD

Our general method is based on the notion of the *relational analysis of schooling and culture*. This approach derives from the belief that cultural phenomena are the products of economic, political, and cultural conflicts; to treat people or cultural institutions "as isolated objects of study is also to risk tearing them out of the fabric of history" (Apple, 1986, p. 5). In calling for a critical sociology of cultural forms, Apple and Wexler (1978) emphasize the need to analyze such texts as novels, films, magazines, and curricula in terms of their connections to specific societies and the socioeconomic configurations to which they are linked. Our analysis of character education programs thus situates each initiative in a general discourse stream and within the local contexts in which it was developed.

Apple (1986) notes the inherently political nature of schooling. From his perspective, schools and the culture at large are best understood when examined in relation to the particular social, historical, political, and economic conditions that shape, define, and sustain them. These conditions contribute to the ideologies of both participants and observers of social action and thus help to produce the discourses through which arguments about education are carried out. Gee (1990) argues that discourse is ideological and thus by nature imbued with political power and intent. When tacit, he argues, ideologies are "the root of human evil and leave us complicit with, and thus responsible for, the evil that is in the world" (p. 24). He finds discourse analysis to be a moral enterprise because it endeavors to explicate tacit and removed or deferred theories and ideologies. Our study uses a form of discourse analysis to characterize the discourse of character education as revealed through a study of a sample of OERI-funded proposals for character education curricula.

Data Collection

We wrote to the state department of education of each state that had received an OERI grant for a character education curriculum, requesting documents that described its curriculum. Of the 31 states receiving funding at the time of our request, 11 provided documents. Of these 11, 8 provided detailed information about their programs (including the proposal submitted to OERI) whereas three provided only brief pamphlets and/or fliers. In addition, we read Web site descriptions of five other OERI-funded state ini-

Americanism is a question of principle, of purpose, of idealism, of character. It is not a matter of birthplace or creed or line of descent.

—Theodore Roosevelt

> *To arrive at a just estimate of a renowned man's character one must judge it by the standards of his time, not ours.*
>
> —*Mark Twain*

tiatives. For the remaining funded state curricula, we were unable to get access to program descriptions.

Data Analysis

Question Generation. Following principles of the constant comparative method (Glaser & Strauss, 1967), we read the documents several times in order to generate our analytic questions. Initially, we read each set of documents provided by each state independently, using weekly meetings to discuss our impressions and begin generating questions. During this initial reading, for instance, we noted that many documents opened with some kind of declaration of youth depravity, citing figures on increases in teen violence, pregnancy, and drug use, much like those with which we open this volume. Our informal characterization of this rhetorical approach was that they provided a rationale based on alarms about sex, drugs, and violence. From this observation, we became interested in the kinds of discourses in which each proposal was couched. Ultimately, we generated the research question, "In which discourses is the document situated?" This question addressed both issues raised in the documents themselves and our own mutual interests in discourse, authority, ideology, and the social construction of reality which we have explored in other projects (see, e.g., Smagorinsky, 1995a, 2001a; Taxel, 1981, 2002).

In this initial reading we developed a set of analytic questions that included:

- What is the rationale for character education (e.g., sex, drugs, and violence)?
- What are described as the root causes of problem (e.g., the Sixties)?
- What are the anticipated effects of a character education initiative (e.g., safe schools, orderly classrooms, virtuous citizens)?
- What values do the curricula promote (e.g., respect, justice)?
- What is the source of those values (e.g., community consensus, objective criteria of virtue)?
- What assumptions about teaching and learning are behind the curricula (e.g., didactic instruction will change students' character, students answer honestly to surveys about at-risk behavior)?
- Whose character is at stake (e.g., students, school community members, larger community members)?

- How is character education implemented in the curriculum (e.g., integrated in coursework)?
- How is the program tied to other initiatives (e.g., government programs, private foundations, local initiatives, etc.)?
- How is the program's effectiveness assessed (e.g., reduced disciplinary referrals, better grades, etc.) and how are claims substantiated? (e.g., testimony, statistics, etc.)?

In using this framework to analyze the documents, in subsequent readings we refined these questions to interrogate what ultimately became the focus of the study:

1. *Discourse:* In what ways are the curricula in dialogue with the call for proposals? More broadly, in what discourses are the curricula situated? Within these discourses, what assumptions are embedded? Within these assumptions, on what issues are the proposals silent?
2. *Curriculum:* What does the educational program look like? What is their conception of character? What is the rationale for a character education curriculum? What tensions or conflicts are exhibited in the curricula?
3. *Assessment:* What are the anticipated effects of the program? How do the programs determine that character has been educated or that other program goals have been achieved?

Our continued rereading of the proposals according to these questions led us to recognize a continuum of beliefs about character and character education across the initiatives. Based on this recognition, we selected curricula that clearly articulated different conceptions of character and character education and decided to use them as the basis of the profiles that we present in this study. In Parts III and IV of this book, we describe these profiles and how they are revealed through the discourses in which they are embedded.

Discourse Analysis.   With our research questions developed and refined, we then needed to find a systematic way of coding the documents to reveal what was both explicit and tacit within them. Our research questions

---

Our people even answer the phones, "Thank you for calling Tom Gill Chevrolet, a business of character."

—Tom Gill, owner of Tom Gill Chevrolet and Tom Gill MotorSports Plus, Florence, Ohio.

suggested one level of coding, that being our three categories of analysis: *discourse, curriculum,* and *assessment.* Often, these were identifiable by the area of the proposal in which they fell. The opening rationale typically revealed the discourse of the proposal, although this discourse in turn provided the ideology for the curriculum and means of assessment. The curriculum and means of assessment were often made explicit by subject headers in the proposals.

The more interpretive part of the analysis came in classifying discourse. Our approach was to read the documents together and discuss what was implied by the authors' declarations about the nature of character and of character education. For example, one state document specified the following groups as being particularly in need of character education: those of low-income status or below poverty guidelines, juvenile offenders, groups with high infant mortality, those with high teen-birth rates, groups frequently charged with child abuse, those in economic distress, those exhibiting behavior problems, groups receiving free and reduced lunches, recipients of Title 1 funding, those with problems managing their anger and controlling their behavior, those who lack social and behavior skills, people who are geographically and socially isolated, people with limited English proficiency or speakers of "broken" English, the unemployed, recipients of food stamps, inhabitants of rural areas, those scoring below the state average on the Iowa Test of Basic Skills, speakers of the Cherokee language, minority students, students who are unsupervised after school, students with records of violence, students from single-parent homes, students who are sexually active, and students from undereducated homes. We inferred from this list of at-risk students that the proposal authors believed that those most in need of character education were largely poor students from uneducated families in which standard English is not spoken at home. These young people, according to the proposals, tend to be sexually active, have histories of violence, abuse drugs, and have absentee parents. We further inferred that the document authors assumed that people not fitting these categories were not particularly in need of character education. We then classified this discourse as being in the category of class-based morality.

Classification of Proposals. Based on this analysis, we found that the proposals fell along a continuum. At one end were proposals with the following traits:

• Character is located within the individual.

What a man's mind can create, man's character can control.

—*Thomas Edison*

- *Character* can be defined according to a set of stable, universal traits, and moral relativism is to be shunned.
- Those most in need of character education are poor people of color and those with limited English proficiency.
- Character education proceeds didactically, with virtuous adults instructing children in proper moral behavior.

At the other end of the continuum were proposals in which

- Character is located in communities of people and is a shared responsibility.
- Character traits are generally stable but can vary situationally.
- Character education benefits all.
- Character education proceeds inductively and reflectively, with moral behavior emerging from consideration of moral situations.

Proposals tended to fall somewhere along this continuum, which are polarized according to the two major positions (didactic and individualistic, and reflective and communitarian) found in academic publications propounding opinions about character education. For our report, we decided to take two proposals from each end of the continuum and provide profiles of them according to our research questions. By focusing on the most clearly articulated position at opposite ends of the continuum, we hope to identify the ideological nature of different conceptions of character and how to educate for its betterment.

PRODUCING THE STUDY

Following our analysis, we produced profiles of the two regions. These included attention both to the character education proposals themselves and to what we inferred to be the cultural factors contributing to their development. For instance, we noticed that the southern states' proposals emphasized *civility* (defined as good manners and deference to adults). On the other hand, the upper midwestern states emphasized *agency*, which might include questioning adults' authority. As former residents of the Upper Midwest and current residents of the Deep South, we saw a clear relation between these different ideologies and what we had under-

---

Son! Develop good character because it is beneficial in this world as well as hereafter. Allah has described the good character of the Holy Prophet (s.a.w.a.) as his special attribute. Good character is half the religion.

—Wasaelus Shia

stood to be the different cultures of the regions. Based on these informal observations, we began to look more deeply into the cultural context of each region and began to see many relations between local ideologies and local conceptions of character.

We also began to wonder how the OERI Request for Proposals (RFP) had influenced the proposals' conceptions of character. As we looked more closely at the RFP, we began to see its ideological orientation and wondered how it had come into being. Using the web-based Congressional Record, we were able to trace congressional discussions of character back to the Aspen Conference hosted by Michael Josephson of the Josephson Institute of Ethics. Our investigation of the origins of the OERI RFP thus helped us identify its ideological origins and political trail through Congress.

These factors led to insights about the character education movement and informed our analysis. We present the results of our analysis in Parts II through IV of this book. Our purpose in creating and contrasting these profiles of two distinct regions is not to construct a binary, but to identify the two most distinct conceptions of character revealed in the proposals and use them to understand the ideological nature of different notions of character. We hope that this effort contributes to what Knoblauch (1988) calls *dialectic inquiry:* "[T]he stipulation of 'difference' among competing classes is the fundamental ground of dialectic inquiry. In other words, what might be regarded as 'the trap of oppositional thinking' is also the very quality of dialectic that moves us toward enriched understandings and interpretive resolutions" (Nystrand, Greene, & Wiemelt, 1993, pp. 273–274). We hope that our outline of these distinct perspectives contributes to at least a trialectic as readers engage with these conceptions of character and seek their own resolutions and new understandings.

Before getting to the analysis itself, however, we next provide a framework for our study, first with a historical overview of character education in the United States, then with an outline of character education at the turn of the twenty-first century, and finally with a more detailed outline of our theoretical perspective on our topic.

Monicagate made many of us ever more cynical when anyone chimes that character matters. Because we all now know that, for too many voters, character only matters if it's not your guy who's the lecher or the liar.

—Myriam Marquez

Chapter 3

Historical Framework

> The concern for moral education has never really diminished through the course of American history. It was urgent in the seventeenth century as it is today. Constant through the ages is the sense of "moral crisis" that attends the young. Panic, outrage, passionate admonitions from the moral gatekeepers of society—so it has been in each generation. (Hunter, 2000, p. 77)

Many in the United States believe that the nation has entered the twenty-first century in a time of moral decline. They find evidence for this belief in school shootings, unsafe streets, corporate corruption, malfeasance by public officials, widespread drug abuse, the ubiquitous celebration of sex and violence in the media, a perceptible loss in civility in public interactions, and countless other indicators that people in the United States are losing their moral grip. These events, such as the infamous breast-bearing climax to Janet Jackson's 2004 Super Bowl half time performance, "have left many Americans wholly desensitized to the civil and moral grotesqueness that stalks so many of our streets" (Ryan, Sweeder, & Bednar, 2001, p. 3). Incidents of violence are also not limited to our nation's inner cities, which are the locus of immorality in the minds of many despite the occurrences of suburban school shootings, middle-class gang rapes, infanticide among affluent teens, and other problems occurring outside urban centers of poverty (Pitts, 2001).

A second belief held by many in the United States is that a "pervasive relativism and an ultraliberal view of morals, a belief in the absolute right and freedom of the individual to choose his or her own lifestyle, have

---

How can they expect a harvest of thought who have not had the seed time of character.

—Henry David Thoreau

19

eroded the best of what a more traditional view of ethics and morality once provided" (Nash, 1997, p. xi). Turiel (2002) attributes the claim that contemporary U.S. society is in a "dire moral state" and in urgent need of "renewal, revival, and recommitment" to "abandonment and loss: abandonment of traditions, a loss of sense of community, and a sharp decline in civic participation and trust." He argues that these traditional values have been replaced by "a pervasive orientation to individualism ... that has taken hold in such a way that it has become radical and threatening" (p. vii). Some critics believe that this extreme form of individualism actually is an "increasingly pathological" form of narcissism that is characterized by

> Feelings of entitlement, perfection and grandiosity, devaluation of others; a disregard for courtesy, etiquette, and traditional ritual; a need for immediate gratification, self-absorption; the use of deceit and manipulation to control others; and the inability to make commitments. (Ryan et al., 2001, p. 38)

Thomas Lickona (1997), a leader of today's character education movement, summarizes the perception held by many of the state of morality in present-day U.S. society:

> It is painfully clear that our contemporary society suffers from severe social and moral problems: the breakdown of the family, an epidemic of violence, the deterioration of civility, rampant greed in a time when one child in four is poor, dishonesty at all levels of society, a rising tide of sleaze in the media, a plague of problems stemming from the breakdown of sexual morality, widespread drug and alcohol abuse, the physical and sexual abuse of children, declining respect for life, and the moral schizophrenia of championing the rights of children while permitting their violent destruction before birth. These societal problems have deep roots that require systemic solutions, but it is not possible to build a virtuous society if virtue does not first exist in the minds, hearts and souls of individual human beings. (pp. 45–46)

The systemic solution promoted by Lickona and others is to employ that most systemic of institutions, the public schools, as an instrument for effecting radical changes in the morality of U.S. youth that restore a worldly order and sensibility that they believe has been lost.

Character is the culmination of basic, fundamental values that guide our lives. They are uncompromising beliefs, beliefs we rarely change or distort. Murder is bad. Kindness is good. Michael Bolton is evil. This is the stuff of character.

—Mark Joseph Goldenson

CHARACTER EDUCATION:
SOLUTION TO THE PERCEIVED CRISIS

Given the gravity of the deterioration of traditional values and morals, say the critics, responsible members of society must intervene and help to restore the national character. As has often been the case throughout the history of the nation, schools have been identified as the vehicle through which a high sense of morality will be restored (Purpel, 1997; Smagorinsky, 1995b). In the present instance the solution is character education. Funded at unprecedented levels by the federal government, character education is now institutionalized in the curricula of well over one half of the states in the United States.

A number of individuals, groups, and institutions have tried to address perceived character deficiencies of youth in the United States:

- academics such as Doris (2002), Lickona (1991), Ryan and McLean (1987), and many others;
- university-based centers such as the Center for the Fourth and Fifth Rs at SUNY-Cortland, the Institute for Character Development at Drake University, and the Boston University Center for the Advancement of Ethics and Character;
- private organizations such as the Character Counts! Coalition, the Jefferson Center for Character Education, and the Character Education Partnership;
- political leaders such as George W. Bush, Bill Frist, and Joseph Lieberman;
- athletes such as Nate "Tiny" Archibald, Rebecca Lobo, and David Thompson;
- celebrities such as 2001 Miss America Angela P. Baraquio, actor Tom Selleck, and musician Peter Yarrow;
- public figures such as William Bennett, Colin Powell, and Laura Bush;
- religious leaders such as Rev. Jesse Jackson, Rabbi David Saperstein, and Rev. Edwin Leahy;
- business leaders such as Sanford N. McDonnell of the McDonnell Douglas Corporation, Larry E. Knox of General Motors, and John E. Pepper of Procter & Gamble;
- academic journals such as the *Journal of Research in Character Education,* the *Journal of Character Education,* and the *Journal of College and Character;*
- annual academic conferences such as the Character Education Leadership Academy sponsored by the International Center for Character Education at the University of San Diego, the Annual Character Education Conference in St. Louis, and the Character Education Partnership National Forum;

- countless Web sites promoting character education in both profitable and nonprofit ways;
- and commentators speaking from a host of other professional and ideological perspectives.

In addition, over the past few years 48 states have introduced character education programs "in the hope of bolstering students' resolve to resist the temptation to lie, cheat, bully, use drugs and behave immorally in other ways" (Gilbert, 2003). These efforts have been promoted by the United States Department of Education that, since 1995, has allocated $27 million for character education programs, although not all states' programs have been federally funded. Although all character educators make claims about character and how best to promote it, the conceptions of character, human nature, and education that motivate these efforts span a wide range of beliefs. We next review how these beliefs have informed understandings of character historically and how these conceptions are realized in the current character debate.

HISTORICAL PERSPECTIVE

Contemporary alarms about character and character education belie the fact that these concerns are hardly a recent phenomenon. Indeed, discussions about character are so ancient as to be of indeterminate origin. Wynne (1997) maintains that "The for-character approach to education is older than written history. Anthropological and archaeological studies disclose that even preliterate cultures have applied teaching methods congruent with for-character principles" (p. 65). Wynne and others find evidence of character education in the writings of Socrates, Aristotle, Xenophon, Plato, and Plutarch among the ancient Greeks. Plato, for example, held up character as the defining qualification for the ruling class (Hunter, 2000) while his pupil Aristotle was the first Western educator to "express interest in teaching children to be good human beings" through such texts as *Nicomachean Ethics* (Nash, 1997, p. 3; cf. Noddings, 1997).

Despite this enduring emphasis on educating for character, many in the United States believe the current crisis to be, first of all, a crisis, and second, unprecedented in history. Yet Hunter (2000) argues that every U.S. genera-

---

The presence of a noble nature, generous in its wishes, ardent in its charity, changes the lights for us: we begin to see things again in their larger, quieter masses, and to believe that we too can be seen and judged in the wholeness of our character.

—George Eliot (Marian Evans Cross)

tion for at least the past two centuries has believed its youth to be in a state of crisis and that the project of moral development "has long been infused with urgency and gravity even as it has been almost completely transformed over generations" (p. 31). Purpel (1997) maintains that the current character education movement "represents a long-standing tradition of using schools as agents of social stability, political stasis and cultural preservation" (p. 140) and that "deliberate intervention in the behavior and character of students is a central if not dominating theme in the history of public schooling in the United States" (p. 141). Despite this historical belief in the need for character formation among the nation's youth, many contemporary considerations of character lack a broad perspective, making it appear that today's character "crisis" is unique and unprecedented.

We next review the role of character education in the history of U.S. schooling, drawing on Leming's (2001) observation that character education in the United States has gone through five distinct phases: The era prior to the 1830s, the period from the 1830s through roughly 1900, the post-World War I years in the 1920s and 1930s, the values and moral education movement of the 1970s and 1980s, and the character education movement of the 1990s.

The United States Prior to the 1830s

In the United States discussions about the role of character predate the founding of the nation itself. A Massachusetts law of 1642, for example, sought to assist parents in establishing a model society characterized by civility, piety, and religion by giving town officials the right to fine negligent parents and place children in apprenticeships where they could be instructed in the moral and legal principles of society (Ryan et al., 2001).

Moral education in the era leading up to the founding of the United States was thoroughly Calvinistic and entrusted to the family and local church. Although primarily mediated by parents, moral life was defined by and said to emanate from the Christian God. As a result, obedience to and respect of parents was viewed by colonial Christians as an expression of obeying and being reverent toward God (Hunter, 2000). At the same time, notes Purpel (1997), the early Puritan schools were established "in response to fears that families were increasingly unable or unwilling to inculcate their children with the spiritual beliefs and moral virtues of the Puritan Commonwealth" (p. 141).

> *There is nothing in which people more betray their character than in what they laugh at.*
>
> *—Johann Wolfgang von Goethe*

The revolutionaries rejected the notion that sovereignty was located in the monarchy, believing instead that it resided with the people and that "strength of character" was "essential to the vitality of their experiment in democracy" (Hunter, 2000, p. 7). Thomas Jefferson, a fascinatingly complex and contradictory man who was one of his era's leading advocates of democracy, argued that "the steady character of our countrymen is a rock to which we may safely moor" and that "it is the manners and spirit of a people which preserve a republic in vigor." Setting the stage for the inflammatory rhetoric of the current character movement, Jefferson stated that "a degeneracy in these is a canker which soon eats to the heart of its laws and constitution" (quoted by Hunter, pp. 5–6).

Character education had an especially rich history in the early public schooling of the fledgling republic (Field, 1996). The founders of the new nation called on schools to develop and nurture a new national identity and believed that its cultivation would include character education that would "erect the scaffolding" for a "democratic personality" (Ryan et al., 2001, p. 7). Leming (2001) contends that before the 1830s, "moral instruction had been placed in schools merely to assist the church in insuring the salvation of youth" (p. 64) primarily by homogenizing "an increasingly ethnically and socially diverse population" (p. 65) to insure social control. Thomas Jefferson stated that this early goal of the republic to devise an educational system would "educate men to manners, morals, and habits perfectly homogeneous with those of the country" (cited in Leming, 2001, p. 65).

The 1830s Through the Turn of the Twentieth Century

Leming (2001) argues that beginning in the 1830s, "an important purpose for the schools was as a place where immigrants were to be socialized into a common national culture" (p. 65). The textbooks of the early republic were the primary pedagogic instrument by which character and a new national identity were encouraged. Thus, a central purpose of the McGuffey Readers, published from 1836 onward and used by more than 200 million readers from 1900 to 1940 alone, was to help U.S. children become good citizens (Field, 1996; Moser, 1965; Nash, 1997). Elson (1964) contends that an explicit purpose of virtually all U.S. textbooks of the nineteenth century was to inculcate students with both good character and patriotism, even as these books were rigidly stereotyped by race, class, and gender.

> *A man never describes his own character so clearly as when he describes another's.*
> —*Jean Paul Richter*

Ryan et al. (2001) view the McGuffey Readers as the foundational texts of character education from the 1840s through the early twentieth century. They contend that the McGuffeys encouraged readers to value learning and to practice charity, honesty, courage, and industriousness while eschewing gluttony, alcohol, envy, and insolence. These traits not only were believed to be an essential basis for a stable republican society based on law but also were "well-suited for productive participation in the nation's rapidly expanding industries. Referred to as industrial virtues, character traits such as honesty, industriousness, punctuality, and deference to authority embodied the attitudes of the ideal nineteenth century factory worker" (p. 11). Hunter (2000) concurs, believing that the term character gained its greatest currency in the nineteenth century and always was related to an explicitly moral standard of conduct oriented toward building, expanding, achieving, and sacrificing on behalf of a larger good—all those "producer values" (p. 7) described by Weber (1930) as central to the Protestant work ethic.

Purpel (1997) connects the values taught in the formative years of U.S. schooling to the Puritan traditions of obedience, hierarchy, and hard work, values that correspond to the requirements of an economic system that requires a workforce that is compliant and industrious (Bowles & Gintis, 1976). These values, hoped educators, could be enculturated in the increasing numbers of immigrants who came to the U.S. in the late-nineteenth century. These immigrants' diverse cultures, concentrated in urban centers, created a conflict between the Christian orientation of earlier character education movements and the increasingly multicultural makeup of the new population. The result was what Leming (2001) calls "pan-Protestantism" (p. 66), a secularized version of Christian morality that affected the content of even the McGuffey Readers. This curriculum was designed to help socialize immigrants into a common national culture, allowing schools to become "museums of virtue" (Tyack & Hansot, 1982, p. 7). This common culture was often realized in conformity to the most atomistic of academic endeavors; the Illinois State Board of Education, for instance, opined in 1874 that "Laxness in

---

Not rank, but character, is birth;
It is not eyes, but wits, that see;
True learning 'tis, to cease from wrong;
Contentment is prosperity.

The character of sons
The father e'er reflects:
Who, from a screw-pine tree,
An emblic fruit expects?
The Panchatantra

such matters as spelling betrayed a weakness in [students'] character or a moral lapse" (cited in Lindblom & Dunn, 2003, p. 168).

Post-World War I

By the close of the nineteenth century, moral instruction became increasingly detached from the traditions, beliefs, and ritual practices of religious communities, and character was being conceptualized as something that was amenable to development, rather than something that was fixed by nature (Hunter, 2000). Although the commitment to moral education remained a central feature in classrooms as the twentieth century began and educators continued to believe that religion had a role to play in it, there was a new-found insistence that the democratic institutions of capitalism itself constituted an important moral influence. Ideas such as justice, individual liberty, and the consent of the governed; personal character including promptness, truthfulness, courtesy, obedience, and industry; and the superiority of Protestant civilization all occupied a "sacred place in mainstream discourse and social life" (Hunter, 2001, pp. 59–60).

A number of formative circumstances of the early twentieth century drove and shaped the era's approach to character education. These included

- the United States' nativist response to World War I, leading to such developments as the repression of second language instruction in schools and the creation of the national origins quota system, which favored Anglo Saxons and English-speaking people in immigration (Higham, 1988). These efforts to assimilate people in the United States were part of a broader effort to limit the linguistic and cultural diversity that followed from indiscriminate immigration policies and thus establish a more clearly defined national character;
- the rise of Bolshevism in the new Soviet Union, a movement designed to overthrow the tsarist order, dismantle free enterprise, eradicate the social-class structure, centralize decision-making, and replace religion with communist ideology. Fear of Bolshevist ideology and practices led to the Red Scare in the United States. During this period reaction to such developments as labor strikes—presumed to originate in the activities of communist sympathizers—led eventually to McCarthyism, blacklists, and other efforts to suppress the influence of communism. Among the consequences of the early Red Scare was the deportation of those believed to be radicals. Ironically, such socialist thinkers as Rosa Luxemburg (1918) argued at the time that

    the worker in a socialist economy must show that he can work hard and properly, keep discipline and give his best without the whip of hunger and without the capitalist and his slave-driver behind him. This calls for inner self-discipline, intellectual maturity, moral ardor, a sense of dignity and responsibility, a complete inner rebirth of the proletarian. One cannot realize socialism with lazy, frivolous, egoistic, thoughtless, and indifferent human beings. A socialist society needs human beings from whom each one in his place, is full of passion and enthusiasm for the general well-being, full of self-sacrifice and sympathy for his fellow human beings, full of courage and tenacity in order to dare to attempt the most difficult.

A socialist dissident in the early USSR who was imprisoned for her criticism of Lenin's Bolshevism, Luxemburg outlines many of the very qualities central to the U.S. notion of good character—particularly as prescribed for the working class—even while socialism has been identified by many critics as the breeding ground of weak character (e.g., Wagner, 2001); and

- the "Roaring 20s" of speakeasies, bootlegging, gangland activities, and other responses to the Eighteenth amendment to the U.S. constitution, established in 1919 to prohibit the production and consumption of alcohol and thus contribute to a sober and pious populace. Prohibition was repealed in 1933.

As a result of these and other threats to the Western value structure in the wake of the new world order that followed World War I, virtually every school in country responded in some way to the demands that education play a role in the formation of good character (Leming, 1993).

The early part of the twentieth century simultaneously saw the rejection of religion as the basis of educational practice. John Dewey was especially influential in this movement, believing that faith in a divine authority and related ideas of a soul and destiny were no longer reasonable foundations of Western civilization, stable institutions, or social progress. For Dewey, "experience itself is the sole ultimate authority," and he and his colleagues insisted that definitions of moral behavior depended more on the circumstances of individuals rather than in pre-established rules (Hunter, 2000, pp. 60–61). Dewey's faith in "values verifiable in social experience" implied a shift away from morality as something that could be didactically imposed on the child. In practice, this paradigm change led to children being regarded as "having the capacity to determine their own moral standards" (p. 60). The conflict between the belief that there are universal moral truths as opposed to truths arising in the context of complex social experience and circumstances remains at the heart of contemporary debates about character and character education.

The United States further experienced a shift from a focus on industrial production to one based of mass consumption in the early twentieth century. This transformation led to a change in the psychological and ethical demands placed on the individual. More emphasis on accumulation, leisure, and cultivation of personal preferences led to change in attention from character to personality. The concept of personality reflected a self no longer defined by austerity but by emancipation for the purposes of expression, fulfillment, and gratification. As Hunter (2000) argues,

> The progressive period marks the early ascendancy of psychology and the simultaneous retreat of moral theology. The concept of character was discredited and the very idea of moral excellence was displaced by the idea of personal effectiveness. Accordingly, the classic and religious virtues associated with strong moral character (such as courage, loyalty, truthfulness and integrity) had now given way to the grammar of psychological well being (self confidence, social, integration, adjustment). (p. 70)

At the heart of this "Copernican" change in how children were perceived was the conception that children "were no longer regarded as degenerate but rather as innocent, vulnerable, and malleable" (Hunter, 2000, p. 66). Moral instruction was now to be predicated on the belief that children needed to be protected and molded to live responsibly and rationally. Hunter argues that the retreat of Christian traditions "inexorably to the margins" (p. 67) came in concert with the rise of psychology as a way to explain human behavior. He maintains that the early decades of the twentieth century saw the discrediting of the concept of character and the classic and religious virtues such as courage, loyalty, truthfulness, and integrity. These traditional qualities of character gave way to such newly developing psychological concepts as self-confidence, integration, and adjustment. To a very significant degree, the character education movement of today is a reaction to this very eclipse of what had been believed to be transcendent, eternal moral virtues by a malleable, increasingly relativistic set of beliefs about human development.

Lickona (1993) identifies two additional causes for the decline of character education. One was Darwinism, featuring what Lickona terms the "metaphor" of evolution "that led people to see all things, including morality, as being in flux" (p. 1). The second was the advent of logical positivism, which distinguished between facts and values and accorded a lower status to values which were "mere expressions of feeling, not objective truth." Morality was thus "relativized and privatized—made to seem a matter of personal 'value judgment,' not a subject for public debate and transmission through the schools" (p. 1).

Perhaps the best known moral educator of this period was Lawrence Kohlberg. Kohlberg (1958) identified six moral stages that people go through in sequence, with a refined sense of justice representing the height of morality. He argued that students' progress through these stages could be scaffolded and their understanding honed through the consideration of scenarios. In Heinz's dilemma, for instance, the impoverished Heinz has to choose between letting his cancer-stricken wife die or stealing a drug that can save her. Students considering this quandary could both be assessed according to their stage of development and, from an educational standpoint, be assisted in sharpening their moral understanding, at least as defined by Kohlberg. To Kohlberg, who worked in the tradition of Piaget (e.g., 1932), these stages corresponded to biological development (i.e., one could not reach Kohlberg's postulated higher stages of development at a relatively young age).

Turiel (1983) contested this claim, arguing that Kohlberg's advanced stages were available to children much younger than Kohlberg theorized. The critique that provided the most severe and enduring challenge to Kohlberg's theory, however, came from Gilligan's (1983) dispute with Kohlberg's all-male sample. Gilligan replicated Kohlberg's methods with women and found that because of their communitarian orientation they typically did not reach Kohlberg's highest levels of morality, which privileged an individual's abstractions of laws at the expense of a more relational contextualization of issues. Gilligan argued that Kohlberg's use of an exclusively male sample provided a particular profile that did not correspond to the population as a whole. She has since developed this idea by expanding her original sample of White middle-class women to include women from across the racial and social class spectrum (e.g., Taylor, Gilligan, & Sullivan, 1995).

In response to criticisms that people's abstract reasoning did not necessarily correspond to their social behavior, Kohlberg and colleagues (Power, Higgins, & Kohlberg, 1989) proposed what they called *Just Communities:* schools in which students participated in democratic communities in which decision making required consensus. These schools tended to be small so as to promote a sense of belonging and included community meetings in which issues pertaining to both personal and school business were discussed and democratically decided, with teachers and students having equal voice in these discussions. Adults were not simply discussants but played a central leading role in identifying democratic norms and helping to sustain them.

Importantly, Kohlberg rejected both the tradition of didactic instruction in moral absoluteness and the alternative of unfettered relativism. Rather, Kohlberg (Kohlberg & Turiel, 1971) believed that certain principles of justice and fairness represent the highest stage of his moral progression in a variety of cultures around the world. This emphasis on justice has led to questions about why this virtue should be paramount rather than among a set of qualities of equal importance.

Kohlberg, while an important figure in discussions of moral thinking, has had less lasting impact in the arena of character education. Just Communities—Kohlberg's primary contribution to educational practice—had their heyday but have now faded into obscurity. His work fit well with the

> *In later life as in earlier, only a few persons influence the formation of our character; the multitude pass us by like a distant army. One friend, one teacher, one beloved, one club, one dining table, one work table, are the means by which his nation and the spirit of his nation affect the individual.*
>
> —*Jean Paul Richter*

secular approach to moral development of his era and the ascendance of Piaget as education's primary psychologist in this period, and likely contributed to the values clarification movement of the 1970s and 1980s. Ironically, his work has ultimately been damned by both multiculturalists, who find his work too narrowly concerned with the values of White Western males, and the cultural traditionalists, who find his work too relativistic. Despite these criticisms, Kohlberg remains a near-obligatory citation for anyone writing about morality and character education in the past 40 years, a testimony to the intellect and insight that he brought to his project.

The 1970s and 1980s

Hunter (2000) argues that "the vocabulary of psychology frames virtually all public discussion" (p. 81) of children's moral development at the turn of the twenty-first century, powered by the rhetoric and methods of science and its presumed neutrality. The new emphasis on psychology and relativism paved the way for the ascendance of the values clarification movement. Presumably, this approach would help young people sort through the myriad of complex moral perspectives emanating from various political, religious, and ideological sources and develop personal codes of conduct. This purportedly unbiased approach to values, argue its advocates, overcomes the problems of ideology inherent to doctrinaire approaches to morality and allows for different perspectives to emerge as young people interact with their worlds.

As is the case with much educational research conducted on the effectiveness of character education, research on values clarification is inconclusive. Proponents, argues Leming (1997), rely primarily on anecdotal evidence to support its use. The debate is thus driven largely by ideology. Leming concludes that "it was not empirical research that resulted in the decline of the values clarification process; rather it was careful scholarly critique that exposed the flaws at the heart of values clarification." Chief among these flaws was the ambiguity of moral relativism in which "everyone's values resulting from the clarification process must be treated as acceptable." Furthermore, critics argued that values clarification sanctioned the schools' intrusion into private matters. These critiques, fueled by an emerging conservative political climate, contributed to values clarification becoming "anathema in most schools" (p. 38).

Along with the new emphasis on psychology, many in the U.S. began to attend to the role of emotions in the development of moral understanding in the 1960s. Hunter (2000) argues that the concept of self-esteem was central to this new thinking and that it "has become virtually unassailable as a general prescription in child rearing." (p. 84). The psychological regime, he maintains, is "overwhelmingly therapeutic and self-referencing" and features a moral framework whose center point is the "autonomous self" (p. 86).

SUMMARY

Changing ideas of the self both reflect and help to reproduce social structures, structures that impose different requirements upon the role and presentation of the self. The older ideas of the self surrounding the character ideal suited the personal and social ideas of an older political economy. The newer ideas reflected in the concept of personality emerged because they better fit the demand of a developing consumer economy. As we next review, the idea of regarding morality as a puzzle to be solved and young people as sensitive beings in need of stronger senses of self has become the object of scorn for many current proponents of character education. In an effort to restore the more authoritarian approach to character available in the early part of the twentieth century, these critics reject relativism and feelings and endorse a more didactic role for adults in teaching values to their society's young. This set of values has provided the impetus for the current state of affairs in character education, which we review next.

We begin to see [in a child's development] the little rills of moral consciousness, the germinal roots of rectitude and, perchance, the sense of shame. These serve as the alphabet of that large moral sense, which, through precept and example, develop into noble character; and which, based upon these elementary facts as a foundation of the soul's spiritual training, expands in the family, into love and truthfulness; and in the church, blossoms into reverence and sacred worship.

—Alexander Crummell

Chapter 4

The Current State of Affairs

John Dewey, the 1960s, and values clarification are often named as central causes of moral decline in youth among those who have spearheaded the character education movement that began in the 1980s and reached maturity in the 1990s. The discourse streams that run through the two profiles we provide are related to a history of discourse that suggests different epistemologies with regard to character education, education in general, social relationships, and other aspects of society. In this chapter we review the factors that contribute to the current disagreements about what sort of nation the United States ought to be, and how the character education movement is situated within those debates.

THE CULTURE WARS

These broader ideological differences are popularly known as the Culture Wars, described by Hunter (1991) as the struggle to define the United States in terms of its values relative to public education, abortion, homosexuality, the courts, and other issues that distill value systems into policy and practice. Hunter identifies the polar perspectives on these topics that con-

---

Character cannot be summoned at the moment of crisis if it has been squandered by many years of compromise and rationalization. The only testing ground for the heroic is the mundane. The only preparation for that one profound decision which can change a life is those hundreds of self-defining seemingly insignificant decisions made in private. Habit is the daily battleground of character.

—Dan Coats

stitute the Culture Wars as *Orthodoxy* and *Progressivism,* labels more commonly known as conservative and liberal. Similarly, Lakoff (2002) views the United States as comparable to a family who might be led by either a strict or permissive parent, approaches that he argues correspond with conservative and liberal perspectives on national leadership. Significantly, these positions correspond to the two perspectives on character education that we have found in the states from the Deep South and Upper Midwest.

As with character education, these extreme positions represent points on a continuum rather than the only perspectives available. Just as the majority of character education initiatives we studied represent hybrid versions of the two polar views, the majority of citizens likely hold moderate views on the disposition of the United States, despite the inflammatory terms of the public debate by both conservatives (e.g., Bernstein, 1994; Bork, 1996) and liberals (e.g., Conason, 2003; Franken, 2003).

In Hunter's (1991) analysis, those who embrace Progressivism find morality and politics to be protean, a function of conditions that people face in their cultural milieus, historical time periods, and particular circumstances. Truth, rather than being absolute, is constructed by individuals based on their experiences with what life offers them. This perspective is fundamentally liberal, seeing society as continually in flux. People's adaptation to these changes requires ongoing reconsideration of the meaning of existence as new knowledge is gained and aggregated and old knowledge is reformulated. For those who adopt an Orthodox perspective, morality and politics are fixed and divinely inspired. Morality in particular is the province of the Almighty, rather than a mortal construction. This perspective is fundamentally conservative, seeking to preserve cherished institutions, structures, and beliefs in an increasingly chaotic world.

Court appointments are of particular concern to both Progressive and Orthodox believers. A Supreme Court case on an issue such as abortion, or the legality of homosexual marriages, or any number of other contested issues, writes ideology into law. In 2003, for instance, the U.S. Supreme Court decriminalized what is known as "sodomy" (i.e., same-sex intercourse or opposite-sex oral or anal intercourse), a term we set aside in quotation marks to highlight its pejorative origins based on the Biblical censure of homosexual men in ancient Sodom. Televangelist Pat Robertson issued a televised prayer to God to urge the termination of three physically vulnerable Supreme Court justices who voted with the majority of six in the case. In a published statement on July 17, 2003, Robertson wrote that

> A growing number of Americans see the Supreme Court for what it truly is. After all, no matter how much a legislature may debate, negotiate, compromise, and discuss a significant social issue, a mere five-member unelected majority of the Supreme Court is always free to impose what it thinks is really best for

the American people.... The idea of a "living Constitution"—whose heart and
breath ends up being nothing more than the ideological predilections of the
Supreme Court's sitting members—is contrary to fundamental principles of
the Rule of Law. (http://cbn.org/about/pressrelease_030717.asp)

Robertson's (2003) solution was to replace three judges he characterized
as *liberal* and as having health problems with judges with a conservative perspective and presumably robust health. Robertson believed that he had access to the "truth": that ideologically liberal justices were distorting the
framers' original intent, which coincided with Robertson's own reading of the
Bible and the U.S. Constitution. Conservative justices would uphold his
views, which unlike those of liberals were not colored by ideology. A prayer to
God would contribute to the restoration of laws that would conserve timeless
ideals of morality such as heterosexuality. Robertson's assessment highlights
the critical nature of court appointments to those who believe that court rul-
ings set the direction U.S. society will take, with or without godly sanction.

Public schools, because they are the one legally required site of attendance and compliance for young U.S. citizens, often serve as the nexus of
the Culture Wars (Apple, 1993; Cope & Kalantzis, 1993; Taxel, 1997), as
suggested by debates over the appropriateness of the Biblical Ten Commandments and Lord's Prayer, and of the wording of the Pledge of Allegiance in schools. Those who hold Orthodox views feel that schools—once
the site of assimilation into Christian morality—have fallen into the hands
of secular humanists. They blame many of society's shortcomings on the
Progressives whose moral relativity and rejection of religion as the sole
source of moral guidance have led, they believe, to the decline of civilization
and education. We also see these issues at play in relation to controversies
over the placement of the Ten Commandments in public areas, especially
courtrooms. The dispute over character education—in conjunction with
beliefs about the separation of church and state, the morality of such behavior as same-sex intercourse, the role of discipline, and other issues—is but
one of many instantiations of the larger struggle over whether schools will
be guided by a secular or theocratic vision.

Taxel (1993) argues that the controversies surrounding sensitivity to
others (a.k.a. *political correctness*) and multiculturalism in art, literature, and
curriculum—among the banes of modern education in the views of D'Souza
(1991), Bernstein (1993), and others from the orthodox tradition—are centrally concerned with how people in the United States define themselves as
individuals and understand their nation's past and present and its future
possibilities. Because these controversies involve issues that simultaneously
are aesthetic, relate to questions of historical interpretation, and involve
myths that are basic to U.S. citizens' beliefs about themselves and their nation, they are fundamentally political and increasingly contentious. Taxel

maintains that literature for young people, his specific area of interest, is best understood and appreciated when a wide range of factors, political as well aesthetic, are considered. We believe that this effort to situate issues culturally can enrich an analysis of any aspect of education, including character education.

A good example of the ways in which these factors may converge comes from the controversial "West as America: Reinterpreting Images of the Frontier, 1820–1920" exhibition at the Smithsonian Institution's National Museum of Art (see Truettner, 1991). Criticism was directed especially at what were characterized as *revisionist* wall texts that accompanied the paintings and photographs in the exhibit, which portrayed mythic images of the era known as Western expansion. For example, Remington's 1903 painting, "The Fight for the Water Hole," depicts an incident in which a group of White Texans defended themselves from an attack by Comanche Indians. The work is interpreted by the wall text "as an allegory in which a native-born white elite is surrounded by menacing and uncivilized immigrants" (Foner & Weiner, 1991, p. 164).

Reactions to this exhibit vary widely. According to Foner and Weiner (1991), the controversy over the Smithsonian exhibit is but the latest manifestation of "the assault on 'politically correct' thought by longtime conservatives, onetime radicals, and academics" (p. 163) who lament the passing of the days when White males dominated college campuses and other centers of intellectual and cultural significance. Displeasure over the Smithsonian exhibit even led to threats by influential members of Congress to cut off funding for the Institute and to the cancellation of plans for the exhibition to visit a number of major U.S. cities. Foner and Weiner find evidence from this response that political conservatives are just as likely to act as thought police as the liberals that D'Souza (1991) and others believe are limiting freedom of speech through campus injunctions against discrimination and bigotry. Pinkerton (2001), on the other hand, writes that

> In the 80s, the same cancers of multiculturalism and political correctness that afflicted American universities metastasized into the Smithsonian Institution. The Museum of Natural History, for example, spent much of the last two decades in an increasingly obsessive quest to purge itself of any display that anybody might deem "racist" or "sexist." In 1991 the Museum of American Art put on an exhibit, "The West as America: Reinterpreting Images of the Frontier, 1820-1920" that denigrated U.S. expansion; the eminent historian Daniel Boorstin called it "a perverse, historically inaccurate, destructive exhibit." (http://www.newamerica.net/index.cfm?pg=article&pubID=498)

The presence of such different perspectives, both in this case and many others, suggests that culture wars are in fact *interpretive* wars, that is, strug-

> *If you were to sell your character, would you get full retail or would it go for a bargain-basement price?*
>
> —*H. Jackson Brown*

gles to incorporate the voices and viewpoints of historically powerless, oppressed, and marginalized groups into the narratives accorded status and respect in this society, and the reaction of dominant social groups to these efforts (Taxel, 1997). From this perspective, attempts to alter or amend particular definitions and conceptions of the U.S. experience are understood as part of the long standing and determined struggle of minorities and women to compete with historically dominant groups for control of the historical and literary narratives that are so significant to a nation's understanding of itself, and of efforts to resist such presentations of new histories and revisions of old. The character education movement epitomizes this struggle for interpretive supremacy, drawing from the same discourse streams that flow through other debates about the direction of U.S. society.

THE IMPETUS FOR CHARACTER EDUCATION TODAY

Lickona (1993) identifies three broad reasons for the current interest in character education: "the decline of the family," "troubling trends in youth character," and "the desire for a recovery of shared, objectively important ethical values" (pp. 3–4). Among the leaders in the effort to restore a more authoritarian conception of character education are Kevin Ryan, Thomas Lickona, William Bennett, Lynn Cheney, and many others. We see this perspective as consistent with what we have called a *conservative* or *orthodox orientation,* given the explicitly Christian orientation of many such moral leaders—Kohn (1997) more specifically identifies them as Catholic—and their wish to return to a distant, more pristine time in the past. Leming (1994) describes this yearning for "an ideal state that existed at some indeterminate point in the past. At that time, a set of cultural values was effectively taught to all children and there was a shared consensus in society regarding those values" (p. 124). Today's focus on character education has as its impetus a perceived "crisis in society" that is the result of "the culture's inability to transmit a set of core values and virtues to youth" (p. 123).

Like many popular movements, the character education effort has achieved its effect through a mixture of academic theoreticians and political rhetoricians capable of influencing convictions through populist rhetoric spoken from the bully pulpit. This movement has gained momentum through the shared commitments of its adherents, including the need for both individual rights and a pledge for shared public re-

> *Happiness must be cultivated. It is like character. It is not a thing to be safely let alone for a moment, or it will run to weeds.*
>
> —*Elizabeth Stuart Phelps*

sponsibilities and the transcendence of personal interests in service of the larger social good (Hunter, 2000).

The current interest in character education, argues Lockwood (1991), is a "revivification of the CE movement of the 1920s. Then, as now, there was much handwringing over the irresponsible behavior of youth" (p. 246; cf. Leming, 2001). There are striking similarities, for instance, between Mary Beth Klee's (2000) Core Virtues program—an outgrowth of E. D. Hirsch's (1996) Core Knowledge Curriculum—and the McGuffey Readers in their effort to combine historical knowledge with moral lessons (Ellington & Rutledge, 2001). Given the presence of a socializing institution such as school available to engineer values among young people—the sort of institution absent in the pluralistic and highly differentiated adult world—both young people and schools seem logical vehicles for addressing perceived problems in society, even if young people's morals are simply a reflection of the values and behavior of their elders as some believe (e.g., Males, 2001).

LATE-TWENTIETH AND EARLY-TWENTY-FIRST CENTURY CONCEPTIONS OF CHARACTER

We next review the terms of three perspectives on character education available at the turn of the twenty-first century. The first, and by far most widely endorsed in publications on the topic, is based on the belief in an authoritative creed of objective values that is didactically transmitted. We associate this approach with Lakoff's (2002) notion of the strict parent as advocated by those who endorse a conservative, orthodox, and usually Republican position. The second—an alternative expressed primarily through critique of the first—is predicated on the assumption that character education is achieved when young people develop concern for others and attempt to build a just and diverse community of character. We see this approach as consistent with Lakoff's characterization of the nurturing or permissive parent, usually emanating from a liberal, progressive, typically Democratic perspective. The third approach comes from outside the Western purview, a Native American

> *The person of intellect is lost unless they unite with energy of character. When we have the lantern of Diogenes we must also have his staff.*
>
> —*Sebastien-Roch Nicolas de Chamfort*

perspective that sees morality as a set of reciprocal spiritual relationships between people and all earthly things. Each approach yields a different approach to education based on different conceptions of character.

The Strict Parent: Instilling Character in Errant Youths

The approach advocated by today's most influential character education proponents is an effort to abandon the relativism spawned by the cultural changes of the 1960s, the advent of poststructuralism, the emergence of multiculturalism, and other movements predicated on the decentering of authority and recognition of multiple perspectives on moral issues. Although a good bit of discussion in the literature on character education speaks of the need for a "comprehensive holistic approach" that includes the creation of a "moral community," the practice of "moral discipline," and the creation of "democratic classrooms" (Lickona, 1993, p. 10), most character education programs are didactic in nature and explicitly endorse the inculcation of traditional values. Ryan (1996), a leading spokesperson in the revival of character education, argues that character education programs must embrace indoctrination since "a fundamental mission of the schools is to indoctrinate children with the community's best values" (p. 1). (See Schwartz, 2002, for an argument for transmission rather than indoctrination.)

The prologue to the Character Education Manifesto (Ryan, Bohlin, & Thayer, 1996) of the Center for the Advancement of Ethics and Character at Boston University, founded by Ryan, opens by asserting that

> American schools have had from their inception a moral mandate. Moral authority, once vested firmly in both our schools and teachers, has receded dramatically over the past few decades. While many teachers are valiantly working to promote good character in their classrooms, many are receiving mixed and confusing messages. Attempts made to restore values and ethics to the school curriculum through values clarification, situational ethics, and discussion of

---

A good educational system should help in the development of good character. When the character building duty of education is ignored, it becomes incomplete education. Therefore, if India has to emerge from the ongoing character crisis, it has to revive the value-based education. In the philosophical context, "value" has ethical, moral and spiritual relevance. In general, the factors that shape an ordinary individual into a person of good character can be called values. Values should enable an individual to distinguish between good and bad, justice and injustice, cruelty and kindness and protect him from destructive activities. In other words, a person with values will have humanism in attitude and actions.

—Rameeza A. Rasheed

moral dilemmas have proven both weak and ephemeral, failing to strengthen the character and behavior of our young people. Still our schools too often champion rights at the expense of responsibility and self-esteem at the expense of self-discipline. (http://www.bu.edu/education/caec/files/manifesto.htm)

This unambiguous approach to character education is central to a didactic perspective. As we will demonstrate, the views of Kevin Ryan, Thomas Lickona, and others holding this view have explicitly been codified in the federal government's requirements for character education funding.

We next outline what we understand to be the assumptions behind what we term a *didactic conception* of character education.

Human Nature Is Flawed and Needs Correction.   Among the premises stated at the Web site of Lickona's Center for the Fourth and Fifth R's is the belief that "People do not automatically develop good character. Intentional and focused efforts must be made—by families, schools, faith communities, youth organizations, government, and the media—to foster the character development of the young" (http://www.cortland.edu/c4n5rs/ce_iv.htm). Rather than being the youthful innocents proposed by Rousseau in *Emile,* young people are afflicted by original sin. According to Headmaster Reverend William F. Washington Jarvis of Boston's Roxbury Latin School, kids are "mean, nasty, brutish, selfish, and capable of great cruelty and meanness" (cited in Herbert, 1996, p. 58; cf. Sommers, 2002). Jarvis is among the educators lauded by Ryan (1993) for outstanding achievement in character education. This assessment of the inherently uncivilized nature of youth is confirmed in the lists of youth vices that frame the arguments of Ryan (2003), Lickona (1993), and others who argue for the necessity of character education in an era of declining morality. Because of this naturally antisocial disposition in young people, Kilpatrick (1992) argues that "a comprehensive approach [to character education] is based on a somewhat dim view of human nature" (p. 96; cf. Wynne, 1989). As the next assumption outlines, this dim view of personal virtue suggests the need for educators to attend to individuals who lack character as they socialize young people into adult value systems.

Individuals are the Proper Focus of Character Education.   Although acknowledging the role of culture and community in shaping character, ad-

---

When President Clinton touts national standards, he talks as if he is the virtuous, most ethical pursuer of educational excellence in the world. Yet he never really addresses the question of what kind of person or character or self will be produced by the imposition of such rote standards.

—Wayne C. Booth

herents of this perspective foreground the individual as the locus of character education. In the 1960s, argues Lickona (1993), "Personalism ... delegitimized moral authority, eroded belief in objective moral norms, turned people inward toward self-fulfillment, weakened social commitments (e.g., to marriage and parenting), and fueled the socially destabilizing sexual revolution" (p. 2). This emphasis on personal fulfillment spawned a pervasive narcissism (Ryan et al., 2001) that flaunts traditional values and undermines respect for established institutions and their guardians. Similar to the character education movement following World War I, the emphasis of character development is "on personal character, rather than civic character" (Leming, 2001, p. 71).

Sommers (2002), for instance, regards the Columbine shooting tragedy as the sole responsibility of "two badly socialized boys" (p. 35) whose actions are clearly traceable to "the views of the progressive-education theorists who advocated abandoning the traditional mission of indoctrinating children in the 'old morality' and persuaded the American educational establishment to adopt instead the romantic moral pedagogy of Rousseau" (p. 35). To Sommers, "Teachers and parents who embraced this view badly underestimated the potential barbarism of children who are not given a directive moral education. It is not likely that a single ethics course would have been enough to stop boys like Harris and Klebold from murdering classmates" (pp. 35–36). Sommers argues that these two bad boys, and not the many students who taunted and ostracized them on a daily basis or the nihilistic culture in which they immersed themselves, were the cause of the problems at Columbine (see Espelage & Swearer, 2004, for a different perspective on bullying in schools).

Purpel (1997) argues that from this perspective, "social problems are *not* so much rooted in the failures of our social, economic, and political structures as in the attitudes and behaviors of individuals" (p. 140). He continues,

> The basic explanation that the character education movement offers for moral decline is a psychological one, that the problems are rooted in an inflated sense of personalism and self-centeredness rather than in social, economic, and cultural institutions ... [the assumption is that] what we have to do is not make structural changes in the economic system, the social class structure, or the political hierarchy but instead insist that individuals change. According to this ideology, society is being victimized by unvirtuous (lazy, selfish, indulgent, and indolent) individuals rather than seeing indi-

---

In addition to the physical benefits that Tae Kwon Do offers (healthy body, better balance, strength, flexibility), Christian Tae Kwon Do also develops the mind (focus, concentration, perseverance), and spirit (a closer relationship with God, character development).

—Christian Tae Kwon Do, An Omega Martial Arts School

viduals as victims of an unvirtuous (rapacious, callous, competitive, and heartless) society. (p. 150)

Improving the behavior of these unvirtuous individuals who disrupt societal norms is the focus of character education. These norms are the topic of the next assumption we outline.

There Is a Single, Objective, Universally Valid Notion of Human Character. To some, society has moved beyond the question of which values ought to constitute the character curriculum. Schwartz (2002) declares that "Although there remain a few skirmishes here and there, the reports from the front lines are decisive: the battle over the question 'Whose values?' has ended" as a consequence of consensus among "the primary stakeholders in our schools" who have "answered this thorny question ... [w]ith remarkable clarity and unity" (p. 1; cf. Damon, 2002). The Web site of Lickona's Center for the Fourth and Fifth R's maintains that

> These core ethical values are not mere subjective preferences like taste in music or clothes. They have objective worth (they are good for us whether or not we know it), universal validity, and a claim on our personal and collective conscience. They are affirmed by religious traditions around the world and transcend religious and cultural differences. They are rooted in our human nature and express our common humanity. (http://www.cortland.edu/ c4n5rs/ce_iv.htm)

These universal values are identified by the Character Counts! Coalition as the Six Pillars of Character: trustworthiness, respect, responsibility, fairness, caring, and citizenship (http://www.charactercounts.org/defsix.htm). For Lickona and others, the objective worth and universal validity of these values provides the imperative to indoctrinate students into them, as advocated by Ryan (1996) and others. Toward this end, Lickona (1997) argues that

> the peer culture is a powerful influence on student conduct and character. If teachers do not take the initiative to shape a positive peer culture—one that supports the virtues adults are trying to teach—the peer culture will often develop in the opposite direction, creating peer norms that are antithetical to good character (e.g., cruelty to schoolmates who are different, lack of academic responsibility, and disrespect for legitimate authority). (p. 49)

The deviant peer culture provides a mandate for adults to socialize young people—through harsh means if necessary—into the universally valid virtues of the adult community.

Purpel (1997) argues that this perspective is fundamentally conservative, that is, designed to maintain existing norms rather than allow young people to reconstruct them. Ryan (2003) maintains that by asserting authoritarian roles, teachers can help restore the virtue lost in the unruly 1960s:

Character is the sum total of all our everyday choices.

—Margaret Jensen

The current generation of students—and yes, of teachers—has been brought up on a heavy fare of movies and television shows in which high schools are seen as adolescent playpens and the adults who inhabit them are portrayed as banal and inept misfits masquerading as teachers. To reclaim this indispensable status, teachers will need a clear and ringing mandate from school administrators—and the behavior codes to back it up. (p. 3)

This authoritarian conception of character education suggests our final assumption from this perspective, that character education is didactic.

Character Education Should Be Didactic. Wynne (1997) identifies loyalty as a key trait in a character curriculum and recommends that educators "have the curriculum in literature and history solicit such loyalty, for example, keep revisionism under control (*revisionism,* in this context, means historical materials with an undue interest in deprecating the contributions of previous traditional leaders and notable past achievements)" (p. 69). In this conception, authoritarianism is placed at a premium, with young people accepting established traditions and exemplars on the basis of their portraiture in existing texts. Presumably, then, an exemplar such as Thomas Jefferson would not have his morality placed under the same scrutiny as more recent leaders such as Bill Clinton; rather, their virtue would stand as established in the depictions of prior eras.

Wynne (1997) also advocates the trait of obedience, toward which teachers should "Develop written rules of behavior for the classroom and/or the whole school which prohibit all reasonably foreseeable forms of disruption and/or specify the behaviors required" (p. 68). This emphasis is part of Wynne's (1989) hope to return to "traditional values," that is, "the panoply of virtues connoted by phrases such as the work ethic and obedience to legitimate authority and by the important nonreligious themes articulated in the Ten Commandments." Toward this end he argues that "adults who routinely deal with children and adolescents are gradually driven to recognize that adult-child relationships in schools cannot and should not be governed by so-called democratic theories" (p. 19). This belief in the power of adults and cultural icons is central to a character education approach in which adults have unassailable authority in providing direction to young people's moral development.

Ryan (2003) argues that one requirement for effective character education is "The institution of a schoolwide language system that uses the language of character (respect, responsibility, commitment, and right and wrong), rather than the soft language of therapy (self-esteem, inappropriate behavior, adjustment)" (p. 4). This value on adult and established authority contributes to the perspective that didactic instruction in values ought to constitute character education. Benninga (1997) concurs, saying that

> throughout the history of our country, Americans have always had faith that their schools could "close the floodgate of corruption and ... arrest the torrent of public immorality" [Curti, 1959] through character education, believing that the nation could not survive unless its citizens were virtuous as well as intelligent. The recent emphasis on self-discovery, values clarification, and consensual morality thus may be only a blip in an otherwise long and consistent history of more directed teaching for character formation. (p. 87)

This more directed teaching consists of "defining, communicating, modeling, teaching, and consistently upholding the school's professed moral values in all areas of school life" (Lickona, 1997, p. 57). To Bennett (1980), inculcating values in such a way results in habitual behaviors that do not require reflection or judgment: "emphasis on morality as 'cognition' can lead to a serious error in a child's understanding of what a moral life consists ... it is often the case that the more a person has a fixed and steady disposition, the less, not the more, he has to make a decision at all" (p. 30). Wynne (1997) is confident that such authoritarian means are entirely appropriate for moral education:

> The concept of the construction of children's character ... implies some environments should be deliberately managed to form children's character. Some readers may see this as manipulative, totalitarian, or stifling. Yet, educators who want to help pupils acquire good character must manage school and classroom environments that are more likely to help produce outcomes associated with good character, in effect, to construct them. (p. 63)

Kohn (1997) argues that character education programs that emerge from a didactic perspective are collections of "exhortations and extrinsic inducements designed to make children work harder and do what they're told" (p. 2). Their goals, he says, are not concerned with supporting or facilitating children's moral and social growth, but are designed to control students' behavior. We next review the alternative view outlined by Kohn and others.

Three characters can be found in a man about to perform a good deed. If he says, "I shall do it soon," his character is poor. If he says, "I am ready to do it now," his character is of average quality. If he says, "I am doing it," his character is praiseworthy.

—Hasidic saying

> *Character is simply habit long continued.*
>
> —*Plutarch*

The Nurturing Parent: Creating Communities of Character

Molnar (1997) outlines a fundamental difference between the two dominant approaches to character education in the current debate. In describing
didactic approaches, he says that "although there is the occasional bow to
the need for people of good character to act collectively, our collective social character and our common social responsibilities are generally of less
interest in character education programs than reinforcing 'good' individual behaviors and censoring 'bad' ones" (p. ix).

The collective approach suggested in Molnar's (1997) remarks is at the
heart of the other main approach to character education articulated in publications about character education, one rooted in Deweyian progressivism.
Its articulation has come largely in response to didactic approaches, often
in the form of critiques; and its influence has been relatively marginal in the
national character education movement. This perspective is reminiscent of,
though not replicative of, the psychological approaches superceded in the
late-twentieth century by authoritarian conceptions of character education.
Rather than demanding the compliance of individual children, Kohn
(1997), Lockwood (1997), Smagorinsky (2000, 2002a), and others argue
that the focus of character education needs to be on the way the school environment works and feels. They argue that emphasis ought to be on transforming educational structures rather than forming individual characters.
This approach includes the following assumptions.

Conventions Must Be Distinguished From Morality. Turiel (2002)
makes a key distinction for those who take community-based perspective, that
between social conventions and moral codes. Moral judgments, he argues,

> need to be distinguished from judgments about social organization and the
> conventions that further the coordination of social interactions within social
> systems. Conventions are shared behaviors (uniformities, rules) whose

> *If there is righteousness in the heart there will be beauty in the character; If there is
> beauty in the character there will be harmony in the home. When there is harmony
> in the home there will be order in the nation. When there is order in the nation
> there will be Peace in the world.*
>
> —*Bhagavan Sri Sathya Sai Baba*

meanings are defined by the social system in which they are embedded. Therefore, the validity of conventions lies in their links to existing social systems. Morality, too, applies to social systems, but contrasts with convention in that it is not determined by existing uniformities. (pp. 109–110).

Turiel argues that many character traits of the sort emphasized in the proposals we studied (e.g., punctuality, loyalty) serve to socialize young people into existing social conventions, rather than to engage them in moral behavior. From this we infer that much of what is offered as character education is instead socialization into a particular value system. Whether that system is moral or not is a separate question, in the view of Turiel and others.

Ethical Behavior Follows From Judgment of Situations.   Commentators on character education from a didactic perspective (e.g., Lickona, 1993; Ryan, 1993; Wynne, 1985) often target relativism—the idea that there are multiple legitimate perspectives on events—as a construct that must be abandoned in order for character education to proceed. Indeed, Bennett (1980) argues that judgment of ethical situations may result in moral confusion because it may lead to the questioning of established rules and traditions. These critics typically refer to values clarification as an example of relativistic approaches undergirded by the uncritical assumption that any belief is as good as another. This inclusive perspective, they argue, renders students incapable of making moral judgments about even the grossest of human misconduct: the Holocaust, the slave trade, the attacks on the World Trade Center, and so on. As a result of such ambivalence about morality, argues Nisbet, liberal solutions to societal problems emerge from a "vacuum of values" (cited in Noddings, 1997, p. 6).

Those arguing from a community-based perspective distance themselves from radical moral relativism, yet allow for and often encourage perspective-taking as a way to understand different constructions of the same situation. Further, they argue that circumstances may require choices about which virtue to act on, resulting in what their critics would likely characterize as *situational ethics* that produce the sort of moral ambiguity and inaction not available in didactic approaches. Hartshorne's and May's (1928) primary finding in their study of character education in the years following World War I was that children cannot be divided into honest and dishonest categories. It was found that honesty in one situation does not predict well to other situations. That is, "character was found to be situationally specific." Such a conclusion contradicts the assertion that ethics are immutable, as Lickona (1993) argues. Lockwood (2001) maintains that the complexity of many moral situations requires a curriculum that "can address the reality of value controversy and not be limited by the view that value questions invariably have clear right answers ... a view that is unrealistic, simplistic, and stifling of moral growth" (p. 60).

Smagorinsky (2002a), for instance, offers the example of slaves and abolitionists on the Underground Railroad who disrespected and violated the values and laws of plantation society, violated U.S. law after the passage of the Fugitive Slave Act of 1850 and ruling on the Dredd Scott v. Sandford case of 1857, developed textual codes (conveyed through spirituals, quilts, and other media) designed to facilitate deception and escape to the North, were disloyal and dishonest to slave masters, and otherwise transgressed the moral codes promoted by didactic character educators. At the same time the slaves and abolitionists were courageous, responsible to one another, respectful of the idea of freedom, and imbued with other traits that, in other circumstances, would not have resulted in what the South treated as criminal behavior. Such complex moral dilemmas, argue these character educators, are not well served by absolute moral codes, an idea that Turiel (2002) identifies as a distinctly Western concept; rather, they require reflection on moral choices that must be weighed against one another. As such, they require flexibility relative to situations and must be resolved in order to make appropriate action (cf. Walker, 2000). This example illustrates Turiel's distinction between conventions (oppressing African Americans) and morality (resisting injustice). More recent examples include nonviolent civil rights demonstrators, antiwar protestors, antiglobalization activists, nonviolent abortion clinic protestors, and others who have been jailed for protesting what they believed to be unjust laws and social practices.

Lickona (1993) argues that "Values clarification said, don't impose values; help students choose their values freely. Kohlberg said, develop students' powers of moral reasoning so they can judge which values are better than others." Neither is sufficient to Lickona in distinguishing between "personal preferences (truly a matter of free choice) and moral values (a matter of obligation)" (p. 2). For runaway slaves, however, the "matter of obligation" needed to be resolved in terms of the question, obligation to whom? Such

Having good character is one of the 5 Powers of a Champion.™ It means to act in a manner that is honorable, courageous, compassionate and ethical. It results in being viewed with respect, overcoming the difficult and feeling good about yourself. But achieving that goal can be a challenge due to outside forces and your own destructive attitudes. Your character is based on the opinion of others, as well as your own view. When you have a reputation of having good character, people tend to treat you with respect, trust and admiration. This increases your esteem and self-respect, as well as allows you to prosper. Having good character is important to us all in maintaining a good position in society and a favorable opinion of yourself. A bad reputation can even affect your confidence and relationship with others.

—School for Champions website

questions stand outside the dichotomy between personal preference and moral values outlined by Lickona, suggesting the need for a more complex, flexible, and situational understanding of moral action. Turiel (2002) argues that such an approach is responsive to the ways in which people act morally:

> Individuals make complex moral, social, and personal judgments that often entail taking into account the context of people's activities. Research also has demonstrated that in their moral decisions people take circumstances into account—not in the relativistic sense nor simply as accommodation to the situation. Rather, people often weigh and struggle with different and competing moral considerations, as well as try to balance nonmoral with moral considerations. (p. 15)

Constructivist Perspectives Best Account for Human Learning and Development.   Kohn (1997) and Smagorinsky (2000, 2002a) criticize the dominant approach to character education for its reliance on a transmission (Shannon & Weaver, 1949) or banking (Freire, 2000) model of education, that is, one predicated on the assumption that when teachers and texts say things, students receive and internalize them intact. In one of the few systematic studies of character education conducted in U.S. schools, Hartshorne and May (1928) found that "the mere urging of honest behavior by teachers or the discussion of standards and ideals ... has no necessary relation to conduct.... The prevailing ways of inculcating ideals probably do little good and may do some harm" (p. 413; cited in Leming, 1997, p. 34). This study and many like it across the field of education raise questions about how effectively a curriculum can work when it relies so heavily on didactic indoctrination.

Kohn (1997) and Smagorinsky (2000, 2002a), citing such communication researchers as Barnes (1992), offer instead a constructivist conception of communication (cf. Turiel, 2002). In this view people interpret new information on the basis of prior knowledge developed through formal and informal experience, an emphasis that is derived from the progressive beliefs of John Dewey, the architect of cultural decline in the eyes of many orthodox commentators (e.g., Hirsch, 1987). Kohn, for instance, argues that education, including character education, ought to engage students in "deep, critical reflection about certain ways of being" (p. 2). He sees traditional character educators as viewing "children as objects to be manipulated rather than as learners to be engaged" (p. 8). Both Kohn and Smagorinsky (cf. DeVries & Zan, 1994) advocate reflection as a central component of character education, one that invites them to consider moral dilemmas and all their complexity as a way to arrive at moral action. This sort of deep, engaged, critical reflection allows individuals and groups to construct meaning differently from the same text, depending on how their cultural and

> *There is a wonderful Hasidic story about a rabbi who was asked whether it is ever proper to act as if God did not exist. He responded, "Yes, when you are asked to give charity, you should give as if there were no God to help the object of the charity." I think the same is true of morality and character: in deciding what course of action is moral, you should act as if there were no God. You should also act as if there were no threat of earthly punishment or reward. You should be a person of good character because it is right to be such a person.*
>
> *—Alan Dershowitz*

personal experiences have shaped their perspectives (Smagorinsky, 2001a). This idiosyncratic conception of textual interpretation has been widely accepted by teachers of literature (Beach, 1993), an ironic development given the importance placed on stories as vehicles for cultural assimilation and character development (Bennett, 1993).

A constructivist emphasis suggests the role for relativism to play in moral development. The challenge for character educators is then to allow for moral interpretation and perspective-taking while encouraging students to question the morality of mass murderers and other societal pariahs. To help negotiate the grey areas in between clear instances of moral and immoral behavior, teachers operating from this perspective might indeed avail themselves to the sorts of moral dilemmas developed by Kohlberg (1976), employed in values clarification and denounced by today's character education leaders.

The Community of Practice Is the Focus of Attention. Both didactic and reflective approaches to character education give attention to the individual and the community. They are distinct in which of the two they foreground, however. As we have noted, didactic approaches to character education focus on individuals who exhibit poor character, striving to change them so that the community is a more stable and moral arena. Leming (1997) cites May and Hartshorne (1927) to argue that character education

> needed to be improved somewhat by focusing less on direct methods of instruction such as lecture and exhortation and more on indirect methods such as the creation of a positive school climate and service-oriented activities for students ... given the relative constancy of the teacher-centered method of instruction in American schools, it appears unlikely that the use of the traditional direct method of character education changed substantially in the direction suggested by the May and Hartshorne study. (p. 35)

Again arguing for less didactic teaching methods, Leming and May and Hartshorne seek to shift the focus from the deviant individual to the social context in which behaviors are deemed deviant. Kohn (1997) concurs, maintaining that:

> the accumulated evidence from the field of social psychology [demonstrates] that much of how we act and who we are reflects the situations in which we find ourselves" and that educators should strive to transform the structure of the classroom rather than try to remake the students themselves. (p. 4)

Noddings (1997), extending her studies of the notion of care (1984, 1992) to character education, emphasizes the key role of community in the development of character: "As social beings, we are products of, as well as contributors to, traditions of behavior. We are not first disengaged, rational mechanisms and *then* participants in a society; rather, whatever rationality we eventually exhibit is itself a product of the tradition in which we are raised and educated" (p. 2). Purpel (1997) sees this notion of community as being quite broad, including the various social, economic, and political structures that serve as cultural institutions. To Purpel, "bad behavior" is less a function of bad values as it is a failure of these institutions to carry out their responsibilities to the whole of the population. As a consequence, mainstreamers construe non-normative behavior on the part of the socially marginalized as immoral and in need of character education. Purpel is troubled by the absence of attention by didactic character educators to

> The harshness and cruelty of an increasingly unbridled free market economy, of growing economic inequality, of the systemic nature of poverty, of the enormous disparity in the quality of medical care, of ecological devastation, of the ever-increasing desperation of have-not nations, or of the continuing dangers of international conflicts. The basic explanation that the character education movement offers for moral decline is a psychological one, that the problems are rooted in an inflated sense of personalism and self-centeredness rather than in social, economic, and cultural institutions. (pp. 149–150)

These institutions, argues Purpel, ought to be the focus of change so that people are less likely to act out against them.

To counteract the harsh world identified by Purpel (1997), Schaps, Battistich, and Solomon (1997) believe that school ought to be transformed into a "caring community of learners," which

> means they are valued contributing members of a group dedicated to shared purposes of helping and supporting each other as they work, learn, and grow together. It means that they care about their learning and care about each other. At the heart of a caring community of learners are the following: *Respectful, supportive relationships among students, teachers, and parents.... Emphasis on common purposes and ideals.... Frequent opportunities to help and collaborate with others.... Frequent opportunities for autonomy and influence.* (pp. 128–129)

> *All need to become good persons. Good character is essential. In order to keep this good conduct (sila) permanently, we all need right understanding as a guide. Sila alone is not sufficient. So the Buddha teaches that the practice of samadhi concentration and the use of mindfulness to watch the changing phenomena of our daily lives must be the greatest concern for all mankind. Only the Buddha can teach the fact of Anatta which can be known by means of Vipassana practice.*
>
> *—U Han Htay*

These educators advocate transforming the climate of school so that it is less punitive and more nurturing, enabling the sort of engagement that Kohn (1997) and others believe is important in thinking deeply about issues of character. Such an approach is dismissed by Ryan (2003) as relying on the "soft language of therapy" rather than the presumably strong "language of character" (p. 4).

Character Education Should Contribute to a Just, Democratic Society.
In keeping with their emphasis on the quality of the environment of character development, those who advocate a reflective approach to character education are interested in the formation of a just, democratic society. Presumably, in such a setting one's character will flourish given the diminished tendency to denigrate and marginalize individuals and groups who then resist the community and its values. Gay (1997), for instance, argues that "Rejecting or demeaning the cultural heritage of individuals constitutes an act of psychological and moral violence to their human dignity and worth … character development … includes a combination of *egalitarian* ethics, morality, and behaviors evident in personal, social, and civic conduct" (p. 105). The establishment of a just and equitable society, then, is among the primary goals of character education from a communitarian perspective. This goal is quite compatible with this approach's focus on the community of practice rather than on the individual actor within that community.

Suggesting a Deweyian influence, Schubert (1997) sees the goal of a just society as necessarily following from experience-based learning:

> Students do need an experientialist curriculum, but one that centers inquiry and action together (praxis) on the experience of injustice—on first exposing it and then on working to overcome it. To engage in such work with students *is* the most important project of character education, because doing so requires the exercise of courage and commitment to overcome injustice. Through such work character is forged. (p. 27)

To Kohn (1997), such efforts produce character education that is "principally concerned with helping children become active participants in a democratic society (or agents for transforming a society into one that is authentically democratic) [and to] help students develop into principled and caring members of a community or advocates for social justice" (p. 5).

Noddings (1997) anticipates how such a program might be received by many in the United States, saying that "conservative critics have seen the form of liberalism that stresses equality (instead of freedom) as the precursor of communism" (p. 6). Although fear of communism might not have the same mobilizing effect on people in the United States now that it had before the early 1990s, this fear of a society of equals runs counter to the principles of free market capitalism that have long driven U.S. consumerism and competition. Popular among academics, calls for equality have had less currency among those who benefit from the capitalist enterprise. We should not be surprised, then, that this approach finds relatively little support among members of Congress who helped to institute funding for character education.

Character Education Should Have a Strong Affective Dimension.
Noddings (1997), long a champion of emphasizing an ethic of care among education's primary goals, argues that in the sort of communities she envisions, "the virtues to be prized will be relational rather than personal. Relational attributes such as trust, good cheer, equality, peace, and compatibility may be more important than personal virtues such as courage, honesty, and industry" (p. 8). Relationships, a staple of feminist psychology since the early work of Gilligan (1983) and Belenky, Clinchy, Goldberger, and Tarule (1986), require attention to the affective dimensions of experience. Good character, in this view, is in great part a function of good relationships.

Toward this end, character educators who take a reflective or community-based approach have begun suggesting emotional character traits that are absent from the lists generated by the mostly male set of character commentators. Berkowitz (2002) finds the beginning of empathy to be among the most significant hallmarks of the development of character. Meier and

---

"Do as I say, not as I do:" this is considered the very motto of hypocrisy. But does anyone believe that having a good character is as easy as wanting it? If virtue is as difficult as other excellences, there must be few or none who are perfectly virtuous. If the rest of us are not even to talk about virtue or express admiration for it, how shall anyone improve? A hypocrite is one who claims virtue beyond what he possesses, not one who recommends virtue beyond what he claims. If a man's principles are no better than his character, it is less likely to be a sign of an exemplary character than a sign of debased principles.

—Mark Thompson

Schwarz (1995) offer empathy and skepticism as traits that enable young people to see situations from the perspectives of others and consider the validity of those perspectives. Similarly, Smagorinsky (2002a) suggests compathy as an essential trait. Whereas *empathy* refers to the projection of oneself into the personality of another in order to achieve better understanding, and *sympathy* describes an affinity of feelings between people, *compathy* refers to feeling with another person. It requires not simply projecting and understanding but making an effort to live through that person's emotions, to resonate with that person's experiences and responses. Such a trait, although extremely difficult to achieve, is important in order to understand how marginalized or alienated people are affectively experiencing social situations and offer them inclusion and acceptance.

In a related move, Kohn (1997) offers autonomy as an important trait that leads to feelings of self-determination, which he argues is the antithesis of what authoritarian approaches to education hope to instill in young people. The idea that students should take responsibility for the directions of their lives is central to the idea that character education should contribute to students' capacity to negotiate the world with some degree of authority and self-direction.

On the whole, these commentators agree on the notion of the caring community as a way to construct what Berkowitz (2002) believes to be a moral atmosphere, which he finds to be a critical component of character education effort. He argues that "Relationships are crucial to character development, so character education must focus on the quality of relationships in the school.... Those relationships need to be benevolent

---

The cause of all the miseries we have in the world is that men foolishly think pleasure to be the ideal to strive for. After a time man finds that it is not happiness, but knowledge, towards which he is going, and that both pleasure and pain are great teachers, and that he learns as much from evil as from good. As pleasure and pain pass before his soul they have upon it different pictures, and the result of these combined impressions is what is called man's "character." If you take the character of any man, it really is but the aggregate of tendencies, the sum total of the bent of his mind; you will find that misery and happiness are equal factors in the formation of that character. Good and evil have an equal share in moulding character, and in some instances misery is a greater teacher than happiness. In studying the great characters the world has produced, I dare say, in the vast majority of cases, it would be found that it was misery that taught more than happiness, it was poverty that taught more than wealth, it was blows that brought out their inner fire more than praise.

—Swami Vivekananda

(nurturant, supportive), authentic (honest, open), respectful (inclusive, valuing the student's voice), and consistent (predictable, stable)" (pp. 58–59). Power (2002) concurs, feeling that too may educators perceive such problems as cheating, bullying, and vandalism as existing "in a gestalt that accentuates individual students but not the groups to which they belong. Until we change the culture of schools into democratic communities, these problems are likely to persist and our character education programs to flounder" (p. 130). Power refers to Horace Mann's ironic observation about the presence of authoritarian schools in democratic nations:

> In order that men may be prepared for self-government, their apprenticeship must begin in childhood.... He who has been a serf until the day before he is twenty-one years of age, cannot be an independent citizen the day after; and it makes no difference whether he has been a serf in Austria or America. As the fitting apprenticeship for despotism consists in being trained for despotism, so the fitting apprenticeship for self-government consists in being trained in self-government. (Mann, 1845/1957, p. 58; cited in Power, p. 136)

Although difficult and problematic to implement, argues Power, such caring communities of democratic practice ought to be the goal for schools that hope to teach character.

Character Education Includes Attention to Diversity.

Leming (1994) reports that

> Moral instruction was always tied to questions of the assimilation of immigrants and the development of a national character. It wasn't until the last half of the twentieth century that a solution was sought to the distinctive question of how a pluralist society can simultaneously contain cultural groups with differing values systems, and a national culture built on a shared set of cultural values. (p. 128)

Such an approach requires what Gardner calls "wholeness incorporating diversity" (cited in Noddings, 1997, p. 8), a condition that includes the challenge to honor diversity while emphasizing shared values. To Gay (1997), character education that does not include attention to multicultural education avoids the very issues to which good character is most fruitfully applied, those that require the negotiation of difference and diversity. She says that

> Whereas character education is often centered in "individual attributes and actions," multicultural education emphasizes the "social and the collective." It evokes the promises and perils of the social character of the United States (as symbolized by principles of democracy) in justifying its vision, and its calls for group action and social reform to achieve its goals and objectives. In this sense, multicultural education is consistent with concep-

> *The final forming of a person's character lies in their own hands.*
>
> —*Anne Frank*

tions of character development as "a social and not an individual phenomenon," since "there is no such thing as a solitary, a private human being" [Johnson, 1987, p. 61]. As a social edict multicultural education challenges "the societal power structure that has historically subordinated certain groups and rationalized the educational failure of children from these groups as being the result of their inherent deficiencies" [Cummins, 1996, p. xvi]. At its core are those attributes of a nation's social character which constitute "social justice and equality." (p. 98)

Gay's (1997) views on multicultural education are consistent with other aspects of a community-based approach to character education, particularly the idea that attention ought to be focused on the larger society rather than the aberrant individual. This focus produces not only a multicultural education but a more just and equitable society, one that as a whole has admirable qualities of character that its citizens willingly embrace. Presumably, the care that permeates such a community will extend to all stakeholders and create the affective bonds that hold communities together over time.

Outside the Western Vision:
A Native-American Perspective on Character Education

In *Teaching Virtues: Building Character across the Curriculum*, Native American educators Don Trent Jacobs and Jessica Jacobs-Spencer (2001) outline a perspective on character education that is different in fundamental ways from either approach we have described. In particular, they view character as extending beyond human communities and encompassing "intimate relationships of living things" (p. vii). This belief in the interrelationship among all constituents of the ecology extends to those earthly objects viewed in the West as inanimate, such as stones (Four Arrows [D. T. Jacobs], personal communication, June, 2003). A major goal of character education in this conception is for students to "internalize virtues as a part of their identity and learn how this identity relates to the larger web of life" (p. vii). The distinguishing premises of this perspective are as follows.

> *Nearly all men can stand adversity, but if you want to test a man's character, give him power.*
>
> —*Abraham Lincoln*

All Life and Nature Are Interconnected

Jacobs and Jacobs-Spencer (2001) argue that schools

> do not have policies that see human relationships with nature as dependent
> and morally reciprocal. More inclined toward individualism and mechanis-
> tic structures than community or holistic processes, the dominant worldview
> emphasizes economic utility and consumption rather than diversity and con-
> servation. With such a priority, moral education is not about a commitment
> to life and its interconnections, but is merely another vehicle for enforcing
> conformity on behalf of economic outcomes. (p. vii)

Here Jacobs and Jacobs-Spencer offer a possibility not available through
Western conceptions of character, the idea that moral relationships extend
to the natural environment. Throughout their book they describe encounters with hawks and other creatures whose example informs their development of character and life choices. "From all the noble creatures that
display courage, patience, humility, generosity, or fortitude," they say, "we
learn about the respect and responsibility necessary to keep these intimate
relationships in natural harmony" (p. vii). In this reciprocal view, animals,
not people, are the original teachers of virtues, and remain so in the modern world. This stature as moral exemplars explains why animal stories are
used in most cultures to teach virtues (Four Arrows [D. T. Jacobs], personal
communication, July, 2003).

This view departs dramatically from what they regard as the "overly anthropocentric" orientation of most character education programs (Jacobs &
Jacobs-Spencer, 2001, p. viii). The idea that reciprocal relationships exist
between people and all earthly life, and that attention to these relationships
is central to one's character, is extended in other work by Jacobs (e.g., 1998)
to include not only the whole ecology but all earthly and heavenly elements.
This animistic perspective is not accounted for in Western conceptions of
character and is indeed viewed by traditional Western anthropologists (e.g.,
Clifton, 1990) as lower on the social evolutionary scale than perspectives
that accord spirit life only to people (Deloria, 1995). Jacobs and Jacobs-
Spencer (2001), in contrast, invoke the Lakota expression, *Mitakuye Oyasin*

> *We believe that the ultimate aim of Hapkido and Tae Kwon Do is the building of*
> *character in the student. Classes are physically and mentally challenging at times,*
> *and through patience and determination the student will accomplish feats they*
> *previously thought beyond their abilities. This in turn will increase the student's*
> *self-confidence and self-image and will allow them to treat others with greater*
> *patience and respect.*
>
> *—The Colorado Hapkido and Tae Kwon Do Association*

(We are all related) as among the great awarenesses needed for effective character education.

Character Education Includes the Spiritual Realm. Jacobs and Jacobs-Spencer (2001) stress the importance of the spiritual, by which they mean "a sacred awareness that we are all related and that all things in the seen and unseen universe are interconnected. This, of course, includes our vital relationships and interdependence on the earth and its creatures" (p. ix). They distinguish between religion and spirituality, quoting Paul Byers's assertion that "Religions are particular answers to the universal human questions about the creation and meaning of life. Spiritual refers to the universal personal concern for the questions" (p. xvi). They argue that "Spirituality pervades the entire process of learning that leads to good character. Knowledge ultimately is always connected to our spiritual, ecological, and intrapersonal and interpersonal relationships. However, the overly anthropocentric assumptions of our current culture cause us to forget this fact, even when we use collaborative models for our teaching" (p. 18). Spirituality, they argue, has no beginning or ending, rejecting the linear conception of progress that undergirds Western beliefs about time and space. Rather, they say, it "already exists in our consciousness at birth, even before we participate in life's various learning experiences. In American Indian cultures, this sacred aspect of the child is nurtured from birth so that the sense of interconnections colors all of the person's subsequent learning" (p. 18). Such a belief about human nature runs counter to that of Headmaster Jarvis's view that people are by nature mean, nasty, brutish, and selfish. It is also distinct from Rousseau's view of the young as noble innocents who become corrupted by the effects of society, a view potentially available in the reflective approach to character education we have reviewed.

Character Education Is Built on Universal Virtues. Similar to those working from a didactic conception of character education, Jacobs and Jacobs-Spencer (2001) believe that there is a set of universal values that have been identified in cultures throughout the world. The traits they identify are different, however, consisting of fortitude, courage, patience, honesty, humility, and generosity. Several factors interrelate with these traits. People use the five inner skills of reason, intuition, reflection, humor, and emotional control to master three types of external skills: survival, occupational, and recreational. People use these inner skills to develop the three external skills, mediated by their attention to the six universal virtues in

---

A sense of humor is an important trait of good character; it bespeaks an ability to put things in perspective and to refrain from taking oneself too seriously.

—*James Taranto*

conjunction with experience, respect, and wisdom to form good character. Good character consists of two primary components: integrity (firm adherence to an identity with a code of ethics/virtues) and Wolakota (being genuinely at peace with the self and others). Permeating the entire process is one's sense of spirituality. Character education is the process of formal pedagogy designed to promote this complex process by constantly looking for teachable moments to weave virtue awareness into the daily curriculum and by emphasizing intrinsic motivation over rewards and punishments for acting in virtuous ways.

Such facets of character as feeling humility, being at peace, being spiritual, seeing generosity as the highest expression of courage, and feeling connected with all life forms are absent from Western conceptions of character. As we will review in subsequent chapters, they are not surprisingly absent from proposals funded by OERI for character curricula.

RESEARCH ON CHARACTER EDUCATION

Despite the widespread and long-term interest in character education that we have outlined, the field "is woefully deficient in producing systematic outcomes research" (Berkowitz, 1998, p. 4). The first widespread efforts to study the effects of character education came in the 1920s, following the intervention to assimilate, homogenize, and pacify young people in the years following World War I. Hartshorne and May's (1928) study, to which we have referred previously, found that character education efforts in general did not have the impact on children's behavior that their advocates hoped to achieve. Furthermore, Nickell and Field (2001) argue that "during the 1920s and 1930s ... little systematic program assessment occurred," with "self-reports and narrative generalities" constituting the evaluation of character education initiatives (p. 2). Lockwood (1991) concludes that the character education movement in the wake of World War I failed to live up to its promise, arguing that there is "No evidence that CE had any systematic effect on behavior" (p. 246).

Research since that time has turned up similar conclusions. Leming (1997) argues that "The findings of Hartshorne and May still reverberate among those concerned with the education of character.... To date, there has been no similar inquiry that combines the quality of research and sample size employed in this study" (p. 34). Leming's (1993) review of the research in character education leads to the conclusion that "The current CE

Talent develops in quiet, alone; character is sharpened in the torrent of the world.
—Johann Wolfgang Von Goethe

movement lacks either a theoretical perspective or a common core of practice. The movement is eclectic both in terms of its psychological premises and its pedagogical practices. No common perspective exists to provide a basis for a coherent research program" (p. 41).

According to Purpel (1997), the literature on character education suffers from "the near absence of ideological analysis." Purpel sees this absence as "extraordinarily anomalous, particularly for those who are responding to a sense of cultural and moral crisis, since it would seem that a thoughtful response to a moral crisis inevitably requires some interpretation of its etiology and nature" (p. 146). Leming (1997) concludes that most discussions of character education are driven more by ideology than data:

> Changes in the theory and practice of educational programs designed to affect the character of youth have resulted more from questions of values than from questions of data … the future of character education will likely depend on the values that underlie the chosen approach and the degree to which those assumptions and values are perceived as congruent with the values and needs of the communities served. Research that supports program effectiveness is only one part of the warrant for character education programs. (p. 42)

SUMMARY

On the whole, character education efforts appear to be driven more by values (presumably clarified) than data, suggesting the importance of an analysis of the discourse of character education. Although our analysis does not include studies of the actual implementation of these curricula, we believe that it does reveal much about the concerns and preoccupations of opinion leaders at a particular moment in history regarding the moral education of young people. In this chapter we have reviewed the two major positions on character education. These positions adhere to radically different premises about human nature and social organization. They emerge from competing traditions that govern thought about the purpose and process of society, and each maintains that its assumptions embody fundamental principles of U.S. heritage. These two positions are set in relief by the non-Western perspective provided by Jacobs and Jacobs-Spencer (2001). We see these three distinct positions as operating

---

[The people] have a right, an indisputable, unalienable, indefeasible, divine right to that most dreaded and envied kind of knowledge—I mean of the character and conduct of their rulers.

—John Adams

from different ideologies, employing different discourses, invoking different traditions, and resulting in different conceptions of a good society. In the next chapter, we attend more carefully to the theories that inform our understanding of these issues.

> *How do we acquire character, how do we come to possess good qualities? By living according to the precepts of the vedas and sastras and by following the good customs practiced by our own forefathers as well as by performing the rites that have been passed down to us. Good conduct springs from a good mind. So the mind must be free from evil.*
>
> *—Hindu Dharma*

Chapter 5

Theoretical Framework

In this chapter we review the theoretical lenses through which we view the notions of character and character education. First we discuss the notion of *discourse,* the central term in our analysis. Then, we review Vygotsky's (1987) construct of the *concept,* which informs our analysis of the coherence of the various accounts of character education articulated in the proposals.

DISCOURSE

In this study we analyze the discourse of character education, as evidenced in successful proposals submitted to OERI. Our notion of discourse includes three elements: Gee's (1990) outline of ideology, Bakhtin's (1981) construct of dialogism, and Kristeva's (1984) views on intertextuality. We next review each of these three concepts and their relation to our project, which shares Purpel's (1997) assumption that the current character education movement "represents an *ideological and political* movement rather than a debate about curricular and instructional matters" (p. 140), although we see the curriculum, instruction, and, we would add, assessment offered in service of character education as part of the discourse itself.

To introduce these three elements, we reprint a letter sent to the *Athens Daily News/Banner-Herald* (GA) on Monday, January 8, 2001, in response to an editorial that questioned the Georgia character curriculum's inclusion of "respect for the creator" as one of its essential character traits:

> I read with dismay your (Jan. 5) editorial, "Reference to the 'creator' hurts character education." Far from being an unnecessary addition to Georgia's character education goals, "respect for the creator" is a rudimentary principle from which many other character education goals are derived. Cour-

tesy, compassion and respect for others, for example, all flow from the notion that people have intrinsic worth because they are created beings, rather than simple biological accidents or random combinations of protoplasm. Not only is "respect for the creator" a worthy goal of Georgia's character education program, it is an idea that is foundational to the entire American experiment. The first principle of our republic is that all people are "endowed by their creator" with certain rights that cannot legitimately be taken away. The purpose of government, as stated by the Declaration of Independence, is to uphold the creator's intent. Our national motto, stamped on all our coins and carved in stone in the U.S. House of Representatives, is: "In God We Trust." I find it passing strange that the editorial board of the *Athens Daily News/Banner-Herald* considers this too controversial a concept to be reinforced in our schools.

—Joseph Slife

We will refer back to this letter in our review of the constructs of ideology, dialogism, and intertextuality.

Ideology

Slife's letter is motivated by a clear ideology regarding the role of a creator in the principles behind U.S. democracy. Gee (1990) and others (e.g., Butler, 1997; Fairclough, 1995; Lee, 1996; Weedon, 1987) have argued that language is inherently ideological. In the passage that follows, Gee's capitalization of *Discourse* is deliberate, referring not simply to brief episodes of speech but "ways of being in the world, or forms of life which integrate words, acts, values, beliefs, attitudes, social identities, as well as gestures, glances, body positions, and clothes" (p. 142). Discourse, in other words, embodies a political stance through which a world view is enacted through tacit or explicit means, imparts a stance that it is impervious to question or criticism, and suggests the marginality or dubiousness of values and perspectives central to other Discourses. Gee says,

> Each Discourse incorporates a usually taken-for-granted and tacit "theory" of what counts as a "normal" person and the "right" ways to think, feel and behave. These theories crucially involve viewpoints on the distribution of "social goods" like status, "worth" and "material" goods in society (who should and who should not have them).... Such theories, which are part and parcel of each and every

---

The [ancient] Greeks believed that character was formed in part by fate and in part by parental training, and that character was exemplified not only by acts of bravery in battle but in the habits of daily conduct.

—James Cannon

Discourse, and which thus underlie the use of language in all cases, are what I call … "ideologies." Language is inextricably bound up with ideology, and cannot be analyzed or understood apart from it. (p. xx)

Our study of OERI-funded character education curricula looks at discourse as ideological in Gee's (1990) sense. In reading the curricula, we found that each proposal implied an answer to one of Gee's major questions: *"what sort of social group do I intend to apprentice the learner into?"* (p. 45). Students are not only being instructed about character, they are being socialized into a particular way of being and into the social groups who value those ways of being.

Dialogism

Bakhtin's (1981) notion of dialogism is well-illustrated by Burke's (1941) metaphor of a parlor conversation:

Where does the drama get its materials? From the "unending conversation" that is going on at the point in history when we are born. Imagine that you enter a parlor. You come late. When you arrive, others have long preceded you, and they are engaged in a heated discussion, a discussion too heated for them to pause and tell you exactly what it is about. In fact, the discussion had already begun long before any of them got there, so that no one present is qualified to retrace for you all the steps that had gone before. You listen for a while, until you decide that you have caught the tenor of the argument; then you put in your oar. Someone answers; you answer him; another comes to your defense; another aligns himself against you, to either the embarrassment or gratification of your opponent, depending upon the quality of your ally's assistance. However, the discussion is interminable. The hour grows late, you must depart. And you do depart, with the discussion still vigorously in progress. (pp. 110–111)

Interactive workbook! Know What?®️ We Have Good Character! Ages 6–8

Doing the right thing is a lot easier when kids get a chance to work with the building blocks of good character. This workbook introduces them to simple, key factors in character development that include showing respect to others and oneself, being considerate of others' feelings, treating others fairly, and being trustworthy. Interactive exercises include:

- *showing-respect sentence completion*
- *acts of kindness word match*
- *building-trust maze*
- *ways to talk back to TV shows that depict "wrong" behaviors*
- *parent–child values discussion.*

Bakhtin's (1981) construct of dialogism corresponds to Burke's (1941) idea of an ongoing conversation in which many people intermittently take part. Discourse in this sense does not arise out of thin air but is always a conversational turn directed to others, even if they are only anticipated or imagined.

Dialogism enables the discourse of a particular community (Libertarians, Jungian psychologists, character educators affiliated with conservative Christians) to become normalized in terms of its ideology; that is, their historical, ongoing conversation ceases to question certain axioms that in turn marginalize other perspectives on the topic. Thus, for instance, in ongoing conversations about character education among people for whom a sacred text prescribes morality such as Slife's letter on the Georgia character education initiative, it may be axiomatic that character is composed of a set of fixed traits (e.g., honesty, trust) that are invariant and may be instructed to youth and sinners through didactic methods. Those who believe that notions of character are relative and situated are marginalized and dismissed among such discussants.

Dialogism may be exhibited explicitly (e.g., as part of an actual conversation) or through what Bakhtin (1984) calls *hidden dialogicality*. Here, texts are produced as conversational turns that take into account prior texts even if those texts are not present or acknowledged (Wertsch, 1999). In this sense texts are *emplotted* (Ricoeur, 1983) within a continuum of narratives or lines of argument, that is, a text or utterance never stands alone but is always in conversation with prior and anticipated conversational turns. In our study we see both narratives and arguments at play in successful OERI-funded character education initiatives. Narratives are presented about the bygone days of virtue and modern decline of morality, the story of the United States' civic heritage and its current demise, and so on. Typically, these narratives, as Loewen (1996) points out, are selective, presenting the United States according to its most glorious mythology and ignoring its many contradictions and those events that might promote feelings of shame and anger (e.g., the legacy of slavery). The proposals typically include a counternarrative that will follow from a character education curriculum, one in which a well-funded curriculum will reform errant youths and society's ethics will return to their halcyon days of yore. The proposals are further situated within arguments about the state of society, the notion of character, the role of schooling, the U.S. heritage, and so on.

In addition to being emplotted in these narratives and dialogically situated within ongoing arguments about the state of U.S. youth and education, the proposals that we analyze are in dialogue with the OERI Request for Proposals (RFP). As part of our analysis we will look at the kinds of discourses distilled in the RFP, the congressional discussions in which those discourses were invoked, and the ways in which the RFP shaped the discourses evident in the proposals submitted by the states.

> *This is what we call character—a reserved force which acts directly as presence, and without means.*
>
> —*Ralph Waldo Emerson*

Slife's letter incorporates all of these principles. He locates himself as a respondent to the newspaper's editorial and situates his argument within a creationist discourse stream. Other perspectives are dismissed because they are outside the axioms of this perspective. His letter illustrates the emplotted, dialogic nature of discourse.

Intertextuality

Like the notion of dialogism, intertextuality refers to the ways in which any newly produced texts derive from prior texts. Although *dialogism* refers to the fact of this ongoing conversation, intertextuality refers to the forms and social practices from which new texts take shape. Intertextuality thus helps account for the enduring traits of discourse as well as the variations made in conventional forms by particular communities of practice.

The OERI character education curricula we analyze for this study are connected with discussions of values, ethics, and morality and their relation to education, U.S. nationalism, multiculturalism, and other discourses with which they interact, and they do so through particular historical ways of addressing these issues. They typically indicate their membership in social groups and disdain for groups who hold different worldviews, particularly when it comes to character, morality, education, and civic behavior. And so, for instance, when Lickona (1991) is invoked to support a particular approach to character education, he traces the current demise in youth character to the 1960s, a time in which adult authority was questioned, feminism was boldly revived, minority groups asserted their Constitutional rights, a youth drug culture developed, "the Establishment" was questioned, sexuality lost its historical relation to marriage, multiple forms of birth control became widely available, and other pillars of society were undermined in a way that, he argues, only effective character education can restore.

The discourse Lickona employs about effective character education relies on special *topoi* (Fahnestock & Secor, 1991)—a reification of adult authority, an unequivocal view of sin, and so on—that make him an authoritative speaker in a particular, ongoing discussion about morality and education and provide him a prominent platform on conference podiums and in the pages of journals. Taking on the hortatory tone of authoritative discourse, his argument assumes the marginality or foolishness of those whose ideologies follow from different assumptions about these matters.

> *People of character don't allow the environment to dictate their style.*
>
> *—Lucille Kallen*

We see this authoritative tone reflected in Slife's letter regarding the necessary relation of "the creator" to character education, the Declaration of Independence, and the founding of the United States. Our notion of discourse, then, is centered on the particular ideologies, conversational streams, and forms that language takes when applied to the question of character education.

CONCEPT, PSEUDOCONCEPT, COMPLEX

We have referred to the ways in which character and character education are conceptualized by various stakeholders in the public debate. To inform our understanding of the construct of the concept, we borrow from Vygotsky's (1987) distinctions among concept, pseudoconcept, and complex.

Vygotsky (1987) was concerned with the ways in which people develop concepts over time. To Vygotsky word meaning is the appropriate unit of analysis for studying the development of consciousness, which he equates with the development of concepts. Through the meanings that they attribute to words, people reveal the degrees of abstraction that they have achieved in their thinking. Vygotsky argues that "the speech of those who surround the child predetermines the paths that the development of the child's generalizations will take" (p. 143). To become a member of a community of practice with normative ways of acting and being understood, a learner needs to come to the same understanding for words that elders and other societal veterans have for them.

The development of concepts thus involves growing into a culture's values and practices, with the culture in turn growing and changing as its practitioners contribute their understanding of its concepts. To borrow from the previous section, a person's use of a particular Discourse reflects not only knowledge of vocabulary but an understanding of the ideology behind that vocabulary. Furthermore, one's Discourse is intertextual, enabling members of the same culture to instantiate similar referents when hearing the same terms and by and large share the same perspective on those referents, an issue of definition that Lockwood (1997) finds problematic in discussions of character education. A person whose understanding of character emerges from the conservative Christian church might find it indisputable, as does Lickona (1997), that "championing the rights of children while permitting their violent destruction before birth" is a sign of "moral schizophrenia" (pp. 45–46). Such a claim is dialogic in relation to many discussions about social relationships emerging from conservative political positions, such as those institutionalized in the Republican Platform of 2002, for example, "We support the traditional definition of 'marriage' as the legal union of one man and one woman, and we believe that federal judges and bureaucrats should not force states to recognize other living arrangements as marriages. We rely on the home, as did the founders of the American Republic, to instill the virtues that sustain democracy itself" (http://www.rnc.org/About/PartyPlatform/default.aspx?Section=4).

Concepts are distinguished by the fact that all of the individual elements they encompass are unified by a single theme. Along the path toward concepts, people develop *complexes* and *pseudoconcepts*, both of which approximate the unity of elements found in concepts but include inconsistencies.

A *complex* lacks the unity of both scientific and spontaneous concepts and the formal, abstract logic that underlies a scientific concept. Vygotsky (1987) argues that

> If empirically present, *any* connection is sufficient to lead to the inclusion of an element in a given complex.... The concept is based on connections of a single, logically equivalent type. In contrast, the complex is based on heterogeneous empirical connections that frequently have nothing in common with one another. (p. 137)

Items grouped within a complex therefore are linked according to shared properties, though not all are linked according to the same property. At the level of the young child (Vygotsky's primary interest as a researcher), a youngster might first encounter a body of water and learn to name it a pond, and then name other bodies of water—swimming pools, water holes, oceans, puddles—ponds as well. For the adult character educator, a complex might occur when conflicting arguments are made to support the same point. As we will review, for instance, proposals submitted to OERI for a didactic character education program typically maintain that the family is the first and most important moral teacher of young people, and that schools need to intervene and act *in loco parentis* because families provide such poor moral guidance for their children—witness the record levels of youth crime, pregnancy, substance abuse, and other depravities. Similarly, the states from the Upper Midwest assume that moral issues are open to interpretation, while conforming to the OERI RFP's requirement to assert that there are six invariable traits that comprise character. We argue that such contradictions suggest the notions of character that we see in both sets of proposals are not fully conceptual. A *pseudoconcept* bridges the complex and concept developmentally. A pseudoconcept is a "shadow of the concept, one that reproduces its contours" (Vygotsky, 1987, p. 144), having all of the appearances of a concept yet connecting the objects "on the basis of simple association" (p. 142).

> *To point out the importance of circumspection in your conduct, it may be proper to observe that a good moral character is the first essential in a man, and that the habits contracted at your age are generally indelible, and your conduct here may stamp your character through life. It is therefore highly important that you should endeavor not only to be learned but virtuous.*
>
> *—George Washington*

Vygotsky distinguishes a concept from a pseudoconcept with the analogy that "the pseudoconcept is as similar to the true concept as the whale is to the fish" (p. 144). Internal contradictions prevent a pseudoconcept from being a concept.

As we will argue, these contradictions occur for a variety of reasons, including the need to conform to the OERI vision of character, the influence of different traditions in the development of the OERI proposals, and other factors. When diverse groups of people attempt to define concepts, they inevitably include inconsistencies as the group attempts to negotiate, accommodate, and resolve individual differences. If, as the adage goes, a camel is a horse designed by a committee, then a pseudoconcept is often a concept designed by an expert panel. At the same time, homogeneous groups are less likely to include inconsistencies but tend to overlook counter discourses that critique and challenge the authority of the dominant perspective and ideology of unquestioned beliefs. Both of these processes, we argue, are likely at work in the development of the proposals submitted to OERI for character education funding.

SUMMARY

Our effort thus far has been to present the general terms in which the question of character education has been debated through academic publications. These positions are well-represented in the proposals submitted to OERI for character education funding. In addition, the proposals incorporated related discourses that provide both detail and contradiction to the basic concepts outlined by academics. In the next part of our analysis, we introduce the discourses of character education in greater detail, reviewing how they are present in broader discussions of education and society in the United States.

Good Character Requirements for Solid Waste and Hazardous Waste Management Permits

---

Permit applicant disclosure statement

Sec. 2. Before an application for the issuance, renewal, transfer, or major modification of a permit described in IC 13-15-1-3 may be granted, the applicant and each person who is a responsible party with respect to the applicant must submit to the department:

a disclosure statement that:

- *meets the requirements set forth in section 3(a) of this chapter; and*
- *is executed under section 3(b) of this chapter; or*

(2) all of the following information:

- *The information concerning legal proceedings that is required under Section 13 or 15(d) of the federal Securities Exchange Act of 1934 (15 U.S.C. 78a et seq.); and the applicant or responsible party has reported under form 10-K.*
- *A description of all judgments that have been entered against the applicant or responsible party in a proceeding described in section 3(a)(3) of this chapter; and have imposed upon the applicant or responsible party a fine or penalty described in section 3(a)(3)(A) of this chapter.*
- *A description of all judgments of conviction entered against the applicant or responsible party within five (5) years before the date of submission of the application for the violation of any state or federal environmental protection law.*

PART II

INTRODUCTION
TO THE DISCOURSES
OF CHARACTER EDUCATION

In these chapters we outline the discourses of character education that we found in the proposals submitted to OERI. In chapters 6 through 9 we review how these discourses are used in daily speech and public statements about the status and direction of U.S. society. We are quite eclectic in the sources we draw on, including letters to newspaper editors, opinions expressed on Web sites, and other sources that often fall outside the purview of formal scholarship. We consult and include these sources because they suggest the breadth of discourse on these topics. Although scholarly work may represent elite versions of the perspectives we define, we hope to reveal that the ideologies and accompanying rhetoric permeate public opinion expressed in a variety of media. In Parts III and IV we will refer back to these discourses and illustrate how they are manifested in the RFP, in the conception of character education found in the two Southern states, and in the conception of character education found in the two states from the Upper Midwest.

In our analysis we identify what the discourses explicitly state and what we believe they leave unsaid. What they do say is relatively easy to identify. What they are silent on requires consideration of how their speakers selectively represent the topic under consideration. Macherey (1978) believes that the ideology of a text is best revealed through its silences—that is, the issues upon which it does not explicitly comment. To illustrate, Loewen's (1999) study of American monuments draws attention to the ways in which public memorials glorify their subjects while either ignoring or distorting other less admirable facets of their lives. The many southern monuments that celebrate Confederate cavalry leader Nathan Bedford Forrest, for instance, suggest a majesty—supported by such widely read historians as Foote (1958)—that is belied by the unstated fact that he founded the Ku Klux Klan (KKK) and helped to undermine Reconstruction through intimidation and violence. Loewen indeed argues that his role in the KKK is the real reason for his glorification, given that the monuments were erected by the United Daughters of the Confederacy and other Southern heritage groups following the abrogation of Reconstruction. Like monuments, character education curricula often valorize their claims without attending to their weaknesses. We feel that what is left unsaid is just as key to our ideological analysis as what is said.

The two profiles we establish draw on both similar and different discourses. We will first outline the discourses that are shared by both notions of character education and, as we will show in chapter 9, in some cases required by the OERI RFP. We will then describe the discourses that are specific to each of the two profiles we draw: the individualistic, didactic approach found in the southern states and the relational, community-oriented approach found in the upper midwestern States.

During these last few months, I've been humbled and privileged to see the true character of this country in a time of testing. Our enemies believed America was weak and materialistic, that we would splinter in fear and selfishness. They were as wrong as they are evil. The American people have responded magnificently, with courage and compassion, strength and resolve. As I have met the heroes, hugged the families, and looked into the tired faces of rescuers, I have stood in awe of the American people.

—George W. Bush, January 29, 2002

Chapter 6

Discourses Shared in Both Regions

In this chapter we outline discourses that we identified in the proposals from both the Deep South and the Upper Midwest. While diverging in clear ideological directions in critical areas, the proposals also shared certain assumptions about character and character education. We found that both sets of profiles included the discourses of what we termed academic achievement, moral absoluteness, the Protestant work ethic, family first, class-based morality, and logical positivism.

ACADEMIC ACHIEVEMENT

The discourse of academic achievement runs throughout the proposals and has long been a staple of rhetoric about education. Given that schools exist *prima facie* to educate, the durability of this discourse should come as no surprise. Historians of education (e.g., Tyack, 1974) have found that schools have, since their inception, been viewed as deficient in meeting this central mission of raising academic proficiency. The discourse of academic achievement is thus often phrased in terms of its corollary (i.e., that schools are academically inadequate). This discourse is well in evidence in the government report *A Nation at Risk,* issued in 1983, which opened memorably with

> Our Nation is at risk. Our once unchallenged preeminence in commerce, industry, science, and technological innovation is being overtaken by competitors throughout the world. This report is concerned with only one of the many causes and dimensions of the problem, but it is the one that undergirds American prosperity, security, and civility. We report to the American people that while we can take justifiable pride in what our schools and colleges have historically accomplished and contributed to the United States and the

73

well-being of its people, the educational foundations of our society are presently being eroded by a rising tide of mediocrity that threatens our very future as a Nation and a people. What was unimaginable a generation ago has
begun to occur—others are matching and surpassing our educational attain-
ments. (http://www.ed.gov/pubs/NatAtRisk/)

This discourse calls upon another discourse that we will review, the discourse of *the good old days,* to argue that the quality schools of bygone times
have given way to a current laxity in standards and performance, leaving
the United States at a competitive disadvantage in the global marketplace.

This discourse is silent regarding evidence that schools service a broader
range of students than ever and do so quite well. Tyack (1974), Applebee
(1974), and other historians of education have found that public education
has always been accompanied by the belief that it is not living up to its potential and is in some or many ways failing its constituencies. As in many ap-
peals to the good old days, the presumed golden age of education never
existed as pined for in yearnings for its revival. Indeed, some have con-
versely argued that given the range of students served and services provided, U.S. schools have never succeeded so nobly, equitably, and
extensively as they do now (Berliner & Biddle, 1995).

Critics of schools point to a number of sources of evidence for the decline in educational quality: falling scores in international comparisons on
standardized tests, complaints in the workplace of poor writing and grammar, and other indicators that students are not expected to perform at
high levels in school. Causes for these declines, say the critics, range from
diversifying (and thus watering down) the curriculum (Stotsky, 1998), the
1960s and the decentering of authority by feminists and other malcon-
tents (Bloom, 1987), poststructural and postmodern worldviews (Gross,
1998), the progressive education movement (Ravitch, 2000), political correctness (D'Souza, 1991), and, in general, other social movements that
have challenged the predominance of European American authority in
U.S. society.

Others have argued that the crisis outlined by these critics is manufactured
(e.g., Berliner & Biddle, 1995). The same data used to substantiate the decline
of schools and society, these countercritics say, can be used to illustrate the
growing excellence of U.S. education. National Assessment of Educational
Progress (NAEP) data on reading achievement, for instance, show that
fourth-grade students have recently recorded all-time high achievement levels
and that U.S. fourth graders finished second in the most recent international
literacy assessments   (http://nces.ed.gov/nationsreportcard/site/home.asp).
Berliner and Biddle (1995), Allington (2002), and others have argued that
most critics who draw on statistical data to condemn public education do so er-
roneously or downright fraudulently in order to forward political agendas or to
shift funding to private education.

> *Good character dissolves sins as water dissolves salt. The majority of the people going to paradise will be those who have refrained from sin (Muttaqi) and those who have good character.*
>
> *—Usul-e-Kafi*

We do not wish to enter this debate at too great a length, given the volumes that have been written on both sides of the issue and the volume at which the debate has been conducted. Our point here is simply to identify this discourse and its centrality to the character education movement, for which it is axiomatic that higher character will produce higher achieving students. This tenet is an explicit requirement of the OERI RFP.

MORAL ABSOLUTENESS

"This is Good versus Evil."

—George W. Bush, 2002

Thomas Lickona, a central figure in the character education movement, is quoted in one proposal we studied as saying, "Character education is directive rather than non-directive; it asserts the rightness of certain values—such as respect, responsibility, honesty, caring, and fairness—and helps students to understand, care about, and act upon these values in their lives." This view of the rightness of certain values illustrates well the discourse of moral absoluteness. The Center for the Fourth and Fifth R's belief that "encouraging right behavior, and correcting wrongful actions" exemplifies the clear distinction that many character educators make between good and bad choices, with no suggestion that the judgment of right and wrong might be complex or relative.

Examples of the discourse of moral absoluteness are abundant in the work of character educators. In his *Book of Virtues*, William Bennett (1993) asserts that

> Moral education—the training of heart and mind toward the good—involves many things. It involves rules and precepts—the *dos* and *don'ts* of life with others—as well as explicit instruction, exhortation, and training. Moral education *must* provide training in good habits…. The vast majority of Americans share a respect for certain fundamental traits of character: honesty, compassion, courage, and perseverance. These are virtues…. We welcome our children to a common world, a world of shared ideas, to the community of moral persons. In that common world we invite them to the continuing task of preserving the principles, the ideals, and the notions of goodness and greatness we hold dear. (pp. 11–12)

Two aspects of Bennett's comments are worth noting for our purposes. First is the way in which the traits are identified as *fundamental*. This notion that there are universal ethics or core values is central to the discourse of moral absoluteness. This discourse was stated clearly by syndicated columnist Maggie Gallagher (2001) following the school shooting in Santee, California. In the "new morality," argued Gallagher,

> Morality is personal. What's right for you isn't necessarily right for me. And who you wrong doesn't matter to me, as long it's not me: "I'm not going to dislike him just because he killed people."
>
> The old moral model that dominated Western civilization was based on the opposite premise: Moral rules are the same for everybody, everywhere. Belief in an absolute moral code transcending personal tastes and affections is not an inevitability. It is the product of two millennia of thinking and teaching about God, reason and human nature. And it can disappear, it seems, virtually overnight.

With this statement Gallagher invokes both the notion of moral absoluteness and the discourse of the good old days when relativism was presumably not available to cloud the issues. A critic might contend that other perspectives were indeed available but not given voice, that what has changed is the availability of floor space to historically marginalized groups for entering their perspectives into the national debate.

The second aspect we find relevant is Bennett's rhetorical move of using *we* in both inclusive and exclusive ways. *We* is inclusive in that it implies that he stands for and with those who are part of the "common world," the "community of moral persons." It is exclusive in that it suggests that those who disagree with this notion are not moral. The positioning of *we* and *they* in a discourse normalizes the values of the speaker and suggests a hierarchical relationship between the speaker and others. Loewen's (1999) study of monuments describes the ways in which artists employ *hieratic scale* to suggest social relationships. Spatially, this relationship occurs with the placement of the valorized group (usually White males) in a dominant position over a marginalized group (e.g., Native Americans). A Native American figure, for instance, might be partially clothed and kneeling at the feet of a White explorer, or positioned behind or beneath him. Viewers then infer dominant and subservient positions relative to one another. We see a rhetorical hieratic scale at work in the character education proposals as well. The positioning is established through descriptions of *we* and *us* as occupying the moral high ground, with people living by a different standard diminished and deficient, beneath and behind.

This hieratical positioning suggests the ideological nature of Bennett's views on virtue, a stance he might deny given his association of goodness with his heavenly mandate. The idea of universality in the discourse of moral absoluteness, then, can be phrased by its adherents so as to *petitio principii* or *beg the question* (i.e., to employ the logical fallacy of assuming that which one sets out to prove).

This discourse is silent on the ways in which different perspectives are available for determining who provides an exemplar for right behavior. One state, for instance, adopted the "50 Ways to Promote Character Education" produced by the Center for the Advancement of Ethics and Character at Boston University. The very first suggestion on this list is to "Hang pictures of heroes and heroines in halls and classrooms," presumably to inspire students to emulate them. Later down the list is the recommendation to "Celebrate birthdays of heroes and heroines with observance and/or discussion of their accomplishments."

This effort is problematic in two ways. First, people are complex. If Andrew Jackson were to be memorialized on a classroom wall because of his significance in expanding U.S. society westward, one would have to overlook his fierce racism and policy of genocide toward and removal of indigenous people. Thomas Jefferson is invoked in many character education curricula, yet was a slave owner who disowned the children he bore by one of his own slaves. Martin Luther King, Jr., helped to effect great changes in civil rights yet plagiarized parts of his doctoral dissertation and had extramarital affairs.

The list goes on and on. Among the 50 recommendations is "Read and discuss biographies of accomplished individuals. For students in upper grades, encourage them to be discerning, seeing that an individual may have flaws but still be capable of much admirable action." This acknowledgment does recognize greater complexity than is suggested in much Right versus Wrong rhetoric. The question, however, of which flaws to overlook is not addressed. President Bill Clinton's peccadilloes offer a good example. To some they provided the primary criterion for judging his presidency, to others they were largely irrelevant to his legacy.

The second way in which this recommendation is problematic concerns the perception of who is and who is not a hero. Ryan (2003), for instance, says that "too many of our students have crafted their characters modeled on such dubious heros [sic] as Eminem, Jennifer Lopez, Adam Sandler, and various professional-sports personalities" who presumably are too profane, sensuous, scatological, and otherwise immoral for Ryan to consider them to be wall-worthy in a character education curriculum. Yet many young people admire these people as heroes precisely for their willingness to transgress societal norms. What sort of heroism is deserving of such recognition and emulation? Who decides who is heroic? The character education curricula we studied typically suggest that these heroes will be selected by adults to exemplify particular traits, especially if they ignore their character flaws in other areas. The notion of displaying selected heroes, then, fits well with the

Right versus Wrong rhetoric, all the while silent on the complexity and contradictions of their behavior.

Finally, the discourse of moral absoluteness is silent on the diverse values that U.S. cultures foster. The "50 Ways to Promote Character Education" issued by Ryan's Center for the Advancement of Ethics and Character at Boston University, for instance, advises, "Don't permit swearing, vulgar or obscene language in classrooms or anywhere on school property." Spears (1998), Ball (1999), and others, however, argue that within some streams of African American English, profanity is an accepted way to provide emphasis. The discourse of moral absoluteness, in contrast, regards profanity as being among the "filth" identified by William Bennett that youth should not be exposed to. Again, the problem with this discourse concerns whose values and perspectives are officially sanctioned and invested with morality.

THE PROTESTANT WORK ETHIC

> Those who study hard ... "live comfortably in good houses," whereas those who are idle and neglect their schoolwork "are poor and dirty and ragged and ignorant and vicious and live in miserable cabins and garrets." (Letter from Benjamin Franklin to his grandson; quoted in Isaacson, 2003, p. 379)

The "50 Ways to Promote Character Education" list includes the recommendation that schools should "Make it clear that students have a moral responsibility to work hard in school." This belief falls squarely within what Max Weber (1930) identified as the Protestant work ethic in *The Protestant Ethic and the Spirit of Capitalism*. Weber described the value attached to hard work, thrift, and efficiency in earthly pursuits that in turn will yield eternal salvation. Weber argued that this ethic accounted for the economic success of Protestant groups in European capitalism because it combined the goals of material success and spiritual deliverance, even if he found that Benjamin Franklin, who epitomized this work ethic in his *Poor Richard's Almanac*, to be overly "colored with utilitarianism" and to be overly invested in "the earning of more and more money combined with the strict avoidance of all spontaneous engagement of life" (quoted in Isaacson, 2003, p. 481). The systematicity and orderliness of this work ethic fit well with the machin-

> *Crazy Horse would not go to the reservation when the tribe was defeated. He wanted to go anywhere in this country to provide for his people with dignity, with character, with pride. He believed no one owned the land; that he could live where he so desired.*
>
> *—Billy Mills*

ery of industrial capitalism, inextricably linking spiritualism and material-ism and suggesting that hard work is itself a virtue.

The Protestant work ethic also stresses that work sustains the individual, who can attain a better life through diligent effort. Given the inherent compet-itiveness of a capitalist economy, society is viewed as a collection of individuals striving for personal advancement, with the greater good resulting from per-sonal achievements that benefit others (e.g., the creation of jobs and products). Like material success, virtue is a quality of the individual. Each person thus has not just a moral responsibility to work hard in school but a moral imperative to work hard in life if he or she is to reach heaven in good stead.

The durability of capitalism and the ethic that sustains it has produced a discourse that runs throughout educational rhetoric. This discourse pro-motes the notion of hard work and disdains frivolity and enjoyment. Charles Sykes (1995) embraces the Protestant work ethic in his scorn for whole language approaches to reading, which he feels are not merely inef-fective pedagogically but will produce a nation of slackers:

> [Jeanne] Chall attributed the resiliency of such ideas [as whole language] to the desire of Americans to avoid pain, hard work, and discomfort, and to shield the tender sensibilities of the young from the rigors of a demanding curriculum. Learning basics can be hard and might entail both effort and disappointment. But basics also imply a set of standards outside of the child himself, a standard that is uncompromising and to which the child must ac-commodate himself. This, of course, is anathema to the democratic, child-centered classroom. Chall's analysis is worth quoting at some length: "Why do these concepts of reading return again and again? Why are they so persistent?" the Harvard professor asked. "I propose that they are deep in our American culture and therefore difficult to change. These conceptions promise quick and easy solution to real learning—reading without tears, reading full of joy. They are the magic bullet that is offered as a solution to the serious reading problems of our times. Further, phonics requires knowl-edge, effort, and work. The whole or whole language way has always prom-ised more joy, more fun, and less work for the child and for the teacher." (http://www.sntp.net/education/The_Reading_Wars.htm)

The views of Chall and Sykes (1995) embrace the Puritanical notion that one must experience pain or tedium in order for learning to occur and its corollary that learning cannot be a joyous experience. Similarly, liberal com-mentator David Callahan (2004a, 2004b) has argued that "The harsh disci-pline of the free market was offered by conservatives as more than just a path toward greater prosperity. It was presented as a savior of America's moral character" (2004b, p. 14). Callahan, however, views the free market as the cause of "a moral crisis of serious dimensions—one that underscores the pov-erty of today's values debates" (2004b, p. 15), rather than viewing free market competition as society's salvation from the permissiveness that Sykes and others blame for moral decline. To Callahan, when competition becomes extreme, it is "poisonous to people's ethics" (2004b, p. 15) because cheating becomes an acceptable way to get ahead. These disagreements underscore the ways in which people of different ideologies are both selective and interpretive in assessing the state of U.S. society: The same perceived problem (i.e., moral decline) is constructed as caused by either rampant liberal socialist indulgence or runaway conservative capitalist competitiveness.

The discourse of the Protestant work ethic does not attend to the ways in which different cultures view industry, productivity, and efficiency. Krueger (1989), for instance, discusses how Native-American notions of time do not fit easily with the Western value on productivity, especially punctuality and time management. She explains that

> In the relief and pleasure of really being taken seriously as a human being, it is also easy to forget that at the very moment one is being helped to feel at ease, the healer may simultaneously be putting off someone else for whom she will then be "late." That kind of time consciousness includes time to be compassionate and human. Taking time and tuning in.... There are benefits to the highly structured time frame: predictability (which makes people feel safe, too); an order and harmony of its own; it can fit and function well in an eight-to-five world. But it does not create "knowing" and comfort. The more *fluid time consciousness* [ital. added] has its own benefits: making real human contact, creating ease, creating comfort through knowing an "other," and faith. This kind of time does not fit as readily into an eight-to-five structured world. (pp. 227–228)

A culture that emphasizes relationships and the time it takes to develop and sustain them, then, might not fit the model of virtue that drives the Protestant work ethic. Whether this culture is associated with race, as Krueger (1989), Delpit (1995), and others argue; or gender, as Belenky et al. (1986) believe; or research perspective, as Lather (1990) argues, it conflicts with the capitalist values that are behind this notion of character. From a multicultural perspective, associating the Protestant work ethic with good character likely stacks the academic deck in favor of those students whose cultural backgrounds have embraced this ethic and instilled it in their children.

FAMILY FIRST

> I know of no other place where happiness abides more securely than in the home. It is possible to make home a bit of heaven. Indeed, I picture heaven as a continuation of the ideal home.
>
> —David O. McKay (http://www.familyforever.com/)

The politics of character tend to drive out the politics of substance.

—Judith Lichtenberg

This remark is typical of the discourse of family first, in which the home is depicted as an idyllic and warm house of virtue. Many character education curricula take the position that parents are one's first and best moral teachers. The kind of home envisioned in the curricula appears to be the traditional nuclear family: presumably monogamous heterosexual parents and children. Representative Steve Largent (R-Oklahoma) argues that families, not the government, know what is best for their children:

> Government should always keep in mind that no one loves children more than their parents. There are many in Washington who believe otherwise, and think that *they* know what's best for your children. The best thing that government can do to ensure children grow up with a mother and father is to recognize that parents—both a mother *and* a father—are fundamental to a child's upbringing in the first place.... We need to acknowledge that government—in any form—can never provide what children need most: love. Only two people are qualified for that—Mom and Dad. (1996, http://www.policyreview.org/sept96/symp.html)

Unfortunately, this home is not available to all students. In 1996 the Department of Health and Human Services reported that the number of confirmed child-abuse cases rose from 737,000 in 1986 to more than 1 million in 1993 and estimated that the actual number (as opposed to reported number) is likely closer to 1.5 million, with family drug and alcohol abuse often implicated in the assaults. Between 1950 and 1993, the number of divorces and children younger than 18 involved in divorces per year more than tripled (http://nces.ed.gov/pubs/yi/y9604c.html).

The notion of family envisioned in this discourse also neglects nontraditional households, including those with gay and lesbian parents and caretakers and families headed by grandparents and extended family members. In some conceptions (e.g., that of the Southern Baptist Church; see chap. 10, this volume), homosexuality is viewed as immoral. For those who strictly follow the teachings of the Southern Baptist Church, a home headed by homosexual parents or guardians would not be capable of providing an exemplary upbringing for youngsters. The discourse of family first, then, must overlook many kinds of families in order to postulate that parents are a child's foremost moral teachers.

This discourse is often contradicted by the discourses of youth depravity and class-based morality that accompany them in the proposals. In these discourses, untamed youth must have a character curriculum in school to overcome the lack of parental instruction in virtue. The discourse of family

---

Sow a thought, reap an act; sow an act, reap a habit; sow a habit, reap a character; sow a character, reap a destiny.

—Charles Reade

first, then, is often undermined by other discourses within the same character education proposals.

CLASS-BASED MORALITY

The poor and the vicious classes have been and will always be the most productive breeding ground of evildoers of all sorts; it is they whom we shall designate as the dangerous classes. For even when vice is not accompanied by perversity, by the very fact that it allies itself with poverty in the same person, he is an object of fear to society, he is dangerous.

—Honore-Antoine Fregier (Paris, 1840)

In mid-nineteenth century Paris, *les classes dangereuses* were considered the bane of the bourgeoisie, who believed that those from society's lower economic strata inevitably gravitated to a life of crime. Those holding this view perceived those in poverty as morally corrupt rather than unfortunate. In *Les Misérables* Victor Hugo challenged this assumption, suggesting that their suffering was intolerable and calling for social action on their behalf. Hugo's literary work and its vision have endured, as has the antithetical belief that poverty and corruption are morally linked.

In a February, 6, 2001 *Wall Street Journal* column, Charles Murray condemns the "'thug code' of the underclass, which celebrates violence, cheating, and vulgarity." Here Murray takes up themes previously developed in such books as *Losing Ground—American Social Policy, 1950–1980* and *The Underclass Revisited* to argue that the social underclass is and remains impoverished not merely because its members are poor but because productive work, family, and community exist for them only in fragmented and corrupted forms. He refers to Toynbee's *A Study of History*, where the author discusses the disintegration of civilizations in terms of the "proletarianization of the dominant minority," that is, the process by which the virtuous elite gravitate to the vulgar morality of society's "trash," as Murray calls them. Although Murray claims that he does not strictly associate the underclass with lower SES groups—his paradigmatic underclass representative is Bill Clinton—most of his examples suggest otherwise. We see this discourse played out in the following letter published in the *Atlanta Journal-Constitution* on January 29, 2004:

Out to stem tide of cultural decline

It's unfortunate that [African American editorial page editor] Cynthia Tucker can only find fault with President Bush's proposed "marriage initiative." The initiative attempts to address two of the more insidious problems facing our society: The decrease in stable marriages and increase in the number of children born out of wedlock. Both problems feed the downward spiral of our culture. The result is higher rates of poverty, physical abuse, incarceration and drug abuse. These problems, symptoms of a society that has lost its moral underpinnings, are acute in the African-American community. Rather than address their underlying source, Tucker makes excuses for drug users, unwed mothers and absent fathers by blaming excessive drug enforcement or inadequate government subsidies. She and other so-called black leaders need to focus on promoting personal responsibility, hard work and integrity.

—Steve Gleason, Tucker

Gleason employs related discourses—family first, the Protestant work ethic, the good old days, and class-based morality—in his broad indictment of African American families and the causes for their misfortune. These commentaries typify the discourse of class-based morality, which complements the discourse of the Protestant work ethic by finding people of lower social and economic classes to be the moral agents of their own circumstances and the instruments of moral degeneracy in society at large.

Eckert (1989), in her study of "jocks" and "burnouts," locates these relative identities in affiliation with social class. She defines a "jock" as any student who

embodies an attitude—an acceptance of the school and its institutions as an all-encompassing social context, and an unflagging enthusiasm and energy for working within those institutions. An individual who never plays sports, but who participates enthusiastically in activities associated with student government, unquestioningly may be referred to by all in the school as a Jock. (p. 3; cf. Apple, 1979; Bowles & Gintis, 1976; Giroux, 1981)

A burnout, on the other hand, is among those "alienated adolescents [who] are 'burned out' from long years of frustration encountered in an institution that rejects and stigmatizes them as it fails to recognize and meet their needs" (p. 4). One problem for the outcasts she calls burnouts is that the adults in the building—themselves primarily from middle class backgrounds—typically identify and sympathize with the jocks, creating a school-wide culture that officially marginalizes those who already feel rejected by the institution.

Eckert (1989) identifies

two main mechanisms for the reproduction of the class hierarchy—the perpetuation of class inequalities through the funnelling of children into their parents' place in society, and the enculturation of children into hierarchical social forms through explicit and implicit educational practices. Through the inequality of resources and practices in schools serving communities of different regions, ethnic groups, and socioeconomic levels, and through the unequal treatment of children of varying backgrounds within the same schools, schooling teaches children both their place in society and how to behave in that place. (p. 7)

She identifies jocks with the middle class and burnouts with the working class, arguing that "each category defines itself very consciously as what the other is not" (p. 5).

The discourse of class-based morality positions middle- and work-ing-class students hieratically, normalizing the values and behavior of the school's insiders and condoning their marginalization of members of sub-cultures. In general, this positioning creates class discrimination within the school (with some exceptions—the shooters at Columbine, for instance, were middle-class students who identified with a subculture of alienation). For the most part, however, students from lower SES and working-class backgrounds are viewed as being deficient in character and are targeted for character education.

The discourse of class-based morality is silent on ways in which "good kids" harass and belittle social outsiders. A dramatic example of this prob-lem comes from the tragic Columbine, Colorado massacre in which two teenage boys from the "Goth" subculture were routinely taunted and ostra-cized by the school's social insiders and responded with an armed assault that killed 13, including themselves. Evan Todd, a football player and con-summate jock at Columbine High School, believed that

> Columbine is a clean, good place, except for those rejects. Sure we teased them. But what do you expect with kids who come to school with weird hair-dos and horns on their hats? It's not just jocks; the whole school's disgusted with them. They're a bunch of homos.... If you want to get rid of someone, usually you tease 'em. So the whole school would call them homos. (*Time*, 20 December 1999, pp. 50–51)

One self-styled Goth who goes by Kaya (n.d.) described his own reaction to anti-Goth prejudice by identifying the instigators of conflict as

> Jocks and Preps: The other root cause for this kind of lashing out. When these mindless minions of the media, with their fashion fads and "in crowds" start excluding certain groups of people, naturally, the rest of the student body (except those excluded by the jocks and preps) will follow along in an attempt to be part of the in crowd. This leads to *forced* isolation from the rest of society and a desire for revenge on the oppressors. If anyone should be blamed, it should be these people. (http://www.storytellers challenge. com/STTruth/ttf033.asp)

We do not condone the kind of violent response that occurred in Colum-bine and other notorious school sites. We do see, however, the "good kids"—the jocks and preps—who treat others as social outcasts as lacking the kind of character emphasized in character curricula. In the discourse of class-based morality, however, these students are part of the group referred to hieratically as "we": those who identify with the social center of the school and whose values determine who has good character.

Writing on school violence, syndicated columnist Leonard Pitts (2001) said that

[W]hen some urban-dwelling black kid has a beef with another black kid, goes gunning for him and inadvertently kills or injures some bystander, we put that kid's culture and environment under a microscope. We debate the effects of fatherlessness in the African-American community, poverty in the African-American community, miseducation in the African American community. We struggle to find out what it is about that specific community that has led him to do this awful thing.

But when some middle-American white kid has a beef, goes out and shoots everything that moves, our questions become conspicuously more generic. We debate video games, movie violence, gun control laws ... non-specific things applicable to kids of all kinds. We never ask what it is about his particular community and culture that has left him so angry, so self-obsessed, so alienated from his very humanity. We never ask if there's something inherently isolating about the suburbs. Or something empty about lives of relative affluence.

Pitts confronts the discourse of class-based morality, turning it back on itself and questioning the morality of the upper and middle classes. Yet his observation is largely ignored among character educators who believe that core community values are modeled and upheld by the White upper and middle classes and that the character curriculum should be directed primarily toward those who do not share "our" values. All this despite the fact that, according to the Centers for Disease Control (2000), White high school students are seven times more likely than Blacks to have used cocaine, eight times more likely to have smoked crack, 10 times more likely to have used LSD, and seven times more likely to have used heroin. White youth ages 12 to 17 are 34% more likely to sell drugs than are young Blacks, are twice as likely to binge drink and drive drunk, and are twice as likely to bring a weapon to school.

LOGICAL POSITIVISM

In the OERI proposals' presentation of the efficacy of their programs, they often rely on the discourse of *logical positivism,* which is primarily concerned with the logical analysis of scientific knowledge. It enlists the verifiability principle (i.e., a statement is meaningful if and only if it can be proved true or false, at least in principle, by means of an experiment) and its consequence, the logical structure of scientific theories and the meaning of probability. Educational research and assessment have long been wedded to the discourse of logical positivism. The National Reading Panel (2000), for instance, issued the following statement about the kinds of research that should be included in its recommendations about reading instruction:

Character is power.

    —*Booker T. Washington*

To make a determination that any instructional practice could be or should be adopted widely to improve reading achievement requires that the belief, assumption, or claim supporting the practice is causally linked to a particular outcome. The highest standard of evidence for such a claim is the experimental study, in which it is shown that treatment can make such changes and effect such outcomes. (p. 29)

The discourse of logical positivism is rooted in the European Enlightenment and, as the views of the National Reading Panel indicate, asserts the superiority of scientific analysis to other forms of inquiry and investigation. The Reading Excellence Program, for instance, requires those seeking funds to conduct scientific research:

(1) ELIGIBLE PROFESSIONAL DEVELOPMENT PROVIDER—The term "eligible professional development provider" means a provider of professional development in reading instruction to teachers that is based on scientifically based reading research....

(5) SCIENTIFICALLY BASED READING RESEARCH—The term "scientifically based reading research"—

    (A) means the application of rigorous, systematic, and objective procedures to obtain valid knowledge relevant to reading development, reading instruction, and reading difficulties; and

    (B) shall include research that—

        (i) employs systematic, empirical methods that draw on observation or experiment;

        (ii) involves rigorous data analyses that are adequate to test the stated hypotheses and justify the general conclusions drawn;

        (iii) relies on measurements or observational methods that provide valid data across evaluators and observers and across multiple measurements and observations; and

        (iv) has been accepted by a peer-reviewed journal or approved by a panel of independent experts through a comparably rigorous, objective, and scientific review. (http://www.ed.gov/offices/OESE/REA/legis.html)

This RFP clearly outlines the values of logical positivism. We do not wish to enter the reading wars here. We quote the rhetoric expressed in the documents of the National Reading Panel and Reading Excellence Program simply to illustrate the discourse of logical positivism. This discourse is found in character education proposals in the area of assessment, where programs are assessed in terms of a variety of indicators that are subjected to statistical tests of significance.

This discourse is silent on the limitations of logical positivism and the way it has been critiqued by scholars operating from a variety of perspec-

> *The best index to a person's character is (a) how he treats people who can't do him any good, and (b) how he treats people who can't fight back.*
>
> *—Abigail van Buren (a.k.a. Dear Abby)*

tives: poststructuralism, ethnomethodology, and others. Much useful research, for instance, does not employ an experimental design, is concerned with the particular rather than the general, involves nonnumerical reduction of data, benefits from depth of analysis in small samples over breadth of analyses in large samples, and otherwise violates the rules embraced by the National Reading Panel and others who valorize what they believe to be scientific research. Furthermore, this discourse overlooks the ways in which many researchers in the hard sciences do not employ experimental designs to test their hypotheses. Astronomers, for instance, cannot arrange the cosmos into control and experimental groups in order to test hypotheses, relying instead on calculations made from observations of phenomena.

SUMMARY

In this chapter we have outlined the discourses that we found in the proposals from both the Deep South and Upper Midwest. As we have noted, often these discourses are ideologically at odds with one another: The discourse of family first, for instance, often contradicts the discourse of class-based morality, which suggests that only particular kinds of families provide the models for good character that sustain U.S. society. As we review the discourses more particular to the two regional cultures we profile, we will identify additional conflicts. At times these conflicts come about because of states' efforts to align themselves with the ideology embedded in the OERI RFP. At others they appear to follow from diverse stakeholders' conflicting priorities in establishing a character curriculum. By and large, these contradictions remain unacknowledged and unresolved in the proposals, resulting in what we have termed, from a Vygotskian perspective, a complex or pseudoconcept rather than a consistent concept for character and character education. Even with these similarities and internal contradictions, the two regions depart dramatically in their development of their character curricula. Those regional visions are the topics of the next two chapters.

> *Competition doesn't create character, it exposes it.*
>
> *—Author Unknown*

Chapter 7

Discourses in Proposals From the Deep South

We next provide an overview of the discourses we found exclusively in the proposals from the Deep South. On the whole, these states conceived of character education as individualistic and authoritarian, predicating their approach on the notion that individual errant youths may have invariant core character traits impressed on them by virtuous adults. In addition to the shared discourses outlined in Chapter 6, those particular to the proposals from the Deep South were youth depravity, authoritarian society, the good old days, and the virtuous individual.

YOUTH DEPRAVITY

It is common for character education proposals for funding to open with an array of claims bewailing the decay of U.S. society and youth character in particular. Youth are increasingly depraved, according to this perspective, especially in the areas of sex, drugs, and violence. The decline and depravity of young people is typically announced in quite alarming terms. The following excerpt from an essay by Ray Cotton, entitled "The Morality of the West: From Bad to Worse," typifies this rhetoric:

> According to a study by Rutgers University, over 70% of all university students admit they have cheated at least once. And there's probably a few more

A vote for Bush is a character flaw.

—Jeanne Garofalo

89

who wouldn't admit it. The most common form of cheating admitted to is plagiarism. Students have always copied from someone else's paper or stealthily brought forbidden notes into the classroom. But the incidence is rising. Nineteen percent admit they have faked a bibliography, and fourteen percent say they have handed in a computer program written by someone else (*Parents of Teenagers,* 1992).

This report highlights the fact that many students today are either unable or unwilling to act in an ethical manner. William Kilpatrick, in his book *Why Johnny Can't Tell Right From Wrong,* brings to light the millions of crimes committed yearly on or near school property. Children go to school scared and intimidated. Many teachers contemplate and actually do leave the profession because of all the discipline and behavior problems (Kilpatrick, 1992). A professor of philosophy at Clark University says: "Students come to college today as moral stutterers. They haven't been taught much respect for what I call 'plain moral facts,' the need for honesty, integrity, responsibility. It doesn't take a blue-ribbon commission to see this. Students don't reason morally. They don't know what that means." (Marquand, as quoted in Cotton, 1988, p. 34) (http://www.leaderu.com/orgs/probe/docs/morality.html)

We see clear parallels between the discourse of youth depravity and the discourse of academic achievement: Both claim that there was once a golden age of youthful morality, educational attainment, and other virtues that society has lost along with societal standards and expectations. Often, the same causes (postmodernism, relativism, popular culture, liberalism, etc.) are cited to explain any changes in values, especially those viewed as degenerate. And often, there is ample evidence to support the view that both the golden age and the current decline are chimeras created to support other agendas (Berliner & Biddle, 1995), or simply curmudgeonly disapproval of a world going to hell in a handbasket (Aronowitz & Giroux, 1988).

There is a very good case to be made that young people are far more civil than the discourse of youth depravity would suggest. The highly publicized school violence in Colorado, Arkansas, Kentucky, Georgia, California, and other states has created horrific images of young people that are belied by statistics on how most of them actually behave. Two criminal justice think tanks, in fact, have issued reports based on federal data concluding that almost all types of youth crime declined in the 1990s. Even though youth are acting in more civil ways, they are getting incarcerated more frequently and punished more severely in school. Justice Policy Institute president Vincent Schiraldi has declared that the pervasive fear of teen crime is based on ignorance rather than knowledge of the facts (http://www.cjcj.org/jpi/crimedrop.html).

The Justice Policy Institute and Children's Law Center (http://www.cjcj. org/schoolhousehype/shh2pr.html) have reported that, even though the most sensationalized cases of school violence have been committed by Whites, the brunt of punishment is meted out to minority youths. The disparities between fact and belief are revealed in the data they report:

> FBI arrest data indicate that there was a 56% decline in juvenile homicides from 1993 to 1998, and a 30% decline in overall juvenile crime. Nearly two thirds of poll respondents (62%) believe that juvenile crime is on the increase.
>
> The number of school-associated violent deaths is small and not increasing. School-associated violent deaths decreased 40% from 1998 to 1999, from 43 down to 26 in a population of 52 million American students. In 1999, there was a one in 2 million chance of being killed in one of America's schools.
>
> Yet Americans' fears about school violence increased. Despite the declines in violence, seven out of ten Americans in recent surveys said they believed that a shooting was likely in their school, and Americans were 49% more likely to express fears of their schools in 1999 than in 1998. One million youth in America were suspended or expelled from school in 1997, or nearly 6.8% of all students. This is up from 3.7% of students in 1974.
>
> School suspensions have fallen disproportionately on African American and special education students. An analysis of recently released data from the Applied Research Center reveals that black students are suspended from schools in Phoenix, AZ at 22 times the rate of white students, and in Denver, San Francisco, and Austin at 3 to 4 times the rate of white students. (Sullivan, 2000)

As this report reveals, what has changed is the perception of youth violence, rather than the actual behavior of young people. One of the major premises supporting the funding of character education initiatives, then, appears to be seriously flawed.

There are also good reasons to doubt that there is an increase in youth drug use. Indeed, statistics show that young people are far less likely to engage in substance abuse than their parents. Mike Males (2001), a Justice Policy Institute senior researcher, reports that

> A high schooler is five times more likely to have heroin-, cocaine- or methamphetamine-addicted parents than the other way around; far more senior citizens than teenagers die from illegal drugs. Accordingly, a "war on drugs" that truly cared about protecting children would make treating parents' addictions its top priority.
>
> The "teenage heroin resurgence" repeatedly trumpeted in headlines and drug-war alarms is fabricated; it shows up nowhere in death, hospital, treatment or survey records. The Drug Abuse Warning Network's most recent hospital survey reports 84,500 treatments for heroin abuse nationwide in 1999; just 700 of these were for adolescents. Of 4,800 Americans who died from heroin abuse, only 33 were under 18 years old. Media panics over supposed teenage heroin outbreaks in Portland and Seattle last summer collapsed when the Centers for Disease Control and Prevention reported the average overdoser was 40 years old....
>
> Teenage "heroin epidemics" breathlessly clarioned in some California cities are refuted by hospital records that show just nine of San Francisco's 3,100 emergency treatments for heroin overdoses in 1999 were teenagers, as were 17 of San Diego's 1,100 and two of Los Angeles's 2,950. Why aren't there

more teen heroin casualties? Few use it. The National Household Survey on Drug Abuse, released in September 2000, showed that .2 percent of 12- to 17-year-olds had used heroin at any time in the previous year. Nor are the few heroin initiators getting younger (most remain over 21).... Four-fifths of California's heroin decedents are over the age of 30, and three-fourths of them are white, a quintessentially mainstream demographic neither drug warrior nor drug reformer wishes to target.

The truism that youth character is in decline illustrates W. I. Thomas's adage that "If a situation is defined as real, it is real in its consequences." Given OERI's tremendous investment in character education and the flourishing of entrepreneurs selling character education products and services to schools that believe in the decline of youth character, we can only conclude that the discourse of youth depravity has helped to construct a reality that has both educational and punitive consequences for students in school, not to mention a ready market for those with character wares for sale.

In addition to being downright wrong in some assertions, the discourse of youth depravity is silent on key issues that could broaden and enrich the discussion of youth behavior. One is the issue of mental health. Indeed, with rare exceptions (e.g., Sackett, 1997; Smagorinsky & Taxel, 2002a, 2002b), mental health is not mentioned at all as the cause of disruptive or socially undesirable behavior. All problems are attributed to flaws in students' character. Yet the field of mental health is providing both explanations and medical remedies for a host of problems that may affect students' performance in school: anxiety, depression, hyperactivity, attention deficit disorder, oppositional-defiance disorder, Tourette's syndrome, and others. Most health care professionals would argue that many students who act out would benefit from competent diagnosis and treatment through counseling and medication, rather than instruction in core character traits.

This discourse is also silent on the fact that youth has been viewed as having declining morals for many generations. Wynne (e.g., 1979, 1997) has identified the same decline in at least two distinct generations of U.S. children. Turiel (2002) argues that "the theme of moral crisis and decay in society as a whole has recurred in different times and places. Most frequently, it is a nation's youth that are seen as a large part of the problem" (p. 45). Typically such alarms occur during times of change, such as the post-World War I 1920s, or the Vietnam era 1960s, when society becomes more open: the jazz and dancing of the 1920s, the drugs and sexual liberation of the 1960s, and so on. Turiel concludes that

> In generation after generation, there have been complaints about the moral failings of the next generation—whether it be those in the 1920s or 1990s complaining about how youth have produced societal decline and crisis by virtue of their individualism, failure to abide by traditions, lack of respect for authority, and desire to go it alone and forego community ties. (p. 293)

Another issue on which the proposals are silent is the prevalent influence of popular culture and media on students. Senator Joseph Lieberman, a supporter of the legislation that enacted funding for character education, campaigned for the 2000 vice presidency in part on a moral platform in which he took Hollywood and other popular media to task for the vulgar images they presented to people in the United States. During his acceptance speech at the 2000 Democratic convention, he declared that "No parent should be forced to compete with popular culture to raise their children" (Lieberman, 2000). William Bennett, one of Lieberman's allies in the assault on popular culture, said that "Joe Lieberman and I were denouncing the filth, sewage, and mindless bloodletting of the popular entertainment industry, calling it what it is—degrading and dehumanizing" (http://www.unspun.org/bennett-lieberman.html). These denouncements contributed to and were typical of the rhetoric calling for character education, yet what remains unexamined in this discourse are a set of realities related to popular culture:

- The ubiquity of popular culture and its accessibility to young people through media sources, relative to the culture preferred by orthodox character educators;
- The ways in which a strain of popular culture has always been vulgar and subversive relative to current values. Elvis Presley, for instance, seems tame by the standards of Tupac Shakur and Marilyn Manson, but created a similar outrage in the 1950s;
- The ways in which youth popular culture—in particular music—has always challenged and defied adult norms and helped to define the generation gap;
- The fact that the First Amendment to the Constitution allows for freedom of expression and that popular culture has historically pushed the edge of the First Amendment envelope; and
- The ways in which critical reading skills can enable an understanding and critique of popular culture.

The caricature of popular culture and underestimation of the relation between youth culture and popular culture is identified in the remarks of Henry Jenkins, MIT professor who is Director of the Comparative Media Studies Program and Professor of Literature, in his testimony at a hearing on youth violence to the Senate Commerce Committee. Jenkins warned the committee members

> not to succumb to a climate of moral panic and embrace misguided and ineffectual proposals to censor youthful expression or the media.... "The moral panic that currently consumes us," Jenkins believes, is "pumped up" by three factors: Our fears of adolescents and popular culture as a way in which they

define their desire for autonomy from their parents; adult fears of new technologies; and the increased visibility of youth culture as children under 15 now constitute about 30% of the population.

"If these factors shape the policies that emerge from the Senate Committee, they will lead us down the wrong path," Jenkins said. "Banning black trenchcoats or abolishing violent video games doesn't get us anywhere. These are the symbols of youth alienation and rage—not the causes." (National Coalition Against Censorship, 1999) (http://www.ncac.org/cen_news/cn74jenkins.html)

Popular culture, then, rather than being a pariah that must be eradicated, can be a window into understanding the ways in which young people view and experience society. Indeed, some educators (e.g., Gee, 2003; Smith & Wilhelm, 2002) argue that video games in particular—often criticized for their violent and sexual content—require multiple literacies and can provide a model for engaged learning. If educators are to take an empathic approach to their work, they might then seek to understand rather than sanitize and repress popular culture, no matter how crude or obscene they might find it.

Finally, we see this discourse silent on the fact that most discipline problems exhibited by students are modeled by adults. Rather than revealing youth depravity, they reflect societal trends. Adults participate in workplace violence, discrimination, social inequity, violence against women, unethical practices, petty theft, corporate crime, and countless other socially offensive behaviors that are taken up by young people (Callahan, 2004a, 2004b). Youth appear to be following violent trends rather than leading them. Yet the discourse of youth depravity consistently uses moral adults as the models for iniquitous youth to follow, often in the discourse of family first.

If you find from the evidence that prior to the time this case arose, the Defendant possessed a good character and reputation as a peaceful and law abiding citizen in the community in which the Defendant lived, you should weigh and consider such good reputation of the Defendant, if found by you, along with all the evidence, and give to such reputation such weight and credit as you believe it to be entitled to receive in determining the guilt or innocence of the Defendant. If, after weighing and considering all of the evidence, together with and in light of the Defendant's good reputation, you are convinced beyond a reasonable doubt that the Defendant is guilty, then you may so find. If the Defendant's good reputation when considered together with and in light of all of the evidence, raises in your minds a reasonable doubt as to his/her guilt, you should find the Defendant not guilty.

—Proposed Jury Instruction for Good Character, West Virginia

AUTHORITARIAN SOCIETY

The discourse of the authoritarian society has been implied by discourses in which *post* beliefs (poststructuralism, postmodernism, etc.) are vilified for their destructive effects on culture because of their deconstruction of cherished institutions. Criticisms of progressive education, multicultural education, and other efforts to decenter authority regard established customs and relationships as normative and efforts to displace them as signs of deteriorating values (e.g., Bernstein, 1994; Henry, 1994; Schlesinger, 1992). Hirsch (1987; cf. Ravitch, 2000), for instance, argues that Euro-American culture is the definitive culture of the United States and that declarative knowledge of this culture ought to dominate the curriculum. He believes that student-oriented approaches motivated by Deweyian progressivism are responsible for a decline in students' mastery of this knowledge base and argues that only be reinstituting it will schools be restored to the stature they once occupied—yet another appeal through the discourse of the good old days. Hirsch relates his father's ability to convey a belief through a reference to Shakespeare:

> My father used to write business letters that alluded to Shakespeare. These allusions were effective for conveying complex messages to his associates, because, in his day, business people could make such allusions with every expectation of being understood. For instance, in my father's commodity business, the timing of sales and purchases was all-important, and he would sometimes write or say to his colleagues, "There is a tide," without further elaboration. Those four words carried not only a lot of complex information, but also the persuasive force of a proverb. In addition to the basic practical meaning, "act now!" what came across was a lot of implicit reasons why immediate action was important.... The moral of this tale is not that reading Shakespeare will help one rise in the business world. My point is a broader one. The fact that middle-level executives no longer share literate background knowledge is a chief cause of their inability to communicate effectively. (pp. 9–10)

To Hirsch, such educational movements as child-centered teaching, multiculturalism, and other inclusive and nurturing approaches have led to a culturally questionable diffusion of essential knowledge bases such as the quick recognition of Shakespearean allusions that his father relied on to convey a concept or imperative.

In addition to stressing the need for authoritative cultural icons, this discourse reflects the mercantile structure found in most capitalist enterprises in which authority proceeds from the top down. In education this belief leads to a rejection of child-centered teaching that encourages students to be decision-makers and participate actively in the construction of curriculum, rules, and knowledge. British Education and Skills Secretary Charles Clarke (2002), for instance, argues that

Values such as respect, courtesy and consideration are the foundations of a civilized society. That includes respect for others and respect for authority. Heads, teachers and other school staff deserve respect. There can never be any justification for subjecting them to assault—verbal or physical. Residents living near schools and older people also deserve respect—they should not have to put up with being jostled or abused while waiting for a bus, walking near their home or shopping at the local store. In case any one thinks that sounds authoritarian then just reflect on this fact: 45 percent of teachers leaving the profession cited behaviour as one of the main reasons for doing so.... Quite simply, we can't raise educational standards if pupils miss school and behave badly when they are there. These measures are about ensuring that we as a government do all we can to restore order in our classrooms. It is time to restore respect for authority in its rightful place. Discipline and respect for authority may be unfashionable concepts, but let's not be afraid to use them. In the end what matters is the future of our children. We owe it to them to have the chance to grow up in a society that is safe and to learn in an environment where there is respect for all.

This discourse is tied to others central to didactic approaches to character education. The discourse of the good old days is tied in with laments about societal deterioration. The discourse of class-based morality is often implicated with hieratic positioning of those traditionally endowed with cultural capital (upper and middle-class, usually White, citizens) and those positioned beneath them. Those marginalized groups who critique privilege—feminists, civil rights activists, gay and lesbian activists, and so on—are viewed in this discourse as being the agents of the demise of civility and culture. Because they often adopt norms outside those assumed by the traditionalists, they are viewed as lacking character and as having ideological agendas, unlike those whose beliefs are assumed to be normative and bias-free.

This discourse is silent on the question of whether authority figures are always in the right and should be complied with. As Albert Einstein is reported to have said, "Unthinking respect for authority is the greatest enemy of truth." Many authority figures come to mind whose conduct was morally questionable: brutal segregationist Birmingham Police Commissioner Bull Connor, disgraced televangelists Jim and Tammy Faye Bakker, corrupt Panamanian General Manuel Noriega, blackmailing FBI director J. Edgar Hoover, statutory rapist and U.S. Senator Strom Thurmond, gangster-affiliated labor leader Jimmy Hoffa, the many CEOs from Fortune 500 companies and their accountants indicted in the wake of the 2002 accounting scandals, and adulterers Bill Clinton, Newt Gingrich, Jesse Jackson, and many others among the nation's political and opinion leaders. As we have previously noted, many of the United States' most revered leaders (e.g., Thomas Jefferson, John Fitzgerald Kennedy, Martin Luther King, Jr.) have also demonstrated character flaws. Following a leader's lead has not historically benefited all followers or led to moral action.

> *Character cannot be developed in ease and quiet. Only through experience of trial and suffering can the soul be strengthened, vision cleared, ambition inspired, and success achieved.*
>
> *—Helen Keller*

THE GOOD OLD DAYS

What has happened to the days when we could let our children play outside unsupervised? What has happened to the days when the only guns and knives our children possessed were plastic and came with a Halloween costume? Don't tell me those days are gone forever—I don't believe that. I believe that the history of America shows a country and a people that has, time after time, walked up to the very edge of the abyss, looked over, and stepped back. We have done so in the past and we can do so in the future…. We are still a nation at risk. Why is it that a survey in the 1940s listed the top five disciplinary problems in public schools to be talking, chewing gum, making noise, running in the halls, and getting out of turn in line, while a more recent survey listed the top five discipline problems to be drug abuse, alcohol abuse, pregnancy, suicide, and rape? Why is it that education today is all too often about fear, and not about hope? (Owens, 2000)

Mrs. Byrne's Dictionary of Unusual, Obscure, and Preposterous Words includes *hesternopothia*, defined as "a pathologic yearning for the good old days" (Byrne, 1974, p. 92). We found a discourse running through the proposals that, if not necessarily pathological, indeed expressed a yearning for the good old days. The discourse of the good old days is recurrent in human history. People have consistently felt that a golden age has passed and that society's goal should be to return to a period of higher purpose. We have the Golden Age of Spanish poets (the Sixteenth century), of Dutch painting (the Seventeenth century), of France (the Eighteenth century), of radio (the Forties), of jazz (1938–1942), of comic books (the 1940s), and so on. One source describes the Roman mythological Golden Age as "an era at the beginning of the world, when *Saturn* ruled Latium. It was a period of perfect harmony and prosperity. War and battle were unknown, as were crime and injustice. Laws were redundant. The earth itself brought forth fruits and even among animals there was peace" (Lindemans, 1997).

The hesternopothiac character Lou, played by Burt Lancaster in the film *Atlantic City*, illustrates this yearning for the good old days well. At one point, in response to a remark about the beauty of the Atlantic Ocean, he wistfully says, "You should have seen the Atlantic Ocean in those days." As noted, the discourse of the good old days is often found in combination with the discourses of youth depravity, moral absoluteness, academic achievement, and others. In terms of morality, the old days have seemed better to many observers in many time periods. In the early twelfth Century, for instance, historian Orderic Vitalis "frequently bemoaned the contemporary decline of moral standards and ... looked back, as people often do, to a better and idealized past" (Bates, 1989, p. 146).

The discourse of the good old days typically neglects the problem that the old days weren't so good for some groups of people. Turiel (2002) finds that nostalgia for times past often entails a form of stereotyping that airbrushes out complexity and disconfirming evidence. In one southern state whose proposal pined for "a saner, simpler time in history," there was a legacy of slavery, a long history of lynching, and a century of Jim Crow laws that made life for African Americans cruel and bleak. In the "good old days," women were denied the right to vote and were subjected to stifling gender-based discrimination. The discourse of the good old days overlooks the fact that racial minorities and the working poor typically were denied a quality education and had limited opportunities for prosperity. Many of the Founding Fathers often held up as exemplars were slave owners. Before legislation mandating safe work environments, workplaces were dangerous and oppressive for members of the working class and reforms were resisted by management. The good old days, then, were good primarily for those with power and capital, but not so good for the remaining majority of citizens. Will Rogers captured well these reservations about the good old days when he said, "Things ain't what they used to be and never was."

THE VIRTUOUS INDIVIDUAL

Immediately following the school shooting at Santana High School in Santee, California in March, 2001, President George W. Bush condemned the shooting as a "disgraceful act of cowardice." He continued: "When America teaches her children right from wrong and teaches the values that respect life in our country, our country will be better off." Syndicated columnist Mona Charen (2001) praised Bush's remarks, adding that "in our time, some key mechanism of social inhibition has gone missing, and even kids who seem normal and balanced are capable of the worst depravity."

> *All good and evil things in humanity have their roots in human character, and this character is, and has been, conditioned by the endless chain of cause and effect. But this conditioning applies to the future as well as to the present and the past. Selfishness, indifference, and brutality can never be the normal state of the race—to believe so would be to despair of humanity—and that no Theosophist can do. Progress can be attained, and only attained, by the development of the nobler qualities.*
>
> *—H. P. Blavatsky*

She argued that "the twisted minds of some borderline kids" who are "without basic morality" are responsible for school violence.

This remark exhibits the discourse of the virtuous individual, in conjunction with the discourses of moral absoluteness and the good old days: Morality is a quality possessed by individual people in varying degrees. Colorado Governor Bill Owens (2000), in reflecting on the Columbine shootings of 1999, said that the task of "healing our culture ... must be done one man and woman of character at a time." The violence committed in school, in this conception, is a function of the degree of virtue held by the students who act out: They are cowardly, do not know right from wrong, are depraved, have twisted minds, and lack basic morality. In this view of morality, the social circumstances with which the person acts in relation are irrelevant; morality is within the individual.

The dismissal of relational factors in student behavior is expressed by Ayn Rand Institute analyst Edwin A. Locke (2001), who locates society's dysfunction in a collectivist, rather than personal, approach to social relationships. Locke's area of concern is the national debate over the validity of standardized tests, which he feels are good indicators of students' ability. In response to criticisms of these tests as being culturally biased, he says that

> The root cause of racism is collectivism. Collectivism means viewing people as interchangeable units of a group. For the collectivist the individual is not really "real," but only an insignificant and interchangeable part of a superorganism (the gender, the race, the party, the nation). For the collectivist only group statistics count, because what any given individual does is not important.
>
> The racial collectivist ignores the self-made qualities of a person (character, ambition, knowledge, skill) and considers only genetic factors to be important. To quote Ayn Rand: "Racism is the lowest, most crudely primitive form of collectivism. It is the notion of ascribing moral, social or political significance to a man's genetic lineage.... Which means, in practice, that a man is to be judged not by his own character and actions, but by characteristics and actions of a collective of ancestors."
>
> If we really want to eliminate racism in this country, we must replace it with individualism. (Locke, 2001)

We characterize this discourse as the discourse of the virtuous individual. Social problems result from individuals who lack character; the child who acts out in school, rather than the social relationships in which he or she participates, is what must be addressed through character education. This discourse lies at the basis of McPherson's (1962) theory of possessive individualism, which includes the tenets that

a. Individuals are by nature equally free from the jurisdiction of others.

b. The human essence is freedom from any relations other than those one enters with a view to her or his own interest.
c. The individual's freedom is rightly limited only by the requirements of others' freedom.
d. The individual is proprietor (owner) of her own person, for which she owes nothing to society. One is free to alienate her or his capacity to labor, but one cannot alienate her whole person. (One cannot sell herself into slavery.)
e. Society is a series of relations between proprietors. Political society is a contractual device for the protection of proprietors and the orderly regulation of their relations. (p. 269)

This libertarian view of the individual is often linked to the U.S. notion that society is composed of a collection of competitive, enlightened, self-interested individuals, a view found in much conservative ideology. The discourse of the virtuous individual is quite compatible with the emphasis on individualism inscribed in U.S. political documents. It has been espoused by Ralph Waldo Emerson, Henry David Thoreau, and other architects of U.S. Romanticism and is central to U.S. capitalism (Friedman & Friedman, 2002).

This discourse is silent on the possibility that a person's social circumstances may contribute to his or her possibilities for living a healthy, happy, and productive life as an individual in U.S. society. The discourse is also silent on the ways in which powerful individuals and corporations influence the government, often through such vehicles as campaign contributions, to advance their own interests in the areas of tax law, trade and environmental policies, and other government actions. While Horatio Alger success stories, in which individuals overcome the limitations of their circumstances to lead bold and prominent lives, exist in fact and fiction, the corollary that those who do not overcome such obstacles lack character is questionable to many (e.g., Ryan, 1971). In the next chapter we outline discourses that suggest that, if it does always not take a village to raise a child, it is incumbent on

---

Clearly, we need to teach young people to behave as good human beings, and not like animals, and let them know they possess the God-given ability to develop purity of heart, mind and soul. For it is because we truly love others that we must remain pure until giving of ourselves lovingly and selflessly within the sacrament of marriage. By remaining pure until marriage, we never will have to feel guilty about past indiscretions, nor will we have to feel ashamed of looking into the eyes of our husbands and wives. If we were unfaithful to our spouses before marriage, will we possess the strength and nobility of mind, spirit and character to remain faithful to them after marriage?

—*Haven Bradford Gow*

communities to share responsibility for the welfare of all of their members. This vision in turn suggests a different approach to character and character education based on the sorts of premises rejected by those who embrace individualistic notions of virtue.

SUMMARY

This chapter has reviewed discourses found in the OERI character education proposals that were included in the vision of states from the Deep South but not from states from the Upper Midwest. These discourses generally follow a conservative or orthodox perspective on U.S. society in which virtuous adults from upper and middle-class nuclear families impress upon young people the values that teach them right from wrong, generally using exemplars that illustrate positive traits of virtue and avoiding models of what they consider to be negative behavior. Through this effort society will restore the virtues of a bygone era, one that has vanished in these times of rising youth depravity.

We should stress that in establishing these profiles, we are not attempting to make value judgments on the regions or the people who inhabit them. We have sought to avoid, as much as possible, describing one region at the expense of the other. As we stated in our Preface, we have both lived in both regions and find each to have advantages and disadvantages. We now make our homes in the Deep South, and do so with great appreciation for the region's many attractions yet concern for the persistence of racism and inequality. We are also well aware that racism and inequality have existed in the Upper Midwest and virtually everywhere else (see, e.g., Litwack, 1961), if not without the institutionalization that obtained in the Deep South for so long.

Our goal, in other words, is not to critique the Deep South at the expense of the Upper Midwest but rather to explain the southern states' conceptions of character in terms of the regional cultural that helped to produce them. Although our sympathies undoubtedly lie more comfortably with many tenets of the states from the Upper Midwest, we recognize them as problematic as well. We hope that our presentation, then, can be regarded as an effort to contextualize and situate the discourses of character education as we find them in the proposals we analyzed. We cannot entirely set aside our own biases in doing so, but hope to approach this task with as open a mind as we can muster.

> *Our country's founding fathers' ... passionate plea was, and still is, that if the wondrous political experiment called democracy is to succeed, it will require more than any other form of government a higher degree of "virtue"—of ethical character—in its citizens. For you and me and our fellow Americans, the hard-hitting reality of this plea couldn't be more timely or critical.*
>
> *—Russell Gough*

Chapter 8

Discourses in Proposals
From the Upper Midwest

The states from the Upper Midwest produced initiatives grounded in discourses derived from a consistently different set of ideologies than those that drive the southern states' proposals. We next outline these discourses and illustrate them with rhetoric from public statements of their adherents, including the discourses of citizenship, community, diversity, relationships, student agency, local control, and reproduction of the social division of labor.

CITIZENSHIP

> Enlighten the people generally, and tyranny and oppression of body and mind will vanish like evil spirits at the dawn of day … the diffusion of knowledge among the people is to be the instrument by which it is to be effected. (Thomas Jefferson, 1816; cited in Mapp, 1991, p. 266)

The states from the Upper Midwest explicitly tied their character education proposals to the concept of citizenship, invoking Thomas Jefferson as their inspiration. To Jefferson, education was the cornerstone of a democracy and prerequisite to the right to vote; Jefferson even believed that society had the right to disenfranchise those who did not take advantage of their right to a free education (Malone, 1981).

> *'Tis true that tho' People can transcend their Characters in Times of Tranquility, they can ne'er do so in Times of Tumult.*
>
> —*Erica Jong*

Jefferson's belief in the visionary possibilities of an enlightened elector-ate extended to his belief in their ability for self-governance. He said, "only popular government can safeguard democracy." "Every government de-generates when trusted to the rulers of the people alone. The people them-selves are its only safe depositories. And to render them safe, their minds must be improved to a certain degree.... The influence over government must be shared among all people" (cited in Koch & Peden, 1972, p. 265). Jefferson's belief in the political liberty afforded by education rests on four principles:

- that democracy cannot long exist without enlightenment.
- that it cannot function without wise and honest officials.
- that talent and virtue, needed in a free society, should be educated re-gardless of wealth, birth or other accidental condition.
- that the children of the poor must be thus educated at common ex-pense. (cited in Padover, 1952, p. 43)

Jefferson's notion of democracy was thus extended to each (White male) citizen, investing in the government the obligation to create a citizenry suf-ficiently illuminated to select wise governance.

The sense of democracy found in the states from the Upper Midwest draws on a particular brand of democracy, one that combines a Jeffersonian vision with the progressive ideals of John Dewey. Dewey, who emphasizes the active role of cooperative learners in constructing knowledge, is a pa-riah to many whose ideas contribute to the discourses we found in the au-thoritarian, individualistic notion of character education in the southern states. As stated at the Web site of the John Dewey Project on Progressive Education at the University of Vermont,

> democracy means active participation by all citizens in social, political and economic decisions that will affect their lives. The education of engaged citi-zens, according to this perspective, involves two essential elements: (1) *Respect for diversity*, meaning that each individual should be recognized for his or her own abilities, interests, ideas, needs, and cultural identity, and (2) the develop-ment *of critical, socially engaged intelligence*, which enables individuals to under-stand and participate effectively in the affairs of their community in a collaborative effort to achieve a common good. These elements of progressive education have been termed "child-centered" and "social reconstructionist" approaches. (http://www.uvm.edu/~dewey/articles/proged.html)

Such child-centered approaches are the bane of Ravitch (2000), Hirsch (1987), and others who argue that attending to the interests of students has contributed to the decline of education and U.S. society, displacing the attention to Western cultural knowledge that they believe ought to drive the curriculum.

Among Dewey's beliefs is that democratic communities work collaboratively toward ends that elevate all citizens instead of having individuals compete against one another for resources. He argues that

> the conception of the school as a social center is born of our entire democratic movement. Everywhere we see signs of the growing recognition that the community owes to each one of its members the fullest opportunity for development. Everywhere we see the growing recognition that the community life is defective and distorted excepting as it does thus care for all its constituent parts. This is no longer viewed as a matter of charity, but as a matter of justice—nay even of something higher and better than justice—a necessary phase of developing and growing life. Men will long dispute about material socialism, about socialism considered as a matter of distribution of the material resources of the community; but there is a socialism regarding which there can be no such dispute—socialism of the intelligence and of the spirit. To extend the range and the fullness of sharing in the intellectual and spiritual resources of the community is the very meaning of the community. Because the older type of education is not fully adequate to this task under changed conditions, we feel its lack and demand that the school shall become a social center. The school as a social center means the active and organized promotion of this socialism of the intangible things of art, science, and other modes of social intercourse. (http://www.uic.edu/jaddams/hull/urbanexp/ documents/Dewey_SchoolAsSocialCenter.htm)

As we will review in chapter 14, many of the original white settlers of states from the Upper Midwest were Scandinavian immigrants. These pioneers institutionalized a number of communal practices in their governments and community organizations from the mid-1800s to the present. The particular version of democracy and citizenship in these states, then, draws on a communitarian belief in society indebted to both Jeffersonian principles of a fully educated citizenry and Deweyian notions of using collaborative, inductive, discovery-oriented, action-based instructional methods that help people become better individual citizens and more compassionate neighbors.

Another notable facet of this statement from Dewey is his rejection of the discourse of the good old days. Rather, he says, "the older type of education is not fully adequate to this task under changed conditions" and must be adaptable to developing circumstances in society. Instead, then, of seeking the re-establishment of bygone cultural values, Dewey would have schools be more protean institutions that work in conjunction with changing times to provide appropriate education for the world that awaits its graduates and that they in turn help to construct as they participate in its democratic practices.

The link between the culture of the upper midwestern states and the discourse of citizenship pertaining to progressive democracy was revealed by R. Freeman Butts in a speech at the University of Wisconsin-Madison in

1995, in which he discussed the Civitas project and the national civics standards. Butts referred to

> a speech delivered to the alumni of the University by Governor Robert M. La Follette, Sr. in 1901. His theme was "The Wisconsin Idea." Let me read a few sentences:
>
> [T]he greatness of a state does not lie in its area, its commerce, its … accumulated splendor. It lies back of all these in the character of her citizenship…. [The national civics standards] set forth the key organizing questions that students at various grade levels from kindergarten through high school should study and be able to answer if they are to become rationally committed to the fundamental values and principles set forth in *CIVITAS*. They are:
>
> I. What is government and what should it do?
>
> II. What are the basic values and principles of American democracy?
>
> III. How does the government established by the Constitution embody the values and principles of American democracy?
>
> IV. What is the relationship of the United States to other nations and to world affairs?
>
> V. What are the roles of citizens in American democracy?
>
> *CIVITAS* certainly fits nicely with the goal of "community learning" that Chancellor David Ward has outlined in "A Vision for the Future" of the University in the next decade. One of his priorities is "Updating the Wisconsin Idea," which surely must include the "character of citizenship." And Dean Philip R. Certain has explicitly stated that one of the four goals of the College of Letters and Science is: Education for Citizenship. The Jeffersonian ideal of a liberal education is that it enables the citizens to choose from among them leaders best able to serve the democracy. This is also the essence of the Wisconsin Idea: education in service to the state. (http://www.civiced.org/civitas-butts.html)

The discourse of citizenship that we found in the proposals from the Upper Midwest, then, includes the ideology that each individual has a deep and abiding affiliation with the nation, state, and community. This affiliation requires enlightenment in order to make the greatest possible contributions to the common good. Included in these contributions is the obligation to assist each other citizen in reaching greater levels of knowledge and agency so as to contribute to a more insightful, morally powerful whole.

This discourse is silent on a number of issues that have made Dewey and his intellectual progeny the villain in many criticisms of education. Communitarianism is at odds with the cherished U.S. ideals embodied in capitalism, in which people compete to gain material advantages. This competition, argue the critics, is healthy for individual growth and beneficial for the nation because it produces industriousness and inventiveness as vehicles for personal advancement and, as a consequence, the nation's global stature and competitiveness.

This discourse is also silent on the question of how to set performance standards and accountability measures when work is cooperative. Not all group members contribute equally, and some take credit for the efforts of others in group projects. From this perspective, the group suffers because each individual is not pressed to perform at his or her highest level, resulting in an aggregate drop in performance. Because the goals of such approaches are difficult to articulate, verify, and measure, individual performance is hard to assess.

From an educational standpoint, this approach is silent on the likely mismatch between cooperative approaches to education and the competitive nature of U.S. commerce and society. Students acclimated to cooperative education may have a difficult time with the transition to individualistic school and work environments where they are pitted against one another for rewards.

COMMUNITY

The upper midwestern emphasis on communities as the locus of values stands in direct contrast to the southern states' focus on family first. Presidential candidate Bob Dole declared during his acceptance speech at the 1996 Republican national convention that

> After the virtual devastation of the American family, the rock upon which this country was founded, we are told that it takes a village—that is, the collective, and thus, the state—to raise a child. The state is now more involved than it has ever been in the raising of children, and children are now more neglected, abused, and mistreated than they have been in our time. This is not a coincidence, and, with all due respect, I am here to tell you: it does not take a village to raise a child. It takes a family. If I could by magic restore to every child who lacks a father or a mother, that father or that mother, I would. And though I cannot, I would never turn my back on them, and I shall, as president, promote measures that keep families whole. I am here to tell you that permissive and destructive behavior must be opposed, that honor and liberty must be restored, and that individual accountability must replace collective excuse. I am here to say to America, do not abandon the great traditions that stretch to the dawn of our history, do not topple the pillars of those below. (see http://www.pbs.org/newshour/convention96/floor_speeches/bob_dole.html)

> *With the child naturally social and with the skillful teacher to stimulate and guide his purposing, we can especially expect that kind of learning we call character building.*
>
> *—William Kilpatrick*

These comments appeared to be a response to the views expressed by Hillary Rodham Clinton (1996), who invoked the African aphorism that "it takes a village to raise a child" in the title of a book she published the year of husband's second presidential race. During her speech to the 1996 Democratic convention, Clinton said:

> For Bill and me, family has been the center of our lives. But we also know that our family, like your family, is part of a larger community that can help or hurt our best efforts to raise our child. ... Of course, parents, first and foremost, are responsible for their children. But we are all responsible for ensuring that children are raised in a nation that doesn't just talk about family values, but acts in ways that values families. Just think—as Christopher Reeve so eloquently reminded us last night, we are all part of one family—the American family. And each one of us has value. Each child who comes into this world should feel special—every boy and every girl. (http://www.pbs.org/newshour/convention96/floor_speeches/hillary_clinton.html)

The Dole–Clinton exchange highlights another key distinction between the ideologies driving the two conceptions of character education we profile, that being the roles of families and communities in raising children. Clinton seeks a community that provides a safe, caring environment for young people whose families are fractured, whose parents work long hours, whose parents provide poor role models for virtuous behavior, whose parents lack the resources to care for their critical needs. Dole believes that the best approach is for government to promote traditional family structures through economic incentives. Clinton believes that government should support services that provide what many families cannot.

The conception of community outlined by Clinton is consistent with that offered in upper midwestern notions of character education: The community has a collective responsibility to empower each individual to become a productive member of the whole, sharing and redistributing resources when necessary to help those with the greatest disadvantages. This approach echoes the socialistic stance reviewed previously that, as we will review in chapter 14, has been engrained in life in the Upper Midwest for a century and a half.

This discourse is silent on several issues. Bob Dole's response to Hillary Clinton identifies one area of critique, that being that many parents do not want the state interfering with their child-rearing in any way, preferring instead to instill their own values in their own children. The state's willingness to act *in loco parentis* is offensive to many in the United States who view the state as ideological in ways likely opposed to their own worldviews, and therefore poor surrogates for their parenting goals.

Another area in which this discourse is silent is the historic low regard in which most in the United States have held socialism and Marxism. While

> *If I had my life to live over again, I would have made a rule to read some poetry and listen to some music at least once a week; for perhaps the parts of my brain now atrophied would thus have been kept active through use. The loss of these tastes is a loss of happiness, and may possibly be injurious to the intellect, and more probably to the moral character, by enfeebling the emotional part of our nature.*
>
> *—Charles Dickens*

having considerable currency in academia, collectivist values are viewed by many citizens as antithetical to U.S. individualism and freedom. Its association with Soviet communism has made collectivism a dubious form of social organization, in part because of Cold War hostilities and in part because of the failure of any communist regime to escape the often murderous totalitarian tendencies of its leaders. No socialist economies have produced the wealth that U.S. capitalism has provided, even though in many instances socialism has better provided for society's forsaken. On the whole, however, government interventions have been entangled with enough failures and inefficiencies that many people in the United States regard them with skepticism if not outright disdain.

DIVERSITY

The sort of democratic community central to this discourse also relies on the discourse of diversity. As revealed through previous quotes, these communities are expected to be pluralistic, with each individual equally valued regardless of his or her social class origins. Charles F. Bahmueller (1998) of the Center for Civic Education states this perspective well:

> The majority has not, as in liberal democracy itself, decimated the minority; a plurality of voices is heard, not a monotone. The roots of this liberal message are nearly as old as democracy itself. In this presentation of plural voices some will hear an echo of Aristotle's famous criticisms of the notorious unity—and consequent decimation of liberty—found in Plato's *Republic*. Plato erred, in Aristotle's view, in searching for social harmony by driving out all dissident sounds from his "closed society," mistaking a single note for a chord. Real harmony consists of more than one note. By the end of the twentieth century we have come to believe that, like the fabric of liberal democracy, musical integrity is undiminished by dissonance. (http://www.civiced.org/cbframe.html)

Bahmueller's association of pluralism with liberalism is not a surprise; support for cultural diversity has been a hallmark of democratic (i.e., liberal) social policies in the lifetimes of most U.S. citizens. The idea that a democracy should be multivoiced is consistent with most of the other discourses we identify in the Upper Midwestern proposals: Each individual is valued and supported and given floor space in the public forum. Those who are voiceless deserve particular attention amidst the collective concern for equality and merit assistance in sharing the resources afforded by a community's prosperity.

An inclusive society ideally does not discriminate against any of its constituents. As stated at the Web site of the California Department of Education, "We are distinguished and united by differences and similarities according to gender, age, language, culture, race, sexual identity, and income level—just to name a few. Such diversity challenges our intellect and emotions as we learn to work and live together in harmony" (http://www.cde.ca.gov/iasa/diversity.html). Not only is such a society nondiscriminatory, it actively protects the rights of its most vulnerable citizens. The Tolerance.org Web site, for instance, speaks out against "bias incidents":

> any acts directed against people or property that are motivated by prejudice based on race, religion, ethnicity, sexual orientation, gender, social affiliation, ability or appearance. These include hate crimes, ranging from violent assault and harassment to vandalism and graffiti, as well as hate speech, hate literature and derogatory language and imagery in all media. (http://www.tolerance.org/rthas/index.jsp)

The following description of diversity education from *Education World* reporter Linda Starr (2002) illustrates one typical approach to promoting an appreciation for difference:

> On January 12, 2000, a school bus pulled out of the parking lot of McGee Middle School in Berlin, Connecticut.... At each stop, it will be boarded—and transformed—by the efforts and idealism of middle school students of all ethnicities, races, religions, abilities, and social and economic backgrounds. The *Town-to-Town C.A.R.E.-A-VAN* is on the road to a new world—a world in which people share and celebrate diversity....
>
> In an activity developed by Joseph Geisler, the art teacher at Slade Middle School, 30 students—ten from each of the participating schools—were provided with *bus templates* and asked to create visual metaphors that would convey both the concept of diversity and the idea of a school bus as a vehicle for ideas. After creating individual designs, the students collaborated on an overall design, combining aspects of each metaphor into a single image. They eventually settled on the metaphor "We are all an important 'peace' in the same puzzle." Puzzle pieces, the students noted, are different in shape, size, and color, and no puzzle is complete unless all the pieces are in place.

As this account illustrates, the discourse of diversity is alive and well in schools. Diversity education greatly displeases such cultural critics as Bernstein (1994), D'Souza (1991), and Stotsky (1999), who argue that multiculturalism—a component of diversity education—dilutes the quality of education by displacing canonical works and knowledge with an inclusive curriculum. In general, diversity education is silent on the question of how diversifying the curriculum will affect what Hirsch (1987), Bloom (1987), and others believe to be the core knowledge that each child ought to know in order to grow into a productive citizen. This discourse is also often silent on the question of what constitutes the U.S. culture. The discourse of diversity, focused on celebrations of pluralism, does little to address the consequences of abandoning traditional conceptions of nationality that help to create kinship among citizens of a nation, at least those with access to education, opportunity, and authority (e.g., Schlesinger, 1992). The discourse also overlooks more progressive conceptions of multiculturalism, which link the construct to notions of social reconstruction (McCarthy, 1991). It further is often silent on the notion of representation, that is, the degree to which any given text may represent the cultural group that the diversity curriculum is attempting to recognize through inclusion (Smagorinsky, 1992).

Critics of diversity education also argue that by viewing everything as equal, young people do not learn to make important discriminations, particularly on moral issues such as genocide as practiced in Bosnia, Russia, Nazi Germany, and other societies. Many critics would include the European settlement and expansion on the American continents, and subsequent decimation and internment of native people by the U.S. government, as illustrations of genocide as well. Instead, diversity education can engender the belief that all cultures have something equally useful to offer and that criticism of other cultures may do more to reveal one's own biases than problems in other societies. Diversity education can thus make it difficult to be critical of such practices as the radical subjugation of women by the Taliban in Afghanistan, the genocide committed by Saddam Hussein and Idi Amin toward their own people, and other events easily condemned by critics who are not ambivalent about the value of other cultures. While generous, this posture clouds the effort to make decisions about what is right and wrong, a central aspect of moral education.

RELATIONSHIPS

The discourse of relationships stresses the need to develop a strong ethic of care among young people and to enact this vision of care by spending con-

---

One of the troubles of our times is that we are all, I think, precocious as personalities and backward as characters.

—W. H. Auden

> *You can tell a lot about a fellow's character by his way of eating jelly beans.*
>
> —*Ronald Reagan*

siderable time with young people to cultivate their virtues. The notion of developing caring relationships with students is typically referenced to the work of Nell Noddings (e.g., 1984, 1992, 2002). While not without critics (e.g., White, 2002), Noddings's conception of caring as the central goal of schooling has gained much currency in discussions of education.

On the whole, what we call the discourse of relationships stresses the quality of time that people spend together over time. By taking a caring, nurturing approach to young people, adults can demonstrate an interest in their development and commitment to their well-being. Richard G. Tiberius argues that attention to relationships relies on a belief that learning has a strong affective dimension:

> the more we know about learners, the better we can connect with them and the more likely they will be able to benefit from our experience in reconstructing their world. The knowledge that teachers need about learners in order to connect with them is gained through interaction.... Effective teachers form relationships that are trustful, open and secure, that involve a minimum of control, are cooperative, and are conducted in a reciprocal, interactive manner. They share control with students and encourage interactions that are determined by mutual agreement (Tiberius and Billson, 1991, p. 82). Within such relationships learners are willing to disclose their lack of understanding rather than hide it from their teachers; learners are more attentive, ask more questions, are more actively engaged. Thus, the better the relationship, the better the interaction; the better the interaction, the better the learning.... Key features underlying the alliance are mutual respect; shared responsibility for learning and mutual commitment to goals; effective communication and feedback; cooperation and willingness to negotiate conflicts and a sense of security in the classroom.... The key to all these features, however, is a recognition of the reciprocal nature of the teaching-learning process. Both parties must participate; both must learn to trust the other. But the nature of the academy and students' past interactions with faculty may require the teacher to take the first step toward that mutuality and possibly to continue to lead the way until the students are sufficiently confident to become full partners in the process. (http://www.cte.umd.edu/library/podresourcepackets/studentteacher/why.html)

Tiberius thus argues that strong relationships between adults and young people will affect students' grades by improving the quality of interactions, thus tying this discourse to the discourse of academic achievement. As with many discourses employed in service of character education, claims of improving academics—as required by the OERI RFP—contribute to the rationale for a character curriculum.

This discourse is silent on the ways in which relationships at times do not work. Some students are cynical and manipulative and may perform in ways that suggest a relationship but instead are designed to work the system to the student's advantage. The discourse of relationships is imbued with a certain Romanticism about the nobility of young people that many adults find unjustified.

Another area of silence is the way in which a close relationship with a student may compromise a teacher's ability to make judgments about the quality of academic work. The discourse of relationships stresses the motivational benefits of engaging with students in caring, reciprocal transactions over time, under the assumption that by feeling included and cared for students will take their academic work more seriously. What advocates of this approach tend to ignore is the possibility that a teacher's judgment of the quality of this work may become conflated with judgments about the worth of the individual student, resulting in leniency and grade inflation that in the long run may detract from students' self-esteem—an issue we take up next in the discourse of student agency—because they receive rewards for work that falls short of broader expectations.

STUDENT AGENCY

Connected to the Jeffersonian notion of education for democracy is the idea that through intellectual empowerment students will develop greater agency to act honorably as members of society. Jefferson identified six objectives for primary education, which he believed to be the most democratic arena given its likelihood of reaching the broadest citizenry:

- To give every citizen the information he needs for the transaction of his own business;
- To enable him to calculate for himself, and to express and preserve his ideas, his contracts, and accounts, in writing;
- To improve, by reading, his morals and faculties;
- To understand his duties to his neighbors and country, and to discharge with competence the functions confided to him by either;
- To know his rights; to exercise with order and justice those he retains; to choose with discretion the fiduciary of those he delegates; and to notice their conduct with diligence, with candor, and judgment;
- And, in general, to observe with intelligence and faithfulness all the social relations under which he shall be placed. (cited in Peterson, 1960, p. 239)

Here Jefferson explicitly links intellectual prowess to moral development: The intelligent, knowledgeable citizen will gain a clear moral understanding and act in accordance with rational moral principles. Not only will individual citizens become more moral personally, the aggregate of educated citizens will comprise a moral whole.

The proposals from the Upper Midwest explicitly named *self-esteem* as a quality that provides agency to act morally. Robert Reasoner (n.d.) of the National Association of Self-Esteem, in an attempt to outline "The True Meaning of Self-Esteem," argues that

> we need to develop individuals with healthy or high self-esteem characterized by tolerance and respect for others, individuals who accept responsibility for their actions, have integrity, take pride in their accomplishments, who are self-motivated, willing to take risks, capable of handling criticism, loving and lovable, seek the challenge and stimulation of worthwhile and demanding goals, and take command and control of their lives. In other words, we need to help foster the development of people who have healthy or authentic self-esteem because they trust their own being to be life affirming, constructive, responsible and trustworthy.... A close relationship has been documented between low self-esteem and such problems as violence, alcoholism, drug abuse, eating disorders, school dropouts, teenage pregnancy, suicide, and low academic achievement.... The National Association for Self-Esteem ... define[s] self-esteem as "The experience of being capable of meeting life's challenges and being worthy of happiness."... This concept of self-esteem is founded on the premise that it is strongly connected to a sense of competence and worthiness and the relationship between the two as one lives life. The worthiness component of self-esteem is often misunderstood as simply feeling good about oneself, when it actually is tied to whether or not a person lives up to certain fundamental human values, such as finding meanings that foster human growth and making commitments to them in a way that leads to a sense of integrity and satisfaction. A sense of competence is having the conviction that one is generally capable of producing desired results, having confidence in the efficacy of our mind and our ability to think, as well as to make appropriate choices and decisions.... [I]t is critical that any efforts to build self-esteem be grounded in reality. It cannot be attained by merely reciting boosters or affirmations, and one cannot give others authentic self-esteem. To do so is likely to result in an inflated sense of worth. Most feel that a sense of competence is strengthened through realistic and accurate self-appraisal, meaningful accomplishments, overcoming adversities, bouncing back from failures, and adopting such practices such as assuming self-responsibility and maintaining integrity which engender ones sense of competence and self-worth. (http://www.self-esteem-nase.org/whatisselfesteem.shtml)

This notion of self-esteem fits well with many conceptions of strong character. Those with self-esteem are less likely to engage in the kinds of high-risk behaviors generally believed to be endemic to those presumed to be of low character: sex, drugs, violence, and other potentially dangerous activities. They instead develop the sorts of traits institutionalized in the OERI RFP—respect, trustworthiness, responsibility, and so on—that will enable them to find healthier alternatives to their needs.

They also exhibit resiliency in the face of difficulty, a quality explicitly identified in one upper midwestern state as a skill that can be taught as part of a character education intervention. Resiliency research is concerned with the ability to bounce back from life's obstacles by cultivating strengths to meet challenges in positive ways. Resiliency research looks at individuals, families, and communities as interdependent and complementary and in need of resiliency, which involves both building competencies and avoiding unnecessary negative stressors (Bogenschneider, Small, & Riley, 1993). These competencies include the development of values, attitudes, and behaviors that enable one to bounce back from and adapt to negative experiences (Werner & Smith, 1992).

A final dimension of agency found in the proposals is critical thinking ability. Richard Paul (n.d.), chair of The National Council for Excellence in Critical Thinking, identifies the following principles of the ability to think critically:

1. There is an intimate interrelation between knowledge and thinking.
2. Knowing that something is so is not simply a matter of believing that it is so, it also entails being justified in that belief....
3. There are general as well as domain-specific standards for the assessment of thinking.
4. To achieve knowledge in any domain, it is essential to think critically.
5. Critical thinking is based on articulable intellectual standards and hence is intrinsically subject to assessment by those standards.
6. Criteria for the assessment of thinking in all domains are based on such general standards as: clarity, precision, accuracy, relevance, significance, fairness, logic, depth, and breadth, evidentiary support, probability, predictive or explanatory power....
7. Instruction in critical thinking should [lead] to a disciplining of the mind and to a self-chosen commitment to a life of intellectual and moral integrity.
8. Instruction in all subject domains should result in the progressive disciplining of the mind with respect to the capacity and disposition to think critically within that domain....
9. Disciplined thinking with respect to any subject involves the capacity on the part of the thinker to recognize, analyze, and assess the basic elements of thought: the purpose or goal of the thinking; the problem or question at issue; the frame of reference or points of view involved; assumptions made; central concepts and ideas at work; principles or theories used; evidence, data, or reasons advanced, claims made and conclusions drawn; inferences, reasoning, and lines of formulated thought; and implications and consequences involved.
10. Critical reading, writing, speaking, and listening are academically essential modes of learning....

11. The earlier that children develop sensitivity to the standards of sound thought and reasoning, the more likely they will develop desirable intellectual habits and become open-minded persons responsive to reasonable persuasion.

12. Education—in contrast to training, socialization, and indoctrination—implies a process conducive to critical thought and judgment. It is intrinsically committed to the cultivation of reasonability and rationality. (http://www.criticalthinking.org/ncect.html)

This notion of critical thinking is compatible with the character education initiatives, tying academic achievement to moral development. The more clearly one can think through complex moral problems, the more moral one's actions will presumably be.

The discourse on student agency is silent on the ways in which such faculties as critical thinking do not necessarily produce judgment that most of humanity deems moral. Adolf Hitler, for instance, displayed critical thinking abilities in conjunction with personal charisma and the leadership needed to exploit post-World War I German nationalism. His critical thinking did not appear to extend, however, to the moral questions behind his quest for world dominance and the eradication of the Jewish people. History has provided many clear thinkers of dubious moral integrity: Theodore Kaczynski, Saddam Hussein, Timothy McVeigh, Osama Bin Laden, Kim Jong II, and many others. The assumption that critical thinking necessarily extends to moral issues, then, can be contradicted by extensive historical evidence.

This discourse is also silent on the threat to authoritarian societies that student agency may create. Students with agency may question adult authority in ways that those who support authoritarian societies may find disrespectful, rebellious, and otherwise deficient in character.

Finally, this discourse is muted, if not silent, on the disrepute into which self-esteem has fallen in the eyes of many as an educational goal. Although Robert Reasoner stresses that self-esteem is not produced by coddling, the self-esteem movement often foregrounds young people's immediate feelings at the expense of their long-term emotional needs. To Ryan (2003), emphasizing self-esteem reflects "the soft language of therapy" (p. 4) that undermines efforts to instill values in children (cf. Hunter, 2000). This skepticism is well-expressed in a letter published at the website of no-nonsense parenting guru John Rosemond, the paradigmatic embodiment of Lakoff's (2002) strict parent:

> I am one of eight children. My parents did not have time to consider if our self-esteem was being injured. We knew what the rules were and if we broke one, we suffered the consequences. Our rules were simple. You will respect

adults, authority and your parents. You will do chores in this family because it is required. I remember using a chair to reach the sink to do the dishes. We had to hang out clothes, iron and our summers were spent working in the garden and canning. The older ones had to help with the younger children. We slept two and sometimes three in a bed. We never had more than three bedrooms and one bathroom. We knew we would get a spanking if we disobeyed. There weren't that many because we always remembered why we got the last one and never did it again. Our parents may have seemed strict, but we had fun and we were always taught that family was everything. Always love and respect each other … my siblings and I were raised as "Grandma" taught and we weren't damaged and we didn't grow up with low self-esteem. We didn't grow up to be child abusers because we were spanked or whiners because we had such a hard life. But we did grow up to pass on to the 21 grandchildren and five great-grand children a legacy of moral wealth and values that will grow from generation to generation.—Sharon C. Scheu, Richmond, Virginia, 10/18/2000. (http://www.rosemond.com/)

The notion of self-esteem, then, at the very least requires better articulation and operationalization in order to overcome the doubts of its skeptics.

LOCAL CONTROL

The Web site of the No Child Left Behind legislation (http://www.nclb.gov/start/facts/local.html) provides a clear example of the discourse of local control. The legislation, it argues, "empowers your school" because it promotes local control and flexibility:

- This encourages local solutions for local problems.
- *No Child Left Behind* encourages federal money to be used to solve problems, rather than to subsidize bureaucracy.
- That means principals and administrators will spend less time filling out forms and less time dealing with federal red tape and more time focusing on student progress.

Whether this act indeed encourages local control is a matter of disagreement. David Boaz of the conservative Cato Institute argues that the legislation "trashes local control of schools" (http://www.cato.org/dailys/06-23-01.html) because funding is tied to a host of federal requirements. Our purpose here is not to debate whether this government program admits or denies local control. Rather, we use this exchange to illustrate the ways in

Character is that which reveals moral purpose, exposing the class of things a man chooses and avoids.

—Aristotle

which the discourse of local control is present in broad discussions about social life in the United States.

These contradictory views of the degree of local control available through No Child Left Behind reveal a fundamental tension in a free market society: the notion of unfettered liberty versus the range of commitments any individual or community has to the larger society. This tension is revealed in Boaz's libertarian concern that government funds are available only to those who yield to government's requirements, themselves typically forged in the fires of compromise. In perhaps its most extreme form this tension was realized in the old southern policy of nullification, which led to the rejection of national laws that white leaders of southern states felt were antithetical to their regional culture: laws supporting integration of the races in all facets of life.

A current example of this tension comes from the state of Texas over the question of whether cities or the state should make local policy regarding concealed weapons, which produced the following editorial arguing for local control of this issue:

> Texas' concealed weapons law is pitting the will of the Legislature against local control. The House Committee on Criminal Jurisprudence approved HB 878 Tuesday, a bill prohibiting cities from banning licensed concealed weapons on city property. Rep. Suzanna Gratia Hupp, D-Lampasas, who authored the bill that still faces a vote in the House, said cities that institute a concealed weapons ban are "ignoring the intent of the Legislature" and that such bans make it difficult to determine where a licensed carrier can legally carry a concealed weapon .... it should be the responsibility of the city to specifically designate areas where concealed weapons are not allowed .... it is best left to city officials to determine public safety and not be hamstrung by a broad, all-encompassing state law that fails to meet local priorities. (February 20, 2003, http://www. amarillonet.com/stories/022803/opi_takingaim.shtml)

In this discourse, centralized decision making is viewed as unresponsive to the local needs of communities and superimposes a single ideology on large and diverse populations. The great tension revealed through this discourse is that between what is good for the collective and good for local populations. As the issue of gun control in Texas reveals, at times communities reject the wisdom of the representative legislature, invoking the discourse of local control to justify their departure from the common good.

The discourse of local control typically overlooks the advantages of abiding by rules established to equalize opportunity within diverse social organizations. We can think of incidents in which we find centralized decision-making to contribute to a more just society (e.g., the Civil Rights legislation that required southern institutions to integrate). In making this judgment we recognize that our own ideologies are at work in favoring this imposition of federal will over states' rights to maintain segregation. Often people who

> *Because it is the most character-building, two-letter word in the English language, children have the right to hear their parents say "No" at least three times a day.*
>
> —*John Rosemond*

favor local control with respect to one issue (e.g., establishing site-based school management, eliminating laws governing industry pollution) might favor centralized control with respect to another (e.g., instituting laws against abortion, developing a national core curriculum). The discourse of local control, then, is selective, subject to the critique that it supports particular agendas rather than the general idea of unfettered local decision making. Although liberals, for instance, have historically tended to favor centralized decision making, during the 2004 presidential race Democratic candidate John Kerry argued that the opportunity for gay and lesbian marriage should be decided at the state level and not be addressed at the constitutional level. On the same issue, Republicans who traditionally have argued that the government should not interfere with personal decisions sought to legislate a constitutional amendment preventing gay and lesbian marriages. We see neither agenda, then, as being concerned with national or local control but as tied to broader ideological commitments and goals, regardless of how they are achieved.

REPRODUCTION OF THE SOCIAL DIVISION OF LABOR

In reviewing the discourse of class-based morality, we referenced Eckert's (1989) views on the ways that jocks and burnouts—roughly corresponding to students from white and blue collar families—experience school and society. Eckert argues that class structures are typically reproduced from generation to generation, with "the perpetuation of class inequalities through the funnelling of children into their parents' place in society, and the enculturation of children into hierarchical social forms through explicit and implicit educational practices" (p. 7). This sort of social categorizing is known as the reproduction of the social division of labor, in which people tend to be channeled toward particular types of experiences and outcomes depending on their social class of origin.

Apple (1982) and other curriculum theorists argue that systems of domination and exploitation persist and are reproduced in schools most often without conscious recognition by the people involved. This condition obtains despite the fact that "commonly accepted practices ... clearly seek to help students and to ameliorate many of the 'social and educational problems' facing them" (p. 13). This reproduction is effected not only by the formal and hidden curriculum in schools but by the broader cultural apparatus of society, what Williams (1977) refers to as an effective dominant culture. Bowles (1972) argues that schools play an important role in reproducing and legitimizing social class stratification across generations, meeting the needs of capitalist employers for a disciplined and skilled labor force and providing a mechanism for social control to create political stability.

An interesting twist on this tendency is revealed during an interview with Frederick W. Smith (1998), founder of Federal Express, who describes his military experience in Vietnam:

> When I was in the Marine Corps as a lieutenant, I had come up from a good background, went to a fine university at Yale. I wasn't exactly exposed to folks that were in the blue collar professions and occupations. And then here I was in the Marine Corps, and became a platoon leader, and I was surrounded by kids like that. I maybe was three years older than they were. I was 21, they were 18. But these were youngsters from very different backgrounds than I was. You know, blue collar backgrounds, steelworkers, and truck drivers, and gas station folks. And there we were, out in the countryside in Vietnam, living together, eating together and obviously going through all sorts of things. I think I came up with a very, very different perspective than most people that end up in senior management positions about what people who wear blue collars think about things and how they react to things, and what you should do to try to be fair to those folks. (http://www.achievement.org/ autodoc/page/smi0int-2)

Smith describes the ways in which the life trajectories of management and workers rarely cross paths in substantive ways. Rather, those from blue collar backgrounds, such as the soldiers with whom he served, are most vulnerable to being drafted into front line military service and are likely to return ultimately to the working class ranks. Meanwhile, Smith himself was destined for upper management as social reproduction theory would predict for someone of his station in life.

The discourse of the reproduction of the social division of labor is evident in a "Summary of Concepts" provided by the Self-Discover School on the web, designed to assist students who fail in school so as to relieve society from the burden they may pose as criminals. Among the concepts they stress are:

- All of us have different natural talents, intellectual, artist, mechanical, to name some. For this reason, there needs to be alternative learning environments to meet different natural talents. In the right learning environment, anyone can excel.
- For intellectuals, the academic base education system inspires a vision, discovery of natural talent, opportunity to develop it, career guidance, and job placement. The system does not provide the same opportunity for non intellectuals. (http://www.motivation-tools.com/ school/concepts_summary.htm)

The approach advocated by the Self-Discover School is to separate "intellectual" from "nonintellectual" students in the curriculum because

- A student who has natural talent to be a first class lawyer will never make it as a machinist. He does not have the required mechanical natural talent.
- A student who has natural talent to be a first class machinist will never make it as a lawyer. He does not have the required academic natural talent.

According to this logic, one's professional inclinations are natural rather than socially constructed. Career tracks thus channel people into professions that match their presumed abilities, identities, and dispositions, which not coincidentally often match the jobs held by their parents. Instead of being perpetuated through cultural assumptions, as argued by Eckert (1989), these class distinctions are presumed to be a function of natural ability. This belief resonates with the long-cherished U.S. ideal that people from all backgrounds have the same access to and opportunity for success in school and work. One need not be a socialist or even a liberal to see that a child born into great wealth and privilege has a great head start in the competition for economic goods relative to a comparably talented child born into poverty.

This discourse normalizes such expectations and stands in contrast to the democratic ideals of Jefferson and Dewey that motivate most of the discourses found in the proposals from the Upper Midwest. As we will review in Part IV, these proposals find provisions for students to engage in school-to-work arrangements that move them from vocational educational programs to the workforce, presumably as a way to develop character through the fostering of a positive work ethic. Typically, this discourse is silent on the economic limitations and anti-democratic nature of such programs: Rather than using the educational system to provide paths for Horatio Alger success narratives, such students find that school matches a curriculum to their presumed station in life and then establishes channels to the workforce that keep them in the lowest salaried, least authoritative tier of the economy.

Every person in America has done or said something that would keep him or her from being president. Maybe a nation that consumes as much booze and dope as we do and has our kind of divorce statistics should pipe down about "character issues."

—P. J. O'Rourke

SUMMARY

In this section of the book, we have reviewed the discourses of character education as found in public discussions of education. Our purpose has been to establish the existence of these discourses in general practice so as to situate the discourses of character education within them.

Consistent with our motivating theory, we have found that the discourses represent two distinct ideologies. The southern states predicate their approach to character education on a related set of discourses that position adults and young people in authoritarian relationships. Moral adults guide individual students toward virtuous behavior of the sort long lost in our increasingly coarse and vulgar society. This society has contributed to the moral delinquency of individual students whose values must be restored by character education. The educational approach is primarily didactic, with core values inculcated into students through exhortation, modeling, and other efforts by adults. Families are the first moral teachers of their children, but the ill effects of society call for assistance through the efforts of schools. Reductions in school-based offenses that result in punishment indicate the effects of character education on the moral development of young people. This approach might be deemed *conservative* both in terms of the political affiliations of those most likely to produce this discourse and in terms of the conserving nature of beliefs that support authoritarian relationships and hearken to times of old when that authority was believed to be beyond question.

The states from the Upper Midwest rely in contrast on a set of discourses that emphasizes a communitarian set of relationships. Adults both model appropriate behavior and engage in reciprocal exchanges with young people to both understand them better and learn from them. The community, rather than the individual, is the primary, if not exclusive, locus of attention on the part of character educators, so that constructing a healthy moral climate becomes the vehicle for empowering young people to reflect on their circumstances and behavior and derive a moral code to govern it. Understanding the pluralistic perspectives of diverse community members is critical to developing a comprehensive understanding of what makes up good character. These diverse perspectives often come from members of different socioeconomic groups, the least affluent of whom are provided ready access to the workforce and the benefits that accrue to the steadily employed. We might term this approach *liberal*, again in terms of those whose ideologies make up the discourse and in terms of the approach's tendency to embrace change, particularly in response to the needs of disenfranchised citizens and societal newcomers whose diverse perspectives may potentially enrich the broader community's beliefs. However, as we have noted, this liberal approach is contradicted by the discourse of the reproduction of the social division of labor, which would consign the disenfranchised to jobs in the lowest tiers of the economy with little chance for social mobility. The opportunity to advance both socially and economically is central to the ideology of the United States as the land of opportunity with equal possibilities for all for access to success.

In both conceptions these dispositions are fostered in order to promote academic achievement and thus position young people for the best possible circumstances afforded by the economy. The virtues that they learn will limit the likelihood that they will engage in at-risk behaviors such as substance abuse, premarital or extramarital sex, and violence. Thus imbued with moral reasoning and behavior, they will contribute to a body politic that makes up a strong nation of respectable citizens.

In Character and Health: Cultivating Well-Being Through Moral Excellence, John M. Yeager, clinical assistant professor, aims to help educators and health-care professionals think about the influences that character formation has on health behavior. Yeager ... hopes to see health education evolve from teaching "disease-of-the-week" content to stressing the link between good character and good health.... Yeager has closely examined health education and determined that well-being rests not only in the development of isolated skills and behavior, but also in acquiring an enduring disposition to act in a right and healthy manner.... Developing good character built on life experiences, he says, will create the foundation for enduring, positive, healthy patterns of behavior. Yeager proposes changing the vision of traditional health education from a value-neutral perspective to one that cultivates good health through moral excellence. Teaching health education without paying attention to the character of the student, he believes, is misguided. And since character is formed from the first day of life, the teaching of values falls into the hands of parents and primary caregivers as well as early childhood educators. Stressing well-accepted desirable character traits—for example, respect, responsibility, integrity, justice, courage, moderation, and compassion—to students gives them a healthy foundation with which they can inspire their future students.

—Boston University School of Education Newsletter • Fall 1998

Chapter 9

Discourses of the OERI Request for Proposals

All proposals submitted to OERI for character education funding were produced in dialogue with the Request for Proposals (RFP; see Appendix 9.1) and the Partnerships in Character Education Pilot Project Program description (see Appendix 9.2) issued by OERI. In order to be funded, proposals needed to be conversant with the specific requirements and the discourses called for in these documents. We next analyze the congressional discussion through which the OERI documents were produced and the conversational turns provided by OERI. We then review the discourses embedded in the RFP in relation to the political landscape in which it was produced.

DISCOURSE STREAM THAT PRODUCED THE OERI RFP

The RFP itself emerged from ongoing congressional discussions taking place over a number of years, which themselves arose from notions and discussions of character education that date to the origins of U.S. schooling (see Part I). Here we draw on the web-based version of the United States Congressional Record to document the conversational stream that resulted in the RFP for character education funding.

Character is like a tree and reputation like its shadow. The shadow is what we think of it; the tree is the real thing.

—Abraham Lincoln

The event that defined the terms for OERI-funded character curricula was the production of the Aspen Declaration in July, 1992. In Senate Resolution 176 proclaiming National Character Counts Week in 1998 (see Appendix 9.3), Senator Pete Domenici (R-NM) and colleagues described this declaration to be the work of "an eminent group of educators, youth leaders, and ethics scholars for the purpose of articulating a coherent framework for character education appropriate to a diverse and pluralistic society" (see Appendix 9.4 for a list of the document's authors). The Aspen Declaration came out of the Aspen Conference, sponsored by the Josephson Institute of Ethics.

One can indeed trace the vision of character in OERI-funded character curricula to Michael Josephson, founder and president of the Josephson Institute of Ethics. Josephson established the institute in honor of his parents in 1987 as a public-benefit, nonpartisan, nonprofit membership organization whose funding comes from individual memberships and gifts, foundation and corporate grants, fees and contributions for services, and sales of publication, curricular materials, and other products. The institute is dedicated to conducting programs and workshops designed to bring ethical awareness to schools and the workplace.

The Aspen Conference that Josephson sponsored produced an 8-point manifesto that summarized the participants' views of character education:

1. The next generation will be the stewards of our communities, nation and planet in extraordinarily critical times.
2. In such times, the well-being of our society requires an involved, caring citizenry with good moral character.
3. People do not automatically develop good moral character; therefore, conscientious efforts must be made to help young people develop the values and abilities necessary for moral decision making and conduct.
4. Effective character education is based on core ethical values rooted in democratic society, in particular, respect, responsibility, trustworthiness, justice and fairness, caring, and civic virtue and citizenship.
5. These core ethical values transcend cultural, religious, and socioeconomic differences.
6. Character education is, first and foremost, an obligation of families and faith communities, but schools and youth-service organizations also have a responsibility to help develop the character of young people.
7. These responsibilities are best achieved when these groups work in concert.
8. The character and conduct of our youth reflect the character and conduct of society; therefore, every adult has the responsibility to teach and model the core ethical values and every social institution has the responsibility to promote the development of good character.

> *Character is indeed displayed in pressure-packed situations, but not merely so. For better or worse, every display of character contributes to character.*
>
> *—Russell Gough*

The year following the production of the Aspen Declaration, the Josephson Institute formed the Character Counts! Coalition, a group dedicated to the advancement of character education. Significant for the OERI character education initiative, the Character Counts! Coalition used the "Six Pillars of Character" identified in the Aspen Declaration—respect, responsibility, trustworthiness, justice and fairness, caring, and civic virtue and citizenship—as the basis of its approach to character education (see Appendix 9.5 for a concise definition of each, and http://www.josephsoninstitute.org/MED/med6P.htm for elaborated definitions). These six traits, along with the view that they are invariant across culture, social class, and faith system, were ultimately institutionalized in the OERI RFP.

The name *Character Counts* was also adopted by the U.S. Congress in its approval of the annual National Character Counts week each October. The sponsors of this dedicated week—Republicans Pete Domenici, Robert Bennett, Thad Cochran, William Frist, and Dirk Kempthorne, and Democrats Christopher Dodd, Byron Dorgan, Joseph Lieberman, and Barbara Mikulski—helped to write the Josephson Institute's axioms into the federal requirements for funding.

STATUTORY ORIGIN OF THE OERI RFP

In order to provide funding for character education, OERI needed to house the awards within one of its bureaucratic categories. The funding apparatus was placed under the auspices of the Funds for the Improvement of Education (FIE), the purpose of which is "to conduct nationally significant programs, to improve the quality of education, assist all students to meet challenging state content standards, and contribute to the achievement of national education goals" (http://www.ed.gov/pubs/TeachersGuide/oeri.html.) Because the funding was located in the FIE, character education proposals were by necessity obligated to meet its criteria. All applicants for character education funding, therefore, had to claim that the programs would lead to increases in student academic achievement. The budget line (FIE) was designed to fund something other than character education, yet character education initiatives are bound to meet this budget line's goals.

The bureaucratic decision to fund character education in a student achievement bill creates seemingly insoluble problems for states writing proposals, for they must claim that a character education curriculum will

> *The politics of crime is not about a party's record or a candidate's proposals, but about perceived character and values.*
>
> *—Susan Estrich*

not only improve character but grades and standardized test scores as well. The proposals submitted to OERI must therefore claim an effect that is nearly impossible to document, given that in a school environment there are too many variables at work to link student achievement empirically to a character education curriculum. Yet without such a claim in the proposal, a state could not get funded, and without some claim of success in an annual report, the chance of getting a grant refunded would be compromised. As we will report, states admitted in their documentation to OERI that assessments showed no gains in students' character, yet they claimed success nonetheless based on anecdotal evidence from stakeholders.

The bureaucratic placement of the CE funds in the FIE, then, creates a Procrustean bed for program administrators. Procrustes was an Attican thief who laid his victims on his iron bed. If a victim was shorter than the bed, he stretched the body to fit. If the victim was too long, he cut off the legs to make the body fit. In either case the victim died. The RFP requires applicants to meet the FIE subject indexes. Given that it is quite a stretch to claim that character education correlates with academic achievement, program administrators must engage in various bureaucratic and rhetorical contortions to make their proposals appear to fit the funding source's priorities.

THE DISCOURSES OF THE OERI RFP

Discourses of the Congressional Discussions

From the Aspen Declaration we identified four discourses that were streamed throughout the discussions, had dialogic roots in ancient discussions of morality, and were ultimately incorporated in part into the OERI RFP for character education initiatives. The four discourses fall in the realms of moral absoluteness, youth depravity, family first, and academic achievement. We outline each of these next.

> *Our people are slow to learn the wisdom of sending character instead of talent to Congress. Again and again they have sent a man of great acuteness, a fine scholar, a fine forensic orator, and some master of the brawls has crunched him up in his hands like a bit of paper.*
>
> *—Ralph Waldo Emerson*

Moral Absoluteness.   A key notion emerging from the Aspen Declaration was that there are six stable, invariant *core elements* of character. In language that recurs throughout the Congressional Record and is instituted in the RFP, "these values are universal, reaching across cultural and religious differences" (see Appendix 9.6, Sense of Congress Regarding Good Character) and "transcend cultural, religious, and socioeconomic differences." The Hon. James M. Talent of Missouri, on Nov. 18, 1999, introduced to congress a speech by Governor and presidential candidate George W. Bush called "The True Goal of Education," in which Bush criticized relativistic notions of morality:

> The real problem comes, not when children challenge the rules, but when adults won't defend the rules. And for about three decades, many American schools surrendered this role. Values were "clarified," not taught. Students were given moral puzzles, not moral guidance. But morality is not a cafeteria of personal choices—with every choice equally right and equally arbitrary, like picking a flavor of ice cream. We do not shape our own morality. It is morality that shapes our lives (Bush, G. W., October 26, 1999, campaign speech in Gorham, NH, http://nytimes.com/library/politics/camp/110399wh-gop-bush-text.html).

Bush's remarks include the discourse of the authoritarian society in which virtuous adults impose on youngsters rules that enculturate them into society's core values. Bush went on to say that "We must tell our children—with conviction and confidence—that the authors of the Holocaust were evil men, and the authors of the Constitution were good ones." This conviction about moral absoluteness reveals a straightforward and uncomplicated view of moral behavior, overlooking such contradictions as the fact that many of the Constitution's authors were slaveholders, wished to deny women and unlanded men the right to vote, engaged in bitter political rivalries, exhibited profound vanity, and otherwise revealed themselves to be complex human beings rather than plainly "good" people (see, e.g., Ellis, 1997; Vidal, 2003). This notion of universal, invariant traits of character, however, must be incorporated into any application for federal funding for character education.

Youth Depravity.   According to Senate Resolution 176, "concerns about the character training of children have taken on a new sense of urgency as violence by and against youth threatens the physical and psychological well-being of the Nation." This notion of youth depravity appears in

---

Good character is not formed in a week or a month. It is created little by little, day by day. Protracted and patient effort is needed to develop good character.

—Heraclitus

the expected outcomes of a character education curriculum identified by Senator Domenici and colleagues in proposed Amendment No. 3020 to Senate Concurrent Resolution 1001: "antisocial behavior being reduced, attendance improving, attentiveness in class going up, substance abuse declining, schools becoming safer places, and even academics improving." Senate Concurrent Resolution 89 asserts that "record levels of youth crime, violence, teenage pregnancy, and substance abuse indicate a growing moral crisis in our society," a statement repeated verbatim in the Sense of Congress Regarding Good Character.

Whether these alarms are real or perceived is questioned in other assertions contained in the Congressional Record. Governor Bush, for instance, maintained that "In spite of conflicting signals—and in spite of a popular culture that sometimes drowns their innocence—most of our kids are good kids. Large numbers do volunteer work. Nearly all believe in God, and most practice their faith. Teen pregnancy and violence are actually going down" (Bush, 1999). Yet the discourse of youth depravity was streamed throughout the discussion in Congress and recurrent in proposals for OERI funding. As we will show, the rhetoric of youth depravity also served as the prologue to a number of applicants for federal funding. In the minds of many, youth must be presumed to be increasingly corrupt in order to justify funding for a curricular intervention, whether statistics support this claim or not.

Family First.   The Aspen Declaration asserts that "Character education is, first and foremost, an obligation of families and faith communities, but schools and youth-service organizations also have a responsibility to help develop the character of young people" (http://www.charactercounts.org/aspen.htm). This notion that family is the first teacher of morality runs throughout the congressional discourse leading to the RFP. Senate Concurrent Resolution 89 declares that "parents will always be children's primary character educators; ... good moral character is developed best in the context of the family." We also see this discourse in a number of proposals.

The family first rhetoric is coupled with the discourse of youth depravity, although rarely juxtaposed. Families are the first source of moral instruction, yet today's youth are depraved, necessitating an intervention in school. As we will show, this tension between believing in the family as soci-

---

The partisan strife in which the people of the country are permitted to periodically engage does not tend to the development of ugly traits of character, but merely discloses those that preexist.

—*Ambrose Bierce, referring to election campaigns, November 8, 1884*

Character is the only secure foundation of the state.

—*Calvin Coolidge*

ety's moral cornerstone and believing that schools need to atone for familial shortcomings is present throughout the proposals. And according to a number of OERI-funded proposals, certain kinds of families—those who live in poverty, speak variant forms of English, and have dark skin—do a particularly poor job of educating for character, thus requiring the state to intervene through the institution of the schools.

Academic Achievement. As noted, the budget line for character education is in the FIE, which is funded to support academic standards. A proposed amendment to the Title X portion of the FIE (Section 1001) stipulates that character education programs "would be required to be linked to the applicant's overall reform efforts, performance standards, and activities to improve school climate." Governor Bush argued that "Our children must be educated in reading and writing—but also in right and wrong." As funded by OERI, proposals must adopt the view that by educating for the latter they will raise achievement in the former. We have already discussed the empirical infirmity of that relation.

Discourses Embedded in RFP

The discourse of the RFP was dialogic in ways that invited a particular ideology on the part of applicants. We found the following discourses to be manifested in the call for proposals.

Moral Absoluteness. The following statement appears in both the RFP and the Partnerships in Character Education Pilot Project Program document that accompanies the RFP: "Among the programs supported through FIE competitions are State Partnerships for Character Education, which are designed to teach caring, civic virtue and citizenship, justice and fairness, respect, responsibility, and trustworthiness to elementary and secondary students." This information is reiterated in the accompanying document: "Each project will design activities to incorporate six elements of charac-

If you will think about what you ought to do for other people, your character will take care of itself. Character is a by-product, and any man who devotes himself to its cultivation in his own case will become a selfish prig.

—*Woodrow Wilson*

> *In the last analysis, the all-important factor in national greatness is national character.*
>
> *—Theodore Roosevelt*

ter—caring civic virtue and citizenship, justice and fairness, respect, responsibility, and trustworthiness. Projects may add other elements of character deemed appropriate by the members of the partnership." By requiring proposals to include statements affirming these six elements, the RFP stipulated agreement with a conception of character education based on a belief in moral absoluteness.

Academic Achievement. The RFP states that "This program provides funds to conduct nationally significant programs to improve the quality of education, assist all students to meet challenging state content standards, and contribute to the achievement of the National Education Goals." This goal must be documented with data showing that "improving student grades" will follow from a character education intervention (http://www.ed. gov/pubs/TeachersGuide/oeri.html). As we have noted, then, the FIE budget line required states to promise that by instituting a character education program they would improve character and that by improving character they would improve grades. As Hartshorne and May (1928) found some time ago, demonstrating the former is difficult to do and as subsequent character educators have found, claiming to have demonstrated the latter is tenuous. Yet all proposals included the promise that academic achievement would rise as a result of a character intervention.

Authoritarian Society, Reproduction of the Social Division of Labor, and Class-Based Morality. Related to the discourse of moral absoluteness is the discourse of the authoritarian society. In this view, a child of good character is one who does not defy the rules of the system. The Partnerships in Character Education Pilot Project Program document states that "Each project must ... include an evaluation designed to determine the success toward reducing discipline problems [and increasing] participation in extracurricular activities" (http://www.ed.gov/offices/OERI/

> *The function of education is to teach one to think intensively and to think critically. ... Intelligence plus character—that is the goal of true education.*
>
> *—Martin Luther King, Jr.*

ORAD/fie.html). We see several issues at work here. One concerns the operationalization of good character in terms of obedience: A virtuous student is one whose behavior is not viewed by teachers and administrators as disruptive. Given that students have been disciplined for such reasons as dating students of a different race, presenting anti-administration viewpoints in school newspapers, and otherwise engaging in defiant acts of passion and conscience, we see declines in disciplinary actions as questionable measures of increased character.

The second concerns the assumptions behind participation in extracurricular activities, which one might regard as a privilege of upper and middle-class students who do not need to work after school. Roughly one-third of teenage students hold full-time or part-time jobs, according to figures reported by the National Center for Educational Statistics (1996; see Appendix 9.7). Furthermore, as Eckert (1989) argues, students from "burnout" culture, most typically affiliated with lower SES and other socially marginalized groups, are less apt to participate in school-sponsored activities. Given that students from upper and middle-class backgrounds are more likely to have the leisure, affinity for school, and disposition to participate in extracurricular activities, this measure appears to be grounded in the discourses of the authoritarian society, the reproduction of the social division of labor, and class-based morality.

SUMMARY

In this chapter we have reviewed the ways in which the OERI RFP embeds discourses that privilege particular notions of morality that began with the efforts of a private foundation and its entrepreneurial consultants—including Thomas Lickona, Kevin Ryan, and others who maintain an authoritarian perspective on character education—were co-opted by politicians and ultimately written into policy. We also noted that proposals had to demonstrate an explicit causal connection between growth in character and academic achievement. Through our analysis we have identified the ideological underpinnings of the OERI RFP's notion of character, with which all proposals needed to be in dialogue. In the next two sections of our book, we more specifically analyze the con-

---

Character is always lost when a high ideal is sacrificed on the altar of conformity and popularity.

—Anonymous

> *Basic standards of good character, conduct and health applicable to all registrants*
> *The purpose of this statement is to set out the standards of good character, conduct and health to which all registrants and prospective registrants ("health professionals") must commit themselves. It is also the standard against which the [Health Professions Council] will assess complaints made against a health professional. A health professional who breaches the standards set out in this statement is at risk of being struck off the Register....*
>
> *It is the prime duty of all health professionals to safeguard the health and well being of those who use or need their services. Health professionals must therefore always: Act in the best interests of patients and clients; Discharge their duties in a professional and ethical manner; Recognise and respect patients and clients as equal partners in their care; Keep their professional knowledge and skills up to date; Behave with integrity and probity; Act within the limits of their knowledge, skills and experience and, if necessary, refer on to another professional; Maintain proper and effective communications with patients, clients, careers and other professionals; Obtain, except in emergency situations, informed consent to treatment; Respect the patient's or client's confidentiality; Maintain accurate patient or client records; Effectively supervise tasks delegated by them to others; Limit or cease their practice if their performance or judgment is affected by their health; Avoid bringing their profession into disrepute; Disclose to the Council any material information in relation to conduct or competence.*
>
> *—Health Professions Council, London*

versational turns produced by the states from the Deep South and Upper Midwest in their efforts to secure character education funding from OERI. As we will note, the ideology behind the southern states' conception of character education appears better aligned with the notion motivating the RFP than does the ideology behind the upper midwestern states' proposals. We will attempt to ground these different conceptions in the dominant cultural practices of each region, themselves grounded in worldviews guided by ideology.

> *Most parents know that the self-esteem of children is not built by low standards, it is built by real accomplishments. Most parents know that good character is tied to an ethic of study and hard work and merit—and that setbacks are as much a part of learning as awards.*
>
> *—George W. Bush*

APPENDIX 9.1: OFFICE OF EDUCATIONAL RESEARCH AND IMPROVEMENT REQUEST FOR PROPOSAL BASIC INFORMATION

Topical Heading: School Improvement

Administering Office: Office of Educational Research and Improvement (OERI)

CFDA #: 84.215

Program Title: Fund for the Improvement of Education (FIE)

Who May Apply(Categories): Institutions of Higher Education, Local Education Agencies, Nonprofit Organizations, Other Organizations and/or Agencies, State Education Agencies

Who May Apply(Specify): Other organizations include public and private organizations and institutions.

Current Competitions: The following information about competitions is based on the President's Budget request in FY 2000. This information will be updated when the FY 2000 appropriation bill is enacted. It is anticipated that a competition for State Partnerships for Character Education grants will be announced in December of 1999. Only state education agencies are eligible to apply for State Partnerships for Character Education Grants. Applications will most likely be due in February of 2000. The contact for this competition is Beverly Farrar (202) 219-1301. No other grant competitions for FY 2000 are planned at this time. The remainder of the funds will be used for continuation grants and other initiatives.

Type of Assistance(Categories): Discretionary/Competitive Grants, Contracts

Appropriations

Fiscal Year 1998: $108,100,000

Fiscal Year 1999: $139,000,000

Fiscal Year 2000: $139,500,000

Awards Information

Number of New Awards Anticipated: 10 each year

Average Award: $350,000

Range of Awards: $100,000–$1,000,000

Note: The Department is not bound by any estimates in this notice.

Program Details

   Legislative Citation: Elementary and Secondary Education Act of 1965 as amended, Title X, Part A, (20 U.S.C. 8001-8007)

Program Regulations: EDGAR, 34 CFR 700

   Program Description: This program provides funds to conduct nationally significant programs to improve the quality of education, assist all students to meet challenging state content standards, and contribute to the achievement of the National Education Goals.

   Types of Projects: Among the programs supported through FIE competitions are State Partnerships for Character Education, which are designed to teach caring, civic virtue and citizenship, justice and fairness, respect, responsibility, and trustworthiness to elementary and secondary students. FIE also supports the Blue Ribbon Schools program which identifies and gives public recognition to outstanding public and private schools throughout the United States. FIE also makes a grant to the Council of Chief State School Officers to operate the Christa McAuliffe Fellowship program that awards fellowships to outstanding teachers. In FY 1999, there will be one competition under FIE for State Partnerships for Character Education as described above.

   Education Level: K–12

   Subject Index: Academic Standards, Academic Subjects, Demonstration Programs, Educational Assessment, Educational Change, Educational Improvement, Educational Innovation, Elementary Secondary Education, Recognition (Achievement)

Source. Office of Educational Research Improvement Request for Proposal (www.ed.gov/legislation/FedRegister/announcements/1996-1/fr01fe6a.html)

APPENDIX 9.2: PARTNERSHIPS IN CHARACTER EDUCATION PILOT PROJECT PROGRAM

The Partnerships in Character Education Pilot Project Program is authorized under Title X, Part A, Section 10103 of the Elementary and Secondary Education Act as amended. Part A is the Fund for the Improvement of Education (FIE).

The Secretary may make a total of 10 grants annually to state educational agencies (SEA) in partnership with one or more local educational agencies (LEA). Each state is limited to a total of one million dollars over a period of no more than 5 years. The state may retain no more than 30% of the funds. The remainder must be given to the LEAs. There are currently 28 states funded by the Department of Education.

Parents, students, and community members, including private and nonprofit organizations, can participate in the design and administration of the projects. The projects will help states work with school districts to develop curriculum materials, provide teacher training, involve parents in character education and integrate character education into the curriculum. Each project will design activities to incorporate six elements of character—caring, civic virtue and citizenship, justice and fairness, respect, responsibility, and trustworthiness. Projects may add other elements of character deemed appropriate by the members of the partnership. Each project must also establish a clearinghouse for the distribution of materials and information about character education and include an evaluation designed to determine the success toward reducing discipline problems, and improving student grades, participation in extracurricular activities, and parent and community involvement.

Program Title: Fund for the Improvement of Education (FIE)

Current Competitions: The following information about competitions is based on the President's Budget request in FY 2000. This information will be updated when the Fiscal Year (FY) 2000 appropriation bill is enacted. It is anticipated that a competition for State Partnerships for Character Education grants will be announced in December of 1999. Only state education agencies are eligible to apply for State Partnerships for Character Education Grants. Applications will most likely be due in February of 2000. The contact for this competition is Beverly Farrar (202) 219-1301. No other grant competitions for FY 2000 are planned at this time. The remainder of the funds will be used for continuation grants and other initiatives.

Program Description: This program provides funds to conduct nationally significant programs to improve the quality of education, assist all students to meet challenging state content standards, and contribute to the achievement of the National Education Goals.

Types of Projects: Among the programs supported through FIE competitions are State Partnerships for Character Education, which are designed to teach caring, civic virtue and citizenship, justice and fairness, respect, responsibility, and trustworthiness to elementary and secondary students. FIE also supports the Blue Ribbon Schools program which identifies and gives public recognition to outstanding public and private schools throughout the United States. FIE also makes a grant to the Council of Chief State School Officers to operate the teachers. In FY 1999, there will be one competition under FIE for State Partnerships for Character Education as previously described.

Education Level: K–12

Subject Index: Academic Standards, Academic Subjects, Demonstration Programs, Educational Assessment, Educational Change, Educational Improvement, Educational Innovation, Elementary Secondary Education, Recognition (Achievement)

Source. Partnerships in Character Education Pilot Project Program (www.ed.gov/offices/OERI/ORAD/fie.html)

APPENDIX 9.3: SENATE RESOLUTION 176— PROCLAIMING "NATIONAL CHARACTER COUNTS WEEK"

Mr. Domenici (for himself, Mr. Dodd, Mr. Cochran, Ms. Mikulski, Mr. Bennett, Mr. Lieberman, Mr. Kempthorne, Mr. Dorgan, Mr. Frist, and Mr. Cleland) submitted the following resolution, which was referred to the Committee on the Judiciary: S. Res. 176

Whereas young people will be the stewards of our communities, Nation, and world in critical times, and the present and future well-being of our society requires an involved, caring citizenry with good character; Whereas concerns about the character training of children have taken on a new sense of urgency as violence by and against youth threatens the physical and psychological well-being of the Nation; Whereas more than ever, children need strong and constructive guidance from their families and their communities, including schools, youth organizations, religious institutions, and civic groups;

Whereas the character of a nation is only as strong as the character of its individual citizens; Whereas the public good is advanced when young people are taught the importance of good character and that character counts in personal relationships, in school, and in the workplace; Whereas scholars and educators agree that people do not automatically develop good character and, therefore, conscientious efforts must be made by institutions and individuals that influence youth to help young people develop the essential traits and characteristics that comprise good character; Whereas although character development is, first and foremost, an obligation of families, the efforts of faith communities, schools, and youth, civic, and human service organizations also play a very important role in supporting family efforts by fostering and promoting good character; Whereas the Senate encourages students, teachers, parents, youth, and community leaders to recognize the valuable role our youth play in the present and future of our Nation and to recognize that character is an important part of that future; Whereas in July 1992, the Aspen Declaration was written by an eminent group of educators, youth leaders, and ethics scholars for the purpose of articulating a coherent framework for character education appropriate to a diverse and pluralistic society; Whereas the Aspen Declaration states, "Effective character education is based on core ethical values which form the foundation of democratic society."; Whereas the core ethical values identified by the Aspen Declaration constitute the 6 core elements of character; Whereas the 6 core elements of character are: trustworthiness, respect, responsibility, fairness, caring, and citizenship;

Whereas the 6 core elements of character transcend cultural, religious, and socioeconomic differences; Whereas the Aspen Declaration states, "The character and conduct of our youth reflect the character and conduct of society; therefore, every adult has the responsibility to teach and model the core ethical values and every social institution has the responsibility to promote the development of good character."; Whereas the Senate encourages individuals and organizations, especially those who have an interest in the education and training of our youth, to adopt the 6 core elements of character as intrinsic to the well-being of individuals, communities, and society as a whole; and Whereas the Senate encourages communities, especially schools and youth organizations, to integrate the 6 core elements of character into programs serving students and children: Now, therefore, be it

Resolved, That the Senate—

(b) proclaims the week of October 18 through October 24, 1998, as "National Character Counts Week"; and (2) requests that the President issue a proclamation calling upon the people of the United States and interested groups to embrace the 6 core elements of character and to observe the week with appropriate ceremonies and activities.

NATIONAL CHARACTER COUNTS WEEK

Mr. DOMENICI: Mr. President, fellow Senators, today, for the fifth consecutive year I am going to submit a resolution on behalf of myself, Senators Dodd, Cochran, Bennett, Lieberman, Mikulski, Kempthorne, Dorgan, Frist, and Cleland. This resolution that we have introduced 5 consecutive years sets aside the week of October 18–24 of this year for what we call National Character Counts Week.

Source. Senate Resolution 176—Proclaiming "National Character Counts Week" (www.charactercounts.org/senate_cc!_week1998.htm)

APPENDIX 9.4: ASPEN CONFERENCE PARTICIPANTS

Jane A. Amero: Chair, Maine State Board of Education; board member, Maine Excellence in Education and Maine Partners in Education

Sharon Banas: Values Education Coordinator, Sweet Home Central School District, New York

Marvin W. Berkowitz, PhD: Associate Professor of Psychology and Associate Director, Center for Ethics Studies at Marquette University, Milwaukee; board member, Association for Moral Education; Associate Director, Wisconsin Center for Addiction Studies

Diane Berreth: Deputy Executive Director, Association for Supervision and Curriculum Development, Alexandria, Virginia

Beth Brainard: President, Good Idea Kids, Inc.; board member, Cornell Museum of Fine Arts and Rollins College, Florida

B. David Brooks, PhD: President and CEO, The Jefferson Center for Character Education, Pasadena; member, Presidential Advisory Council Working Committee on Ethics and Self-Esteem

Mike Carotta: Executive Director, Department of Religious Education, National Catholic Education Association; author; former Director of Religious Education, Boys Town, Nebraska

Gary Edwards: President, Ethics Resource Center, Inc., Washington, DC

H. Dean Evans, PhD: Indiana Superintendent of Public Instruction; member, President's Advisory Committee on Education; Board of Trustees, Franklin College; Chairman, Indiana State Board of Education

Margaret Gates, Esq: National Executive Director, Girls, Inc., New York; cofounder and board member, Center for Women's Policy Studies; former chairperson, National Collaboration for Youth

John H. Green: National Director, Learning for Life, Boy Scouts of America, Irving, Texas

Frances Hesselbein: President and CEO, Peter F. Drucker Foundation, New York; Chairman, Josephson Institute of Ethics Board of Governors; former CEO, Girl Scouts of the U.S.A.; board member, Mutual of America Life Insurance

Gary Heusel: Director, National 4-H Council, Chevy Chase, Maryland

Geneva Johnson: President and CEO, Family Service of America, Inc., Milwaukee; board member, The Foundation Center, Chairman's Council, and Mutual of America Insurance Co.

Michael Josephson, Esq: President and Chief Executive, Joseph & Edna Josephson Institute of Ethics, Marina del Rey, California

Mary Jean Katz: Character Education Specialist, Oregon Dept. of Education; Treasurer and Executive Committee member, Oregon Council for the Social Studies

Thomas Lickona, PhD: Professor of Education, State University of New York at Cortland; former President, Association for Moral Education

Joanne Livesey: Director, Ghostwriter Outreach, Children's Television Workshop, New York; member, National Assn. Of Broadcaster's Children's Advisory Committee and Scarsdale Youth Advisory Board

Mary Rose Main: National Executive Director, Girl Scouts of the U.S.A., New York

Sylvia L. Peters: Founding Partner, Edison Project, Whittle Communication, Nashville; former principal, Alexandre Dumas Elementary School, Chicago

Kevin Ryan, PhD: Director, Center for the Advancement of Ethics and Character, Boston University

Eric Schaps: President, Developmental Studies Center, San Ramon, California; Director, Child Development Project

Dr. Michael Schulman: Supervising Psychologist, Leake & Watts Children's Homes, New York; Chairman, Columbia University Seminar on Moral Education; Director of Ethical Education for the Ethical Culture Schools, Queens, New York

Thomas H. Smolich, SJ: Executive Director, Proyecto Pastoral at Dolores Mission, Los Angeles; member, Coalition for Humane Immigrant Rights of Los Angeles, Jesuit School of Theology at Berkeley, and Community Involvement Board of LEARN

Keith M. Sovereign, EdD: Executive Director, Community of Caring, Joseph P. Kennedy, Jr. Foundation, Washington, DC; board member, National Organization on Adolescent Pregnancy and Parenting

Norman A. Sprinthall: Professor, North Carolina State University; member, Assn. For Moral Education; editorial board member, Journal of Teacher Education and Journal of Moral Education

Dennis Van Roekel: Executive Committee member, National Education Association, Washington, D.C.; President, Arizona Education Association

Don Whatley: National Representative, American Federation of Teachers; President, Albuquerque Teachers Federation, Albuquerque

Jane Willsen: President, Sports Learning Systems, Inc., Carmichael, California

Dick Wilson: National Executive Director, American Youth Soccer Organization, Hawthorne, California; President, Centinela Valley School Administrators and Trustees Association; former president, Wiseburn School Board, California

Note. Aspen Conference Participants (www.charactercounts.org/aspen.htm)

APPENDIX 9.5: THE SIX PILLARS OF CHARACTER

Trustworthiness: Be honest • Don't deceive, cheat or steal • Be reliable—do what you say you'll do • Have the courage to do the right thing • Build a good reputation • Be loyal—stand by your family, friends and country

Respect: Treat others with respect; follow the Golden Rule • Be tolerant of differences • Use good manners, not bad language • Be considerate of the feelings of others • Don't threaten, hit or hurt anyone • Deal peacefully with anger, insults and disagreements

Responsibility: Do what you are supposed to do • Persevere: keep on trying! • Always do your best • Use self-control • Be self-disciplined • Think before you act—consider the consequences • Be accountable for your choices

Fairness: Play by the rules • Take turns and share • Be open-minded; listen to others • Don't take advantage of others • Don't blame others carelessly

Caring: Be kind • Be compassionate and show you care • Express gratitude • Forgive others • Help people in need

Citizenship: Do your share to make your school and community better • Cooperate • Stay informed; vote • Be a good neighbor • Obey laws and rules • Respect authority • Protect the environment

Source. The Six Pillars of Character (www.charactercounts.org/defsix.htm)

APPENDIX 9.6: SENSE OF CONGRESS REGARDING GOOD CHARACTER.

(b) Findings.—Congress finds that—

(b) the future of our Nation and world will be determined by the young people of today;

(2) record levels of youth crime, violence, teenage pregnancy, and substance abuse indicate a growing moral crisis in our society;

(3) character development is the long-term process of helping young people to know, care about, and act upon such basic values as trustworthiness, respect for self and others, responsibility, fairness, compassion, and citizenship;

(4) these values are universal, reaching across cultural and religious differences;

(5) a recent poll found that 90 percent of Americans support the teaching of core moral and civic values;

(6) parents will always be children's primary character educators;

(7) good moral character is developed best in the context of the family;

(8) parents, community leaders, and school officials are establishing successful partnerships across the Nation to implement character education programs;

(9) character education programs also ask parents, faculty, and staff to serve as role models of core values, to provide opportunities for young people to apply these values, and to establish high academic standards that challenge students to set high goals, work to achieve the goals, and persevere in spite of difficulty;

(10) the development of virtue and moral character, those habits of mind, heart, and spirit that help young people to know, desire, and do what is right, has historically been a primary mission of colleges and universities; and

(11) the Congress encourages parents, faculty, and staff across the Nation to emphasize character development in the home, in the community, in our schools, and in our colleges and universities.

(b) Sense of Congress.—It is the sense of Congress that Congress should support and encourage character building initiatives in schools across America and urge colleges and universities to affirm that the development of character is one of the primary goals of higher education.

Source. Sense of Congress Regarding Good Character (www.ed.gov/policy/highered/leg/hea98/sec863.html)

APPENDIX 9.7: EMPLOYMENT
OF 16- AND 17-YEAR-OLD STUDENTS
Employment status of 16- and 17-year-olds enrolled in school, by sex and race: 1970 to 1993

Year	Males			Females		
	Total	*White[1]*	*Black[1]*	*Total*	*White[1]*	*Black[1]*
Percent employed[2]						
1970 ...	32.5	34.9	15.5	28.1	30.3	13.9
1975 ...	34.4	38.2	10.6	31.5	34.7	12.4
1980 ...	35.3	39.3	14.6	34.1	38.5	10.5
1985 ...	30.2	34.0	13.4	31.4	35.6	11.8
1989 ...	36.3	40.0	20.2	39.1	42.6	23.8
1990 ...	31.6	35.5	15.1	31.3	35.1	16.6
1991 ...	29.1	33.8	10.2	32.7	37.9	10.3
1992 ...	29.4	33.6	11.7	28.8	33.2	10.0
1993 ...	28.9	33.3	9.8	31.1	36.0	13.0
Percent employed full time[2]						
1970 ...	2.1	2.3	1.0	1.0	1.1	1.6
1975 ...	2.8	3.1	1.0	1.6	1.7	1.4
1980 ...	2.0	2.1	1.7	0.8	0.8	0.6
1985 ...	1.3	1.5	0.4	0.9	1.1	0.2
1989 ...	2.5	2.9	1.2	1.2	1.2	0.8
1990 ...	2.1	2.3	3	1.1	1.3	0.4
1991 ...	0.9	1.1	3	1.1	1.3	0.6
1992 ...	1.6	1.9	0.4	0.9	1.0	3
1993 ...	1.0	1.1	0.6	1.1	1.2	1.2
Percent employed part time[2]						
1970 ...	27.1	29.1	12.6	26.5	28.6	11.8
1975 ...	27.4	30.3	8.4	29.1	32.3	9.8
1980 ...	29.7	33.0	12.1	32.8	37.0	9.9
1985 ...	27.2	30.5	12.8	30.2	34.1	11.6
1989 ...	33.8	37.1	19.2	37.9	41.4	23.0
1990 ...	29.5	33.2	15.0	30.1	33.8	16.3
1991 ...	28.2	32.8	10.2	31.5	36.6	9.6
1992 ...	27.8	31.7	11.3	28.0	32.2	9.9
1993 ...	27.8	32.2	9.1	30.0	34.8	12.0

(continued on next page)

Year	Males			Females		
	Total	White[1]	Black[1]	Total	White[1]	Black[1]
			Unemployment rate[4]			
1970 ...	16.5	15.1	33.3	16.0	14.9	32.1
1975 ...	17.4	16.9	25.7	19.2	17.9	36.1
1980 ...	19.8	17.4	43.3	16.8	15.3	39.6
1985 ...	20.8	18.7	41.2	19.0	15.6	50.8
1989 ...	16.7	15.1	27.0	10.7	9.3	22.5
1990 ...	16.8	15.4	31.8	16.0	13.9	34.0
1991 ...	21.0	18.5	40.7	18.6	15.4	50.0
1992 ...	20.7	17.3	48.1	20.1	17.9	44.7
1993 ...	21.5	18.4	51.0	18.0	16.0	35.3

[1]Includes Hispanics.
[2]Full-time and part-time employment figures through 1985 exclude agricultural employment, but they are included in the percentage employed.
[3]Less than .05 percent.
[4]The unemployment rate is the percentage of those in the labor force who are not working and are seeking employment.

Note. Part-time workers are persons who work less than 35 hours per week.

Source. U.S. Department of Labor, Bureau of Labor Statistics, *Special Labor Force Reports*, nos. 16 and 68; and unpublished data.

Source. National Sporting Goods Association, *Sports Participation in 1986*, Series I; and *Sports Participation in 1988–1991*, Series I; and unpublished data.

Source. Employment of 16- and 17-year-old students (http://nces.ed.gov/pubs/yi/y9642a.html)

PART III

THE DEEP SOUTH: DIDACTIC, INDIVIDUALISTIC, AUTHORITARIAN APPROACHES TO CHARACTER EDUCATION

We use the term *didactic* for this approach because of its hortatory effort to instruct young people in proper morals. Moral adults are viewed as the guardians of a set of universal ethical values and standards. They have an obligation to impress these values upon a generation of youngsters who are immersed in an increasingly coarse and corrupt culture. Young people are ever more tempted to succumb to the temptations afforded by a self-serving media and to defy the wisdom of knowing and authoritative adults. These adults include their parents, regarded as their first and most important moral teachers, and other wise elders throughout the nation and community, including the school. The United States of America is regarded as an especially virtuous nation, founded by judicious and moral leaders and established by a Declaration of Independence written in the name of God. Good character is not innate but must be achieved through hard work by both individuals and those who persistently instruct them in morality. Particularly at risk for poor character are those from communities outside the upper and middle classes, who are exposed to greater and more varied temptations and who have fewer moral role models to emulate. Through a strong and concerted effort to instruct youth in good character, moral adults can restore society to a time when people of virtue occupied a simpler, more noble, less profane world. This restoration requires the return to a higher standard, not just of morality but of academic

> *Between ourselves and our real natures we interpose that wax figure of idealizations and selections which we call our character.*
>
> *—Walter Lippmann*

147

achievement, which will rise as students develop a stronger work ethic, take greater pride in themselves and their schools, and approach school more purposefully and productively.

In this section of the book we look at how the character education proposals from two adjacent states in the Deep South forward this vision of character education. Our analysis will first take into account two key influences on the curricula: the cultural context in which they were produced and the ancillary curricula drawn on to develop them. We then analyze the discourses embedded in the curricula, first in the program rationales and descriptions and then in the program assessments.

Chapter 10

Cultural Context of the Deep South

> *The shell is America's most active contribution to the formation of character. A tough hide. Grow it early.*
>
> —*Anaïs Nin*

Region is a concept that is used to identify and organize areas of Earth's surface for various purposes. A region has certain characteristics that give it a measure of cohesiveness and distinctiveness that set it apart from other regions ... regions are human constructs whose boundaries and characteristics are derived from sets of specific criteria.... Understanding the idea of region and the process of regionalization is fundamental to being geographically informed. (http://www.nationalgeographic.com/xpeditions/standards/05/)

Character curricula do not emerge in a vacuum but represent the cultures in which they are developed. In making this claim we situate ourselves in a tradition that dates at least to 430 B.C., when Herodotus's *History* of the Greco-Persian wars was published (Cole, 1996). In these volumes Herodotus attempted to describe the wars through an understanding of how the two cultures originated and developed to shape distinctive perspectives and ways of life that came into conflict. From this perspective, worldviews are regarded as functions of engagement in cultural practice. In this chapter we describe some key cultural practices from the regions where the curricula were developed that we found inscribed in the discourses of the character education proposals.

Both states featured in this category are geographically and culturally located in the Deep South, an area generally considered to consist of Alabama, Georgia, Louisiana, Mississippi, North Carolina, and South Carolina, and more broadly including parts of Arkansas, Florida, Tennessee, Texas, and Virginia. Before proceeding, we should affirm that we wish to avoid regional stereotyping. We fully recognize that any U.S. state is composed of diverse people and that there is disagreement among its citizenry on many issues. Furthermore, with the increasing mobility afforded by the modern economy, any U.S. region is less parochial than it once was and has access to multinational and multicultural influences through the media. Both authors of this study have lived in the South for more than 20 years and have grown weary of mass media depictions of Southerners as stupid, inbred, ignorant, and handicapped by innumerable other negative traits. With this recognition we heed the caution of Turiel (2002), who argues that

> It is necessary to avoid the types of broad generalizations often used to characterize particular cultures and to reformulate the concept to include heterogeneity, conflict, and change. [Abu-Lughod (1991)] has made the important observation that generalizing across contexts and people within a culture flattens out differences and homogenizes them. This is another way of saying that generalizations about people in a culture serve to stereotype them. Such generalizations give the appearance of an absence of internal differentiations and distinctions in viewpoints and serve to smooth over existing contradictions, conflicts of interest, ambiguities, arguments, and shifts in views from one context to another. Generalizations that impose a coherence upon cultural groups also serve to exaggerate boundaries and separations between groups. (p. 195)

We recognize that some may take issue with our focus on the discourse of the cultural majority, in this case, the White upper and middle class. We are painfully aware that these states include remnants of the native societies that were destroyed in the 1800s by President Andrew Jackson's policy of Indian Removal. We are also well aware that state demographics include large African American and growing Latino and Latina American and Asian American populations whose cultures are vital in these states. States in this region also include large numbers of poor rural Whites whose perspectives rarely enter into public discourse. As we will show, however, these communities have had little input in the development of character education curricula. Our identification of a regional culture thus focuses on that culture which has become written into policy, whether that inscription is fair and representative or not.

With these caveats, we see the likelihood that regional cultural history contributes to the value systems that generated the conceptions of character manifested in the proposals. Indeed, given the ways in which notions of character are often tied to custom and heritage in these states' proposals, we see their character education movements as vehicles for restoring traditional values—at least, those values believed to be traditional among those with the greatest cultural capital—that are thought by their proponents to have gone awry in an increasingly pluralistic and profane world.

That the South views itself as different from other parts of the country can be easily documented. The South—in particular, the White South—has an identity that has been fiercely asserted and safeguarded during such issues as the debate over the Confederate battle flag's appropriateness as a state symbol. The recent decisions to remove the symbol of the St. Andrews cross from its promontory in some southern states has been regarded by many as an abandonment and profanation of a great and abiding heritage. Given that this perspective permeates the discourse of restoration of the good old days, we see the character education movement and its rhetoric as part of an effort to protect a heritage under increasing attack and compromise by those perceived to lack proper respect for its authority.

The Center for the Study of the American South at the University of North Carolina at Chapel Hill (http://www.unc.edu/depts/csas/csasabt.htm) refers to "The persistent and strong regional identity of the South." The Center

> seeks to sponsor a broad public dialogue that addresses the central challenges to public life in the South: What is this shared Southern history and culture that both divides and unites Southerners? What threats to the region are posed by persistent poverty, a decline in civility, and the fragmentation of communities by racism and migration? How are recent changes to the region redefining opportunity in a global economy, transforming landscapes, and radically reshaping communities?

Issues on which the Center publishes polls include economic conditions in southern communities; cultural issues such as southern accent, the Confederate flag, and "Dixie"; race relations; feelings of natives toward those who relocate to the South; and characteristics of Southerners versus Northerners. Each of these issues is visible daily in letters to the editors of southern newspapers, as is the role of Christianity—or more specifically, denominations of Southern Baptists—in all facets of life, including school. We next review those aspects of southern culture that we found particularly visible in the character education proposals.

Before doing so, we reiterate that the South, as they say, is not as Southern as it once was. Columnist Bill Maxwell (2004) makes the point that the New South "is slowly becoming like the rest of the United States." He cites research by Griffin and Thompson (2003) that suggests that the number of people living in the South who identify themselves as Southerners is declining due to the influences of urbanization and immigration. The groups holding most steadfastly to a southern identity are Republicans, political conservatives, and those living in wealth. For people of color, liberals, Democrats, and those living in poverty, the southern identity is losing its hold. For new southern immigrants from outside the historical centers of political gravity, such as the gay African American men who now regard Atlanta as a "mecca" (Jubera, 2004), the South may be home but does not provide their primary identity. We see this disparity

> *A man's character is his fate.*
>
>   —*Heraclitus*

between conservative and liberal ideological and regional identities as being consistent with our belief that the dominant culture of this region, that consisting of those already in authoritative positions, is most likely to have its values inscribed in the character curriculum.

PRE-COLUMBIAN POPULATIONS AND EUROPEAN SETTLEMENT

Much archeological evidence suggests that humans first arrived on what is now called North America as long as 32,000 years ago. These people migrated from present-day Asia across the land bridge provided by the Bering Straits and gradually dispersed throughout the continent over a period of many thousands of years. As migratory groups split and established homelands, they emerged into separate cultures, each developing in response to the local conditions that shaped their daily lives and thus their cultural practices and beliefs over time (Nash, 1974). The people who ultimately settled in the present-day U.S. Southeast included the Apalachee, Caccamaw, Catawba, Cherokee, Choctaw, Congaree, Coree, Creek, Matamuskeet, Pamlico, Santee, Saraw, Seminole, Tuscarora, Yamasee, and others. Their migrations were often circuitous and a consequence of conflict with other tribes. The Cherokee, for instance, likely moved from present-day Texas or Mexico to the eastern Great Lakes region, then moved southeast to the Allegheny and Appalachian mountains following wars with the Iroquois and Delaware tribes, ultimately settling in what is now North Carolina, South Carolina, Tennessee, Georgia, and Alabama.

Life among these tribes changed dramatically after Europeans established settlements on the continent in the 1500s to 1700s Common Era (C.E.). The first Europeans were Spaniards who set up missions in the 1500s. Within the next hundred years the British began setting up colonies, coming in conflict with both native people and the Spaniards, who finally were driven out in the decades preceding the U.S. Revolutionary War. England's motivation for establishing settlements in the present-day Southeast included efforts to relocate their dispossessed and destitute, desire to expand their empire into what they considered the New World, and ambition to establish colonies where goods such as silk needed in England could be produced (Coleman, 1978). Other European groups settling in this region included German Protestants expelled from their homelands, Scottish Highlanders, and immigrants from Italy, Switzerland, and Wales.

From these settlements emerged an agrarian society that relied on a narrow range of crops such as cotton, rice, or tobacco to sustain its economy.

Whereas the North became industrialized and developed a diverse economy, the South remained largely rural and agricultural and dependent on a limited number of crops. This reliance ultimately had devastating consequences on the overall economy when any crop failed, as cotton did during the boll weevil plague around the turn of the twentieth century.

To help run farms, landowners imported indentured servants from England (http://www.africana.com/archive/articles/tt_269.asp). Eventually this pool of labor thinned and many Southerners increasingly viewed slavery as a solution to the problem of operating farms at a profit. The slavery of indigenous people had begun with the Spaniards in the early 1500s, who either sold them in the West Indies or to landowners in the northern colonies, or used them to carry their provisions during explorations. Native tribes were enlisted and rewarded for conquering neighboring tribes who were then sold into slavery (Nash, 1974). As early as 1670 slavery was well institutionalized throughout the South and Caribbean, with native people and imported Africans making up the slave population.

Cobb (1997) reports the following argument from Thomas Stephens justifying the enslavement of Africans to sustain settlers' farms:

> And indeed the extraordinary Heats here, the extraordinary Expences in maintaining, hiring and procuring White Servants, the extraordinary Difficulty and Danger there is in clearing the Lands, attending and Manufacturing the Crops, working in the Fields in Summer, and the poor Returns of Indian Corn, Pease and Potatoes, which are as yet the only chief Produces of the Land there, make it indisputably impossible for White Men alone to carry on Planting to any good Purpose.... The poor People of Georgia, may as well think of becoming Negroes themselves (from whose Condition at present they seem not to be far removed) as of hoping to be ever able to live without them. (pp. 4–5)

National and racial conflict emanating from these early invasions, settlements, and enslavements continued to characterize the southern region of the continent for decades. The years following the Revolution included political and military efforts to remove Native Americans from their lands to clear the way for White settlement. The Creeks ceded lands in the 1790 Treaty of New York. Treaties were signed between the Cherokee and the United States in 1785 and 1791 that provided the native people with permanent rights to lands. These treaties were ignored by Whites who sought to live in Cherokee territory (Ehle, 1988). In 1802 Georgia yielded its Western territory to the U.S. Government "in exchange for a promise that the United States would remove the Indians from Georgia as soon as it could be done peaceably" (Coleman, 1978, p. 30). President Andrew Jackson's policy of Indian Removal culminated this promise, relocating in 1938 to 1939 most of the Cherokee Nation to the lands west of the Mississippi, primarily the Indian

Territory (present-day Oklahoma). This period is still regarded by many native people as a holocaust due to the great loss of life during the harshly enforced march (over 4,000 lives lost) and seizure of land historically the province of the indigenous people (http://www.shadowwolf.org/cherokee_ nation.html).

Most in the United States are familiar with the Deep South's history of slavery, the Civil War and abolition, the brief period of Reconstruction, the repeal of Reconstruction in 1876 by Rutherford B. Hayes in exchange for electoral votes that gave him the U.S. presidency, more than 80 years of racial segregation and Jim Crow laws, the Civil Rights era of the 1950s to 1960s, and the continuing climate of racial unease as evidenced by the ongoing existence of the Ku Klux Klan and other white supremacist groups both in the South and around the United States. We argue that this history and the culture it has helped to shape have contributed greatly to the particular form that character education has taken in the states we profile from the Deep South.

We next review the major cultural factors that we see contributing to the Southern states' conceptions of character education as revealed through their proposals to OERI for funding.

RELIGION

Both states included in this profile are considered a part of the Bible Belt, that part of the nation that runs across the South and is largely Christian and particularly Southern Baptist. In one of the two states, the director of the character education initiative was identified as a "lay minister" who authored a self-published book called *Teaching Jack and Jill Right vs. Wrong in the Homes and Schools*. Among his listed credentials for leading the character education movement was his previous work with evangelical minister Billy Graham and politician Strom Thurmond.

In one southern state we analyzed, 93% of the population is Christian, with 56% of the state's population members of the Baptist church; in the other, 91% is Christian, with 60% of the total population Baptist (http://www.adherents.com/). Although the Southern Baptist doctrine is not embraced by all who identify as Baptists in these states, the official statement of beliefs is worth reading as a way of understanding some of the cultural origins of these states' notions of character education. These official

---

Crazy Horse was a typical Sioux brave, and from the point of view of our race an ideal hero, living at the height of the epical progress of the American Indian and maintaining in his own character all that was most subtle and ennobling.

—Ohiyesa (Charles A. Eastman)

beliefs are outlined by the Committee on the Baptist Faith and Message, chaired by Adrian Rogers (see Appendix 10.1 for the full text of the committee's views). We next quote extensively from this committee's statement of the Baptist faith and message:

> Our generation faces the reality of a postmodern culture, complete with rampant relativism and the denial of absolute truth. A pervasive secularism has infected our society and its corrosive effects are evident throughout the life of our nation. Moral decay and assaults upon cherished truths dominate the arena in which we must now minister.... We have made the total truthfulness and trustworthiness of the Bible even more explicit.... Given the pervasive influence of a postmodern culture, we are called to proclaim Jesus Christ as the only Savior and salvation is in His name alone. Baptists thus reject inclusivism and pluralism in salvation, for these compromise the Gospel itself.... The Convention has spoken clearly its conviction that while both men and women are gifted and called for ministry, the office of pastor is limited to men as qualified by Scripture.... Our Baptist ancestors of a mere generation ago could not have imagined the need to address the issues of abortion, homosexuality, euthanasia, and all manner of deviant and pagan sexuality. We answer with a clear word of biblical correction. (Rogers, 2002)

These aspects of the Baptist doctrine are reflected in the southern states' character education proposals in several areas. The rejection of postmodernism and its relativistic outlook runs throughout the discourse of moral absoluteness and the authoritarian society. The belief in moral decay and the abandonment of cherished truths in these secular times is found in both the discourse of youth depravity and the discourse of the good old days. The assertion of the total truth and trustworthiness of the Bible and the affirmation that only men can serve in the ministry fit well with the discourse of authoritarian society. The association of abortion and homosexuality with deviant and pagan sexuality is consistent with the discourse of family first, which in this region and the discourse of its dominant culture considers families to consist of a heterosexual man and woman and their children. We describe these discourses and others found in the curricula when we analyze the proposals themselves.

Southerners also employ a discourse that gives the church a special moral authority and links character education to religion. Character education guru Thomas Lickona (1991), although located in upstate New York, expresses this discourse well in his Acknowledgements in his oft-referenced book *Educating for Character:*

> In his book *The Road Less Traveled,* psychiatrist Scott Peck writes about "amazing grace"—all the times in our lives when we feel helped in ways that do not seem attributable to natural causes. For religious believers, such graced moments are experienced as the loving action of a God who holds each of us in His awareness.... For me, such moments call to mind a state-

In a president, character is everything. A president doesn't have to be brilliant....
He doesn't have to be clever; you can hire clever.... You can hire pragmatic, and
you can buy and bring in policy wonks. But you can't buy courage and decency, you
can't rent a strong moral sense. A president must bring those things with him.... He
needs to have, in that much maligned word, but a good one nonetheless, a "vision"
of the future he wishes to create. But a vision is worth little if a president doesn't have
the character—the courage and heart—to see it through.

—Peggy Noonan

ment by St. Thomas Aquinas: All truth comes from the Holy Spirit. For the
errors in this book, I take responsibility. For whatever truth it contains, I
would like to thank the source. (p. viii)

Lickona articulates well the belief that his views on character are divinely
inspired. This faith meshes well with the discourse of moral absoluteness,
which accords its notion of morality a universality that transcends culture,
circumstances, and other contextual factors.

RACE

During the era in which the rice planters ruled the Low Country [of South
Carolina], a distinctive caste system prevailed. Handed down the system, the
planters embraced a social doctrine which pertained not only to economics,
but also to race relations. This caste system, which the planter class held so
dear, would eventually prove to be the principle that led to the demise of
their world. The Georgetown rice culture, as well as the plantation system
throughout the American South, may have been little more than a trans-
plant, or continuance, of medieval European Manorialism. However, because of the addition of race as a determiner of slavery, it was uniquely
American. (Boyle, 1996)

The term *plantation mentality* is still used to describe caste-like social structures in which a small group of elites oversees and oppresses larger groups
not born into privilege, wealth, and power. Both states from which we derive our profile were part of the original Confederacy and have histories of
slavery, segregation, lynchings, Jim Crow laws, civil rights violations, and
other racial inequities committed by Whites against Blacks. As previously
noted, this region was also party to the forced removal of indigenous people
under the presidency of Tennessean Andrew Jackson. To this day both
states still have active groups defending the Confederate heritage, displaying the Confederate battle flag, and in more radical cases seeking Southern
independence (see, e.g., http://www.southernindependence.com/). The
legacy of racial inequity is still manifested in the poverty and educational
levels of Blacks and Whites in each state:

Over 90 percent of the executions that have been carried out in the last 20 years have been in the states of the Old Confederacy.... 98.4 percent of those serving life sentences in [one state] for a second conviction for sale or possession with intent to distribute certain narcotics are African American. Only 27 percent of [this state's] population is African American. Virtually every report that has examined the operation of the death penalty has found racial discrimination and arbitrariness in its infliction. As a result of this discrimination, one-third of African American men between the ages of 18 and 30 are under some type of court supervision. By the turn of the [21st] century one half of all African American men will be in prison or jail, on probation or parole. The majority of victims of crime in many southern jurisdictions are people of color and an even greater majority of those accused of crimes are people of color. Yet despite the importance of the operation of the criminal justice systems to the African American community, most of the decisions in the system are made by white people. (Southern Center for Human Rights, http://www.schr.org/center-info/index.html)

The exclusion of minorities from the judicial system reflects their exclusion from authority in other realms of society. In one of the two proposals from Southern states, for instance, a stated goal for the second year of the funded program was "to include minority representation." The original and definitive conception of character, then, was entirely the work of White residents of the state and their advisors.

The issue of race is key in our analysis because people of color and of the working class are identified as being especially in need of character education. We found this belief particularly at work in the discourses of class-based morality and the authoritarian society. We also found the issues of race and religion to be virtually inseparable. This history is described in the following account:

"In the 1840s, the Southern Baptist Convention was formed because they wanted the right to own slaves. In the 1950s, they stood in opposition to equal rights. The problem most African-Americans have (with this resolution) is when the SBC had an opportunity to stand in favor of equal rights, they didn't," said the Rev. George Glass Jr., pastor of New Pilgrim Baptist Church. "Now when they're presented with certain situations in the future, where will they stand?"

The historic rift in the Baptist Church occurred in the early to mid-1800s. Fundamentally, the issue was a north vs. south, industrial vs. agrarian one. Slaveholders and slavery were central to the debate. Southerners, dependent on slave labor for the economic gifts it produced, demanded the right to chattel property. Northerners, with their industrial base, largely opposed slavery as a moral issue. In 1845, the SBC seceded from the American Baptist Association. The southern secession guaranteed slaveholders would continue to serve as missionaries, something the national body wouldn't allow.

At its 150th anniversary meeting June 20–22 [1995] in Atlanta, the convention adopted an 18-paragraph resolution repenting past racism (Gibson, n.d.).

In 2003 this apology had not yet been realized in substantive action, in the minds of many African Americans, as reported in the *Atlanta Journal-Constitution:*

> several of the SBC's best-known black leaders say they're still being treated as if they're on the plantation—that white Southern Baptists refuse to see them as equals or share power. "If they're going to accept black people and their churches, they're going to have to get rid of the slave master's mentality that's so prevalent in the convention," says the Rev. James Coffee. (June 14, 2003, http://www.ajc.com/saturday/content/epaper/editions/saturday/faith_values_e3ae98d671ff41f90070.html)

As we will report, this skepticism is justified in the fact that minorities were excluded from the initial planning of the character education initiative in at least one of the Southern states profiled, with minority involvement slated as a goal for subsequent years of the project.

POVERTY

As noted by the Center for the Study of the American South, persistent poverty is among the greatest concerns facing southern states. The U.S. Census Bureau (2000) reports that of the four major regions in the United States (Northeast, Midwest, South, West), the South has the highest poverty rate (13.1% compared to the national average of 11.8%), with 12.5 million people living in poverty. The two states profiled in this section had 13.7% and 12.8% of their populations living in poverty. All states regarded as part of the Deep South or Old Confederacy had poverty rates higher than the U.S. average.

Some trace the South's persistent poverty to the antebellum slave-based economy which caused the South to become so dependent on agriculture—and in particular, on a narrow range of crops such as cotton—that it did not provide the diversity necessary to surviving changing economic

> *The relation too of master and slave is fitted to cultivate and foster the most generous and noble traits of character. Legally recognized and settled inferiority, helplessness and dependence on the one side, bring forth as their legitimate fruit, magnanimity, forbearance and generosity on the other; and many of the highest, manliest and most admirable qualities in the Southern character have been preserved in their pristine strength, if not engendered by our peculiar, social and domestic system.*
>
> *—Oration delivered before the Fourth of July Association of Charleston, South Carolina, by William Porcher Miles on The Fourth of July, 1849.*

conditions. This limited agrarian economy resulted in both a tremendous resource deficit compared to the North during the Civil War and poor resiliency in establishing a new economy at the war's end (Donald, 1960).

Southern education's status has always been tied to its economy and to issues of race. Denied formal education during slavery—with both slaves and Whites often brutally punished for efforts to make Blacks literate—African Americans were then segregated into schools that were underfinanced even by Southern standards. The southern economies lagged behind other regions for most of the twentieth century, leading to low investments in all social services including schools. Southern states consistently have ranked toward the bottom in educational spending. According to data compiled by the National Education Association (NEA, 1997), southern states for the most part occupy the lower third of the 50 states and Washington, DC in terms of teacher salaries and per pupil expenditures.

We see the issue of poverty at work in two discourses found in the character education proposals. One is the discourse of Protestant work ethic, in which poverty is viewed as a consequence of poor work habits and thus low character. The second is the discourse of class-based morality, in which people of low economic status are viewed as deserving of their poverty and particularly in need of character education, which could provide their economic salvation.

CIVILITY

The Center for the Study of the American South identifies a decline in civility as a major concern among Southern states. Southern manners and hospitality are part of the lore of the South. Undoubtedly there is great variation among Southerners in the degree to which they practice civility. The extension of mannerly relations has also been a selective custom. Witness, for example, the historic brutality by Whites toward African Americans and forced removal of indigenous people. Yet its consistent identification as a southern tradition suggests that it has been at least an ideal, however inconsistent its application.

The Southern Manners website (http://members.tripod.com/~tcc230/SManners.htm), although surely lacking scientific rigor in compilation, does articulate a paragon of etiquette that distinguishes the Southern sensi-

---

Mankind is made up of inconsistencies, and no man acts invariably up to his predominant character. The wisest man sometimes acts weakly, and the weakest sometimes wisely.

—Lord Chesterfield

> *Yahya related to me from Malik from Salama ibn Safwan ibn Salama az-Zuraqi that Zayd ibn Talha ibn Rukana, who attributed it to the Prophet, may Allah bless him and grant him peace, said, "The Messenger of Allah, may Allah bless him and grant him peace, said, 'Every deen has an innate character. The character of Islam is modesty.'"*
>
> —*Book 47, Number 47.2.9: Glorious Koran*

bility (see Appendix 10.2). While perhaps tinged with the aroma of magnolias and wisteria and recalling the tones of Scarlet and Rhett more than a modern Southerner, this ideal of courtliness has not entirely disappeared from the southern landscape. The author's overt repudiation of politically correct manners is echoed daily in letters to the editor across the South. As noted by the Center for the Study of the American South, the decline in civility is a problem of great concern in the modern South.

The issue of manners and civility appears in several discourses we identified in the character education proposals. It is implied throughout the discourse of youth depravity, with young people increasingly exposed to the corrupting influence of the mass media. The deference shown to elders is part of the discourse of authoritarian society. We also see this issue implicated in the discourse of the good old days, given the way in which civility is associated with southern heritage and is believed to be in decline.

SUMMARY

Our goal has ben to identify factors from the dominant culture that we see represented in the character education proposals from states in this region. In essence, we see the character curricula designed to recenter southern culture on a particular heritage, that of the White upper and middle classes whose values have been challenged in the postmodern era by traditionally marginalized groups. Recalcitrant behavior among the poor, among people of color, and among other historically powerless cultural groups is viewed as an indication of a lack of civility and thus absence of good character, a problem that can be addressed in the school curriculum through the provision of positive role models and exemplars. We next turn our attention to the proposals themselves and outline the specific ways in which they are designed to improve students' character.

> *The world may take your reputation from you, but it cannot take your character.*
>
> —*Emma Dunham*

APPENDIX 10.1: FROM THE CHAIRMAN
OF THE COMMITTEE ON THE BAPTIST FAITH AND MESSAGE

Dear Southern Baptist:

On behalf of the Committee on the *Baptist Faith and Message,* I am pleased to release this report and recommendation to the Southern Baptist Convention. President Paige Patterson appointed our committee by authorization of the Convention as it met in Atlanta last year. Meeting over a period of several months, we reviewed the confessional history of our denomination and considered the challenges faced by the Baptists of this generation. We were guided by the rich heritage embodied in the 1925 and 1963 editions of the *Baptist Faith and Message.* We have sought to retain all the strengths of that noble heritage, to clarify the truths there expressed, and to address the needs of our own times. Baptists cherish our doctrinal inheritance. We are a people of the Book, who recognize no other authority for faith and practice but God's Word. Thus, we receive and affirm those doctrines revealed in the Bible, and we are unembarrassed to take our stand upon the solid rock of biblical authority. Our confessions represent statements of those doctrines revealed in the Bible. The Bible is the source of our authority, not merely a support for our historic doctrines.

In 1925, the Southern Baptist Convention first adopted the *Baptist Faith and Message* as a public statement of our faith and doctrine. Nearly forty years later, faced with new challenges and questions, the Convention adopted a revised edition of the *Baptist Faith and Message* in 1963. Now, again nearly four decades after the Convention's last comprehensive action, a new generation must take up the stewardship of the faith "once for all delivered to the saints" [Jude 3].

Our generation faces the reality of a postmodern culture, complete with rampant relativism and the denial of absolute truth. A pervasive secularism has infected our society and its corrosive effects are evident throughout the life of our nation. Moral decay and assaults upon cherished truths dominate the arena in which we must now minister, and to which we must now proclaim the Gospel.

Our profound respect for the heritage of the previous statements is reflected in the intentional decision of our committee to incorporate language from both the 1925 and 1963 editions in our recommendation. Both of these historic statements speak to the present, as well as the past.

Scripture instructs us always to be ready "to give an account" for the hope that is within us [I Peter 3:15]. This is our motivation and the cause to which we have dedicated this process. As the Baptists of old acknowledged, each generation faces the responsibility of speaking to the issues of its day, and facing the challenges of its own climate.

The preface to our report sets forth the rationale and method for our work. With the 1963 committee, we cite the principle set forth by our forebears in 1925: "As in the past, so in the future, Baptists should hold themselves free to revise their statements of faith as may seem to them wise and expedient."

We now propose a new edition of our honored confession. This generation must set forth its witness to the truths revealed in the Bible. Where necessary, we have proposed changes and additions to certain sections. We have retained the structure of the confession and the substance of each article. We have proposed no new articles. Several of the articles are presented without any revision at all. Our recommendation is intended to clarify our doctrines for this present age, and to define our beliefs against the backdrop of modern confusion.

Our hope is that a rising generation of Baptists will recognize the significance of our biblical doctrines, embrace our Baptist heritage, and own this confession of faith for themselves.

The following is a summary of revised articles included in our report:

1. We have sought to clarify the intention of both previous editions of the *Baptist Faith and Message* as reflected in Article I: The Scriptures. We have made the total truthfulness and trustworthiness of the Bible even more explicit, and we point to Jesus Christ as the focus of divine revelation. We have removed the statement that identified Jesus Christ as "the criterion by which the Bible is to be interpreted," because it has been subject to misunderstanding. Jesus Christ cannot be divided from the biblical revelation that is testimony to Him. We must not claim a knowledge of Christ that is independent of Scripture or in any way in opposition to Scripture. Likewise, Scripture cannot be set against Scripture.

2. In the context of modern denials of the omniscience, exhaustive foreknowledge, and omnipotence of God, we have reaffirmed the teachings of the Bible and the consistent teaching of our Baptist tradition, as reflected in Article II: "God." God has all knowledge. He knows all things simultaneously. His knowledge is immediate, without the process of thought, reason, or inference. His foreknowledge of events does not necessarily mean that He predetermined them. He knows the workings of his natural, physical, moral, and spiritual laws which work toward definite ends. Man is free to choose in the light of them, but is responsible for his choices. God knows these choices beforehand, but does not predetermine them. *Herschel H. Hobbs, The Baptist Faith and Message (1971), p. 36.*

3. We have made clear our embrace of the substitutionary character of Christ's atonement in Article II:B "God the Son."

4. We have clarified God's creation of human beings as male and female, both made in His image. The gift of gender is thus part of the goodness of God's creation. This is reflected in Article III: "Man."

5. Baptists must also make clear our affirmation of the blessing of racial and ethnic diversity, and acknowledge that all races possess full dignity by the creative intention of God. This is also included in Article III: "Man."

6. Given the pervasive influence of a postmodern culture, we are called to proclaim Jesus Christ as the only Savior and salvation is in His name alone. Baptists thus reject inclusivism and pluralism in salvation, for these compromise the Gospel itself. Salvation comes only to those who call upon the name of the Lord, and come to personal faith in Jesus Christ as Savior. Article IV: "Salvation," includes this clarification.

7. We reaffirm the New Testament heritage of Baptist congregationalism in Article VI: "The Church," recovering the language of the 1925 Baptist Faith and Message and affirming the contribution of the 1963 statement as reflected in the last paragraph of the article. The church comprises all the redeemed, and will include "believers from every tribe, and tongue, and people, and nation."

8. The Convention has spoken clearly its conviction that while both men and women are gifted and called for ministry, the office of pastor is limited to men as qualified by Scripture. This is included in Article VI: "The Church."

9. Our Baptist ancestors of a mere generation ago could not have imagined the need to address the issues of abortion, homosexuality, euthanasia, and all manner of deviant and pagan sexuality. We answer with a clear word of biblical correction. This is found in Article XV: "The Christian and the Social Order."

In other articles we have made minor clarifications, adjusted language to modern usage, and added phrases from the 1925 statement as appropriate.

Sincerely,

Adrian Rogers, Chairman

Source. From the Chairman of the Committee on the Baptist Faith and Message (www.sbc.net/bfmchairman)

APPENDIX 10.2: PROPER SOUTHERN MANNERS

Proper Southern Manners

Make no mistake about it, manners matter in Dixie! Good manners make life more pleasant for everyone. Good manners are what make Southerners different from those who aren't from here. You cannot take good manners too seriously in the South.

The Fundamentals of Good Manners

These five fundamentals should set you in good stead. Good manners are extended to everybody, regardless of whether you know them, on which side of town they live, or whether they tithe.

1. Be Humble: Others first, yourself last. Self-denial and deference to others ("After you") are the cornerstone of good manners, acting selfish or uppity is not. This commandment is indisputably rooted in the Bible Belt theology ("the first shall be last, and the last shall be first").
2. Be Courteous: Remember the Golden Rule. Go out of your way to be helpful and kind to everyone you encounter.
3. Behave Yourself: Don't be uncouth, rude, brash, loud, coarse, or cause a commotion in public. Only trashy types do such things ... and obviously this is because they weren't raised to know better.
4. Be Friendly: Put your friendliest foot forward, whether you've been properly introduced or don't know the person from a hole in the ground. Be sociable and neighborly, just like you learned in Sunday School ("Thou shalt love thy neighbor as thyself").
5. Be Modest: Never be highfalutin'. Practice modesty in all situations. "Why, shucks, I guess I was in the right place at the right time" would work just fine upon learning that you had won the Pulitzer Prize. "Of course I won it, I deserve to" would absolutely categorize you as too big for your britches.

Common Courtesies in Dixie.

- Say "please" without fail. Please, always say "please" when you make a request, no matter how trivial or important.
- Always ask, never tell. The only way to make a request is to ask for it, directives are much too surly. "Would you please carry me up the road a piece?" is correct. "Give me a ride to the market" is most assuredly not.
- Say "Thank you" without fail. Upon being granted your request—be it a personal favor or impersonal transaction—always look the other party

in the eye, give them a pleasing smile, and cheerily say, "Thank you." To show them you're really grateful, dress it up with "Thank you kindly," "Thanks a whole lot," "Preciate it." If your request is denied, say "Well, thank you anyway." Using your best turn-the-other-cheek manner.

- Say "ma'am" and "sir" without fail. If any adult your senior addresses you (or vice versa), automatically attach the appropriate title to your response ("Yes ma'am," "I reckon so, Sir," "Pardon me ma'am"). Neglecting this rule is apt to be interpreted as arrogance or insolence or just plain bad upbringing.
- Always refer to those of the female gender as Ladies. The descriptive *woman* is usually reserved in Dixie for females of questionable respect. If you are a gentleman, then treat all ladies with courtness, deference, and respect you'd accord members of the royal family since, in the South, ladies occupy such status. This is an immutable rule of order in Dixie, no matter what may be happening elsewhere on this planet.
- Chivalry may not be well appreciated outside the South today, but you can be sure that around home territory a true gentleman will so honor a lady:
- Hold the door open for all members of the fairer sex, regardless of their social station.
- Stand when a lady enters or leaves a room.
- Walk on the streetside of a side-walk, when accompanying a lady.
- Order for both of you when at a restaurant (excluding business meals).
- Always call his mother "Mamma" or "mutha" or "Mrs. _____ " never by her first name, no matter what his age.

My Daddy Said

- As my daddy told me many years ago, "Good manners do not cost you anything to exercise, but the lack of them may cost you dearly further down the road."
- My daddy also told me "Treat all ladies as ladies, no matter what you have heard and continue to do so until she proves to you that she is not a lady."
- He also said "A man's word is his bond and that you come into this world with only your name and will leave this world the same and how you are remembered is how you kept the honor of your name."
- The last quote that I will make of my daddy's is "The manners that your children exhibit to you and the public are a direct reflection of you."

Political correctness is a cop-out to explain away the failures of our leaders, clergy, teachers, and most of all PARENTS. Morals and Manners are never out of style and are a prerequisite of all Southern Ladies and Gentlemen!

Thomas C. Cardwell

From the book *Having It Ya'll,* 1993, by Ann Barrett Batson, published by Rutledge Hill Press. Reprinted with permission.

Source.   Proper Southern manners (http://members.tripod.com/~tcc230/SManners.htm)

Chapter 11

Ancillary Curricula of the Deep South

In our analysis of the discourses included in the curricula, we include attention to the ancillary curricula identified as being sources for the ideas in the proposals. We next review the programs identified in the proposals as having been purchased or incorporated into the character curricula included in the southern states' OERI proposals. States from this region drew on services provided by Aspen Declaration authors, one commercially available curriculum, two staff development services and programs, and one program designed to help prevent violence and substance abuse.

SERVICES PROVIDED BY ASPEN DECLARATION AUTHORS

Character Education Partnership's 11 Principles of Effective Character Education

As required by the OERI RFP, the southern states drew on the Six Pillars of Character identified by the Character Counts! Coalition to inform their character curricula. In addition, one of the states borrowed the 11 Principles of Effective Character Education put forward by the Character Education Partnership (CEP) (http://www.character.org/). The CEP's 11 Principles of Effective Character Education were outlined by Tom Lickona, Eric Schaps, and Catherine Lewis (see Appendix 11.1). Lickona and Schaps were participants

---

I know [Saddam Hussein's] character. The defense of Baghdad would not have collapsed so quickly if he was not dead.

　　　　　　　　　　　—Sami Sadoun, Iraqi ambassador to Serbia-Montenegro

in the Aspen Conference that provided the conception of character adopted by Congress and written into the OERI RFP; at the time of our study, Schaps was President-elect of CEP. Given the key role of Lickona and Schaps in articulating the conception of character adopted by the federal government, it is not surprising to see their ideas incorporated into the curricula written in response to the government's call for proposals. The documents assert, for instance, a belief in core ethical values which, as the annotated version of the 11 principles states, a school "promulgates ... to all members of the school community ... and upholds ... by making all school members accountable to standards of conduct consistent with the core values.... The school makes clear that these basic human values transcend religious and cultural differences and express our common humanity."

The 11 principles also assert an inherent relation between good character and academic success: "Character education and academic learning must not be conceived as separate spheres; rather there must be a strong, mutually supportive relationship." As we have noted previously, there is no empirical basis for this claim. Indeed, we can find no empirical evidence offered to support the 11 principles in general. Rather, we find a priori assertions about character and character education that we argue are a function of their authors' ideology rather than any universal truth.

A third principle outlined by the CEP that appears in the character education proposals is the belief that character education ought to be streamed throughout the curriculum, rather than being an add-on program. Furthermore, exemplary character should be modeled by adults and practiced by all within the community.

A fourth area that appears in the curricula is stated clearly in the annotation for the tenth principle: "A school's character education mission statement should state explicitly what is true: Parents are the first and most important moral educators of their children," a belief firmly located in the discourse of family first. The assumption is that schools should support families in their moral instruction and also enlist parents' support in the school-based character education effort. This assumption is often contradicted by other beliefs about the quality of students' homes.

In addition to these general claims, the 11 principles have a clearer and more specific influence on the curricula we studied. The eleventh principle, for instance, treats the issue of assessing both students' character and the effects of a character education intervention. The general approach to assessment and the illustrative items provided by Lickona and colleagues are reproduced verbatim in the assessment instruments in one of the states we profile here. Later we will return to the issue of the commodification of character education (i.e., the ways in which it is packaged and sold for profit). Here we will simply note the direct influence of the CEP on the curricula we studied.

> *The measure of a man's character is what he would do if he knew he never would be found out.*
>
> —*Thomas Babington Macaulay*

Center for the Fourth and Fifth R's

Lickona also influenced the character education curricula through their adoption of ideas from The Center for the Fourth and Fifth R's, which he directs at the State University of New York at Cortland (http://www.cortland.edu/c4n5rs/). The fourth and fifth Rs are respect and responsibility. The center's home page outlines its mission:

THE CENTER FOR THE 4TH AND 5TH RS serves as a regional, state, and national resource in character education. A growing national movement, character education is essential to the task of building a moral society and developing schools which are civil and caring communities.

THE CENTER disseminates articles on character education, sponsors an annual summer institute in character education, publishes a **Fourth and Fifth Rs** newsletter, and is building a network of **"Fourth and Fifth Rs Schools"** committed to teaching respect, responsibility and other core ethical values as the basis of good character.

CHARACTER EDUCATION holds that there are universally important ethical values such as **respect, responsibility, trustworthiness, fairness, caring, courage, self-control, and diligence.** Character means living by these core values—understanding them, caring about them, and acting upon them. *"It is character that will conquer materialism, demonstrate respect for life and property, and stem the tide of violence in our land. And it is character that will search for truth and demand diligent scholarship."*
David L. Davenport

This mission statement reprises several of the values written into the OERI RFP. The center asserts the presence of a set of universal values, consistent with the discourse of moral absolutism. The Davenport quote associates good character with academic achievement. And the center's work to "disseminate" articles on character education suggests aspects of the authoritarian society, which we outline later.

Elsewhere at their Web site, under the banner headline *SIGNS OF A NATIONAL CRISIS OF CHARACTER*, reads the following:

Because the character of our nation depends on the character of the young people now coming to maturity, ten current trends in youth character are cause for deep concern:

1. Rising youth violence

2. Increasing dishonesty (lying, cheating, and stealing)
3. Growing disrespect for parents, teachers, and other legitimate authority figures
4. Increasing peer cruelty
5. A rise in prejudice and hate crime
6. The deterioration of language
7. A decline in the work ethic
8. Declining personal and civic responsibility
9. Increasing self-destructive behaviors such as premature sexual activity, substance abuse, and suicide
10. Growing ethical illiteracy, including ignorance of moral knowledge as basic as the Golden Rule and the tendency to engage in destructive behavior without thinking it wrong

This rationale employs several discourses found in the proposals. Most prominently is the discourse of youth depravity, in support of which they offer statistics from the FBI on increasing rape crimes and a variety of surveys that report rises in cheating and drug use. This set of claims also enlists the discourses of the Protestant work ethic and authoritarian society.

Specifically adopted by the curricula we studied was a 12-point comprehensive approach to character education that includes nine classroom strategies and three whole-school strategies, adapted from Lickona's (1991) *Educating for Character* and promoted by the Center for the Fourth and Fifth Rs:

9 CLASSROOM STRATEGIES:

The teacher as caregiver, model, and ethical mentor: Treating students with love and respect, encouraging right behavior, and correcting wrongful actions.

A caring classroom community: Teaching students to respect and care about each other.

Moral discipline: Using rules and consequences to develop moral reasoning, self-control, and generalized respect for others.

A democratic classroom environment: Using the class meeting to engage students in shared decision-making and in taking responsibility for making the classroom the best it can be.

Teaching values through the curriculum: Using the ethically rich content of academic subjects as vehicles for values teaching.

Cooperative learning: Fostering students' ability to work with and appreciate others.

The "conscience of craft": Developing students' sense of academic responsibility and the habit of doing their work well.

Ethical reflection: Developing the cognitive side of character through reading, research, writing, and discussion.

Conflict resolution: Teaching students how to solve conflicts fairly, without intimidation or violence.

3 STRATEGIES FOR THE WHOLE SCHOOL:

Caring beyond the classroom: Using role models to inspire altruistic behavior and providing opportunities for school and community service.

Creating a positive moral culture in the school: Developing a caring school community that promotes the core values.

Parents and community as partners: Helping parents and the whole community join the schools in a cooperative effort to build good character.

These strategies include several discourses found in the curricula, including the discourse of moral absoluteness (encouraging right behavior, and correcting wrongful actions), of the authoritarian society (moral discipline), of the Protestant work ethic (the conscience of craft), and of academic achievement (ethical reflection).

Center for the Advancement of Ethics and Character

Another source drawn on in the proposals is The Center for the Advancement of Ethics and Character (CAEC) at Boston University (http://www.new horizons.org/ofc_bucace.html), founded by Kevin Ryan. Ryan was a participant at the Aspen Conference and at the time of our study was President of the Character Education Partnership.

The vision of the CAEC is well articulated in their Character Education Manifesto (see Appendix 11.2). This manifesto includes a number of discourses found in the proposals we studied. The discourse of moral absoluteness is found in their rejection of the relativism of values clarification and other reflective approaches. The discourses of the Protestant work ethic and virtuous individual appear in their dismissal of self-esteem and valorization of self-discipline. Claims of increasing rates of violence, adolescent suicide, and teen pregnancy fall squarely within the discourse of youth depravity. The claim of a relation between character education and academic excellence reveals the discourse of academic achievement. The discourse of family first is revealed in the affirmation of parents as the primary moral educators of their children. The moral authority granted to principals and teachers, and to adults in general, suggests the discourse of an authoritarian society.

Character is an essential tendency. It can be covered up, it can be messed with, it can be screwed around with, but it can't be ultimately changed. It's the structure of our bones, the blood that runs through our veins.

—Sam Shepard

> *[The qualities of a great people are] vision, integrity, courage, understanding, the power of articulation, and profundity of character.*
>
> —*Dwight David Eisenhower*

CURRICULUM

One southern state borrowed the Heartwood Ethics Curriculum for Children (http://151.201.61.19/index.html) for the substance of its character education program. The Heartwood Institute was founded in 1986 by Eleanore Childs, a criminal defense attorney and mother of seven; Patricia Wood, Childs' children's best teacher in Zelienople, a small town in Western Pennsylvania; Wood's daughter Susan; and two elementary teachers, Barbara Lanke and Patti Flach. They settled on stories as the most effective way to teach character. They collected developmentally appropriate stories for children that involved ethical themes, could be related to the broader curriculum, and could contribute to a kinder classroom climate. Careful choices were made in each aspect of the curriculum:

- seven universal concepts, color coded
- read-aloud stories to build character, to inspire, to motivate and especially to nurture hope for the future
- positive human story characters to provide clear role models for ethical behavior
- fine multicultural literature to build understanding and respect for the diverse cultures sharing these ethical concepts.

The seven universal attributes they stress are courage, loyalty, justice, respect, hope, honesty and love. "These attributes," they say, "indeed have universal appeal, nurturing body, mind and spirit. They represent the essence of human community and a foundation for right action." (See Appendix 11.3 for recommended Heartwood books.)

The Heartwood Institute was ultimately bought out by Scholastic, Inc. Under Scholastic the Heartwood effort is codirected by Childs and Dr. Martha Harty, formerly of the Center for Applied Ethics at Carnegie-Mellon University (see http://www.lcl.cmu.edu/). Scholastic's resources have enabled wider marketing and distribution of the curriculum beyond its original influence in western Pennsylvania. None of the Heartwood founders or directors was involved with the Aspen Conference, which was dominated by men and included no classroom teachers. On the sponsoring Josephson Institute of Ethics' Board of Governors, there are 11 men and 6 women, and at the Aspen Conference there were 18 men and 12 women. Some might interpret this gender balance as suggestive of the authoritarian society.

> *With all the power that a President has, the most important thing to bear in mind is this: You must not give power to a man unless, above everything else, he has character. Character is the most important qualification the President of the United States can have.*
>
> *—Richard M. Nixon*

The Heartwood Curriculum fits with didactic approaches to character education in several ways. First of all, it identifies a set of attributes with "universal appeal" that "represent the essence of a human community." This assumption is central to the discourse of moral absoluteness that is written into the OERI RFP and required in funded character curricula. More than other sources, Heartwood tries to soften the absolute nature of these attributes, listing moral codes at their Web site that includes Ma'at—the Right Way (an Egyptian goddess who personified the concepts of truth, cosmic order and justice), the Boy Scouts, Character Counts!, the Eight Confucian Virtues, 4H Clubs, the 7 Principles of Kwanzaa, Tae Kwon Do, the YMCA, and the YWCA. Although they specify that they do not necessarily endorse these codes, they do present them.

Heartwood also fits the discourse of moral absoluteness with its emphasis on clear role models for ethical behavior. As we note in our discussion of this discourse, this discourse eschews human ambiguity in favor of pristine moral exemplars. We discuss the consequences of this approach later.

STAFF DEVELOPMENT SERVICES AND PROGRAMS

B-ROW (Basic Right Over Wrong), Inc.

B-ROW, Inc. (http://www.b-row.com/pages/index.html) claims to offer "the only complete comprehensive plan of its kind, designed for all people, especially our children. It is the solution to America's Character Education/Development needs." It provides a character development self-help plan designed to "restore, instill and maintain the Original Principles Basic 'Right" over Wrong. With 'B-ROW' Common Courtesy Tools, Common Sense Values and positive people working together, we will provide to both children and adults the tools needed for acceptable conduct and appropriate behavior." At the B-ROW, Inc., Web site, the expertise of their management is described as follows: "The vast experiences and commitment of our management team, which consists of a diverse group of men and women, greatly lends itself to the success of the mission of B-ROW, Inc." We wrote them for more specific information about the makeup of this management team and received the following response:

The experiences of which we speak are the business experiences of the team that will provide simple, top quality products and services to help facilitate the character development process. The B-ROW team consists of experienced educators headed by Ms. Anita Robinson, a retired educator with over 30 years in various capacities within secondary education. Educators, parents, and students are a part of the annual Think Tank from which our lesson books and support materials are drawn.

Their experiences in character education are the ordinary life experiences that come from rearing children, caring for aging parents, teaching, working, employer-employee relationships, community involvement and volunteering in multiple charitable organizations. These life experiences inevitably affect the development of character.

B-ROW, Inc. provides products and workshops for the prekindergarten through higher education curriculum, the family, and the workplace. These services are designed to promote honesty, respect for self and others, dependability, kindness, cooperation, courage, tolerance, love/loyalty, respect for the environment, perseverance, self-control, compassion, citizenship/patriotism, punctuality, courtesy/patience, and team work. As they say,

At minimal cost, implementation of the "B-ROW" Self-Help Plan in your school system will:

- first address student's [sic] everyday basic peer pressures
- acknowledge "It's Right or It's Wrong"
- develop well disciplined, respectful students
- increase test scores
- reduce teen pregnancy
- reduce crime, violence, hatred, and disrespect

When we describe the assessment of character education programs, we will include instrumentation provided by B-ROW, Inc. For now, we will review the discourses embedded in their self-description.

The company's title includes the discourse of moral absoluteness with its clear division of right and wrong. The idea that notions of right and wrong follow from using common sense suggests the belief that there is no cultural variation in what is right or wrong, that the notion of being punctual (one of their character traits) follows the same principles regardless of variations in cultural values. Elsewhere, Smagorinsky, Cook, and Reed (2005) have argued that common sense is a cultural construct, rather than a way of thinking that is eminently reasonable.

The discourse of academic achievement is present in the goal of increasing test scores. We see the discourse of the Protestant work ethic in the idea that punctuality is a matter of good character. The call to patriotism fits with the discourse of the authoritarian society. The discourse of youth depravity

---

Be On Time

Objectives: To introduce the concept of "Be On Time," to help students understand that this concept can help them achieve success, and to learn that being on time can have a positive affect [sic] on their lives in school and at home in their communities.

Example Vocabulary:
ON TIME
LATE
PUNCTUAL
TARDY
PROMPT
TIMELY

Lesson Examples:

- *Discuss what Being On Time means, and the importance of it*
- *Discuss places where you need to Be On Time, and what happens when you're not*
- *Discuss ways to teach yourself to always Be On Time*

   http://www.legalpadjr.com/partner/teachers/no2.htm

---

is found in the claim that they can reduce teen pregnancy and student violence. In our discussion of the assessment of character education programs, we will give more specific examples of how the B-ROW curriculum manifests these discourses.

Character Development Group

The proposals drew on materials produced by the Character Development Group (CDG; http://www.charactereducation.com/), directed by Dr. Philip Fitch Vincent in Chapel Hill, North Carolina. Vincent is the director of the Center for Ethics, Public Policy and Leadership at Greensboro College, Greensboro, North Carolina (http://www.gborocollege.edu/academics/ethics.htm). The CDG Web page includes an endorsement from Kevin Ryan, who says that Vincent "knows children; he knows schools; he knows his theory, he also knows how to put them all together." The CDG describes itself as

> the country's leading provider of character education staff development resources, including Dr. Philip Fitch Vincent's *Character Education Series* of books, curricula, and workshops. We also publish materials from other

leading character education experts. The company distributes the best-selling *Developing Character in Students: A Primer for Teachers, Parents and Communities,* and 19 other publications used extensively in schools throughout the U.S.

Their view of character is stated as follows:

Dr. Vincent's approach to character education fosters school civility by structuring the student experience around certain key concepts. These concepts provide a "moral compass" for students, guiding them in their choice of behavior and attitudes. As Dr. Vincent says, "Character education helps young people to know, love and do the good."

Five concepts guide and structure a meaningful character education program:

RULES AND PROCEDURES—As Harry Wong reminds us, the problems in our schools are not the result of a lack of rules but of a lack of procedures.

COOPERATIVE LEARNING—It is not just a nicety: it is essential for both social and intellectual development. Well-designed cooperative learning activities give students the chance to develop vital skills for succeeding in real life.

TEACHING FOR THINKING—What are the thinking skills needed to master the curriculum and prepare for life? What guidelines can help students analyze ideas and determine the right thing to do?

QUALITY LITERATURE—Doesn't it make sense that if we want our students to develop character, we should include readings which reinforce moral lessons?

SERVICE LEARNING—Students must engage in service learning both inside and outside the school environment.

Character education works: School systems across the country have implemented effective character education elements and have seen the results: a more civil school, fewer absentees, and higher grade averages.

We could find little specific information about Vincent's conception of character and character education at this Web site. He does claim, however, that his program will raise students' grades, invoking the discourse of academic achievement.

It is our character that supports the promise of our future—far more than particular government programs or policies.

—William J. Bennett

PREVENTING VIOLENCE AND SUBSTANCE ABUSE

Second Step: A Violence Prevention Program for Children

Second Step (http://hadm.sph.sc.edu/Students/KBelew/comstep.htm), developed by the national Committee for Children and approved for use by the National Safe and Drug-Free Schools program, is designed to encourage children to get along well with others. Second step emphasizes:

- Empathy—Each child learns to identify and understand others' feelings in order to be a more caring person.
- Impulse Control—means using problem solving skills. Children learn to slow down and think through options when faced with problems.
- Anger Management—In most families anger and conflict are a normal part of family life. The anger management steps help children recognize, understand, and control anger in a healthy way.

This program does not fall so easily within the broad set of discourses found in the character education curricula of the southern states. Its attention to empathy, for instance, is unusual, suggesting a discourse of relationships. In our effort to seek disconfirming data in the proposals, the inclusion of this program appears to move away from the notion of moral exemplars and recognize that anger is a normal human emotion that can be reflected on in productive ways, rather than be quieted by attention to a pacifying exemplar.

SUMMARY

For the most part, these ancillary curricula fit well with the discourses that permeate the proposals from the Southern states. Given their close identification with key members of the Aspen Conference, their compatibility should not be a surprise.

The purchase of collateral services, particularly from a recurring group of character education gurus who influenced the original OERI conception of character, reveals the way in which character education has been commodified. Although the curricula often talk about the importance of local control, many services are purchased from national vendors of character education paraphernalia. Character education conceptions, products, and

> *Character is the result of two things: mental attitude and the way we spend our time.*
> —*Elbert Hubbard*

> *We talk about talent all along, but the thing that set this [Miami University football] team apart is character. They refused to give in, refused to flinch, and they got the job done week in and week out.*
>
> —*Larry Coker*

services are held in somewhat of a monopoly by a small group of character education entrepreneurs, limiting the notions available about character and character education and further reinforcing the discourses employed in the advancement of their perspective. We next look more specifically at how these notions were written into the proposals of the southern states as they engaged in dialogue with the OERI RFP.

APPENDIX 11.1: ELEVEN PRINCIPLES OF EFFECTIVE CHARACTER EDUCATION BY TOM LICKONA, ERIC SCHAPS, AND CATHERINE LEWIS

There is no single script for effective character education, but there are some important basic principles. The following eleven principles serve as criteria that schools and other groups can use to plan a character education effort and to evaluate available character education programs, books, and curriculum resources.

   1. Character education promotes core ethical values as the basis of good character. Character education holds, as a starting philosophical principle, that there are widely shared, pivotally important core ethical values—such as caring, honesty, fairness, responsibility and respect for self and others—that form the basis of good character. A school committed to character education explicitly names and publicly stands for these values; promulgates them to all members of the school community; defines them in terms of behaviors that can be observed in the life of the school; models these values; studies and discusses them; uses them as the basis of human relations in the school; celebrates their manifestations in the school and community; and upholds them by making all school members accountable to standards of conduct consistent with the core values.

   In a school committed to developing character, these core values are treated as a matter of obligation, as having a claim on the conscience of the individual and community. Character education asserts that the validity of these values, and our obligation to uphold them, derive from the fact that such values affirm our human dignity; they promote the development and welfare of the individual person; they serve the common good; they meet the classical tests of reversibility (Would you want to be treated this way?) and universality (Would you want all persons to act this way in a similar situation?); and they define our rights and responsibilities in a democratic society. The school makes clear that these basic human values transcend religious and cultural differences and express our common humanity.

   2. "Character" must be comprehensively defined to include thinking, feeling, and behavior. In an effective character education program, character is broadly conceived to encompass the cognitive, emotional, and behavioral aspects of the moral life. *Good character consists of understanding, caring about, and acting upon core ethical values.* The task of character education therefore is to help students and all other members of the teaming community know "the good," value it, and act upon it. As people grow in their character, they will develop an increasingly refined understanding of the core values, a deeper commitment to living according to those values, and a stronger tendency to behave in accordance with those values.

3. Effective character education requires an intentional, proactive, and comprehensive approach that promotes the core values in all phases of school life. Schools committed to character education look at themselves through a moral lens and see how virtually everything that goes on in school affects the values and character of students. An *intentional* and proactive approach plans deliberate ways to develop character, rather than simply waiting for opportunities to *occur. A comprehensive* approach uses all aspects of schooling—the teacher's example, the discipline policy, the academic curriculum (including the drug, alcohol, and sex education curriculum). The instructional process, the assessment of learning, the management of the school environment, relationships with parents, and so on—as opportunities for character development. "Stand alone" character education programs can be useful first steps or helpful elements of an ongoing effort but must not be considered a substitute for a holistic approach that integrates character development into every aspect of school life.

4. The school must be a caring community. The school itself must embody good character. It must progress toward becoming a microcosm of the civil, caring, and just society we seek to create as a nation. The school can do this by becoming a moral community that helps students form caring attachments to adults and to each other. These caring relationships will foster both the desire to learn and the desire to be a good person. All children and adolescents have a need to belong. And they are more likely to internalize the values and expectations of groups that meet this need. The daily life of classrooms, as well as all other parts of the school environment (e.g., the corridors, cafeteria, playground, and school bus), must be imbued with core values such as concern and respect for others, responsibility, kindness, and fairness.

5. To develop character, students need opportunities for moral action. In the ethical as in the intellectual domain, students are constructive learners; they learn best by doing. To develop good character, they need many and varied opportunities to apply values such as responsibility and fairness in everyday interactions and discussions. By grappling with real-life challenges—how to divide the labor in a cooperative teaming group, how to reach consensus in a class meeting, how to carry out a service learning project, how to reduce fights on the playground—students develop practical understanding of the requirements of fairness, cooperation, and respect. Through repeated moral experiences, students can also develop and practice the moral skills and behavioral habits that make up the action side of character.

6. Effective character education includes a meaningful and challenging academic curriculum that respects all learners and helps

them succeed. Character education and academic learning must not be conceived as separate spheres; rather them must be a strong, mutually supportive relationship. In a caring classroom and school where students feel liked and respected by their teachers and fellow students, students are more likely to work hard and achieve. Reciprocally, when students are enabled to succeed at the work of school, they are more likely to feel valued and cared about as persons. Because students come to school with diverse skills, interests and needs, a curriculum that helps all students succeed will be one whose content and pedagogy are sophisticated enough to engage all learners. That means moving beyond a skill-and-drill, paper-and-pencil curriculum to one that is inherently interesting and meaningful for students. A character education school makes effective use of active teaching and learning methods such as cooperative learning, problem solving approaches, experience-based projects, and the like. One of the most authentic ways to respect children is to respect the way they learn.

7. **Character education should strive to develop students' intrinsic motivation.** As students develop good character, they develop a stronger inner commitment to doing what their moral judgment tells them is right. Schools, especially in their approach to discipline, should strive to develop this intrinsic commitment to core values. They should minimize reliance on extrinsic rewards and punishments that distract students' attention from the real reasons to behave responsibly: the rights and needs of self and others. Responses to rule-breaking should give students opportunities for restitution and foster the students' understanding of the rules and willingness to abide by them in the future. Similarly, within the academic curriculum, intrinsic motivation should be fostered in every way possible. This can be done by helping students experience the challenge and interest of subject matter, the desire to work collaboratively with other students, and the fulfillment of making a positive difference in another person's life or in their school or community.

8. **The school staff must become a learning and moral community in which all share responsibility for character education and attempt to adhere to the same core values that guide the education of students.** Three things need attention here. First, all school staff—teachers, administrators, counselors, coaches, secretaries, cafeteria workers, playground sides, bus drivers—must be involved in learning about, discussing, and taking ownership of the character education effort. All of these adults must model the core values in their own behavior and take advantage of the other opportunities they have to influence the character of the students with whom they come into contact. Second, the same values and norms that govern the life of students must govern the collective life of the adult members of the school community. If students are to

be treated as constructive learners, so must adults. They must have extended staff development and many opportunities to observe and then try out ways of integrating character education practices into their work with students. If students are given opportunities to work collaboratively and participate in decision-making that improves classrooms and school, so must adults. If a school's staff members do not experience mutual respect, fairness, and cooperation in their adult relationships, they are less likely to be committed to teaching those values to students. Third, the school must find and protect time for staff reflection on moral matters. School staff, through faculty meetings and smaller support groups, should be regularly asking: What positive, character-building experiences is the school already providing for its students? What negative moral experiences (e.g., peer cruelty, student cheating, adult disrespect of students, littering of the grounds) is the school currently failing to address? And what important moral experiences (e.g., cooperative learning, school and community service, opportunities to learn about and interact with people from different racial, ethnic, and socioeconomic backgrounds) is the school now omitting? What school practices are at odds with its professed core values and desire to develop a caring school community? *Reflection of this nature is an indispensable condition for developing the moral life of a school.*

9. Character education requires moral leadership from both staff and students. For character education to meet the criteria outlined thus far, there must be leaders (a principal, another administrator, a lead teacher) who champion the effort and, at least initially, a character education committee (or several such support groups, each focused on a particular aspect of the character effort) with responsibility for long-range planning and program implementation. Over time, the functions of this committee may be taken on by the school's regular governing bodies. Students should also be brought into roles of moral leadership through student government, peer conflict mediation programs, cross-age tutoring, and the like.

10. The school must recruit parents and community members as full partners in the character-building effort. A school's character education mission statement should state explicitly what is true: Parents are the first and most important moral educators of their children. Next, the school should take pains at every stage to communicate with parents about the school's goals and activities regarding character development—and how families can help. To build trust between home and school, parents should be represented on the character leadership committee that does the planning, the school should actively reach out to "disconnected" subgroups of parents. And all parents need to be informed about—and have a chance to react and consent to—the school's proposed core values and how the school proposes to try to teach them. Finally, schools and families will enhance the effectiveness of their partnership if they recruit the help of the wider community—businesses, religious institutions, youth organizations, the government, and the media—in promoting the core ethical values.

11. Evaluation of character education should assess the character of the school, the school staff's functioning as character educators, and the extent to which students manifest good behavior. Effective character education must include an effort to assess progress. Three broad kinds of outcomes merit attention:

The character of the school: To what extent is the school becoming a more caring community? This can be assessed, for example, with surveys that ask students to indicate the extent to which they agree with statements such as, "Students in this school [classroom] respect and care about each other," and "This school [classroom] is like a family."

Student character: To what extent do students manifest understanding of, commitment to, and action upon the core ethical values? Schools can, for example, gather data on various character-related behaviors: Has student attendance gone up? Fights and suspensions gone down? Vandalism declined? Drug incidents diminished? Schools can also assess the three domains of character (knowing, feeling, and behaving) through anonymous questionnaires that measure student moral judgment (for example, "Is cheating on a test wrong?"), moral commitment ("Would you cheat if you were sure you wouldn't get caught?") and self-reported moral behavior ("How many times have you cheated on a test or major assignment in the past year?"). Such questionnaires can be administered at the beginning of a school's character initiative to get a baseline and again at later points to assess progress.

Source. Eleven Principles of Effective Character Education by Tom Lickona, Eric Schaps, and Catherine Lewis (2003) (http://www.character.org/principles/)

APPENDIX 11.2: CHARACTER EDUCATION MANIFESTO, CENTER FOR THE ADVANCEMENT OF ETHICS AND CHARACTER

Is there no virtue among us? If there be not, we are in a wretched situation. No theoretical checks, no form of government, can render us secure. To suppose that any form of government will secure liberty or happiness without any virtue in the people is a chimerical idea.

—James Madison

To educate a man in mind and not morals is to educate a menace to society.

—Theodore Roosevelt

In his January 23rd State of the Union address, President Clinton echoed the concerns of Madison and Roosevelt with an urgent call: "I challenge all our schools to teach character education, to teach good values and good citizenship." American schools have had from their inception a moral mandate. Moral authority, once vested firmly in both our schools and teachers, has receded dramatically over the past few decades. While many teachers are valiantly working to promote good character in their classrooms, many are receiving mixed and confusing messages. Attempts made to restore values and ethics to the school curriculum through values clarification, situational ethics, and discussion of moral dilemmas have proven both weak and ephemeral, failing to strengthen the character and behavior of our young people. Still our schools too often champion rights at the expense of responsibility, and self-esteem at the expense of self-discipline.

Distressed by the increasing rates of violence, adolescent suicide, teen pregnancy, and a host of other pathological and social ills assaulting American youth, we propose that schools and teachers reassert their responsibility as educators of character. Schools cannot however, assume this responsibility alone; families, neighborhoods, and faith communities must share in this task together. We maintain that authentic educational reform in this nation begins with our response to the call for character. True character education is the hinge upon which academic excellence, personal achievement, and true citizenship depend. It calls forth the very best from our students, faculty, staff, and parents.

We, the undersigned, believe the following guiding principles ought to be at the heart of this educational reform:

- Education in its fullest sense is inescapably a moral enterprise—a continuous and conscious effort to guide students to know and pursue what is good and what is worthwhile.
- We strongly affirm parents as the primary moral educators of their children and believe schools should build a partnership with the

home. Consequently, all schools have the obligation to foster in their students *personal and civic virtues* such as integrity, courage, responsibility, diligence, service, and respect for the dignity of all persons.

- Character education is about developing *virtues*—good habits and dispositions which lead students to responsible and mature adulthood. Virtue ought to be our foremost concern in educating for character. Character education is *not* about acquiring the right *views*—currently accepted attitudes about ecology, prayer in school, gender, school uniforms, politics, or ideologically charged issues.

- The teacher and the school principal are central to this enterprise and must be educated, selected, and encouraged with this mission in mind. In truth, all of the adults in the school must embody and reflect the moral authority which has been invested in them by the parents and the community.

- Character education is not a single course, a quick-fix program, or a slogan posted on the wall; it is an integral part of school life. The school must become a community of virtue in which responsibility, hard work, honesty, and kindness are modeled, taught, expected, celebrated, and continually practiced. From the classroom to the playground, from the cafeteria to the faculty room, the formation of good character must be the central concern.

- The human community has a reservoir of moral wisdom, much of which exists in our great stories, works of art, literature, history, and biography. Teachers and students must together draw from this reservoir both within and beyond the academic curriculum.

- Finally, young people need to realize that forging their own characters is an essential and demanding life task. And the sum of their school experiences—in successes and failures, both academic and athletic, both intellectual and social—provides much of the raw material for this personal undertaking.

Character education is not merely an educational trend or the school's latest fad; it is a fundamental dimension of good teaching, an abiding respect for the intellect and spirit of the individual. We need to re-engage the hearts, minds, and hands of our children in forming their own characters, helping them "to know the good, love the good, and do the good." That done, we will truly be a nation of character, securing "liberty and justice for all."

Source.   Character Education Manifesto, Center for Advancement of Ethics and Character (http://www.newhorizons.org/restr_charman.html)

APPENDIX 11.3: HEARTWOOD BOOKS

At the core of the Heartwood Ethics Curriculum is the belief that reading aloud is a nurturing act—one that helps teachers establish a warm caring classroom environment in which to explore issues of character and ethics. The titles selected for inclusion in the program include classics, folk literature, legends, and contemporary tales in which students can discover similarities in values among children from many cultures.

In Addition to the Ethics Curriculum Book List, there is also the *Heartwood BridgeBuilders Library*, which consists of additional ethical literature for children.

Level A	Level B
Brave Martha	Thunder Cake
Salt Hands	Ira Sleeps Over
Lucy's Picture	Dogger
Jessica	A Chair for My Mother
Doorbell Rang	Amazing Grace
On Mother's Lap	Mike Mulligan and his Steam Shovel
Miss Tizzy	Masai and I
Two Eyes, a Nose, and a Mouth	Silent Lotus
At the Crossroads	Owl Moon
The Carrot Seed	Too Many Tamales
The Empty Pot	Sam Bangs and Moonshine
Jamaica's Find	Mama, Do You Love Me?
Mom and Me	Wilfrid Gordon McDonald Partridge
The Leaving Morning	

Level C	Level D
Abiyoyo	The Boy Who Held Back the Sea
The Very Last First Time	Follow the Drinking Gourd
The Legend of Bluebonnet	The Two Brothers
The Seven Chinese Brothers	Teammates
Androcles and the Lion	Nettie's Trip South
Sam and the Lucky Money	The Tale of the Mandarin Duck
How My Parents Learned to Eat	The Great Kapok Tree
Miss Rumphius	Chicken Sunday
Angel Child, Dragon Child	Fly Away Home
We Be Warm 'Til Springtime Comes	Grandfather's Journey
The Empty Pot	A Day's Work
Maggie and the Pirate	Our King Has Horns!
The Rag Coat	Mufaro's Beautiful Daughters
Honey, I Love	Magical Hands

Level E

The Flame of Peace
The People Who Hugged The Trees
Cornrows
The Nightingale
Prince Boghole
The Warrior and the Wiseman
Crow Boy
The Wall
How Many Days to America
Knots on a Counting Rope
The Gold Coin
Fire on The Mountain
Annie and the Old One
The Gingerbread Doll

Heartwood Book Selection Criteria

The following criteria are used in selecting books for our ethics curriculums. An annotated *list of Heartwood books* by kit is available in our online libraries.

ETHICAL CONTENT: The story must model one of the seven attributes. The concept must be clear and positive.

TEACHABILITY: The story must be developmentally appropriate for the children and can be related to the broader curriculum.

EMOTIONAL APPEAL: The story must touch the heart.

ROLE MODELS: The story's characters must be "real" to the listener (no animal stories).

STUDENT UNDERSTANDING: The story must engage children and help them understand how the attribute relates to their own lives.

ILLUSTRATIONS: The story's illustrations must assist visual learning through strong visual impact.

READ ALOUD: Stories must be short enough to read in one sitting.

MULTICULTURAL IN SETTING: The stories as a set must represent a variety of cultures; the attributes represented must be universal.

SENSITIVE ISSUES: The story must be sensitive regarding stereotypes of gender, age, race, etc., and other potentially offensive material.

Source. Heartwood Books (http://www.heartwoodethics.org/resources/libraries/hw_ books.asp)

The Discourses of the Deep South's Conception of Character Education

Both proposals from the Deep South included all of the criteria called for in the RFP: They included the six required aspects of character, they established partnerships with Local Educational Agencies (LEAs), they provided a clearinghouse for distributing materials and information about CE, and they included an evaluation designed to determine the success toward reducing discipline problems, improving student grades, increasing participation in extracurricular activities, and raising parent and community involvement.

One of the southern states, in addition to the required six aspects of character, identified 30 additional concepts or qualities that must be included in state character curricula. These 36 traits were required by legislation passed in the state congress of any character education initiative. The proposal classified the traits under the three broad headings of Citizenship, Respect for Others, and Respect for Self "for promulgation throughout the public schools." The other proposal included the following highlighted statement: "*Character education is the long-term process of helping young people develop character, i.e., knowing, caring about and acting upon core ethical character traits such as: Fairness, Honesty, Respect for Others, Trustworthiness, Courtesy, Cooperation, Compassion, Citizenship, Responsibility*." Both states, then, explicitly positioned themselves in dialogue with the OERI RFP and, in turn, were dialogically related to the discourses that produced the Aspen Declaration and the discourses engaged in by the character education consultants who helped to generate it.

We next turn to the proposals themselves, identifying the discourses woven into the conceptions of character education and illustrating them

> *Respect for character is always diminished in proportion to the number among whom the blame or praise is to be divided.*
>
> —*James Madison*

with examples from the documents. We first review discourses shared by proposals from both the Deep South and Upper Midwest, analyzing how they are incorporated in the southern states' proposals to OERI. We then turn to the discourses exclusive to the states from the Deep South as they appear in the proposals.

DISCOURSES FOUND IN THE DEEP SOUTH AND UPPER MIDWEST

Academic Achievement

In compliance with the RFP's mandate to improve academic success, the proposals claimed that their character curricula would maintain or improve student academic achievement. One document argued that an effective character intervention "can provide important support for the academic mission of schools by reducing problems of school violence, improving discipline and raising student achievement." The other maintained that their curriculum would

> provide important support for the academic mission of schools by reducing problems of school violence, improving discipline and raising student achievement. National surveys of schools with effective character education programs show substantial improvements in student–teacher relationships, student discipline classroom and playground behavior, student attendance and even student test scores;

Details of these national surveys were not provided. The programs' goals are well summarized in one document's bold-faced, centered, prominently located declaration:

> **"Effective character education is a doable job which improves students' behavior, makes schools more civil communities, and leads to improved academic performance."**

What these claims overlook is that, even if grades and test scores were to rise concurrent with the implementation of a character curriculum, it would not be possible to establish a causal correlation between the two. We recall Ackerman's (1993) argument that any particular pedagogical intervention cannot bring about widespread change; rather, it is instituted as one part of a multidimensional restructuring of instructional values. It cannot be isolated as a variable that effects change because it is so heavily implicated in a host of other changes taking place simultaneously, particularly overarching attitudinal and conceptual changes. The effective institution of a character curriculum, then, would become part of a wholesale effort to attend to a broad range of student behaviors in school, including their academic performance.

The proposals also do not mention the Hawthorne effect, which posits that improvement is possible because of the introduction of something new, regardless of what that might be. Initial improvement in a process of production is thus caused by the interest in and active observation of that process. The effect was first noticed in the Hawthorne plant of Western Electric, in which management introduced new working conditions in order to improve productivity. Researchers found that the increase that they observed was due not to the changes themselves but instead to management's dedicated interest in seeing the plan work. Because the character curricula are introduced without comparison groups and tightly controlled variables, it's difficult to claim that the character curriculum itself, on its own merits, is responsible for change. Without such comparative data, we do not see how it is possible to make comparative claims.

As we will discuss later, the curricula produce little discernable change in the desired outcomes anyhow. Not only would improvements in academics and behavior be difficult to attribute solely to the character curriculum, the improvements do not show up in the programs' assessments, a problem that does not deter the program administrators from claiming success.

Moral Absoluteness

In the abstract of its program, one document we studied refers to its "alignment with the universal values that have been identified in both the federal statute and the [state] character education legislation." This rhetoric of moral absoluteness was streamed throughout the proposals. As noted, the curricula adopted the RFP's six chosen character traits, as would be expected. Other claims solidified the proposal authors' belief in the constancy of these traits. This view of the rightness of certain values illustrates well the discourse of moral absoluteness. It is on display in a "Quote of the Day" offered as part of an exemplary Language Arts and Literature Curriculum: "No one has a right to do as he pleases, except when he pleases to do right."

> *I can tell you without hesitation being president of this country is entirely about character.*
> *—President Andrew Shepherd in the film "The American President"*

Another illustration of the discourse of moral absoluteness comes in the documents' insistence on a clear distinction between Right and Wrong. One state describes the issue by quoting its state superintendent of education as saying, "We need a clear, consistent and emphatic focus in society on knowing right from wrong, and choosing right. Schools have always had an important role to play in reinforcing that emphasis, and we have never needed their contribution more." As noted, the state's CE director authored a book called *Teaching Jack and Jill Right vs. Wrong in the Homes and Schools*. The Right versus Wrong dichotomy is played out in one state's "Character Education in the Curriculum" document, which asserts that in the reading of literature, students ought to read about exemplary moral characters, rather than complex ones or negative examples. The Center for the Fourth and Fifth Rs's belief that "encouraging right behavior, and correcting wrongful actions" exemplifies the clear distinction that many character educators make between good and bad choices, with no suggestion that the judgment of right and wrong might be complex or relative.

We see several implications of this recommendation. One is that there is a single kind of morality that can be exemplified. Another is that one is either moral or not; moral dilemmas can then easily be resolved by adhering to the presumably universal traits of responsibility, respect, and so on. We also see an implication that books such as *The Catcher in the Rye*, with the morally complex protagonist Holden Caulfield, would be excluded from the curriculum and possibly banned from the library, as has happened often in the past. The curriculum from this state includes recommendations for character education lesson plans. In one, students are instructed to revise stories so that they conclude with more peaceful, respectful, responsible, satisfactory endings (see Appendix 12.1 for the whole range of curriculum ideas). We thus see the discourse of moral absoluteness reducing the complexity that many people believe to be inherent to the human condition to a set of clear, unambiguous choices.

The Protestant Work Ethic

The documents we studied outlined expectations for students in terms of the virtue of work. One document spells out the following required aspects of character to be included in the state-mandated character curriculum:

- Work Ethic: belief that work is good and that everyone who can, should work;

What is character but the determination of incident? What is incident but the illustration of character?

—Henry James

- Punctuality: being on time for attendance and tasks;
- Accomplishment: appreciation for completing a task;
- Cooperation: working with others for mutual benefit;
- Dependability: reliability; trustworthiness;
- Diligence: attentiveness, persistence, perseverance;
- Pride: dignity, self-respect, doing one's best;
- Productivity: supporting one's self, contributing to society;
- Creativity: exhibiting an entrepreneurial spirit, inventiveness, originality, not bound by the norm; and
- School pride: playing a contributing role in maintaining and improving all aspects of a school's environment, programs and activities within the context of contributing to the betterment of the city, county and state.

At the risk of belaboring the obvious, we would point out the clear relation established between virtue and capitalism through the emphasis on productivity, punctuality, task completion, the entrepreneurial spirit, and other traits relating to free market values. This notion of economy is linked to a value on nationalism, with productivity of the individual associated with school pride: Through hard work youngsters can produce the machinery that in turn contributes to better homes, communities, and nations.

Another illustration of the Protestant work ethic comes in one state's adoption of a staff development model, Steven Covey's (1990) "7 Habits of Highly Effective People" training program, licensed by the state and described as "a perfect fit" with The Eleven Principles of Effective Character Education developed by Tom Lickona, Eric Schaps, and Catherine Lewis (2003) for the Character Education Partnership (see Appendix 12.2 for the 7 Habits of Highly Effective People). According to the document,

> Dr. Covey has created a model that puts a premium upon ethical functioning. As Larry Wilson has stated when referencing the 7 Habits material, "Not only does the 'character ethic' win hands down every time over the 'personality ethic' in the battle of effectiveness, it also will bring greater fulfillment and joy to individuals seeking meaning in their personal and professional lives."

We infer from this document that the "personality ethic" refers to an ethic of self-fulfillment, what Sykes (1995) and others might consider self-indulgence, self-celebration, and self-centeredness at the expense of productive labor. Covey's work is designed to help people improve personal and professional management and form quality relationships with other people. We see the state's decision to approach character education from the standpoint of providing better business management principles as being well-aligned with the discourse of the Protestant work ethic.

> *Faced with crisis, the man of character falls back upon himself.*
>
> —*Charles de Gaulle*

Family First

Many OERI proposals we analyzed share a belief in the home as the principal arena for the teaching of morality. One curriculum from the Deep South recognizes "the primary role of the home in character development"; the other reports extensively on a model curriculum in an elementary school in which "Central to character education ... is the belief that the family is the primary influence on young children. Parents, therefore, are the most powerful role models." Furthermore, parents should teach "righteous ideas and ideals." The document says later that "Parents are a child's first and most important moral teachers. The school must do everything it can to support parents in this role." Parents are involved "in setting expectations in terms of behavior" for children to follow.

Yet the documents also reveal a belief that homes are not always good environments for teaching morality. The same document that identifies parents as a child's primary moral teachers says that the schools must "battle the negative effects of the unsupportive environments that some children call home," which turn out to be the homes of poor and minority children. One irony of this discourse is that if homes were doing a good job of teaching character, there would be no need for a character curriculum in school. We see this as a fundamental tension in the documents: one discourse stressing family first yet a rationale for character education based on youth depravity and class-based morality.

One issue that the curricula overlook is the fact that families may depart from the nuclear family that the proposals idealize. One proposal states that it aims to "Help high schoolers—someday to be parents—learn the responsibilities and commitments of marriage and parenting and how to care for young children." This heteronormative claim precludes the idea that gay and lesbian students can have character—it refers only to heterosexual students headed toward marriage and parenthood. We see here an implied developmental trajectory toward an ideal outcome, what the Greeks called *telos,* in which heterosexual marriage and parenthood are essential experiences. As Cole (1996) notes, societies structure life in implicit and explicit ways to encourage those outcomes. Cole uses the term *prolepsis* to describe the subtle ways in which people are guided toward society's desired ends. Not all people, however, are heterosexual or aspire to marriage or parenthood. The curricula are mute on the existence of such people and on the ways in which they might experience an environment in

> *Politics ruins the character.*
> —*Otto von Bismarck*

which their own lives and identities are not merely omitted but characterized as unnatural.

Another area that the discourse of family first neglects is the effects of their values on those populations likely to have children out of wedlock: those who are poor, members of cultural minorities, and less likely to resort to birth control or abortion. Given the hortatory nature of a didactic approach to character education, we infer that admonitions about good character are expected to socialize students into the adult community's singular and stable value system, even if they do not have the kinds of stable, monogamous parental models assumed by the family first discourse.

Class-Based Morality

In the rationale for a character curriculum, certain targeted types of families are identified as deficient. The current values of public discourse prohibit naming those populations (minority, poor), and so the documents suggest that, although the family is the basis of morality and virtue, the schools need to work *in loco parentis* for children from homes that provide no such foundation. These populations are named obliquely. One state, for instance, targeted for character education an area in a rural setting with a 70% minority population and 6 public housing projects. According to documents describing the character curriculum,

> Our children associate with people every day who do not live by the codes we live by here. The greatest challenge we face is to ensure that our children learn to transfer skills and habits of character into environments that don't support them.... [Following character education we] see a difference in the children's understanding of what character is. They come to school without any skills at all. They don't know manners, how to express their feelings appropriately. No one talks to them much. What we see now is their ability to handle things, to work cooperatively, to come up with a product without arguing. They share in the effort and reap the benefits. We see growth, especially in children with emotional behavioral problems. We have seen remarkable changes.

Other documents we studied shared this belief that those most in need of character education were from poor backgrounds, did not speak standard English, were from a cultural or racial minority, and otherwise departed from the white middle-class values that govern U.S. schools. In the preceding paragraph *we* speak on behalf of a particular group of people,

> *A good character carries with it the highest power of causing a thing to be believed.*
>
> *—Aristotle*

those who represent the middle-class values of the schools. They are positioned hieratically relative to *they:* those who come to school with a different enculturation to appropriate social behavior, who are viewed in deficit to *our* values, and who are in need of education so they may adopt "the codes we live by here."

Logical Positivism

The character curricula we studied relied on the discourse of logical positivism to make claims about the replicability and sustainability of their programs and their programs' potential for serving as national models for other states to adopt. The notion of producing a replicable model is clearly stated throughout the documents. One state, after describing the breadth of its efforts to institute a character curriculum, says that

> As a result, the timing is perfect for the development of carefully validated character education models through the Partnerships in Character Education Pilot Projects.... We have a powerful national model of both interagency cooperation and public/private partnerships, with great potential for replication in all fifty states.

This discourse assumes that if it is demonstrated as effective in one setting, a curriculum could be exported wholesale as a "model" to be administered in another.

The notion of validation is also central to the character curricula we studied. One state sought to develop "Three state validated K–12 character education models.... Our intent is to demonstrate that effective character education will be related to the communities [sic] core values. There are basic principles of effective character education but no single script for quality implementation efforts." We see a tension in the proposals between the goal of developing replicable models and their emphasis on local control, described by one state "as one of DOE's priorities."

Another recurrent term in the program descriptions was that of *dissemination,* for example, "the [State] Innovation Program ... has become highly successful in developing, evaluating, and disseminating effective programs," and "All programs will also be validated, with information disseminated through the character education clearinghouse." Many have found this word to be "phallologocentric," that is, locating the procreation of ideas in men, whom some affiliate with a scientific worldview. It further suggests

> *From the beginning we in this nation have had the good fortune to find the right leader, often from an unexpected quarter, whose character, ability, and experience fit the tide of history.*
>
> *—James Cannon*

the kinds of generalization privileged in scientific research; that is, the belief that results can be distributed for adoption in new contexts regardless of mitigating local factors. This idea is congruent with the notion that research should be replicable, suggesting that what happens in one circumstance will be identical to what happens in another, a classic feature of Enlightenment rationality central to the discourse of logical positivism.

DISCOURSES PARTICULAR TO THE SOUTHERN STATES' PROPOSALS

Youth Depravity

The two southern states, like many others, used a rhetorical strategy of asserting the depravity of youth as a rationale for funding a character curriculum. One state began by saying that it

> ranks number one in teenage pregnancy, [the state's major city] leads the nation in violent crime statistics, [the state's major city's] young black males are more likely to die from violence than from all others causes of death combined, [the state's] students have consistently scored in the bottom quartile on standardized tests, dropout rates are high and prisons and youth detention centers are filling up faster than they can be built.

They continued, "Character development is a key intervention with the young people who come under the supervision" of the Department of Juvenile Justice. The increasingly degenerate character of youth must be addressed, say the proposals, and a character curriculum is the means for reversing the moral decline.

They assert that the effectiveness of a character curriculum can be determined by, among other measures, changes in the deviant behavior, evidenced by decreases in the number of discipline referrals, dropout rates, juvenile delinquency rates, and student pregnancy rates; and changes in prosocial behavior, evidenced by increases in participation in extracurricular activities, student volunteerism, and community perceptions of student behavior and activities.

We see here a belief that through character education students will learn to be responsible and respectful and turn away from the images and morality of popular culture. This belief is suggested in a statement from one character education program on the need to shelter young people from the pernicious effects of popular culture:

> As teachers, caregivers, businesspersons, community members and students, we must work to transform our schools and communities into a caring community of learners. We must guard our children's growth and maturity as protectively as a gardener watches over the ground that produces his garden. We must shelter students from the strong winds of neglect; we must weed that which chokes their brains with rubbish, and we must water and fertilize their minds with a sound education.

Through the character intervention, the trend toward youth depravity will be reversed as young people are exhorted to take on the virtues modeled by virtuous adults.

Authoritarian Society

One document we studied included the following curricular idea: to study "Effects of colors on behavior, i.e. Do some make us quiet?" We understood this lesson to mean that a good child of exemplary character is a quiet one. The same curriculum document asserted that in mathematics, students exhibit character by using "Self-discipline in using formulas and correct processes." This value was part of another discourse streamed throughout the documents, one that equated good character with obedience to established authority. For example, one of the state documents identified, in addition to the core traits specified by the RFP, a host of traits that included patriotism, punctuality, and school pride. In this discourse, it is presumed that a good person is one who does not cause trouble or upset the established order of things.

This discourse fits well with general authoritarian conceptions of schooling that have a top-down administrative structure that places students and their interests at the bottom. Student-centered approaches to teaching and learning are often reviled by critics who feel that schools ought to transmit and assess an established culture and its values and history, rather than have students engage in a process of discovery in the Deweyan tradition. Adopting a more business-oriented approach to schooling, with tests of accountability in meeting external standards, is often advocated in this approach (e.g., Finn, 2000). An authoritarian society, then, not only positions author-

---

A person's character is what it is. It's a little like a marriage—only without the option of divorce. You can work on it and try to make it better, but basically you have to take the bitter with the sweet.

—Hendrick Hertzberg

> *Character is what you are in the dark.*
> —*Rev. Dwight Moody*

ity at the top but employs measures to keep its agencies (e.g., schools) and actors (e.g., school personnel and students) in line with its priorities.

The Good Old Days

Character education curricula often employ the discourse of the good old days. The lay minister who directs one southern state's character education curriculum is quoted as saying,

> When people reminisce about "the good old days," their nostalgia usually reflects the bygone values of a saner, simpler time in history. Character education provides a cornerstone to enable upcoming generations to return to those values in a realistic way. Character education could be the saving of America's future—one child at a time.

Character education, the state superintendent of education says, is "not as much a new focus for schools and teachers as a return to one of our most traditional roles."

How good the old days were, however, is a matter of perspective. In one of the states profiled, there were 531 recorded lynchings and other mob slayings between 1882 and 1964—roughly 6.5 per year—among the 4,700 or so lynchings nationwide during that period, according to the Tuskegee University archives. One such slaying is perhaps typical, the July 25, 1946 murder of two African American couples (including one 7-month pregnant woman) who were shot hundreds of times, their bodies so mutilated that they were barely distinguishable from one another. Said a relative of one of the deceased, the murderers "did it 'cause they knew nothing was going to be done about it. Shooting a black person was like shooting a deer" (quoted in Suggs, 2001, p. 4). Similarly, in perhaps a typical county in one of the states profiled, in the 1940s white residents were provided 30 school buses to transport their children to school. Black residents had none and had to walk up to 9 miles to and from school each day. When they were refused a single bus for their children by the school board, they bought a dilapidated vehicle of their own, which soon broke down. They again asked for a school bus and were told by the school board chair, "We ain't got no money for nigger children." These events and thousands like them occurred during the "saner, simpler time in history" yearned for by the state character education director previously quoted.

> *How a man plays the game shows something of his character, how he loses shows all of it.*
>
> —*Anonymous*

The Virtuous Individual

The lay minister's belief that "Character education could be the saving of America's future—one child at a time," is indicative of the discourse of the virtuous individual. The nation is composed of a collection of individuals who either do or do not possess character, and the objective of character education is to instill the proper traits in those who do not. A principal included in the other southern state's pilot program wrote a letter of support for the proposal, saying that her school "continues with two ambitious goals related to student behavior: (1) Zero suspensions for all students, and (2) Reduction in the number of students referred to the office for disruptive behavior." This emphasis on modifying the behavior of individual students is consistent with the discourse of the virtuous (or in this case, virtuous-in-waiting) individual, with conformity to authoritarian expectations serving as proof of the effectiveness of the character curriculum.

Included in one state's second year performance report was a Character Education Initiative Logic Model. This model "begins with the problem identification within the school and includes an increase of disrespectful, dishonest, and disruptive behaviors among students." It makes the following claims about the results and impact of the program:

The results of intervening with a Character Education initiative include:

- Improved student attitudes
- Improved student behavior
- Enhanced student performance
- Increased parental satisfaction
- Enhanced teacher motivation
- Increased classroom productivity
- Enhanced school/community partnership

The impact of the Character Education intervention includes:

- Students develop positive character traits.
- Students reach their full academic potential.
- Students can successfully enter and compete in the workplace.
- Students can make meaningful contributions to their communities.

Elsewhere in the same report the authors say that

Trends and positive directions are beginning to confirm the success that those familiar with the merits of Character Education have long expected. The outside evaluators hired through the grant are hesitant to state that Character Education is making a difference; however, evaluations and measures within the four pilot districts do trend in that direction. In [the state] the momentum is building among teachers, educators and students. Schools and districts in [the state] are on the march toward building schools and districts of character across the state.

In the same report, then, the authors state that independent evaluators question the efficacy of the program and that the program is having great positive effects that merit additional funding. The focus of concern, regardless of the success of the effort, is the individual student's behavior.

SUMMARY

Our primary concern in this section has been to identify the assumptions made about the location of character, which include the idea that character is the province of individuals whose morality may be improved through exposure to the character curriculum. This discourse is complemented by the discourse of the Protestant work ethic (increased classroom productivity and ability to compete in the workplace) and academic achievement (students reach their full academic potential). By focusing on individual deficiencies in character, the character initiative will help the community to become a better place. In contrast, the states of the Upper Midwest assume that by creating a stronger, more moral community, schools will produce individual students who will gravitate to socially acceptable moral norms through their engagement with other morally sensitive people. Before moving to our analysis of the discourse of the character education proposals of the states from the Upper Midwest, we will conclude this section by looking at the curriculum and assessments used by the southern states to implement and evaluate their character education efforts.

There never was a strong character that was not made strong by discipline of the will; there never was a strong people that did not rank subordination and discipline among the signal virtues. Subjection to moods is the mark of a deteriorating morality. There is no baser servitude than that of the man whose caprices are his masters, and a nation composed of such men could not long preserve its liberties.

—Ralph Waldo Emerson

APPENDIX 12.1: CHARACTER EDUCATION IN THE CURRICULUM

CHARACTER EDUCATION IN THE CURRICULUM

Central questions for teachers:

What are the ethical issues in my subject matter? How can I help students identify desirable character traits in my subject? How can I model the kind of character traits essential to the "common good" of society?

LANGUAGE ARTS AND LITERATURE

- Story revisions with more peaceful, responsible, satisfactory endings.
- Character analysis for desirable and undesirable characteristics.
- Discussion and understanding of the meaning of "character"
- Teaching perspective as a function of class, education, religion, family, region, etc.
- Role-plays of outstanding character with desirable character traits
- Analysis of conflicts, moral dilemmas
- Analysis of "great moments" in literature to identify desirable character traits
- Composition of bumper stickers, poetry, songs, stories, essays, and journalism articles emphasizing good character or desirable traits
- Quote of the day— "No one has a right to do as he pleases, except when he pleases to do right."

SOCIAL STUDIES

- Discussion of examples of courage, responsibility, respect, honesty, etc. in famous people in history or in current events or discussion of the lack of these characteristics
- Study of immigration policy as examples of respect
- Effect of various events in history—Does the peace treaty end the war or do bad relationships continue?
- What is necessary for groups to exist in peace? Authority? Rules? Law? Common good? Goals? Common culture?
- International questions or issues, human rights, refugee issues
- Jury systems—ways of settling disputes, remuneration, reciprocity, reparations?
- Teaching perspective as a function of time, place, class, socioeconomic status
- Prejudice—its origins, effects, events

- Religious beliefs—good, evil, treatment of others, respect for self
- Analysis of examples of courage, honesty, perseverance, etc. in history

SCIENCE

- Characteristics of animals which mimic human behavior—aggression, territoriality, mating, fear
- Interdependent relationships in nature—systems
- Human nature—animal nature
- Issues among nations or groups which stern from contradictory view of environmental or scientific concerns
- Ethical issues in transplants, organ donations, artificial insemination, etc., artificial life support
- Respect for the environment—conservation
- Safety in public places
- Scientific fraud

MATHEMATICS

- Respect for accuracy in computation as well as in use of process or formulas
- Self-discipline in using formulas and correct processes
- Student construction of line graphs of their own scores for self-evaluation
- Study of outstanding mathematicians and their character traits

MUSIC

- Emphasis on one's role as a part of the group
- Cooperation as necessity for choirs, bands, orchestras, etc.
- Self-discipline in performers
- Persistence of composers
- Musicians who have overcome difficulties, handicaps, hardships
- Characteristics of "good music," reasons why it is revered
- Examples of evidence of character traits in lyrics or composition
- Compositions of songs or raps concerning character traits or the lack of them
- Studies of music which encourages certain kinds of behavior

ART

- Students can draw or paint examples of good character traits.
- Drawings which show different perspectives
- Study of art, which encourages certain kinds of behavior

- Effects of colors on behavior, i.e. Do some make us quiet?

PHYSICAL EDUCATION/HEALTH

- Respect for self and group as evidenced by good health practice
- The necessity of rules for games and athletic events and the obligation of players to know them
- Courage and persistence to improve one's performance and achieve personal best
- Respect for effort on the part of untalented players or handicapped players
- Compassion for players with little talent or handicaps
- Fair interpretation of rules—discussion of rules, umpires, referees, etc.
- Study of Jesse Owens at the 1936 Olympics
- Examples of suspected "foul play" in organized sports
- Discussion of effects of the behavior of some on society, i.e. Should everyone pay higher insurance rates because of smokers? Should automobile insurance be higher because some people do not wear seat belts? helmets?

MEDIA CENTER

- Book exhibits of people or fictional characters who have desirable traits
- Stories, videos, filmstrips, films of examples of outstanding character
- Posters related to peace, justice, courage, honesty, respect, etc.
- Biography emphasis—by topic, by character trait, by period of history, by genre

COUNSELING

- Reading of stories which emphasize success through responsible behavior, self-discipline, honesty, persistence, etc. Role-play of home or school situations which cause undesirable behaviors and of appropriate responses
- Emphasis on treating others as you would like to be treated
- Discussion of "If everyone acted just like me, would I like it?" or other similar questions
- Discussion of anger and appropriate responses
- Emphasis on resisting impulsive behavior—Count to 10 before …
- Children sharing stories of when they were proud of themselves for exhibiting desirable character traits

APPENDIX 12.2: STEVEN COVEY'S 7 HABITS OF HIGHLY EFFECTIVE PEOPLE

HABIT 1: Be Proactive
Proactivity
Circle of Influence

HABIT 2: Begin with the End in Mind
All Things Are Created Twice
Identifying Your Center
A Principle Center
A Personal Mission Statement
Visualization and Affirmation
Identifying Roles and Goals
Organizational Mission Statements

HABIT 3: Put First Things First
The Time Management Matrix
Quadrant II
What It Takes to Say "No"
Weekly Organizing
Delegation: Increasing P and PC
Paradigms of Interdependence
The Emotional Bank Account
Six Major Deposits
P Problems are PC Opportunities

HABIT 4: Think Win/Win
Six Paradigms of Human Interaction
Five Dimensions of Win/Win

HABIT 5: Seek First to Understand
Empathic Listening
Diagnose Before You Prescribe
Four Autobiographical Responses
Then Seek to Be Understood
One on One

HABIT 6: Synergize
Synergistic Communication
Synergy in the Classroom
Synergy in Business
Synergy in Communication
Fishing for the Third Alternative
Negative Synergy
Valuing the Differences
Force Field Analysis
All Nature is Synergistic

HABIT 7: Sharpen the Saw
Four Dimensions of Renewal
The Physical Dimension
The Spiritual Dimension
The Mental Dimension
The Social/Emotional Dimension
Scripting Others
Balance in Renewal
Synergy in Renewal
The Upward Spiral
Inside-Out Again
Intergenerational Living
Becoming a Transition Person

Source.   Steven Covey's 7 Habits of Highly Effective People (http://userpage.fu-berlin.de/
~tanguay/7habits.htm)

The Deep South's Character Curriculum and Assessment of Character Growth

We next review the curricula described in the proposals from the states in the Deep South to see how they embodied the values expressed through the discourses. We were surprised to find that actual character education curricula were barely outlined in the proposals and reports; rather, we found a set of generalizations about how such a curriculum should work. Finally, we look at the ways in which the states plan to assess the effectiveness of their character intervention.

THE CHARACTER CURRICULA

Curricular Integration of Character Education

One consistent belief expressed in the documents was that "Character education permeates every aspect of the school day." The programs were adamant that character education could only be effective when streamed throughout every aspect of a school's programs. A character curriculum should effect "a positive change in school culture and environment rather than [be] a curriculum add-on or isolated program. Research shows that character education is most effective when it is incorporated throughout a

> *Power is what you do and character is what you are.*
> —*Richard Reeves*

Allegedly raped girl 'is not of good character': Home Ministry

Home Ministry parliamentary secretary Abu Zahar Isnin caused a furore among DAP women MPs in the Dewan Rakyat today when he cast aspersions on the character of the 13-year-old girl who was allegedly raped while in police custody during the deportation of illegal immigrants from Sabah. In answering a supplementary question from Mohd Ali Hassan (Barisan Nasional-Tebrau) on the government's reaction if the Philippines refused to apologise, Abu Zahar said: "We (the Malaysian authorities) have investigated and found that the girl is not of a good character. When she was arrested and put in the detention camp, she could not produce any document."

—Yusof Ghani, October 16th, 2002

---

school's mission and activities." The claim for research support was not identified; among the problems we found with the curricula was that most claims of research-supported effectiveness were not substantiated by reference to specific studies.

Process of Character Education

What we found when looking to analyze the actual curricula was an elaboration of the program's administrative structure, rather than actual character education lessons. We were left to infer what character education might look like in practice. In one state, "Each project is required to develop fifteen lesson plans that incorporate character-building themes." The program sought to have up to 1,200 service-learning lesson plans developed and coded to character education objectives and made available through the state materials center and a web page. The ultimate goal was for character education plans to be developed by local educational agencies (LEAs), "disseminated," and adopted (purchased). What we saw, then, was a plan for schools to develop lessons and submit them to a clearinghouse which would then make them available to other educators.

The documents did give some illustrations of what character education would look like. The following is a description of an exemplary school's general procedure for streaming character education throughout the school day:

[An elementary school] took the initiative in creating a comprehensive integrated character education program. Central to the program are 34 character qualities (e.g., Responsibility, School Pride, and Honesty). These qualities are introduced and defined during the first ten minutes of homeroom. The quality then becomes a focus throughout the week in and out of class and school. Curricular examples of the concept and persons illustrating it (local, school and historic) are studied. Students will engage in related reading, and write and discuss stories. The school has a Character Education Clubroom and a newspaper so that parents may join in the celebration of character education.

Another exemplary elementary school used a literature-based approach adapted from the Heartwood Institute's Heartwood Curriculum. The Heartwood Curriculum is based on the thematic study of what they describe as seven universal ethical attributes: courage, loyalty, justice, respect, hope, honesty, and love. Within each theme students read a set of stories and proceed through a lesson for each. A typical Heartwood lesson proceeds as follows, according to the "sample teaching cards" available at the Heartwood website (see http://151.201.61.19/curriculums/card_fly_away.html).

For a story such as *Fly Away Home* by Eve Bunting, the card lists a set of central concepts (hope, love, courage, thrift), along with a story objective ("The student will be able to define and discuss hope, love, courage, and thrift as they apply to this story.") and a brief story summary. The teaching design calls for the teacher to preview a central attribute from the story and then read the story aloud. Following the reading of the story, there are five learning opportunities:

- *Discussion questions* that focus on the attributes and relate to children's lives (e.g., "Talk about the situation in which Andrew and his father find themselves. Does homelessness force you to be an outsider?")
- *Activities* that include writing, research, creative projects, presentations, and other pursuits that should be both fun and edifying (e.g., "Heartwood uses the color blue to represent hope. Take a sheet of blue paper. Write as many 'hope' connected words as you can. Use these blue hope sheets to create a bulletin board collage.")
- *Wrap-up* designed to encourage students to write, reflect, and share (e.g., "Write about a time when you felt trapped without hope. How did you feel? Do you think Andrew and his father may have felt the same way? How did you help yourself?")
- *Extension* in which students connect with home, community, and the larger world about the attribute (e.g., "Share this story with your family. Tell them how it made you feel.")
- *Interdisciplinary ideas* for exploring cultures and places, analyzing choices and actions, and so on (e.g., for social studies, "Research homelessness in America" and for math, "Make a list of items Andrew will need when he starts school. What will each item cost? (Estimate.) Total your item list.").
- *Vocabulary* (e.g., homelessness)

> *Appreciating the perspective of constituents in the understanding, and practice, of leadership is critical and underscores that leadership is a relationship. This relationship builds upon the character and actions of leaders in meeting and responding to the needs, expectations, and aspirations of their constituents. The most effective leaders cherish this relationship by realizing that the "work" will ultimately not be done by the leader but rests in the hands, minds, and hearts of their constituency.*
>
> *—James M. Kouzes and Barry Z. Posner*

We assume that instruction followed the Heartwood curriculum, which we got from the Heartwood website rather than the character education proposal itself. In general, however, the proposals themselves provided very little information about what character education would look like in practice.

ASSESSING THE EFFECTS OF CHARACTER EDUCATION

In addition to improved student behavior, one of the benefits of integrating character education with school curricula is that the academic achievement of students improves when effective programs are in place. A national study by the Child Development Center in California showed that student achievement improved more in schools with effective character education programs than in schools without such programs.

So states one of the character education curricula we studied. Further investigation revealed that the Child Development Center in California is part of the Josephson Institute of Ethics, sponsor of the Aspen Conference that launched the federal character education initiative and affiliated organization of many who have profited from the character education movement. This further inquiry, however, did not turn up any specifics about the study cited here: how the programs were implemented, how achievement was measured, or how a correlation between character education and student achievement was determined.

In our broader efforts to understand the basis for claims of character education's effectiveness, we typically found that evidence of improved character came from such evidence as statistics about student behavior (declines in discipline referrals, suspensions, etc.) or student's ability to answer questions about word definitions. For instance, Leming, Henricks-Smith, and Antis (1997) based their positive evaluation of the Heartwood Curriculum on students' ability to answer such items as "When I share my favorite things with others, that is: hope or love" and "When I am nice to children who look different from me, that is: respect or hope" (p. 12). In the southern states we are profiling, these means of measuring the effects of character education interventions are adopted or purchased, at times wholesale, from the Character Education Partnership, B-ROW, Inc., and other organizations, entrepreneurs, and vendors.

The curricula that we studied for this research did not find the same degree of effectiveness as the studies cited for character education's effectiveness in the proposals' rationales. One state acknowledges in its Second Year Performance Report that "The outside evaluators hired through the grant are hesitant to state that character education is making a difference; however, evaluations and measures within the four pilot districts do trend in that direction," although they provide no data to support these trends. They continue to say that effective character programs

> must impact academic success for students … discipline must improve and higher standards must be met…. Unfortunately, we do not have specific data which indicates without reservation that the implementation of character education makes a difference in the lives of students and the climate of schools. What we do know from talking to teachers, administrators, community members and students is that they believe that the implementation of character education is making a difference in the academic lives of students as well as in their behavior.

The report's substitution of positive impressions over their own chosen means of instrumentation does raise questions for us about the impact of the programs' success, that is, meeting their stated goals. We next review how character education was assessed in these two programs and what these assessments assume and reveal.

Teachers Registration Board, Tasmania
The Board will at all times be cognisant of the requirements of the Teachers Registration Act 2000, in particular Section 12(2) which describes how the Board is to determine whether an applicant is of good character, and Section 12(3) which says that an applicant is to be given the opportunity to appear before the Board if it is likely that the Board may not be satisfied that the person is of good character.
Definition of Good Character
All applicants for registration are considered by the Teachers Registration Board to be of good character, unless there is evidence to the contrary. Evidence to the contrary could be conviction for an offence or a number of offences, or substantiated information brought to the attention of the Board, that would lead the community to have reasonable doubts about entrusting students into the person's care.

> *Procedures for Determining Good Character*
> *The core process for gathering information for the good character check of an applicant for registration will be via a Record of Conviction check done through Tasmania Police, and interstate and internationally as necessary. The details of the conduct of this check are negotiated between the Board and Tasmania Police, and specified in a Memorandum of Understanding.*
> *Tasmanian employers of teachers will also be given an opportunity to assist in the assessment of applicants' character. The employing authorities will be sent lists of applicants' names and asked if they have any information which would cause the Board to question the good character of any persons on the list.*

Anticipated Effects of the Program

The character education interventions hoped to make changes in such key areas as student attitudes, behavior, grades, and test scores. We see these areas of measurement as being consistent with the goals outlined in the various discourses we have reviewed. One proposal identified the following areas that were assessed by their instrumentation. Some of these areas require interpretation, which we hazard in terms of the discourses in which these goals were embedded and the means of measurement employed to assess them.

- *Improved student attitudes*—attitudes changing toward those traditionally held by the elders whose political, cultural, and economic capital give them authority within the community. This goal employs the discourses of the authoritarian society, virtuous individual, and class-based morality.
- *Improved student behavior*—changes in behavior toward the norm expected by these advantaged community elders, so that these norms are not disrupted. This goal employs the discourses of the authoritarian society, virtuous individual, and class-based morality.
- *Enhanced student performance*—less disruption of established school norms, greater compliance with adult behavioral and academic expectations. This goal employs the discourses of the authoritarian society, class-based morality, Protestant work ethic, virtuous individual, and academic achievement.
- *Increased parental satisfaction*—agreement among parents that students are better meeting adult behavioral and academic expectations. This goal employs the discourses of the authoritarian society, class-based morality, and family first.

- *Enhanced teacher motivation*—less disruption of adult expectations so that behavioral and academic goals may be met more easily. This goal employs the discourses of the authoritarian society and class-based morality.
- *Increased classroom productivity*—more work produced by students and higher quality of the product of their work. This goal employs the discourses of academic achievement, the authoritarian society, and the Protestant work ethic.
- *Enhanced school/community partnership*—greater support of the school's efforts from families, businesses, faith communities, service organizations, and other community stakeholders. This goal employs the discourse of the authoritarian society.
- *Students develop positive character traits*—students do not disrupt dominant norms. This goal employs the discourses of the authoritarian society, youth depravity, moral absoluteness, class-based morality, the Protestant work ethic, virtuous individual, and academic achievement.
- *Students reach their full academic potential*—students get better grades and higher test scores. This goal employs the discourse of academic achievement.
- *Students can successfully enter and compete in the workplace*—students can be productive workers. This goal employs the discourse of the Protestant work ethic and virtuous individual.
- *Students can make meaningful contributions to their communities*—students uphold the traditions and values of their communities through participation in established social and economic avenues. This goal employs the discourse of the authoritarian society and virtuous individual.

In making these interpretations we rely on our knowledge of cultural psychology (e.g., Cole, 1996) and the ideological implications of discourse (e.g., Gee, 1991). To give one example: By the standards of officials of the Southern Baptist denomination, a homosexual person is deviant and could not develop positive character traits. In a community governed by those holding a strict Baptist faith, a homosexual person would violate the norms traditionally established by those whose political, cultural, and economic capital give them authority within the community. Only by renouncing homosexuality and meeting the community's norms for sexuality and presumably morality could such a person be regarded as possessing good character. Our interpretation of these goals is thus neces-

---

Good character is more to be praised than outstanding talent. Most talents are, to some extent, a gift. Good character, by contrast, is not given to us. We have to build it piece by piece—by thought, choice, courage and determination.

—John Luther

sarily grounded in the local cultural norms and political ideologies that establish community standards for virtue.

Data Collected to Measure Change in Character

One state reported that the following measures were used to evaluate the effectiveness of the character education curriculum:

> Student data indicators gathered from pilot districts through the schools has [sic] included the number of absences, the number of tardies to school, the number of tardies to class, the number of after-school detentions, the number of student in-school suspension episodes, the number of student out of school suspension episodes, the number of students referred for services from other agencies, the number of students enrolling in alternative schools, the number of expulsions, the number of disruptive incidents on school buses and the incidence of pregnancy.... School data indicators include the number of Service Learning projects, the number of awards given for citizenship/service and service club memberships.... Parent/Community support data indicators include the number of active volunteers and the number of volunteer episodes.

The other state in this profile used a similar set of measures to evaluate its program. It requires little inference to see that good character is measured primarily in terms of the extent to which students are subjected to school-based disciplinary procedures; additional data come from the degree to which students participate in community-sponsored service projects. Good character, then, is viewed as a student's proximity to behavioral norms of the school's and stakeholders' primary cultural groups, who are the ones who make and interpret the rules that the students follow or violate and who determine what counts as good service.

Despite the proposal's appeal to the notion of moral absoluteness, we see reason to believe that these rules might be subjective and interpreted through cultural lenses. Researchers have found, for instance, that cultural groups—affiliated by race, creed, nationality, gender, social class, and other categories—have different norms for formal social behavior. African American students, for instance, are often disciplined in school in numbers disproportionate to their population (Townsend, 2000). One explanation is that they lack character and need both punishment and character education. Another is that cultural groups within the African American population recognize a different set of norms than those expected in schools, which for the most part follow the social expectations of the White middle class (Eckert, 1989). A number of researchers (e.g., Delpit, 1995; Heath, 1983) have described the ways in which some African American communities encourage performance and spontaneous participation as appropriate social behavior. Kochman (1981) has contrasted White and African American discourse in public forums, finding that African Americans tend to participate with passion and emotion, often at high volume, in contrast to more reserved and rational participation by Whites. Yet being spontaneous, loud, and performative in school may be culturally constructed as disruptive and result in disciplinary measures due to the student's presumed lack of character.

Again, we return to the discourses in which the character education curricula are framed to help with our analysis. In the discourse of family first, parents are the first and foremost teachers of morality. Yet some homes promote different notions of appropriate public behavior than do others. In such cases, the homes with the greatest political, social, cultural, and economic capital are able to institute their norms as a social reality presumed to have universal acceptance (Apple, 1979; Berger & Luckmann, 1966; Gee, 1990; Smagorinsky, 2001a; Taxel, 1981; Williams, 1977). These community "stalwarts," as they are called in one proposal, then employ the discourses of youth depravity and class-based morality to define the cultural minorities as falling outside their notion of moral absoluteness. With proper intervention and work ethic, these students can more closely approximate the prevailing norms and thus become more productive citizens and high achieving students, that is, demonstrate greater character.

We feel that a closer look at these means of measurement will help reveal the notions of character assumed by the states and the beliefs about measurement embedded in the instruments. We next examine the research questions outlined in one proposal and the instruments used to answer them.

Comprehension of Character Education Qualities. The research question posed in the proposal was, "Will students participating in a character education program show greater growth than non-participating students on a measure of *comprehension* of character education qualities?" The instrument they used was a paper and pencil test of comprehension of a sample of the 34 qualities based on behavioral descriptions of equivalent qualities, with t-test used for analysis (see Appendix 13.1 for a sample of this measurement).

This assessment assumes that a student who can correctly define a term is not merely showing academic knowledge but has internalized the concept itself. In reading this measurement and considering its assumptions, we thought of Bill Clinton, denounced by Joseph Lieberman and other authors of character education legislation for his lack of moral leadership. Clinton, we assume, would be able to answer all of these questions correctly

---

Character, in a classic sense, manifests itself as the autonomy to make ethical decisions always on behalf of the common good and the discipline to abide by that principle.

—James Hunter

> *Good Character is a blessing from Allah.*
>
> —*Wasaelus Shia*

and be deemed a man of high character according to this measurement. His marital fidelity while in office, however, might suggest otherwise.

We also see assumptions and discourses revealed in the items. We see the discourse of the Protestant work ethic built into the items about saving, hard work, and promptness. We see the emphases on emotional control, on patience, and on politeness as being cultural artifacts of the white upper/middle class, suggesting the discourse of class-based morality and, given the history of benign neglect in race relations, of the authoritarian society.

Selecting an Appropriate Solution to a Problem. The research question was, "Will students participating in a character education program show greater growth than non-participating students on a measure of *application* of character education qualities?" To measure this quality, students were provided with vignettes for which they selected the alternative that was, in the words of the proposal, "most appropriate for the situation" (see Appendix 13.2 for the instrument). T-tests were used to analyze the students' answers.

We see a number of assumptions at work in this assessment. First of all, the instrument assumes that situations are all the same and that all responses of a type convey the same meaning. Yet we have experienced from our own children a very sarcastic "Yes, sir" that would undoubtedly be considered polite by this assessment though clearly was meant disrespectfully at the time.

This assessment also assumes that each vignette has a most appropriate solution for all students and situations. The item about what to do upon encountering a closed door, for instance, could easily have different answers depending on the circumstances. What if the house is on fire and it is the only way out? What if sounds of distress are coming from the other side? What if sounds of sexual arousal are heard? What if one is not sure whether it is distress or arousal? What if one is a police officer and believes a felon is on the other side? What if the door has a sign on it that says "DO NOT DISTURB"? Each of these calls for a different action, and likely different actions depending on who encounters them, at what time of day, in which building, and so on.

The assessment further assumes that a positive attitude toward school correlates with good character and that growth is equivalent with liking school better. All of this assumes that school is a good and healthy place for all to be and that disliking school is a rejection of a house of virtue. We refer to Eckert's (1989) argument that students on the margins of the school's social center, typically from lower income classes, typically feel rejected by and disaffected with school culture. The discourses of the authoritarian society and class-based morality, however, view students' character to be commensurate with their degree of affiliation with school.

The assessment also assumes that students will willingly sign their names and turn in to administrators a survey in which they indicate that stealing, taking drugs, being disruptive, and so forth, are acceptable behaviors. According to the document,

> All of the data collected will need to include the student's name and student ID number so as to be able to match the information from pretest to posttest. The evaluator will keep the data in a secure location, and will ensure that the ratings given by the students and their teachers are confidential. No student information will be released to anyone unless there is evidence of potential danger to a student or other person.

We imagine, however, that a student who feels disenfranchised by the school or is a member of a cultural group disproportionately disciplined will question the veracity of this claim. In order to treat data from this assessment as valid, one would have to assume that all students respond to it sincerely. Given the circumstances under which the data are collected, however, we can imagine that students—particularly those who engage in the very behaviors viewed as immoral—would be wary of the intentions of the instrument and answer the questions accordingly.

Attitude Toward School. The research question was, "Will students participating in a character education program show greater growth than non-participating students on a measure of *attitude toward school?*" To measure attitudes, students were given a twenty-item self-report attitude instrument, with t-test used for analysis (see Appendix 13.3). Given the research question, we assume that the students would be issued this questionnaire before and after the character curriculum and t-tests would determine whether there were significant gains in the number of "yes" answers relative to answers provided by students not exposed to the curriculum. Such an increase would indicate greater "growth" in attitudes toward school.

We see the same concern for validity in this measurement as we did with the previous one, that is, the assessment assumes that students will give honest answers to the questions rather than safe ones.

On the day of judgment, there will be no other good deed heavier than good character.

—Usul-e-Kafi

> *A man with good character is like a man who is always praying and fasting. His*
> *sawab (reward) is as much as one who is fighting in the way of Allah (Jehad).*
>
> —*Usul-e-Kafi*

Parent and Teacher Evaluations of the Program.   The research question was, "How will parents and teachers evaluate the character education program?" The answer came through semi-structured opinionnaires, with content analysis used for analysis (see Appendices 13.4 and 13.5).

Data were also collected from teachers to understand their perception of changes in students' character. According to the proposal, "Each student is to be rated on the qualities of Politeness, Respect for Authority, Respect for Others, Obedience, Honesty, and Industry (i.e., being hardworking). Each attribute is to be rated on a 5 point scale, according to a provided rubric" (see Appendix 13.6).

We can imagine that this measure could work against the goals of other assessments. If students, for instance, are suspicious of the motives behind surveys on which they must put their names and ID numbers, those suspicions will likely not be allayed by instruments of this type that they might regard as surveillance.

Students' Evaluations of the Program.   To answer the question, "How will students evaluate the character education program?" two measurements were used. One was a set of student focus groups or interviews, with content analysis used for analysis. The second was an adapted version of the Home and School Values Inventory (HSVI) developed by Kevin Ryan (1984; see Appendix 13.7).

We again see an assumption that answers to the surveys will be honest and that those surveyed trust the surveyor. As with other assessments, the inventory is issued in school and the students must identify self by name and student ID. We wonder how answers to some questions would be treated. If a student is a refugee from a country torn by civil war, we see it as conceivable that the statement "People should never steal anything" might not always

> *All these guys came in as good [basketball] players. The thing that we're proud of*
> *is that they all improved and have gotten much better. But, you know, I'm an*
> *old-school guy who thinks that integrity and character and being a good person*
> *are where you start, a foundation. The common denominator with these three*
> *[athletes] is that they're good kids. They're the kind of kids you want babysitting*
> *your kids or going out with your daughter.*
>
> —*Kelvin Sampson*

> *Allah has said: He is ashamed of confining the flesh of a person with good character to hell.*
>
> —*Wasael Shia*

be true, if the student had to steal a gun or food from an enemy to survive. We also wonder how the assessors treat responses to the statement "Belief in a religion is not important to me." We can only assume that people who claim that they are not religious are viewed as having low character. The statement "We should show respect for all our leaders" could surely have a variety of answers, depending on who the leader is and who the follower is. We could imagine, for instance, that Governor George Wallace of Alabama, who vowed never to be "outniggered" in a political campaign, could conceivably not be respected by African American residents of his state.

We see this assessment as being replete with many of the discourses we have reviewed: the discourse of the authoritarian society, given its blind faith in leaders and other societal authority figures; the discourse of moral absoluteness, given its belief in correct answers to moral questions; the discourse of the Protestant work ethic, given such items as "Play is fun, but work is satisfying"; the discourse of family first, evidenced in "My family is the most important thing to me" and similar statements; the discourse of academic achievement, revealed through items such as "Getting good grades in school makes me happy"; and the discourse of logical positivism, as evidenced by the reliance on the use of statistical tests to measure purported changes in attitudes and behaviors following the CE intervention.

Behavior of Students as Evidenced by Discipline Records.   As noted, a large part of the assessment of effective character education comes through records of discipline, detention, suspension, and other punitive measures. One research question was phrased as follows: "Will students participating in a character education program exhibit better school behavior (as evidenced by discipline records) than non-participating students?" We have previously reviewed the assumptions behind using disciplinary records as evidence of greater character. We see this measurement as assessing students' compliance with local norms rather than their adoption of universal core character traits, a point we no doubt needn't belabor further.

> *Bad company corrupts good character.*
>
> —*I Corinthians 33.*

SUMMARY

In this section we have tried to explicate these Southern states' notion of character, locating their conception in regional culture and outlining the character commodities to which they avail themselves in pursuit of operationalizing their beliefs about character. We see a relation between the dominant culture of the region and the dominant discourses through which character education is realized in the proposals, curricula, and assessments. We also see the strong role played by contributors to the Aspen Declaration in informing the OERI RFP and providing products and services that enable these states to work in concert with the Aspen Declaration's values, priorities, ideology, and goals. We see the conception, bureaucratic structure, implementation, and assessment as a closed process; that is, there is widespread agreement among the architects of the movement, the state leaders, and the entrepreneurs as to the nature of character education.

As a result, certain oversights within this conception are either never recognized or never explicated publicly. Primarily, the discourses in which character education is presented do not attend to the cultural variation that could undermine its assumptions or the cultural imperialism that results from diminishing the values and practices of marginalized cultures. We see, then, didactic approaches to character education as working firmly in service of the dominant culture that asserts its own values as universal, core virtues that become institutionalized, preponderant, and perpetuated through their inscription in the school curriculum.

According to the School District Data Book Profile's most recent demographic report (http://govinfo.library.orst.edu/), these states show large populations outside the *dominant minority*, to use Murray's (2001) term. According to the 1990 census, in one state the total population is 70% White and 27% Black, with 14% living in poverty; within the school population 63% of students are White and 33% Black. In the other state 68% of all residents are White and 30% Black, with 15% living in poverty; among school children 60% are White and 38% Black. These racial and economic minority populations have little say in how character is defined and character education is implemented. They are hieratically positioned as *they* in the discourse of the documents and primarily used to illustrate the absence of character and need for character education. Their exclusion from the process of generating a conception of character, however, contributes heavily to the closed and circular process of character conception we have described. By eliminating diversity of perspective, those with cultural capital also limit the discourse available for critiquing their conception of character. And so "the good old days" can be unproblematically forwarded as a sane and simple time without the African American perspective that it was a time of holocaust.

By excluding alternative perspectives, these states have closed themselves off to the ideologies available through other discourse streams. The intertext upon which they draw for their thinking is thus ideologically narrow. Rather than availing themselves to the full heteroglossic array of voices who speak on the topic of character, they listen only to those who echo their own perspective. Ultimately, we see this narrowing of scope as not only limiting but politically oppressive to those who are silenced in and marginalized from the official dialogue.

Humility in our quest for success provides for the strongest sort of sustainable leadership, and facilitates the attainment of true success. It is the core of moral character and is a surprising springboard to both personal and competitive excellence.

—Tom Morris

APPENDIX 13.1: OBJECTIVE TEST OF CHARACTER DEFINITIONS

Name

Grade

Please read the definition and each of the character words to the students. Ask students to circle the word that matches the definition.

1. The power to wait calmly without complaining.

    patience   kindness   commitment

2. Being friendly, considerate and willing to help others.

    cleanliness   self-control   kindness

3. Showing concern or sympathy for others.

    compassion   diligence   perseverance

4. Happy; filled with cheer.

    commitment   joyfulness   sportsmanship

5. To control your actions and emotions.

    respect   conservation   self-control

6. To be useful in helping others.

    helpfulness   citizenship   fairness

7. To save.

    generosity   conservation   responsibility

8. Working hard in a careful, steady manner.

    punctuality   politeness   diligence

9. Being on time, being prompt.

    thriftiness   compassion   punctuality

10. Showing good manners.

    friendly   accomplishment   politeness

Source. Objective Test of Character Definitions.

APPENDIX 13.2: B-ROW EVALUATION INSTRUMENT: BEHAVIOR SURVEY FOR STUDENTS

Name   Student ID   Grade

Please read each item and circle the letter of the choice that you think is most correct. Circle only one choice. This is not a test, and you cannot pass or fail.

Please tell us what you really think, not what you think we want to hear. Your answers will be confidential. That means NOBODY will find out what you said.

1. Saying yes ma'am and yes sir to adults is:

    a. old fashioned

    b. only done in the South

    c. respectful

    d. distasteful

    e. impolite

2. When a door is closed, you should:

    a. open it

    b. knock and enter

    c. knock and wait to be told to enter

    d. enter and look for people

    e. leave

3. To address a judge say:

    a. Mr. Judge

    b. Your Honor

    c. Judge

    d. Your Grace

    e. Your Majesty

4. You should respect:

    1. yourself and your parents

    2. people and animals

    3. property

    4. rules and laws

    5. education

    a. (1 only)

    b. (1, 2, and 3)

    c. (1 and 4)

    d. (1, 4, and 5)

    e. (all of the above)

5. Stealing/shoplifting is:

    a. wrong

    b. all right if you don't get caught

    c. all right to get what you want

    d. all right if you don't have the money to buy something

    e. a way to beat the system

6. The roles of a parent are:

    1. provide food, clothing, shelter

    2. teach children right from wrong

    3. set limits and expectations

    4. provide counseling

    5. provide discipline

    a. (1 only)

    b. (1 and 5)

    c. (1, 3, and 5)

    d. (2 and 4)

    e. (all of the above)

7. Cursing is:

    a. the way to get people off your back

    b. all right when you are mad

    c. all right with friends

    d. okay at home

    e. disrespectful

8. Duties at home are given to:

    a. punish children

    b. do the work parents should do

    c. keep children busy

    d. teach responsibility

    e. keep children off the street

9. Selling drugs is:

    a. a good way to make money

    b. the best way to have fine clothes, jewelry, cars

    c. a way to destroy human life

    d. a way to be accepted and admired

10. Fighting is:
    a. the best way to settle differences
    b. the way to prove you're not a coward
    c. the way to make people respect you
    d. the wrong way to handle conflicts
    e. none of the above

11. Using drugs is:
    a. the way to make your peers accept you
    b. the way to feel good
    c. a good way to escape reality
    d. the way to destroy your mind and body
    e. the way to happiness

12. Being disruptive is:
    a. a way to get attention
    b. a way to hide weaknesses
    c. a way to distract others
    d. a way to save face
    e. all of the above

13. Carrying a weapon
    a. makes people respect you
    b. makes people want to be your friend
    c. makes people fear you
    d. makes you somebody
    e. makes people look up to you

14. Negative actions of gangs:
    a. cause human destruction
    b. involve people in wrong doings
    c. cause fear and violence
    d. make neighborhoods unsafe
    e. all of the above

15. Lying is:
    a. a good way to escape punishment
    b. a good way to get what you want
    c. a good way to get out of trouble

    d. a good way to avoid responsibility

    e. A good way to destroy friendship

16. Cheating is:

    a. okay if you don't get caught

    b. the way to be successful

    c. the way to get what you want

    d. a self destructive habit

    e. the way to make good grades

17. Gossiping makes:

    a. your peers accept you

    b. people distrust you

    c. people want to be around you

    d. people confide in you

    e. people like you

18. It doesn't cost money to:

    a. eat out

    b. show appreciation

    c. go to the movies

    d. travel

    e. ride the bus

19. Which of the following is a Common Sense Value:

    a. greed

    b. hatred

    c. honesty

    d. jealousy

    e. stealing

Source. B-ROW Evaluation Instrument: Behavior Survey for Students.

APPENDIX 13.3: ATTITUDE TOWARD SCHOOL

Please answer each question honestly. Place a check mark (V) or an "X" in the space by your choice. Think about each statement before making a choice

1 Do you expect school to be an enjoyable place to come for learning?

Yes   Somewhat   No

2. Do you feel that this school is enjoyable?

Yes   Somewhat   No

3. Do you expect to receive good grades at school?

Yes   Somewhat   No

4. Do you receive good grades at school?

Yes   Somewhat   No

5. Do you expect teachers to show you respect and not to embarrass you?

Yes   Somewhat   No

6. Do the teachers at this school treat you with respect?

Yes   Somewhat   No

7. Are you involved in activities at school?

Yes   Somewhat   No

8. Should schools make students feel important?

Yes   Somewhat   No

9. Do you feel like an important member of this school?

Yes   Somewhat   No

10. Should students at a school work to get along well together?

Yes   Somewhat   No

11. Do the students at this school get along well together?

Yes   Somewhat   No

Source. Attitude Toward School.

APPENDIX 13.4: SCHOOL AS CARING
COMMUNITY PROFILE (SCCP)

Circle one: Administrator/ Teacher/ Non-teaching professional/ Other staff/
Parent/ Student/ Other

Respond to each item below by filling in the blank on a computer scan sheet for the response that describes how often you see the behavior in your school. (If you have no basis for responding, don't mark that item.) Please write the reason for your rating where you wish to do so.

1 = Rarely

2 = Sometimes

3 = As often as not

4 = More often than not

5 = Almost always

1. Students treat classmates and schoolmates with respect. 1 2 3 4 5

Reason for rating (optional) _____

2. Students respect others' personal property. 1 2 3 4 5

Reason (optional) _____

3. Students behave respectfully toward their teachers (speak
courteously, follow directions, and so on). 1 2 3 4 5

Reason (optional) _____

4. Students behave respectfully toward all other school staff
(including secretaries, custodians, aides, and bus drivers). 1 2 3 4 5

Reason (optional) _____

5. Students treat the school building and other school property with
respect. 1 2 3 4 5

Reason (optional)_____

6. Students behave respectfully toward their parents. 1 2 3 4 5

Reason (optional) _____

7. Students share what they have with others. 1 2 3 4 5

Reason (optional) _____

8. Students care about and help each other, even if they are not friends. 1 2 3 4 5

Reason (optional)_____

9. Students refrain from put-downs. 1 2 3 4 5

Reason (optional) _____

10. Students work well together. 1 2 3 4 5

Reason (optional) _____

11. Students refrain from picking on others or excluding them because they are different. 1 2 3 4 5

Reason (optional) _____

12. Students listen to each other in class discussions. 1 2 3 4 5

Reason (optional) _____

13. Older students are kind to younger students. 1 2 3 4 5

Reason (optional) _____

14. Students solve conflicts without fighting, insults, or threats. 1 2 3 4 5

Reason (optional) _____

15. When students do something hurtful, they apologize and try to make up for it. 1 2 3 4 5

Reason (optional) _____

16. Students help new students make friends and feel accepted. 1 2 3 4 5

Reason (optional) _____

17. When students see another student being mean, they try to stop it. 1 2 3 4 5

Reason (optional) _____

18. Students try to console or comfort a peer who has experienced a sadness. 1 2 3 4 5

Reason (optional) _____

19. Students are patient and forgiving with each other. 1 2 3 4 5

Reason (optional) _____

20. Students show good sportsmanship. 1 2 3 4 5

Reason (optional) _____

21. In their interactions with students, *teachers* display the character qualities the school is trying to teach. 1 2 3 4 5

Reason (optional) _____

22. In their interactions with students, *other professional school staff* (principal, counselors, etc.) display the character qualities the school is trying to teach. 1 2 3 4 5

Reason (optional) _____

23. In their interactions with students, *other school staff* (secretaries, aides, custodians, bus drivers, etc.) display the character qualities the school is trying to teach. 1 2 3 4 5

Reason (optional) _____

24. *In their interactions with each other,* staff display the character qualities the school is trying to teach. 1 2 3 4 5

Reason (optional) _____

25. Teachers treat all students fairly and don't play favorites. 1 2 3 4 5

Reason (optional) _____

26. Teachers go out of their way to help students who need extra help. 1 2 3 4 5

Reason (optional) _____

27. Teachers listen to students' problems, and students feel they can talk to their teachers about things that are bothering them. 1 2 3 4 5

Reason (optional) _____

28. Teachers respect, care about, and help each other. 1 2 3 4 5

Reason (optional) _____

29. The school treats parents in a way that makes them feel respected, welcomed, and cared about. 1 2 3 4 5

Reason (optional) _____

30. Parents support and work with the school. 1 2 3 4 5

Reason (optional) _____

The SCCP is an instrument developed by the Center for the 4th and 5th Rs, SUNY Cortland, P.O. Box 2000, Cortland, NY 13045: (607) 753-2455.

Source. School as Caring Community Profile (SCCP; http://www.cortland.edu/www/c4n5rs/sccp.htm)

APPENDIX 13.5: ELEVEN PRINCIPLES SURVEY (EPS) OF CHARACTER EDUCATION EFFECTIVENESS

The Eleven Principles Survey (EPS) of Character Education Effectiveness is an assessment instrument designed by the Center for the 4th and 5th Rs (Respect and Responsibility) and based on the document "Eleven Principles of Effective Character Education" by the national Character Education Partnership.

The EPS is designed for formative assessment of a school's character education program. It addresses the question, "To what extent is the school implementing the Eleven Principles of Effective Character Education?" Schools undertaking character education will be at varying stages of implementing these principles; they represent an ideal for comprehensive character education to work toward. Information provided by the EPS assessment can be used to plan steps to strengthen a school's character education effort. The EPS can also be used as a framework to guide a school's initial planning of an effective character education program.

The EPS will give you three scores: (1) one score for each subcomponent of each principle; (2) a score for each principle (the average of the subcomponent scores for that principle); and (3) an overall score (the average of the scores for all eleven principles).

Directions to a School Completing the Survey

1. To maximize the validity of the assessment, the school should include as many relevant groups as possible in filling out the survey: administrators, faculty, professional support staff, other staff, and parent representatives. Broad survey participation of this kind will enable the school to see how its character education program is viewed from the perspectives of different groups. (The EPS report will give you overall results as well as a breakdown for different groups.)
2. Each person completing the EPS should do so independently (marking responses on a machine-scoreable answer sheet), so as not to be influenced by the ratings of others.
3. If it is not possible for various school groups to complete the survey, the members of the school's character education leadership group, including the building principal, should each complete it.

Indicate below the number of persons in each category completing the EPS Survey:

_____ Administrators

_____ Teachers

_____ Professional Support Staff

_____ Other Staff

_____ Parents

_____ TOTAL NUMBER

Eleven Principles Survey (EPS) of Character Education Effectiveness

Directions (Please use a No. 2 pencil)

On the NCS Answer Sheet, in the Special Codes section ("K" column), please fill in the bubble indicating your school position. (No names, please. Responses are meant to be anonymous.)

K–0 Administrator

K–1 Teacher or teacher assistant

K–2 Professional support staff (counselor, psychologist, social worker, etc.)

K–3 Other staff (custodian, cafeteria aide, bus driver, etc.)

K–4 Parent

Based on your observations, use a scale of 1, 2, 3, 4 or 5 (with 1 being "LOW Implementation" and 5 being "HIGH Implementation") to rate the degree to which you think the following 11 character education principles are implemented in your school.

1_____2_____3_____4_____5_____

Low Implementation   **High Implementation**

Please give your honest opinion, since candid responses provide the most valid data. If you do not have enough knowledge of a particular item to give a rating, leave it blank. Please record your ratings in two places: on the NCS Answer Sheet, and on the blank line preceding each numbered item on this survey form.

Submit the NCS Answer Sheet to the person gathering the data for your school to machine score. Keep your copy of the survey, with your ratings, to use in staff discussions once you receive the summary of your survey results.

PRINCIPLE 1: CHARACTER EDUCATION PROMOTES AND TEACHES QUALITIES OF GOOD CHARACTER, SUCH AS PRUDENCE (GOOD JUDGMENT), RESPECT, RESPONSIBILITY, HONESTY, FAIRNESS, COURTESY, KINDNESS, COURAGE, DILIGENCE, PERSEVERANCE, AND SELF-CONTROL.

_____ 1. Our school staff and parent community have agreed on the character traits we wish to promote in our character education program.

_____ 2. We have defined these character traits in terms of behaviors that can be observed in the school, family, and community.

____ 3. We have made these character traits and their behavioral definitions widely known throughout our school and parent community.

PRINCIPLE 2: CHARACTER IS DEFINED COMPREHENSIVELY TO INCLUDE THINKING, FEELING, AND BEHAVIOR.

____ 4. We take deliberate steps to help students acquire a developmentally appropriate understanding of what the character traits mean in everyday behavior and to grasp the reasons why some behaviors are right and others wrong.

____ 5. We take deliberate steps to help students admire the character traits, desire to possess them, and become committed to them.

____ 6. We take deliberate steps to help students practice the character traits so that they become habits.

PRINCIPLE 3: CHARACTER EDUCATION IS INTENTIONAL, PROACTIVE AND COMPREHENSIVE.

____ 7. Our program is intentional and proactive; it provides regular, planned, and explicit opportunities for students to learn the qualities of good character.

____ 8. Our program is comprehensive across the curriculum; the character traits are regularly integrated into instruction in all subjects and at all grade levels.

____ 9. Our character program is infused throughout the school day. The character traits are upheld by adults, and taken seriously by students, throughout the school environment: in classrooms, corridors, cafeterias, assemblies, and extracurricular activities, and on playgrounds, athletic fields, and school busses.

____ 10. Our drug, alcohol, and sex education programs are character-based, consistent with the school's highest character expectations of respect, responsibility, and self-control and actively guiding students toward abstinence from drugs, alcohol and sexual activity.

PRINCIPLE 4: THE SCHOOL IS A CARING COMMUNITY.

____ 11. Our program makes it a high priority to foster caring attachments between adults and students. The school schedule, for example, is designed to minimize disruption and stress and to maximize staff time for developing supportive relationships with their students.

____ 12. Our school makes it a high priority to help students form caring attachments to each other, including caring attachments between older and younger students.

____ 13. Our school does not tolerate peer cruelty (persecution, exclusion and the like) and takes steps to prevent peer cruelty and deal with it effectively when it occurs.

PRINCIPLE 5: STUDENTS HAVE FREQUENT OPPORTUNITIES FOR MORAL ACTION.

____ 14. Our program provides students with repeated and varied opportunities for moral action such as cooperative learning, conflict resolution, class problem-solving meetings, classroom helper jobs, peer tutoring, school and community service, and taking personal responsibility for improving one's behavior or learning.

____ 15. Our program helps students consciously take responsibility for developing their own character—for example, by encouraging students to set daily goals to practice the character traits and to assess and record their success in achieving their goals.

PRINCIPLE 6: CHARACTER EDUCATION INCLUDES AN ACADEMIC CURRICULUM THAT BUILDS GOOD CHARACTER.

____ 16. Our academic curriculum is designed to challenge all students to do their personal best and to develop the qualities of character—such as self-discipline, diligence, perseverance, and a concern for excellence—that support personal responsibility and a strong work ethic.

____ 17. Our school respects the way students learn by providing active learning experiences such as problem-solving, cooperative learning, and projects that build on students' interests.

____ 18. Our curriculum recognizes multiple intelligences and helps students of diverse abilities and needs discover and develop their special talents.

PRINCIPLE 7: CHARACTER EDUCATION STRIVES TO DEVELOP THE INTRINSIC MOTIVATION CENTRAL TO GOOD CHARACTER.

____ 19. Our program's approach to classroom and school discipline is centered on developing students' intrinsic commitment to doing what's right—following legitimate rules, for example, because doing so respects the rights and needs of self and others. Logical consequences for wrongdoing are administered in such a way as to strengthen a student's inner character resources: moral reasoning, self-control, and strategies for responsible behavior in the future. Students are also taught to take initiative to make active restitution when they do something wrong.

____ 20. When we deal with discipline problems, we make explicit reference to the character qualities we are trying to teach—with the goal of helping students use standards such as courtesy, kindness, honesty, fairness, and self-control to evaluate and improve their conduct.

____ 21. In our classrooms and school, we recognize and celebrate good character in ways that support rather than undermine intrinsic motivation (by keeping the focus on doing good things because it helps others and oneself); recognition for good character is accessible to all who are deserving and not limited just to a few.

PRINCIPLE 8: THE ENTIRE SCHOOL STAFF SHARES RESPONSIBILITY FOR CHARACTER EDUCATION AND LIVES BY THE SCHOOL'S CHARACTER EXPECTATIONS.

____ 22. All professional school staff (including administrators, counselors, librarians, coaches, and teaching faculty) have been included in planning, receiving staff development for, and carrying out the schoolwide character education effort.

____ 23. All other staff (including secretaries, cafeteria workers, bus drivers, playground aides, etc.) have been included in planning, receiving staff development for, and carrying out the schoolwide character education effort.

____ 24. The character traits espoused by our school are modeled by staff in their interactions with students.

____ 25. The character traits espoused by our school are practiced by staff in their interactions with each other; there is a moral community among adults—including relations between administration and faculty—that is governed by norms of mutual respect, fairness, and collaborative decision-making.

____ 26. Regular and adequate time is made available for staff planning and reflection: to design the character education program, share success stories, assess progress, and address moral concerns, especially gaps between the school's professed character expectations and observed behavior in the school.

PRINCIPLE 9: CHARACTER EDUCATION INVOLVES MORAL LEADERSHIP BY STAFF AND STUDENTS.

____ 27. Our program has a leader (the principal, another administrator, a lead teacher) who champions our character education effort.

____ 28. There is a leadership group (a committee, a task force) that guides the ongoing planning and implementation of our character education program and encourages the involvement of the whole school.

____ 29. Students are involved in leadership roles (e.g., through student government, special councils, and peer mediation) in ways that develop their responsibility and help the school's character expectations become part of the peer culture.

PRINCIPLE 10: THE SCHOOL RECRUITS PARENTS AND THE COMMUNITY AS FULL PARTNERS IN CHARACTER EDUCATION.

____ 30. Our program explicitly affirms that parents are the first and most important character educators of their children. Parents' questions and concerns about any part of our character program are taken seriously; every effort is made to respect parents' rights as their child's primary moral teacher.

____ 31. Our program asks parents to identify the character qualities that should be fostered by the school.

____ 32. Parents are included in our school's character education leadership group.

____ 33. All parents are informed about the goals and teaching methods of our character education program.

____ 34. Our school sends home communications (such as letters from the principal) and suggestions (such as dinner discussion topics and bedtime reading) that help parents reinforce the same character qualities the school is trying to teach. Our school also offers workshops, parenting tips, books, tapes, and other resources that help parents develop their general parenting skills and strengthen their relationship with their child.

____ 35. Our school has involved representatives of the wider community (e.g., businesses, religious institutions, youth organizations, government, and the media) in helping to plan our character education effort.

____ 36. Our school has involved members of the community in efforts to model and promote the qualities of good character in the community.

PRINCIPLE 11: CHARACTER EDUCATION ASSESSES THE CHARACTER OF THE SCHOOL, THE SCHOOL STAFF'S FUNCTIONING AS CHARACTER EDUCATORS, AND THE CHARACTER DEVELOPMENT OF STUDENTS.

____ 37. Our program assesses the character of our school as a moral community (e.g., through school climate surveys using agree-disagree items such as, "Students in our school respect each other" and "Our school is like a family").

____ 38. Our staff periodically engages in systematic formative assessment of our program, using surveys such as this to determine the degree to which we are implementing the intended components of our character education program. The results of these assessments are used to plan program improvements.

____ 39. Our school asks staff to report periodically (e.g., through questionnaires or anecdotal records) their efforts to implement character education.

____ 40. We assess our students' progress in developing an understanding of the character traits—for example, by asking them to define the traits, recognize or produce examples of the traits in action, and explain how these traits help them and others.

____ 41. We assess our students' progress in developing an emotional attachment and commitment to the qualities of good character—for example, by asking students to rate how important the character traits are to them in their lives.

____ 42. We assess our students' progress in behaving in ways that reflect the character traits—for example, by collecting data on observable character-related behaviors, such as school attendance, acts of honesty, volunteering for school or community service, discipline referrals, fighting, vandalism, drug incidents, and student pregnancies, and by asking students to complete anonymous self-report questionnaires on character-related behaviors (e.g., "How many times during the past week have you helped someone who is not a friend or family member?", "How many times have you cheated on a test or major assignment in the past year?", and "How many times in the past month have you stood up for what was right—for example, by resisting peer pressure to do something wrong or by defending a schoolmate against unfair gossip?").

____ 43. We include assessment of student character or character-related behaviors as part of our report card.

Source. Eleven Principles Survey (EPS) of Character Education Effectiveness (www.cortland.edu/www.c4n5rs/eps.htm)

APPENDIX 13.6: TEACHER RATING FORM

Dear Teacher,

As part of the [Anonymous] County Character Education Program, we need to collect information on the values and behaviors of students as judged by the people who spend the most time with them, their teachers. The attached sheets list your students in alphabetical order, with six blanks after each name. Please rate each of your students on each of 6 characteristics, using the rubrics below.

We understand that your time is precious. Do not spend a lot of time making these judgments. Simply respond based on your overall impression of the student. It should not take longer than one minute to evaluate each student, once you have read through the scoring rubric.

Of course, this information is completely confidential and will not become part of anyone's permanent record. Once the data are entered into the computer, these forms will be destroyed.

Thank you for your cooperation.

1. Politeness:
5 = Consistently polite and courteous in dealing with teachers and peers 4 = Usually polite 3 = Often impolite, does not seem to know basic etiquette 2 = Often actively rude to teachers and peers 1 = I have no basis to judge this student on this characteristic

2. Respect for authority
5 = Consistently respectful to teachers and other adults 4 = Usually respectful, occasionally slips 3 = Treats adults as casually as treats peers 2 = Actively disrespectful to teachers and other adults 1 = I have no basis to judge this student on this characteristic

3. Respect for others/peers
5 = Shows active respect for others' opinions, property, and physical space 4 = Respects others 3 = Self-centered, lacks respect for others' opinions, property, and physical space 2 = Actively aggressive towards others 1 = I have no basis to judge this student on this characteristic

4. Obedience
5 = Consistently obedient and well-behaved 4 = Usually obedient, occasionally slips due to inattention 3 = Occasionally violates classroom rules 2 = Often disobeys direct instructions and rules 1 = I have no basis to judge this student on this characteristic

5. Honesty
5 = Consistently honest and truthful, even when not to advantage 4 = Generally honest and truthful 3 = Honest and truthful only when observed 2 = Highly unreliable; has been known to steal and/or tell lies 1 = I have no basis to judge this student on this characteristic

6. Industry
5 = Consistently hardworking; seeks work to do 4 = Completes assignments as requested 3 = Works only when interested in the task 2 = Lazy and passive 1 = I have no basis to judge this student on this characteristic

---

Source. Teacher Rating Form

APPENDIX 13.7: A SURVEY ABOUT VALUES

A Survey about Values

Name: Student ID:

                                   Grade:

We're interested in what students think about personal values. For each sentence on the next two pages, circle the phrase that best describes what you think.

Here's an example:

Dogs are really cool pets.

For sure   I think so   Maybe not   I disagree

Cats are fun to play with.

For sure   I think so   Maybe not   I disagree

Fish are boring

For sure   I think so   Maybe not   I disagree

If you really like dogs, don't like cats very well much, and think fish are really interesting, your paper would look like this:

Dogs are really cool pets.

For sure   I think so   Maybe not   I disagree

Cats are fun to play with.

For sure   I think so   *Maybe not*   I disagree

Fish are boring

For sure   I think so   Maybe not   *I disagree*

Please be honest in your answers. We promise not to tell what anyone said.

1. Getting good grades in school makes me happy.

For sure   I think so   Maybe not   I disagree

2. People should never steal anything.

For sure   I think so   Maybe not   I disagree

3. Students should do their best to get a good report card.

For sure   I think so   Maybe not   I disagree

4. It's OK to get a low grade in a subject you don't like.

For sure   I think so   Maybe not   I disagree

5. I do not like to be with people who have bad manners.

For sure   I think so   Maybe not   I disagree

6. Always put work before pleasure.

For sure   I think so   Maybe not   I disagree

7. It's not so bad to steal small things.

For sure   I think so   Maybe not   I disagree

8. I do not care if people think I have bad manners.

For sure   I think so   Maybe not   I disagree

9. It is important to have some kind of religious faith.

For sure   I think so   Maybe not   I disagree

10. I do not care about learning good manners.

For sure   I think so   Maybe not   I disagree

11. Think about yourself first, then worry about other people.

For sure   I think so   Maybe not   I disagree

12. People worry too much about getting good grades.

For sure   I think so   Maybe not   I disagree

13. Manners don't matter when you're with your friends.

For sure   I think so   Maybe not   I disagree

14. Play is fun, but work is satisfying.

For sure   I think so   Maybe not   I disagree

15. Belief in a religion is not important to me.

For sure   I think so   Maybe not   I disagree

16. I do not mind taking orders from a person who has authority, like a teacher.

For sure   I think so   Maybe not   I disagree

17. Owning a lot of things just ties you down.

For sure   I think so   Maybe not   I disagree

18. We should show respect for all our leaders.

For sure   I think so   Maybe not   I disagree

19. We should relax and enjoy life more.

For sure   I think so   Maybe not   I disagree

20. My family is the most important thing to me.

For sure   I think so   Maybe not   I disagree

21. I would not cheat, even to help a friend.

For sure   I think so   Maybe not   I disagree

22. Most people have broken the rules at some time.

For sure   I think so   Maybe not   I disagree

23. It is better to have fun than to work hard.

For sure   I think so   Maybe not   I disagree

24. People should share their things with others.

For sure   I think so   Maybe not   I disagree

25. You should pay more attention to your family than anything else.

For sure   I think so   Maybe not   I disagree

26. I would rather be with my friends than my family.

For sure   I think so   Maybe not   I disagree

27. My life is guided by my religion.

For sure   I think so   Maybe not   I disagree

28. I don't need money to be happy.

For sure   I think so   Maybe not   I disagree

29. Religions are good guides for how to live a good life.

For sure   I think so   Maybe not   I disagree

30. If I get too much change at the store, I always take it back.

For sure   I think so   Maybe not   I disagree

31. I want to have lots of money.

For sure   I think so   Maybe not   I disagree

32. It's not up to me to help someone I don't know.

For sure   I think so   Maybe not   I disagree

33. I need to have expensive toys and clothes.

For sure   I think so   Maybe not   I disagree

34. I am willing to go out of my way to help others.

For sure   I think so   Maybe not   I disagree

35. Respecting my parents is one way I show that I love them.

For sure   I think so   Maybe not   I disagree

Thank you for sharing your ideas.

Source. A Survey About Values

INTRODUCTION TO THE UPPER MIDWEST: COMMUNITY-BASED, REFLECTIVE APPROACHES TO CHARACTER EDUCATION

In our analysis of various states' conceptions of character education, we found the clearest and most consistent outline of what we termed a community-based, reflective approach in two contiguous states from the American Upper Midwest. The Upper Midwest is an area adjacent to the westernmost Great Lakes, defined most narrowly as encompassing Michigan, Minnesota, and Wisconsin and most broadly as including these states along with northern Illinois, Iowa, Montana, Nebraska, North Dakota, and South Dakota (Ostergren, 1987).

A reflective, community-based approach to character education is designed to promote discussion among all participants about the process and effectiveness of the initiative. Furthermore, character is an issue taken up by the community as a whole, which is recognized as being composed of diverse constituents sharing an equal stake in the quality of community life. The community thus needs to create a caring environment—with exemplary behavior modeled by adults—that in turn helps young people to internalize an ethic of care and a sense of agency in contributing to a better society through good citizenship. The values fostered through character education will presumably lead to greater participation in a productive work force and, as required by the OERI RFP, to greater academic achievement.

As we did with the states from the Deep South, we first attempt to situate the reflective approaches within the cultural context of the states that developed them. We then review the ancillary curricula and other educational programs that the proposals identify as purchased or consulted in operationalizing their vision of character education. Next, we look both to the program rationales and to program assessments to find the discourses central to outlining the authors' assumptions about character education. Finally, we review the programs' curriculum and assessments to get an idea of how the states from the Upper Midwest implement and evaluate a character education intervention.

> *I think if you have people of character that are willing to work hard and are willing to work together and are talented, it's not a question if you will be successful, it's how successful.*
>
> —*Dennis Felton*

Chapter 14

Cultural Context
of the Upper Midwest

The Midwest, too, has its mythic status, one that in part overlaps with some of the mythic elements of the West. It is the land of the "real America" where people are open, friendly and honest; where the predominant feature on the landscape is the small town and the predominant accent is standard American. The Midwestern myth, which in reality began to end as the Northeastern myth took on its full power, continues to influence Americans, including Midwesterners, as we saw this summer in the local response to the terrible problem of flooding in the upper Mississippi Valley and its peripheries.

Each of these myths is based on a kernel of very real truth and, however exaggerated, that truth remains to keep both the myths and the sections alive. (Elazar, 1994)

This observation points to the enduring identity of the Midwest as a region. We repeat the caveat that we presented when introducing the cultural context of southern states in chapter 10, this volume: The states we profile here are more heterogeneous than a simple characterization can capture. Each is composed of multiple cultural groups, political parties, religious affiliations, and other population variables that suggest diversity rather than homogeneity. The Upper Midwest for instance, has been the location for writing about Jewish women (Schloffand, 1996), African

---

Jesus Christ said more about money than about any other single thing because, when it comes to a man's real nature, money is of first importance. Money is an exact index to a man's true character. All through Scripture there is an intimate correlation between the development of a man's character and how he handles his money.

—Richard C. Halverson

Americans (Balfour, Aiken, & Jones, 1986), Native Americans (Pfaff, 1993), Cajuns (http://lanker.home.mindspring.com/), and other groups from outside the White Christian majority now occupying this region. Although Midwesterners may be open, honest, and friendly, the midwestern city of Chicago remains one of the nation's most racially segregated cities, according to Census 2000 figures (Skertic & Dedman, 2001). Our effort to provide a cultural context necessarily applies to characteristics that have had a historical influence on the values of the dominant culture of the area; we recognize that not all share this history or these values. At the same time we recall that regions are human constructs, with the implication that geographic regions such as the Upper Midwest constitute distinctive cultures (Johnson, 1976).

Reflecting early settlement patterns, both states in our profile now have primarily European American populations. Displacing indigenous people were a mixture of British, German, Scandinavian, Slavic, and other European immigrants. In one of the states profiled, for instance, European Americans constituted 93.9% of the population in 2000, with African Americans 2.1%, Latino/a Americans 2.8%, Asian Americans and Pacific Islanders 1.3%, Native Americans 0.3%, and 0.4% not reporting a race or ethnicity. In the other the population included 88.9% European Americans, 5.7% African Americans, 3.6% Latino/a Americans, 1.7% Asian Americans and Pacific Islanders, and .9% Native Americans and Alaskan Natives.

Since White settlement, the Upper Midwest has been an agrarian region with low-population density. One state in our profile had an average population density in 1990 of 50 people per square mile. The other had a population density of 90 per square mile. In contrast, California's population density was 191 per square mile, Illinois's 206, and New Jersey's 1,042. Like the rest of the country, these states have gradually become more urbanized, with over half of the people now classified as living in urban areas, and suburbs and metro-area towns now the fastest growing parts of the states. This trend accelerated after World War II when improvements in farming methods and the use of fertilizers and pesticides, larger equipment, and more productive seeds increased the yield on harvests and created both larger farms and fewer farming families.

The agrarian economy has contributed to the cultures that have evolved in this region. One guide book (USA Study Guide, 2002) characterizes the Midwest as "almost entirely flat, and also very fertile, making it ideal for farming. The region is known as the 'nation's breadbasket.'... Midwesterners are known for being honest, straightforward people of traditional values" (http://www.usastudyguide.com/regionaldifferences.htm). In introducing *Stiller's Pond: New Fiction from the Upper Midwest,* Truesdale (1988) describes the themes that emerge in stories set in the Great Lakes area as grounded in

The Old Midwest of traditional story-telling—the harsh winters, the rootedness of many of these writers in rural communities and agriculture.... There are stories here bred of a nostalgia for an Edenic golden age of plenty or for an unblemished, mythical wilderness that sustains ongoing relationships ... other stories reflect the frontier values of self-denial, isolation, self-effacement, stoicism, and even silence—people isolated from the centers of fashion and cultural trendiness who don't expect life to be easy or even interesting. They are stoical or resigned about hardships they regard as inevitable ... communication—and language itself—is measured, controlled, even strained, where silence often "speaks" the ethos of the tribe. In rural environments, where being a person of few words may still be perceived as a positive attribute, the language act acquires power and bears consequences. And in the city, where social interchange is perhaps livelier but more often a threat than a resource, the human spirit struggles against great odds, successfully or not, for self-knowledge, and dignity. (pp. ix-xi)

While undoubtedly a mythic portrayal, these characterizations are widely depicted in media representations and the arts and likely include the kernel of truth that suggests at least some traits of the region's cultural majority.

We next identify several factors that recurred in our reading about this region and that appeared to contribute to what we characterize as the reflective, communitarian discourse of the character education proposals.

IMMIGRATION AND SETTLEMENT BY GERMANS AND SCANDINAVIANS

The Upper Midwest's first human inhabitants were the Dakota, Fox, Ioway, Menominee, Oneida, Sauk, Winnebago, and other tribes who settled in this region during the lengthy dispersal from the Bering Strait immigration beginning as long as 32,000 years before the arrival of Europeans. Their coexistence was not always idyllic, with continual warfare, encroachment, and migration obscuring any tribe's claim to a territory as its rightful legacy. The Huron and Ottowa, for instance, were driven west by the Iroquois and lived amidst the Dakota before being expelled due to their aggression. The Fox were driven from present-day Michigan to what is now Wisconsin by the Chippewa, who continued their expansion into the present-day St. Croix Valley separating Wisconsin and Minnesota with an invasion of the lands occupied by the Dakota. The Dakota were ultimately driven out following a century of war during a period that coincided with, on a different front, the U.S. Revolution.

Son! I have seen excellent results of good character. Hazrat Imam Jafar-e-Sadiq (a.s.) has said: If you cannot keep good financial relations with people, at least show good character by behaving nicely.

—Usul-e-kafi

Conflict and displacement continued with the arrival of European immigrants. By 1837, native populations had become decimated through war (both intertribal and with Whites, e.g., the Black Hawk War), disease transmitted through contact with Europeans, and the relentless westward expansion of the white population. The Federal government developed a policy of removal and relocation of native people to reservations through treaties that ceded their lands. By the mid-1850s, following the regulations established in the Land Ordinance of 1785 and Northwest Ordinance of 1787, the territories became available for settlement by Whites and for eventual status as states (McMahon & Karamanski, 2002).

During the western expansion of the nascent United States of the mid-1800s, waves of immigrants—primarily Germans and Scandinavians of Catholic, Lutheran, and Methodist faiths—began to occupy the territory in increasingly dominant numbers. These groups joined the French fur traders, who had been among the first Whites to explore and profit from the region and who tended to occupy the northernmost areas of the region where heavily coated beavers, otters, and other fur-bearing creatures dwelt.

The German and Scandinavian immigrants shared a similar history. Unlike the entrepreneurial fur traders to the north, the Germans and Scandinavians departed Europe in order to escape a rigid class structure in their home nations. They found the less forested parts of the Midwest where they settled to be compatible with their agrarian culture and took easily to farming. In contrast to the South, which was dominated by the large enterprises of wealthy plantation owners, the Upper Midwest was settled by peasant immigrants who established small farms.

The preponderance of German and Scandinavians settling in the Upper Midwest in the 1800s still influences Upper Midwestern culture. We next outline the ways in which their experiences and values contributed to the cultural context in which the modern character education movement was developed.

VOX POPULI POLITICAL MOVEMENTS

The growth of industry and mechanization between the close of the Civil War and 1890 brought about changes in agricultural communities and

> It's all about character and teaching. Nothing has ever been taught unless it was learned and nothing has been learned unless it was taught. Pursuing Victory With Honor is about making people understand that we have great integrity and character in our game [of basketball]. We all want to win, but we want to win the right way.
>
> —Kelvin Sampson

contributed to the development of a distinct regional culture in the Upper Midwest. These developments threatened to stratify society along clearer social class lines, the very situation that the immigrants sought to escape by coming to the United States. The German and Scandinavian immigrants appreciated the United States' lack of a hereditary aristocracy, its more fluid class structure, and its stress on individual achievement. At the same time, they opposed the United States' emphasis on wealth as the primary measure of success, which they believed fostered an ethic of greed, predation, oppression, social injustice, and social class distinction. Wefald (1971) quotes an immigrant as writing, "If a man is a cunning businessman and knows how to get the better of you in a bargain, he is called a Yankee" (p. 12). The Yankee business ethic stood in diametrical contrast to and threatened the social structures they were trying to formulate and establish in what was to them a New World.

The German American settlers developed a notion of government as active, rational, honest, and prudent. Beinart (2001) has argued that the German American political tradition

> is most evident in the nation's most German state, Wisconsin. In the early twentieth century, famed Governor Robert LaFollette employed social scientists at the University of Wisconsin to restructure the state's workmen's compensation and tax systems in accordance with "scientific" principles. As Michael Barone and Richard E. Cohen put it in the 2002 *The Almanac of American Politics*, "these programs were an attempt to bring bureaucratic rationality—Germanic systematization—to the seemingly disordered America." (http://www.thenewrepublic.com/punditry/beinart081301.html)

German immigrants had arrived in several waves that followed purges of liberals in their homeland, first in 1848 after the failure of the democratic revolution and again in 1878 following Bismarck's anti-Socialist law. Their status as liberal political exiles strongly influenced the evolving political culture of the Upper Midwest and its emphasis on government planning and reform. The German and Scandinavian desire for a pluralist, non-hierarchical society produced a number of political movements that centered on the role of the common person in democratic decision-making and the role, agency, and stature of the worker in the economy. These movements included:

- *The Farmers' Alliances*—These affiliated organizations worked on behalf of farmer welfare in the late 1800s. Their initiatives included the establishment of cooperatives and labor unions and helped to found the People's Party, also known as the Populists. Populists sought to establish cooperatives through which farmers' costs could be reduced, to create a national cooperative system, to nationalize or regulate monopolies, to institute a graduated income tax, to elect U.S. Senators through popular elections, and to limit the workday to 8 hours, an agenda largely written into law.

- *National Colored Alliance and the Colored Farmers National Alliance and Co-Operative Union*—Because the Farmers' Alliances were reserved for Whites only, these organizations were founded by African Americans to provide similar cooperative services for their members.
- *The National Grange of the Patrons of Husbandry*—This organization, launched just after the Civil War, advocated strongly for community involvement and for agricultural and rural issues.
- *The Progressive Politics of Hazen Pingree in Michigan and Robert "Fighting Bob" La Follette in Wisconsin*—Progressives in the early twentieth century worked to place government more directly in the hands of citizens and improve the lives of farmers, workers, children, and women. Their policies included initiatives to dismantle political machines. They also helped to institute unemployment compensation, social security, progressive income taxation, child labor laws, women's suffrage, and the regulation of the railroad and banking industries.
- *The Socialist Movement in Milwaukee*—Milwaukee elected Socialist party mayors through the 1950s. The city provided the breeding ground for the proliferation of labor unions.
- *Governor Floyd B. Olson's socialist Farmer-Labor party in Minnesota*—Following World War I, the Farm-Labor party advanced the notion of the "cooperative commonwealth," which sought to elevate the political influence of farmers (e.g., the Nonpartisan League), organized labor (e.g., the Minnesota State Federation of Labor), and small business (e.g., the Independent Bankers' Association).
- *The Anti-Monopoly and Greenback-Labor political parties*—These closely-related parties both emerged from the post-Civil War depression known as the Panic of 1873. Their platforms called for regulation of industry, protection of workers, proagriculture policies, and other labor-friendly laws.
- *Finnish American political groups and newspapers*—These organizations, following from Finnish immigration concentrated between 1895 and 1914, included the Finnish Social Federation, Finnish-language Workers Socialist Publishing Company in Duluth, Finnish Worker's Party, Finnish Co-op movement, and Finnish Communist Party. They also included socialist newspapers such as the *Worker* published in Hancock, Michigan, *Truth* published by the Scandinavian Socialists in Duluth, Minnesota, *Industrialisti* published in Duluth, and *Työmies* published by the Finnish-American Socialists in Superior, Wisconsin. These groups and publications furthered the causes of Finnish Americans such as creating better conditions and higher wages for miners,

providing credit for working class people, granting equal rights for women, creating solidarity, and uniting the proletariat.

- *Waldemar Ager*—Ager was a noted agitator for democratic liberalism, women's rights, and moral improvement in Wisconsin from the late 1800s through World War II.

These movements and individual leaders called for the empowerment of ordinary people in all areas of life and for the promotion of economic democracy. They emerged during the economic depression following the Civil War in concert with widespread immigration of people with a community-based orientation to social life. They were also spurred by the Industrial Revolution and expansion of monopolies during this period, and contributed to the movement against industrial capitalism in agriculture (Rothstein, 1988).

Although often interdependent and conflated in the minds of many, these efforts each claimed particular visions. Lasch (1969), for instance, identifies a number of distinctions between populism and socialism, including their reliance on different intellectual sources (for socialists, Europeans such as Marx and Lenin; for populists, U.S. thinkers such as Jefferson and Jackson); their different attitudes toward the ownership of land (for socialists, a commodity to be shared; for populists, a possession to be acquired); their different beliefs about industrialization (for socialists, an example of progress; for populists, an object of hatred); and their different beliefs about the process and degree of social change (for socialists, radical and fundamental; for populists, within

---

What is Character?

As we approach the third millennium of the Christian era, character isn't a priority with many teens. Try talking about character to your peers and you will see from their reactions how odd you look to them. That's not to say there aren't teens who don't put a premium on good character. I know there are others ... who dedicate themselves to living exemplary lives in an increasingly immoral world.

What qualifies as good character? Further, should it be important enough for you to shoot for it, especially if it sets you apart among your friends as a little strange? Here's the definition: Character is a distinctive trait, a pattern of behavior that shows moral strength, self-discipline and fortitude.

The character of a person is his inner makeup. Many young people don't think about character, good or bad. Younger people in our society would probably prefer this slogan: If what I want to do doesn't hurt someone else, then it's okay! Teens pick up on this outlook and adopt it as their own. But is this a good test for you or anyone else?

—Jerold Aust

existing political structures). Some movements were concerned with labor unions and their urban clientele, others with farmers and rural issues. Some supported temperance, others opposed it. But all stressed the value and dignity of the common person in relation to wealthy industrialists and the need for political power through organization.

We see the preponderance of such movements, tied to the values of the immigrants who initiated them, as contributing to the community-based nature of the character education proposals produced in this region. As we will relate, the initiatives sought to include a host of voices in the development of their programs, an effort consistent with these political movements' concern for the welfare and agency of workers, farmers, and other ordinary people in having a say in governance.

RELIGION

As Table 14.1 reveals, the two states profiled from the Upper Midwest are similar in religious makeup, with Catholics, Lutherans, and Methodists constituting the majority of Christian denominations in the states. We next review what we see as relevant tenets of these faiths as a way to understand the value systems that undergird the conceptions of character education developed by these states.

Although different in fundamental ways—in particular Catholicism's deliberate hierarchical structure as opposed to the Protestant view that all believers are part of the church's ministry, and the Methodists' more accepting view of homosexuals (if not homosexuality) than either the Catholics or Lutherans—the three dominant Christian faiths in these states share a compassion toward society's forsaken. Catholics have historically condemned the injustices of the economic and social conditions created by the industrial economy, on both the domestic and international levels, and have sought to remedy them through charitable works. Catholic women have often, for many generations, served as teachers, nurses, and social workers as part of this mission; the Web site of the Catholic women's Regis

TABLE 14.1

	State #1	State #2
Catholic	35%	18%
Lutheran	40%	30%
Methodist	9%	24%
Other Protestant	6%	13%
Baptist	5%	7%

College in Boston, for instance, refers to "our regular curriculum and the training of our students in the role of teachers, nurses, social workers as mandated reporters" (http://www.regiscollege.edu/ar/wn/wn03.html). The protection and promotion of basic human rights in the social, economic, and political spheres have been central to the Catholic faith.

John and Charles Wesley, founders of Methodism, stressed concern for the poor, appealing to working class Protestants who felt removed from the formality and rationalism of the Church of England. This emphasis on common people helped establish Methodism in the United States as a lay movement. The Methodist mission stems from Matthew 28:19–20 and includes the charge that "God has used our Church to save persons, heal relationships, transform social structures, and spread scriptural holiness, thereby changing the world." Methodists are advised to embrace an "Inclusiveness [which] means openness, acceptance, and support that enables all persons to participate in the life of the Church, the community, and the world. Thus, inclusiveness denies every semblance of discrimination." Adherents, according to the United Methodist Church (2000),

> recognize racism as sin and affirm the ultimate and temporal worth of all persons. We rejoice in the gifts that particular ethnic histories and cultures bring to our total life.
>
> We affirm women and men to be equal in every aspect of their common life. We therefore urge that every effort be made to eliminate sex-role stereotypes in activity and portrayal of family life. We affirm the right of women to equal treatment in employment, responsibility, promotion, and compensation. We affirm the importance of women in decision-making positions at all levels of Church life. (http://www.umc.org/faithinaction/)

The communities of faith that predominate in these Upper Midwestern states share key values. Whether as a primary emphasis or a consequence of devotion, all believe in the power of good works, particularly those designed to help the poor achieve basic human rights and a decent standard of living. For Catholics this emphasis comes through charity, for Protestants through the extension of the ministry and access to the Almighty for the most humble follower.

This emphasis on good works designed to elevate the station of society's least privileged and most abject members is evident in these states' character education initiatives. While including a discourse stream that suggests that the poor and marginalized are good candidates for character education and improvement, these initiatives see character education comprising an effort to elevate the whole community and create an environment more conducive to good citizenship by all. This elevation, according to these initiatives, must be achieved by extending access to political involvement to all citizens, not only its prominent stalwarts.

> *Akhlaaq (character) forms one of the most important aspects of Deen. Rasulullah (Sallallaahu Álayhi Wasallam) said, "A Muslim, by virtue of his excellent character, is elevated to the ranks of one who, throughout his life, spends the entire night in Ibaadat and fasts during the day."*
>
> *—Abu Dawood*

COOPERATIVE COMMUNITIES

While adapting to U.S. ways, the German and Scandinavian immigrants also imported and retained important aspects of their home cultures. They maintained their linguistic heritages and promoted their traditional cultures through church, education, and community functions. Home and family were important for survival among individual families, and religion, education, and community contributed to the survival of communities. For Germans settling in the Upper Midwest,

> Land was not just part of the physical environment but the very basis of Cosmology.... Land was seen as an insurance policy. In the days before mechanization, it could only be farmed successfully if you could rely on the cooperation of others. The household or "whole house" [Hoffuss] was the ideal vehicle for ensuring this. Only given this cooperation could the household survive over a number of generations and secure its members a definite place in the village. (Wilke & Wagner, 1981, p.126)

This observation suggests the cooperative nature of agrarian life in the Upper Midwest, both within and among families. Wilke and Wagner (1981) go on to discuss how seasonal farm work was accomplished through cooperation between cow and goat farmers, resulting in a *cooperation for survival* theme in the lives of German-American communities. These farmers relied on cooperation with one another in order to survive the vicissitudes of weather and economy. Their dependence on one another, along with their inclination to bond with fellow immigrants, contributed to a strong sense of community in these settlements. Miller (1992) observes that

> both German and Norwegian immigrants to Wisconsin shared similar history. They left a similar class structure in the Old World, viewed agriculture as a way of life, valued community and offered a similar critique of Yankee culture. They shared adaptation strategies to their new home. Both groups clung to their right to speak a language other than English, to promote traditional culture institutionally through churches, local public and parochial schools and public celebration. Each group maintained its traditional world views, community structure, and many old world traditions in spite of intermittent pressure to conform to "American" ways. (p. 8)

These descriptions suggest the importance of cooperative communities to those immigrants who settled in the Upper Midwest, especially when viewed in the context of the prolabor, profarmer emphasis of the political movements that found voice in this region. In order to gain political power against wealthy and what they believed to be predatory industrialists, they needed to work together for social and economic benefit.

We see clear distinctions between the agrarian cultures of the Upper Midwest and Deep South. In the Upper Midwest families owned their own farms and worked for both personal and community survival and prosperity. The South was ruled by more of a plantation social structure in which a small number of planters owned enormous tracts of land that relied on either forced labor through slavery or through sharecropping, which many consider to be a *de facto* slave system. Although other landowning possibilities existed in the South, the large landowners had the greatest financial and political influence on the evolving culture; whereas in the Upper Midwest, the small farmers and other laborers were able to organize into alliances, unions, and other associations that gave them political power. Such organizations are still rare in the South (http://www.newswise.com/articles/2001/12/LATCLASS.UAR.html).

The notion of cooperative communities appears compatible with the kind of character education initiative we found in the Upper Midwest. Rather than implementing the program through a hierarchical administrative structure as occurred in the Deep South, the upper midwestern states deliberately sought to involve the broadest, most inclusive range of citizens in the development of the program. Such involvement resulted in a multi-voiced effort that was responsive to the interests of a wide range of community members. As we will describe, this expansive effort also produced internal conflicts in the vision of character education developed by these states.

EDUCATION

The Ordinance of 1787, one of the three charters of Wisconsin, established that "religion, morality, and knowledge being necessary for good government and the happiness of mankind, schools and the means of education shall be forever encouraged." The Ordinances helped provide states in the Old Northwest territory with the basis for a strong educational tradition:

> *Every year, every [basketball] team faces adversity either with illness, or injury, or transferring or people just going through tough times where they lose their confidence and the team loses games that you don't think you should lose. Every team has to deal with that. We have talked about the fact that we have always shown great character when we have had to deal with adversity and this is another one of those situations where our character will be tested. We will find out who we are and what we are made of.*
>
> *—Gail Goestenkors*

The Upper Midwest has been distinguished by its support of education at all levels. The region took to heart the provisions of the Ordinances, underwriting education as a primary public goal. By 1890, vital public school systems throughout the countryside reached their climax in excellent state universities with relatively low fees and open access and with a tradition of public service. (Mondale, 1998, http://memory.loc.gov/ammem/umhtml/umessay8.html)

Rousmaniere (n. d.) corroborates this view that historically, education has been a high priority in the Upper Midwest. She maintains that

A commitment to the centrality of education has been a defining feature of Midwestern life for two centuries. Schools and colleges, along with places of worship, were the first institutions created in the European settlement of the Midwest. Its land-grant universities, among the country's most distinguished institutions of higher education, have nourished agricultural and industrial productivity as well as civic-mindedness. (http://www.allmidwest.org/encyclo/education/statement.html)

She continues, "Americans have historically believed social, economic, and political crises can be resolved to a large degree through the educational system," a faith realized through the development of strong public school systems throughout the Upper Midwest. Doudna (1948) argues that Wisconsin's early system of free public education served as the model for the national public school system. Iowa's excellent educational system has been credited for its achievement in 1897 of the nation's highest literacy rate of 99.5% (State Historical Society of Iowa, n. d.). Iowa further developed the Iowa Plan in the 1920s "which asserted various objectives, activities, and character traits to be emphasized" (Nickell & Field, 2001, p. 1). Among the first specific character education vehicles developed for U.S. schools, it was adopted by many states nationwide and was the recipient of awards for its exemplary efforts to shape character.

This historical emphasis on education as a means of social reform, especially in the areas of developing a civic-minded citizenry and a strong economy, is evident in the character education initiatives developed in states from the Upper Midwest. As we will review, these programs are based on the notion of building strong communities that model positive character traits.

SUMMARY

In this chapter we have reviewed what we see as key cultural factors that have helped to shape the regional identity of the Upper Midwest. As we did with

---

Ability may get you to the top, but it takes character to keep you there.

—Tracy Goosey

states from the Deep South, we have focused on the dominant culture, as determined by historical population trends and current population data. Dominant cultures, even those that endeavor to be inclusive, tend to control public institutions and the social practices that accompany them. Understanding the historical development of a region's dominant culture, then, can help to illuminate the social practices that emerge in new initiatives. As we hope to demonstrate, the democratic, communitarian values of the European immigrants who settled in the Upper Midwest more than 100 years ago have contributed strongly to the conception of character education that appears in the proposals of two states from this region for OERI character education funding.

Chapter 15

Ancillary Curricula of the Upper Midwest

The Upper Midwestern states identified ancillary curricula, programs, and government acts that they purchased or requested funding from in the development of their character education initiatives. We next review the programs identified in the proposals as having influence on their efforts. We organize these auxiliaries into the following categories: improving academics, preventing violence and substance abuse, building social and emotional skills, abetting employment, and promoting partnerships.

IMPROVING ACADEMICS

Given that improving academics was a required outcome of the character education programs, it is not surprising that the states from the Upper Midwest consulted sources designed to strengthen curriculum and academics. To help meet the OERI RFP's requirement for demonstrating a correlation between character education initiatives and greater academic achievement, these states drew on four programs to enhance students' performance on assessment measures: The United States' Goals 2000 program, the Improving America's Schools Act, Mid-Continent Research for Education and Learning (McREL) Dimensions of Learning (http://www.mcrel.org/services/dol.asp), and the Northern Trails Area Education Agency (http://www.aea2.k12.ia.us/)

> *The student of good character upholds principles of morality and ethics, is cooperative, demonstrates high standards of honesty and reliability, shows courtesy, concern, and respect for others, and generally maintains a good and clean lifestyle.*
>
> *—National Honor Society—James Lee Martin Chapter*

These programs are all designed to raise academic standards and help schools meet them. They employ a particular discourse and accompanying practices to do so. Goals 2000, for instance, speaks of high expectations and achievement results for all students through a results-focused comprehensive effort known as *standards-based education reform*. Its three overarching principles are:

- Students learn best when they, their teachers, administrators, and the community share clear and common expectations for education. States, districts, and schools need to agree on challenging content and performance standards that define what children should know and be able to do.
- Student achievement improves in environments that support learning to high expectations. The instructional system must support fulfillment of those expectations. School improvement efforts need to include broad parent and community involvement, school organization, coordinated resources—including educational technology, teacher preparation and professional development, curriculum and instruction, and assessments—all aligned to agreed upon standards.
- Student success stems from concentrating on results. Education systems must be designed to focus and report on progress in meeting the pre-set standards. Education reform needs to be results oriented through reliable and aligned means that answer the critical, bottom-line question: to what extent are students and schools meeting the standards? Continuous improvement requires carefully developed accountability systems for interpreting and responding to results and supporting improved student performance for all children.

Both McREL and the Northern Trails Area Education Agency provide programs to help schools get results that are aligned with educational standards, a feature of Goals 2000. McREL's Dimensions model is based on the premise that five types or dimensions of thinking underlie successful learning: developing attitudes and perceptions, acquiring and integrating knowledge, extending and refining knowledge, using knowledge meaningfully, and developing productive habits of mind. McREL regards the first and fifth dimensions as overarching the others. As explained at their Web site,

> all learning takes place against the backdrop of learners' attitudes and perceptions (Dimension 1) and their use (or lack of use) of productive habits of mind (Dimension 5). If students have negative attitudes and perceptions about learning, then they will likely learn little. If they have positive attitudes and perceptions, they will learn more and learning will be easier. Similarly, when students use productive habits of mind these habits facilitate their learning. Dimensions 1 and 5, then, are always factors in the learning process.

McREL consultants provide such services as reviewing standards and benchmarks for clarity, coherence, and content; aligning and translating curricula into sequenced standards and benchmarks; developing standards-based activities; doing staff development in designing performance standards and activities; and advising schools how to collect, analyze, and use assessment data. We see this service as a vehicle for aligning curriculum and instruction with national standards such as Goals 2000. The idea that attitudes, perceptions, and habits of mind are central to academic achievement seems consistent with character education's assumption that good character results in high achievement.

The Northern Trails Area Education Agency's mission is "to provide support and leadership to assist local school districts in helping each child learn to the maximum of his/her potential." Like Goals 2000 and McREL, the Northern Trails Area Education Agency is concerned with the identification of educational standards:

> clear targets for both teachers and students are articulated through standards, benchmarks, and indicators. The standards are what all students should know and be able to do upon graduation from a K–12 school district. The benchmarks describe what the standards look like at either a clustered level (K–2, 3–5, 6–8, 9–12) or a specific grade level. The indicators answer the question for teachers, "What does the benchmark look like at the classroom level?" Together, they encompass what is critical for all students to know and be able to do prior to leaving an educational system. (January 7, 2004, http://www.aea267.k12.ia.us/cia/currinstasssess/stand_ref/stand_ref.htm)

To ensure that high expectations are held for all, one of the states from the Upper Midwest consulted the Improving America's Schools Act, designed "to ensure that districts integrate these federal programs into a comprehensive whole to ensure success for all students." Through this program they accessed funds from Title I (helping disadvantaged youth meet high standards), Title II (Eisenhower Professional Development Program), Title III (technology for education), Title IV (Safe and Drug Free Schools), Title VI (innovative educational program strategies), and Title VII (bilingual education, language enhancement, and language acquisition programs).

From the standpoint of the OERI conception of character and character education, the identification of these standards, benchmarks, and indicators should help structure the curriculum so that students' achievement relative to standards may be defined and assessed. Three of the four programs invoke the notion of educational standards and benchmarks; that is, of structuring curriculum and instruction according to a scope and sequence designed to help students attain the competencies expected of them at each grade level. As one proposal said,

> *For seven births parents will be protected from the effects of demerits because of their children, who are of good character and who are free from vices.*
>
> *—Tiruvalluvar*

By promoting positive character development through an integration into district essential learnings and content standards and benchmarks, and through using curricular materials which invite ethical decision-making and complex reasoning skills, we will promote a wiser and more compassionate group of graduates.

The emphasis on helping students develop proper habits of mind as prerequisite to learning and using knowledge appears congenial to the idea that improvements in character can lead to greater academic achievement.

PREVENTING VIOLENCE AND SUBSTANCE ABUSE

As we have reviewed, much discourse surrounding character education concerns youth at-risk behaviors, particularly in terms of perceived increases in sex, drugs, and violence. This belief is realized in the purchase of a number of services designed to reduce such behaviors among students: the Safe and Drug Free Schools and Communities program (http://ojjdp.ncjrs.org/about/press/ojp990911.html), the Iowa Peace Institute (http://www.iapeace.org/), the Peninsula Conflict Resolution Center (http://www.pcrcweb.org/), and The Iowa Survey of Student Substance Use.

A common theme among these ancillary services is the building of social skills, self-esteem, and strategies for avoiding at-risk behaviors. The Safe and Drug Free Schools and Communities program, for instance, works with school districts to help children show self-control and resist violence and aggression in their interpersonal relationships. Their approach to violence prevention and healthy child development is, according to their literature, community-based, seeking to create a safe school environment by initiating substance abuse and violence prevention programs in conjunction with mental health interventions and social and emotional development programs. Their services, according to their Web site, focus on prevention rather than punishment.

The Iowa Peace Institute has a similar emphasis, attempting to teach skills that allow for negotiation rather than conflict to settle differences. The Peninsula Conflict Resolution Center seeks to provide conflict prevention, management, and resolution services and promotes the use of nonadversarial processes in a wide variety of situations. Consistent with the other approaches we have reviewed, their emphasis is on preventative skill and strategy development so that conflicts may be resolved peaceably. To determine the degree to which students engaged in substance abuse and vi-

> To achieve success in the field of spirituality, good character is essential. Good character can be spoken as having three aspects. The first aspect is best conveyed by the words sacredness, holiness and goodness. The second aspect is best described by the words tolerance, compassion and forbearance. And the third aspect is given by the words resolve, determination and commitment. Whatever education you have, however wealthy you may be, whatever position you may occupy, whether you are a great scholar or a statesman, if you do not have these three aspects of character, you are as good as dead. Whatever else you may have earned, without these three aspects of character, all your attainments and achievements will be worthless. People pay attention to external human beauty, but God recognizes only the inner beauty. Truly speaking, for human beings it is their sterling character which makes up their real beauty. A person devoid of good character is nothing but a stone. You have to follow these seven facets of dharma and let each one of them shine within you, for each one of them is completely natural to you.
>
> —Sai Baba Gita

olence, the Iowa Survey of Student Substance Use surveyed students on their degrees of at-risk behaviors and their perceptions of their peer, family, school, and neighborhood and community environments. This survey was employed, we assume, to gather data so as to assess the degree to which drugs and violence are a problem that may be addressed through the other interventions we have reviewed.

BUILDING SOCIAL AND EMOTIONAL SKILLS

These states also employed programs and interventions designed to help build strong senses of self among young people so that they may weather difficulties in socially responsible and acceptable ways. Such resources can then help young people use obstacles as opportunities for growth into wiser, more mature citizens, friends, and family members. Similar to the programs designed to prevent violence and substance abuse, these programs and interventions use a proactive approach to address the emotional makeup of young people so that they approach life in a healthy and productive manner. These sources include resiliency research, the W. T. Grant Foundation (http://smhp.psych.ucla.edu/lesson22.htm), and the Legacy 150 Institute (http://www.drake.edu/legacy150/index.html).

These programs and bodies of research are employed to provide students with the capacity to cultivate strengths to meet the challenges of life in a positive way. Resiliency research, for instance, helps people "bounce back" by building competence and avoiding negative stress, developing flexibility and learning to use adversity creatively, adapting to unexpected challenges, and developing constructive and healthy ways of interacting and responding. Resiliency interventions are designed to promote commitment, cohesion, adaptability, communication, spirituality, connectedness, time together, and efficacy among families and social groups. This goal is shared by the Legacy 150 Institute, which associates civility with character development and principled decision making in daily life. For those seeking a character curriculum based on these principles, the W. T. Grant Foundation provides curriculum content for enhancing social and emotional functioning, which in turn will presumably prevent and correct social and emotional problems. Their literature emphasizes prevention with children manifesting behavior problems, based on the premise that "the affective domain is critical to increasing student achievement."

Together, these sources help students to develop both strategies for bouncing back and for building the strength and competence to avoid negative stressors and face challenges as they arise. These strategies are developed in concert with values, attitudes, and behaviors that enable one to face challenges strategically. They fit well with the approach of student agency through social skills and tools to reduce and address stress and conflict that we found in programs designed to prevent violence and substance abuse.

ABETTING EMPLOYMENT

In these two states several government programs were called on to help young people make the transition from school to the workforce so that they may begin at the highest level of skill and salary available. These programs presumably help students develop responsibility and other traits that the OERI RFP identifies as necessary for character education so that they may be

---

Good character is a major quality we need in a chief executive. And it has long been so recognized. Thomas Jefferson paid tribute to George Washington's "perfect" character, noting especially his integrity, prudence, dignity, and sense of justice. Every presidential election in our history has contained references to the vital link between character and the White House. Character is what a person really is, at the deepest level. (Personality may or may not be an accurate reflection.) The concept has a venerable heritage, being discussed in the Old Testament, in Plato, Aristotle, Plutarch, Tacitus, the New Testament, the Renaissance, and the Enlightenment. Good character begins with integrity, defined as a "firm adherence to a code of especially moral values," values that are thought to be high and true. Good character begins with integrity. Is the person in question honest? And it includes such qualities as compassion, generosity, prudence, courage, loyalty, responsibility, temperance, humility, and perseverance.

—Thomas Reeves

more successful and productive workers in society and the economy. The programs include the 1982 Job Training Partnership Act, the 1994 School-to-Work Opportunities Act, and the 1999 Perkins Vocational and Technical Education Act.

These government programs are designed to aid the transition from school to the workforce, principally in blue-collar jobs though also through postsecondary education. They are largely targeted to working class or disadvantaged youth to help them find secure, skilled jobs in the workforce. The Job Training Partnership Act, for instance, established a federal program designed to provide states with job training for economically disadvantaged youth and adults, dislocated workers, and others with significant employment barriers to give them the skills necessary to participate in the labor market. The ultimate aim is for participants to achieve permanent self-sustaining employment. School-to-Work includes the feature of maintaining high academic standards through contextual, applied, and focused learning, with the goal of providing students with knowledge and skills that allow them to opt for college, additional training, or a well-paying job directly out of high school. High academic standards are also invoked in the Perkins Vocational and Technical Education Act, with an emphasis on vocational and technical education programs that promote the development of activities that integrate academic and vocational and technical instruction.

We see the possibility that through these states' reliance on such programs for character education, they view character as being realized in young people's honest and steadfast employment. We also see the possibility that they reproduce the social division of labor by stressing workplace readiness over continued education for students from low-SES backgrounds. Although high academic standards are invoked and higher education is among the options, the most likely destination for those enrolled in these programs is the blue collar workforce.

Podiatrists Board Certificate of Good Character

Applicants are required to supply: two Certificates of Good Character from people of good standing in the community who are NOT relatives of the applicant, and who have known the applicant for over one year.

Referee to complete form below:

I hereby certify that I have known (enter applicant's name) _____ for _____ (enter number of years).

Has this applicant had any criminal convictions? _____ (YES / NO)

Please comment on your knowledge of the applicant AND INCLUDE reference to the applicant's character, reputation and any other matters you consider relevant to their application for registration as a podiatrist.

PROMOTING CIVIC PARTNERSHIPS

As required by the OERI RFP, these states promised to develop partner-ships with community groups and businesses. The partnership consultants stress the role of doing community service as a way to demonstrate and en-courage good character among young people. We see here an emphasis on good citizenship through participation in community-benefiting activities that improve the lives of both those served and those serving. To do so these states consulted with Partners in Education, the Center on School, Family, and Community Partnerships (http://www.csos.jhu.edu/p2000/), the Iowa Summit, and Service Learning.

Each of these sources works to establish relationships between schools and communities and involve young people in good civic works. Partners in Education, for instance, was founded in the 1960s as the National School Volunteer Program and endeavors to improve opportunities for compre-hensive youth development through efforts to "increase the number, qual-ity, and scope of effective partnerships; increase the resources to support effective partnerships; increase awareness about the importance of partner-ships for promoting youth success; and promote the importance of effective partnerships to policymakers" (http://www.nwrel.org/partnerships/links). Similarly, the Iowa Summit aspires "To encourage local youth groups in Iowa to partner with at least one other community group to plan and carry out a community service or community improvement project and submit-ting a report at completion so other communities could replicate the pro-ject" (Iowa Commission on Volunteer Service [n.d.], http://www.volunteer iowa.org/promise.html). These projects might include selling food at a farmer's market and contributing proceeds to a food bank, cleaning up trash around the community, caring for a garden at a nursing home, build-ing or repairing benches or picnic tables at a park or nursing home, partici-pating in sportsmanship programs through Boys and Girls Athletic Associations, and getting involved in other good works.

Such projects might become the research focus of the Center on School, Family, and Community Partnerships at Johns Hopkins University, con-sulted by these states and established "to conduct and disseminate research, development, and policy analyses that produce new and useful knowledge and practices that help families, educators, and members of communities work together to improve schools, strengthen families, and enhance stu-dent learning and development." Given that their research is conducted collaboratively with the Center for Research on the Education of Students Placed at Risk, also at Johns Hopkins University, we might assume that these partnerships are designed especially to help youth from disadvan-taged homes to form bonds with the community as a way to create networks for employment and affirmational communities of practice.

Such an emphasis appears to inform the work of the Iowa Summit, funded by The Presidents' Summit for America's Future and based on five basic resources that all young people need to reach their potential: an ongoing relationship with a caring adult, safe places and structured activities in nonschool hours, a healthy start, a marketable skill through an effective education, and an opportunity to give back through community service. Similarly, service learning emphasizes community–school relationships, seeking to meet the needs of the community, foster a sense of civic responsibility and concern for social problems, develop civic and cultural literacy, and enhance personal growth and self-esteem. Ideally, a service learning experience benefits both the community and the students, potentially developing workplace skills and establishing career networks to facilitate postgraduation employment. Service learning is more than simple community service:

> It links "doing" with knowing, thinking, and acting as a citizen. Service learning which is tied to the curriculum enables students to see the connection between working in a soup kitchen and larger issues such as poverty and homelessness and how communities deal with those problems in light of other competing social needs. Service learning enables students to evaluate proposed policy changes that might alleviate the problems. It also should help students learn how to advocate for changes they think will be most beneficial. (Branson, 2000, http://www.civiced.org/articles_mb_june00.html)

We see these partnerships as consistent with other aspects of both the ancillary programs and curricula and the discourses as a whole. The approach is community based and proactive, seeking to build both self-esteem and personal connections that will help students see the value of civic contributions and ultimately become contributing members of their communities. The partnerships appear to be geared toward those without preexisting social and employment networks: disadvantaged and at-risk youth. With the vocational emphasis, the programs run the risk of perpetuating social class distinctions by shepherding economically disadvantaged youth toward blue collar jobs rather than higher education.

SUMMARY

One distinct difference between the states from the Deep South and those from the Upper Midwest, in terms of the ancillary services and curricula

---

Good character increases life span so much so that if in the company of a Jew, then also behave nicely.

—Mustadrak

they consulted, is in terms of the emphasis. The states from the Deep South tended to purchase the curricula themselves, whereas the states from the Upper Midwest tended to purchase programs that provided either the infrastructure for aspects of character education (e.g., the employment vehicles and partnerships) or services to promote human development, particularly as it pertains to developing and maintaining relationships. We see the services consulted by the states from the Deep South working centripetally—that is, designed to instill character by impressing a conception of character from without. In contrast the states from the Upper Midwest appeared to work centrifugally, working to establish strategies so that prosocial behaviors would emerge from within.

We also see the upper midwestern states using these ancillary curricula, programs, and services to promote civic involvement and encourage students to become contributing members of their communities. The emphasis is on the individual as a member of an interdependent, cooperative citizenry rather than an individual whose character can contribute to an orderly society, as is institutionalized in the southern states' character education proposals.

Character is built out of circumstances. From exactly the same materials one man builds palaces, while another builds hovels.

—G. H. Lewis

Chapter 16

The Discourses of the Upper Midwest's Conception of Character Education

One state from the Upper Midwest invoked a range of discourses in describing its primary goals for character education:

Helping children develop to their full potential as citizens is an important priority of families, communities, and schools [*citizenship*]. Developing citizenship means becoming a productive [*Protestant work ethic*], responsible [*student agency*], caring [*relationships*], and contributing member of society [*citizenship*]. It includes:

- Being successful in school [*academic achievement*]
- Making responsible decisions [*student agency*]
- Caring about others [*relationships*]
- Contributing to society [*citizenship*]
- Developing social and personal skills, such as problem solving, accepting a variety of perspectives, and setting and attaining goals [*student agency*]
- Developing a core set of common values [*moral absoluteness*]

The proposal further describes its state's approach as being "about common sense in education—enhancing the total development of children: academic, social, physical, and emotional." If "common sense" is a cultural construction rather than general wisdom (Smagorinsky, Cook, & Reed, 2005), then whatever sense may be attributed to the Upper Midwestern conception of character education is, we would argue, a function of cultural practices specific to the region rather than of a universal sense free of ideology. In some parts of the world, for instance, there is little or no formal academic preparation for children, thus making academic achievement a goal

> A good character is the best tombstone. Those who loved you and were helped by you will remember you when forget-me-nots have withered. Carve your name on hearts, not on marble.
>
> —Charles Haddon Spurgeon

particular to industrialized nations. However people may articulate their conception of character, then, is a function of how they have learned to view the world. Their perspective thus normalized, they then view their own sense as having common application.

We next describe how these states conceptualized character in the proposals submitted to OERI.

IN DIALOGUE WITH THE OERI RFP

Both proposals from states from the Upper Midwest included the elements required by the RFP: the six mandatory aspects of character, partnerships with Local Educational Agencies (LEAs), a clearinghouse for distributing materials and information about character education, and an evaluation designed to determine the success toward reducing discipline problems, improving student grades, increasing participation in extracurricular activities, and raising parent and community involvement. How they went about achieving these ends was quite different from the method proposed by states from the Deep South.

Furthermore, at times the proposals exhibited a strain between following the RFP's requirements and instituting a reflective approach that involved local decision making based on Deweyan principles of local, experience-based learning. We found other tensions as well between the general Deweyan focus and other forces at work in the articulation of the character curriculum. We next review more specifically how the states from

> It is an honor to meet [Miss America 2001 Angela Perez Baraquio] and to have her support in promoting character education in our schools. Ms. Baraquio and I share the belief that emphasizing respect, responsibility, integrity and good citizenship will make our schools safer and more productive while preparing our students to become good citizens. Character education works because it teaches our children to view the world through a moral lens. Character counts in life, and it counts in our schools as well. I am pleased that Ms. Baraquio is promoting this important initiative, and with her high profile support hope Congress will pass my character education legislation this year.
>
> —U.S. Rep. Bob Etheridge (D-Lillington, NC)

the Upper Midwest characterized character education in their proposals in terms of the discourses we identified in their requests for OERI funds.

DISCOURSES COMMON TO BOTH APPROACHES

Academic Achievement

As required by the OERI RFP, both states from the Upper Midwest promised that students' academic achievement would be enhanced as a consequence of their character education initiatives. As one state's proposal said, among their goals is to "keep us evaluating and designing a more informed approach to increasing student achievement through student engagement and climate/culture issues." Increased achievement in this state's conception was, consistent with other aspects of the program, linked to factors in the environment rather than to attributes of individual students. Toward this end they identified a focus on "the vision of developing a caring community for all learners thereby increasing student achievement through student engagement and a positive school culture and climate undergirded by a strong evaluation component to guide the next steps toward the vision." This environment included both high expectations for behavior and academics and strong role models among the adults in the community:

> Students are expected to do their best and experience success. All students and staff are expected to model positive behaviors that embody good citizenship. For students to make the most of their potential, the adults who surround them at home and at school must encourage and expect achievement. Clear expectations for behavior and performance provide students with a picture of the kind of person they and their families want them to be. Having that vision reinforced over and over by teachers and caregivers becomes a self-fulfilling prophesy that helps children overcome difficulties and challenges. Likewise, adults in the school setting should be expected to do their best and model appropriate behaviors. High expectations for youth and adults help everyone in school strive to create an ideal that promotes the best in each person.

Here the discourse of academic achievement is linked to other discourses, particularly citizenship but also including relationships, suggesting a relation among these qualities. A good citizen is one who contributes to the greater good through high achievement and acting with care toward fellow community members. As stated in the other state's proposal, a chief objective was to "Continue to link funding streams in order to capitalize on the synergistic effect of connecting all school improvement efforts into a systemic whole and to promote the connections between positive character development and the achievement of high academic success for all learners," a goal that many might find to be painfully expressed in the jargon of educationese.

The authors of this proposal claimed to have found an empirical link between character and achievement:

> There is a direct correlation between the development of positive character traits (which are often conceptualized by the educational community as "essential learning" or what we want students to be able to know, do, and be like when they graduate; by business, industry, and professional community as "work force readiness skills" which allow them to be meaningful contributors to the effectiveness of the work place; by the faith community as "core values" which define what it means to be fully human; and by parents as simply "being a good kid") and academic achievement. Recent findings from the cognitive sciences and brain research point to the importance of linking positive character development and academic achievement. By promoting positive character development through an integration into district essential learnings and content standards and benchmarks, and through using curricular materials which invite ethical decision-making and complex reasoning skills, we will promote a wiser and more compassionate group of graduates.

The correlation appears to be inferred rather than empirically demonstrated. No references were provided to support this claim, whereas other claims in the proposal were indexed to citations from scholarship. Consistent with the proposals from the Deep South, those from the Upper Midwest made claims of correlations between character improvement and academic achievement without providing any supporting evidence.

One significant aspect of this account of academic achievement is the reference to the importance of benchmarks and standards, as would be expected from this state's reliance on McREL to help them link their character education initiative to a curricular structure based on external criteria for achievement; we review this influence in chapter 15. The discourse was thus linked to a concrete effort to establish levels and measures of performance that helped determine the effectiveness of the program. We see this emphasis as being in conflict with the view of many progressive educators (e.g., Giroux, 1988) that such highly structured curricula are inflexible and insensitive to the developmental needs of individual students, instead serving to superimpose one schedule and line of progression on all students. The student-oriented discourse of student agency, central to the Deweyan vision generally found within this discourse, thus appears to be in opposition to the curriculum and assessment structure that governs the character intervention.

As we will point out often throughout our discussion of the conceptions of the proposals from the Upper Midwest, there are a number of contradictions in the program that suggest the development of a pseudoconcept for the notion of character, rather than a clear concept. The reasons ap-

> *Now with Osama bin Laden calling once again for suicide attacks on the United States and our friends, it seems clear that the root of anti-American hatred in the world is fundamentalist Islam. We must confront this threat sooner rather than later. Waiting will only allow them to attack us in their time, rather than ours. If we are doomed to be at odds with them, we might as well handle the problem as we are now, rather than wait for them to blow up our hospitals and bridges here in our country. Fortunately, we have a president with the character to handle a distasteful chore when it is necessary. I know that the world has noticed that he said he would and then he did. Next time he talks, the bad guys will know he is serious.*
>
> *—Ron Tallon (letter to the Atlanta Journal-Constitution)*

pear to be twofold. First, the upper Midwestern conception of character is at odds with the formulation required by the OERI RFP, thus requiring Procrustean contortions to get funded while retaining a progressive vision. Second, the various stakeholders in the process appear to have diverse values and priorities, resulting in the inclusion of programmatic elements that are at odds with one another. Although we can only speculate, we infer that the planners of the upper midwestern proposals included both Deweyan visionaries and curriculum development experts who worked in the tradition of Tyler (1949), who emphasizes linkages among objectives, assessment, curriculum, and instruction so as to provide a coherent overall structure to students' experiences in school. As a result, the proposal includes both specific structures to promote and measure uniform achievement and a view that each student will construct the curriculum in personally meaningful ways.

Moral Absoluteness

In compliance with the OERI RFP, each state identified a set of core values central to their character education initiatives. "Good citizens," said one, "can be counted on to consistently demonstrate honesty, respect, courage, and other core citizenship values in everyday life." The other state wove its essential traits into a set of broader characteristics that it hoped to encourage in students:

[T]he elements of character are incorporated in the student outcomes or essential learnings:

- Effective Communicator—caring, justice, respect, responsibility, trustworthiness
- Collaborative Worker—civility, virtue/citizenship, respect, responsibility, trustworthiness

- Effective Problem Solver—justice, respect, fairness, responsibility, trustworthiness
- All linked with the individual school/community content standards in Math and Literacy

By instilling these traits in young people, claimed the proposal, school systems could achieve the broader goal required by the OERI RFP, an increase in academic achievement.

These values within the discourse of moral absoluteness appear to be in conflict with the discourses of local control and community that also permeated the proposals. While asserting the existence of core values, these states also declared that the virtues that drive their character education programs will be defined "by staff and students alike and set the standard for acceptable behavior" and by "community members from all ethnic, cultural, religious, socioeconomic, and other groups." While rhetorically sharing the assumption that there are core, invariant, universal values comprising six character traits, one proposal also said that "Students, staff, and family/community members model core values—all three are equally responsible for exhibiting character and should feel ownership for core values (i.e., not superimposed by any one group)." This state's notion of a core value, then, appears to straddle the fence: On the one hand, the authors state agreement with the invariant Six Pillars of Character that transcend culture, nationality, race, gender, creed, and ethnicity written into the OERI RFP. On the other hand, they endorse the idea that the values are core to the community, rather than to humankind, and are determined through a bottom-up process of discussion and consensus.

We see in this contradiction what we might call the discourse of grantsmanship: These states understood the imperative to write in dialogue with the OERI RFP and its funding criteria, even when those requirements went against their core assumptions about character, community, agency, diversity, and so on. As a result the proposals submitted by these states included inherent contradictions over the nature and origins of character, suggesting the Procrustean effect of the OERI RFP on states from the Upper Midwest.

The Protestant Work Ethic

The idea of productivity ran throughout the proposals we reviewed, a key facet of the discourse of the Protestant work ethic. One proposal asserted

> *When we see men of a contrary character, we should turn inwards and examine ourselves.*
>
> *—Confucius*

that "From civic education to teen pregnancy reduction, there is a common belief of what we as a society want our children to know and be able to do. It is common ground that defines citizens as productive, responsible, caring, and contributing individuals." One sees a hint of the discourse of youth depravity in this statement—those who are productive, etc. will presumably be too busy or less inclined to engage in premarital sex. We did not include the discourse of youth depravity within the discourses of Upper Midwestern states because adults were identified as being prone to the same temptations and behaviors as youth and were provided with counseling services to address problems in their own lives. The inclusion of adults as potentially in need of character improvement suggests a broader attention to health issues, recognizing that violence and other at-risk behaviors are exhibited by young and old alike. While adults are encouraged to model positive character, they are not offered as the sole, authoritative model for young people to emulate.

The proposals assert that instilling a work ethic in young people will contribute to a happier workforce: "Children who grow up to be productive and contributing citizens are much more than academically successful. The world of work requires individuals who are capable of managing their own health and well-being, and who have the skills necessary for problem-solving, self-direction, self-motivation, self-reflection, and life-long learning."

The notion of productivity revealed here is tied to other discourses found in these proposals: academic achievement (a necessary but not sufficient condition for productive citizens), citizenship as a consequence of the contributions that accrue from a sound work ethic, and student agency re-

---

"To seek perfection of character!" That line is chanted at the end of many karate classes as the first and foremost rule of karate training. It is the first line of the Dojo Kun *(the karate school oath), as translated by someone in karate's auspicious past. When you open your copy of* Nakayama's Best Karate Volume 1, *you read the following, "Gichin Funakoshi, a great master of Karate-do, pointed out repeatedly that the first purpose in pursuing this art is the nurturing of a sublime spirit, the spirit of humility." Look inside* Dynamic Karate, *also by Nakayama, and you find this, "... the ultimate goal of karate should be the attainment of a developed moral character built through hard and diligent training." Today, the idea that the purpose of karate training is to perfect the character of the participants is widely accepted amongst Shotokan participants as dogma. The commonly believed principle is that through hard work and humbling experiences (humiliation), the karate novice becomes a better human being than he previously was. It is also widely believed that a karate expert has as his personal purpose for his karate training the goal of becoming a better human being.* http://www.24fightingchickens.com/shotokan/mu/perfectcharacter/index.html

sulting from the competence achieved through hard work. Keeping individual noses to the grindstone will ennoble both the person who adopts productive work habits and the greater community who will benefit from each person's contributions to society.

Family First

The discourse of family first provided another contradiction within the proposals from the Upper Midwest, coming in conflict with the discourse of community. One proposal claimed that "Schools are places where these qualities [of character], ideally first taught in the home, can and should be promoted with the support and involvement of the family and community." These states, while recognizing the role of the family, elaborated their proposals to suggest that it takes a village to raise a child. This same state claims elsewhere, for instance, that the school should "Be a resource to families in establishing home environments to support children as students and citizens."

We see ambivalence in their claim that the home is the first teacher of morality. The home is viewed as likely to be inadequate to the task of raising good students and citizens; the school and community are thus invested with the paternalistic role of helping families with this complex task. One proposal claimed that

> Forty-eight percent of Americans believe that people need support from their local communities, beyond their immediate families, to help raise their children. Community efforts to strengthen parental involvement can have far-reaching benefits. This underscores the importance of educators seeking ways to continually engage the community.

So, although the family is the first teacher of character, it is part of an extended community that participates in the raising of children—the *village* of the proverb endorsed by Hillary Rodham Clinton and rejected by Bob Dole.

This vision is articulated in this proposal author's belief that a character education initiative should address societal issues:

> The school is the one institution other than the family that has consistent contact with all children. However, some children are challenged by life issues such as violence, AIDS, teen pregnancy, and AOD [Alcohol and Other Drugs]. Schools, in partnership with families and communities, must help children develop the knowledge, attitudes, and skills they need to make responsible decisions about these behaviors. Children who are dealing with such challenges are simply too preoccupied or distracted to do their best in school.

The other state made a similar declaration:

> The development of positive character traits in young people is a responsibility of the family as first and most important teachers, the schools as a safe

and positive place for young people to grow to their utmost potential, and the community where young people are given opportunities to see positive character traits modeled by the adults, and meaningful opportunities to participate in the life of the community.

The states from the Upper Midwest, consistent with their communitarian approach, see the family as the most important among their youth's moral teachers, but one among many resources that both young people and their families may rely on for support and guidance. Absent from this conflict is the southern states' implication of youth depravity in the moral mix. In general, young people in the proposals from the Upper Midwest are not regarded as the mean, nasty, brutish, selfish, cruel, and mean-spirited creatures in need of adult moral guidance described by Headmaster Reverend William F. Washington Jarvis of Boston's Roxbury Latin School. Rather, they are members of a broader community of flawed but earnest citizens who share responsibility for the outcome of all children raised within its social borders. Although the family is the first teacher of morals, the community also shares responsibility for children's collective upbringing. The line between parental prerogative and community intervention, however, remains unclear as articulated in these proposals. Like the proposals from the Deep South, the proposals from the Upper Midwest are ambivalent on the respective roles of families and communities in raising children. The southern proposals appear to be clearer on when the state should intervene with a character curriculum: when *their* homes are not providing the moral guidance that *ours* do. The upper midwestern proposals provide no such distinction, making it unclear when a family cedes it moral authority to the state.

Class-Based Morality

The discourse of class-based morality was subtle in the proposals from the Upper Midwest yet present nonetheless. Among the class distinctions we inferred from their documents was their reliance on reports on discipline problems, participation in extracurricular activities, and parental and community involvement as assessment measures for the success of the character intervention. As Eckert (1989) argues, students from "burnout" culture tend to view the school as tangential to their financial, emotional, and social needs and tend to resist its efforts to socialize them into middle

> *Be more concerned with your character than your reputation, because your character is what you really are, while your reputation is merely what others think you are.*
>
> —*John Wooden*

class norms. They are more likely to engage in behaviors (e.g., smoking) that may result in disciplinary measures, less likely to participate in extracurricular activities, and less likely to have parents who view school as a place that welcomes their involvement. As a result, students from such families and backgrounds are more likely to be viewed as deficient in character according to these measures.

Minorities and Limited English Proficiency populations were also targeted for some aspects of the character education initiatives, again suggesting that those from such backgrounds would perform better in school if their character were improved. This discourse was tempered by other aspects of the programs, which clearly identified adults from all segments of the population as both worthy participants in the initiative and potentially at risk themselves to the range of vulnerabilities faced by young people. The presence of the discourse of class-based morality, then, provided another internal contradiction, particularly relative to the discourse of community. On the one hand, young people from working class and racial or linguistic minorities are less likely to participate in school activities and so are more likely to be measured as lacking character in the program assessment. On the other, the community is a place of social justice and equality for all citizens and a nurturing extended family that extends caring relationships to all within its range.

Logical Positivism

The discourse of logical positivism was a minor stream in the proposals from the Upper Midwest, primarily in the area of assessment. One state used numerical trends on grades, discipline problems, and so forth to measure the effects of the programs. As we have noted, these measures likely reinforced impressions that those most in need of character education are from socially marginalized populations. This discourse was offset by the abundance of other data sources such as action research teams within schools, which we will review in chapter 17. Again we see the possibility of the discourse of grantsmanship in the employment of statistical indexes of change, given the federal government's beliefs about the superior validity of quantitative, preferably experimental research in such arenas as reading research.

> *Every age, every culture, every custom and tradition has its own character, its own weakness and its own strength, its beauties and cruelties; it accepts certain sufferings as matters of course, puts up patiently with certain evils. Human life is reduced to real suffering, to hell, only when two ages, two cultures and religions overlap.*
>
> *—Hermann Hesse*

> *Character is the combination of moral qualities by which a person is judged apart from intellect and talent. Or to put it in other words, it is the alignment of one's speech and actions with one's core beliefs about reality, life and truth. More simply, character has to do with one's demonstration of virtue.*
>
> *In the challenging arena of organizational change, one's character is quickly revealed. In this arena, leaders with solid character are greatly needed. Their character helps to set the definition of how people will be treated in the collaborative work of the organization. Their character also helps to set the moral and ethical boundaries of the enterprise and its activities.*
>
> *Character development is not a mystical transformation that somehow occurs during childhood and adolescence. It is rather an intentional choice of behavioral alignment to one's core beliefs while in the midst of stressful or demanding circumstances. As one's leadership responsibilities broaden, there must be a revisiting of what one believes about reality, life and truth and how those beliefs must shape one's speech and actions. For any leader, but especially for those who lead in significant organizational change, character development must be a lifetime endeavor.*
>
> *—John Hawkins*

DISCOURSES PARTICULAR TO THE UPPER MIDWEST

Citizenship

One proposal from the Upper Midwest included the belief that "Like Thomas Jefferson, John Dewey's main concern was our democratic way of life, and like Jefferson, he also understood the central role that public education must play if the republic is to remain vital, dynamic, and healthy." The ideas of John Dewey appeared on several occasions in the proposals from the Upper Midwest, though never in those from the Deep South. Dewey's progressivism is regarded as odious in the authoritarian conception of character education found in the Deep South yet compatible with the communitarian approach embodied in the proposals from the Upper Midwest. Dewey's precept that "What the best and wisest parent wants for his or her child, that must be what the whole community wants for all its children. Any other ideal for our schools is narrow and unloving, and acted upon, it destroys our democracy," quoted in one proposal, embodies the belief that character and character education are the domain of the community. (We should note that Dewey (1900) is misquoted here; he actually said, "What the best and wisest parent wants for his own child, that must the community want for all its children. Any other ideal for our schools is narrow and unlovely; acted upon, it destroys our democracy" (p. 3).

The notion of citizenship is not restricted to those in school, but projects a more equitable society when today's youngsters become tomorrow's role models. One proposal stated that

> The call to citizenship is not solely identifying what we don't want young people to do but clearly understanding the kind of people we would like them to become. It is a mission of youth development that engages them in meeting their basic personal and social needs to be safe, feel cared for, be valued, be useful, and be spiritually grounded. Through positive experiences, youth build assets and competencies that allow them to function and contribute in their daily lives. ... Time will pass, and youth will grow into adults regardless of the support they receive. The question is what kind of adults they will become. Positive youth development occurs when adults deliberately create conditions and opportunities for youth to become caring, contributing, productive, and responsible citizens.

This emphasis on community extends the program's goals to all stakeholders. One state argued that schools should "support school employees who may be dealing with similar issues in their own lives through an Employee Assistance Program."

Again, the discourse of citizenship was associated with other discourses: student agency (youth build assets and competencies), relationships (youth become caring and contributing), and Protestant work ethic (youth become productive). All of these discourses contribute to an overall emphasis on the communitarian approach to character education found in the states from the Upper Midwest that at times was contradicted by such discourses as the class-based morality.

Community

Operating on a more local social level than the discourse of citizenship, the discourse of community stresses the need for citizens to contribute to the climate that makes up life in their immediate social and geographical range of relationships. Said one proposal,

> *Character is the aggregate of features and traits that form the individual nature of a person, especially related to ethical or moral values. They make up the inner nature of a person and usually refer to positive qualities. A person with negative, unethical, or slothful attitudes is considered without character. There are a number of unwritten laws or rules that suggest things to do to have good character. Having good character will help establish a reputation of being a person who can be trusted and counted on.*
>
> *—Ron Kurtus*

formal curriculum is not the end but the means to a larger, more important end. Education must seek to help students integrate the knowledge they gain into a coherent vision; help students envision an adult life where they are full, contributing members of a community and society; and help students acquire values and skills that provide leadership and service.

Furthermore, "the overriding vision of a caring community is matched with the philosophy of enhancing student engagement and climate/culture issues in order to increase academic achievement."

The discourse of community included attention to issues of a positive school climate, including safety, mutual care, orderliness, virtue, partnerships, and local control. One proposal referred to the need for family and community involvement in the character education effort: "The contributions of all who make up the school community are honored and celebrated. Parents, caregivers, and community members have a variety of opportunities to make meaningful contributions to school programming and student citizenship development."

A safe and orderly community of character, argue the proposals, will help students perform better academically. One proposal maintained that

> All quality educational programs are built on strong philosophical and theoretical foundations. In designing [the state's] Character Education Initiative three years ago, we built it on a sound academic program based on what we know about expectations for the content of student learning, how students learn, and how teachers can best stimulate that learning. We grounded our approach in our collective knowledge, beliefs, values, and assumptions about teaching and learning leading to a coherent curriculum and authentic teaching that enhances students' ability to achieve. All of this effort to increase student performance is predicated on creating a climate and culture in our schools and communities which exemplifies the tenets character education is designed to promote.

The discourse of community regards values as local and situated. This postulation is different from the authoritarian, universalist premises held by the southern states and institutionalized in the OERI RFP, again creating conflicts between the upper midwestern states' simultaneous needs to write a fundable grant and produce a coherent notion of character. The relativism of the upper midwestern proposal is suggested through one state superintendent of education's recommendation to "Use the [citizenship] tool kit as a resource to help you shape your own efforts. There is no one prescription that fits all communities, but we can all learn from each other, starting in our own communities." One state solicited input from diverse constituents through "community forums to develop a list of character traits for their community."

Presumably this bottom-up approach would lead to the identification of traits representing the interests and values of the community's diverse constituents, rather than universal traits that transcend such cultural variation. The issue of moral relativity is antithetical to the approach taken by the states from the Deep South and their faith in authoritarian social hierarchies. Yet relativity is acknowledged as inevitable in the sort of bottom-up approach found in the Upper Midwest. One state argued that their results and conclusions

> would be very difficult to replicate in schools outside the pilot project because of the lack of a strong value and belief system around teaching and learning. This is a very simple statement and yet the complexities of implementation boggle the mind. Therefore, it is our intent in this part of the dissemination-clearinghouse proposal to incorporate training that looks at values and beliefs followed by incorporation of unit plans that are driven by measurable student outcomes.

This state explicitly distances itself from the claims of replicability that were made by the southern states. Rather, the authors view each community as unique and likely to identify different problems and solutions in its development of a character curriculum. This statement also suggests a different notion of dissemination than that found in the southern profile. In the Deep South dissemination fit with the discourse of the authoritarian society in which powerful people in decision-making positions hand down an effective, replicable way to teach character. In the Upper Midwest what is disseminated is the idea that each school has unique values and beliefs that make replication of any particular program unlikely.

Another facet of the discourse of community comes in these states' desire for school to become a safe and orderly place for all to gather, a haven from the depravity that is available elsewhere: "Students and staff feel respected, and the climate and culture of the school is drug free and safe from any form of violence. Children and adults learn constructive ways to settle differences, and peaceful conflict resolution is the norm." Student agency will help young people resist and bounce back from the negative influences of society and become contributing members of a positive school community. The community has an obligation to help provide both the climate and the coping skills students need to negotiate the vicissitudes of childhood and adolescence: "Policies should include supportive alternatives to help children overcome personal and academic difficulties. Behaviors that threaten the safety of students and staff call for a zero-tolerance approach." Adults should "Continually ask students if they feel that school is a safe place for them," keeping in mind that "Emotional safety is as important as physical safety." If students do not feel safe, all members of the school community should work to adjust the environment so that it provides an appropriate shelter for positive growth.

As is common throughout these proposals, each discourse is implicated in others to produce a generally unified, though inevitably contradictory conception of character education. One state from the Upper Midwest, for instance, argued that

> This country is based on some basic beliefs of democracy [*citizenship*] that include a society where its members care about one another [*relationships*], contribute to the common good [*community*], and participate in sustaining a democratic way of life [*citizenship*]. To be productive citizens in America [*Protestant work ethic*], students need to recognize individual differences [*diversity*]; acknowledge common bonds [*relationships*]; and demonstrate skills related to diversity, inclusiveness, and fairness [*diversity*].

This ideology produced paradoxical proposals that argued for a bottom-up, communitarian conception of character while also asserting contradictory claims about moral absolutism and class-based morality.

Diversity

In the discourse of diversity, a community claims a dedication to including as many of its various constituents as possible in the definition of character and formulation of a character curriculum. Explicit attention to historically marginalized groups was provided in the proposals, as in the following:

> Diversity exists in various forms including but not limited to race/ethnicity, culture, talent, ability and disability, sex/gender, sexual orientations, age, religion, language, socioeconomic status, and learning styles. Inclusiveness involves providing social and economic access to everyone, understanding and appreciating all individuals and groups, learning about the contributions of diverse cultures and times, and developing skills that foster communication. Fairness requires actively challenging prejudice, stereotyping, bias, hatred, and discrimination to ensure a social climate free of favoritism or bias and impartiality and equity to all parties.

These states thus hoped to "Create school environments that reflect and honor the cultural traditions of all people" and "develop a variety of teaching strategies to meet the diverse needs of students" so that "Students will see and experience their own and others' cultures, contributions, and tradi-

---

The Green Party said the Government has set a dangerous precedent in declaring companies involved in whaling to be "of good character" under the 1996 Fisheries Act.

"This will seriously limit our ability to apply the 'good character' test to other companies wanting exemption from our laws and will open the door for companies involved in unsustainable fishing practices to hold New Zealand quota," said [Jeanette Fitzsimons, Green Party Co-Leader, New Zealand].

tions; Staff will support diverse students and families, employ culturally relevant and fair instructional practices; Families and community will honor the cultural traditions and contributions of all groups."

Among the goals of including diverse groups in the character initiative is to ensure social equality:

> We believe the very nature of this Character Education Pilot Project addresses the precursors of discrimination. Research in the field of prejudice has found that children learn prejudice in two basic ways: by adopting the prejudices of their parents, and by absorbing the lessons of the larger cultural environment when that environment fosters suspicion, fear, and hatred of specific groups of people (Allport, 1982). This proposal concentrates on creating a school/community climate that discourages biased acts of any kind and fosters a valuing of diversity that character education qualities exemplify. We believe the results of this Character Education Learning Community Model will show the impact of this new social norm.

We see a contrast between the upper midwestern states' approach to diversity and the southern states' embracing of middle class norms and hieratic positioning of *we*—the upper and middle classes who control the rhetoric and resources of character education—and *they*, the social groups on the margins of that culture whose behavior is the target of a character intervention. We also see the Upper Midwest's embrace of the broadest possible definition of diversity as embodying the sort of relativism rejected by the states from the Deep South.

One state's diversity effort included "an extensive diversity procedure ... in rural and urban [parts of the state] that pays attention to schools/communities that serve minorities, Native Americans, students of limited English proficiency, and disadvantaged students." We see in this effort the implication of the discourse of class-based morality, with specific attention to minority and LEP students for character education. This attention is balanced by such efforts as the Little League Civility Project for "impacting the sports culture including parents, players, umpires, coaches, and fans ... conceived to teach players, parents, umpires, coaches, and fans appropriate behavior for their respective roles and responsibilities." This plan led to an initiative to "put together athletic conference school teams composed of athletic directors, booster club sponsors, athletes, cheerleading sponsors, and cheerleaders to develop an action plan designed around their respective schools for a code of character qualities."

Given the likelihood that Little League is an organization participated in by members of the mainstream community, this project appears designed to address the behavior of participants from across the racial, linguistic, and socioeconomic spectrum. Taking into account this state's largely White population, the Little League Civility Project might be considered to have particular consequences for boorish Whites who dishonor the sporting tradition and

> *Character consists of what you do on the third and fourth tries.*
>
> —*James A. Michener*

the community's cohesiveness. Identifying minorities, LEP students, and other historically marginalized groups for a character intervention, then, was not an exclusive focus of this initiative. Along with other aspects of the proposal, however, this focus suggests the discourse of class-based morality. At the same time, this attention appears to part of a comprehensive effort to identify people from within and without the mainstream population, both young and old, who might benefit from attention to character issues.

Relationships

The discourse of relationships included attention to the quality of long-term interactions among community members, particularly relationships between students and adults. Typical of this discourse is the following statement from the rationale one proposal provided for seeking to develop positive relationships in the schools:

> A collegial relationship among staff and a positive relationship between staff and students contribute to a nurturing, safe, and productive environment. These relationships are critical to helping children overcome difficulty, recognize their talents, and feel individually and collectively valued. School staff understand that they play a critical role in helping students grow and develop as individuals in order to be academically successful.

By developing positive relationships across stakeholders in the school, students will, according to the proposals, internalize the Protestant work ethic and thereby experience academic achievement.

One proposal made an explicit link to Noddings's notion of the caring community in which the emphasis is

> not on the deficit character qualities we see in kids but on the need to develop a caring environment that values all people including children and youth.... This campaign in the pilot project helped facilitate the discussion in town meetings not on the deficit character qualities we see in kids but on the need to develop a caring environment that values all people including children and youth.

Here the proposal rejected the discourse of youth depravity, taking instead an affirmative view of young people perhaps central to a relational approach to character education.

Attention to affect was an explicit part of one state's approach. The proposal authors argue that

The W. T. Grant Consortium on the School-Based Promotion of Social Competence designed programs to increase proactive factors such as bonding to school, resisting antisocial influences, and forming positive social relationships. This research also found that programs designed to have an impact on students' behavior must recognize that change occurs over time, and that learning prosocial skills not only helps young people with their interpersonal relationships but also with their attitudes towards school. In order to increase student achievement we have to focus on student engagement and climate/culture issues (Schlecty, 1997). And in order to increase student engagement, we need to invite creative curricula that encourage innovative teaching practices (Wohlstetter, 1997). The recent breakthroughs in brain research have nudged us to link social, emotional, and intellectual practices thereby setting a strong foundation for the pilot project to embed character education traits into the school culture and curriculum. Howard Gardner (Harvard, 1990) has made a strong link between the cognitive and affective domains, one that is crucial to inform [the state's] pilot project. The works of Goldeman (emotional intelligence) and Pat Wolfe (brain research) look at how the affective domain is critical to increasing student achievement.... This engagement of all of the school/community stakeholders is a long-term process that calls for the building of relationships (Peck, 1990).

The discourse of relationships—undoubtedly the sort of rhetoric that Ryan (2003) would characterize as the soft language of therapy—was tied to the discourse of community, with an emphasis on the "engagement of all of the school/community stakeholders [in] a long-term process that calls for the building of relationships." These relationships include healthy and positive, cultivated and sustained affiliations among all stakeholders in the school system:

Students feel personally known and cared for by at least one adult in the school. Students and community members are viewed as resources for supporting one another. A collegial relationship among staff and a positive relationship between staff and students contribute to a nurturing, safe, and productive environment. These relationships are critical to helping children overcome difficulty, recognize their talents, and feel individually and collectively valued. School staff understand that they play a critical role in helping students grow and develop as individuals in order to be academically successful. [The program will] use older students and community members as tutors or mentors to younger students [and] provide mentors for students as they transition from elementary to middle school and from middle school to high school. Students will feel known and cared for, have a trusted adult to turn to in times of trouble; Staff will take the opportunity to know students personally.

This emphasis on relationships runs counter to the discourse of the authoritarian society, which places students in subservient positions relative to adults. A relational approach to character education instead relies on mutual understanding and personal mentorship so that students are apprenticed into a caring community's value on joint activity and mutual assistance.

> *I have absolutely no problem at all turning my back on the most talented [basketball] player out there if I think he doesn't have the character to put it all together.*
>
> —*Dennis Felton*

Above all, as one proposal stated, this approach "comes from a perspective of being *with* kids, not doing *to* kids." This approach assumes that young people earnestly desire adult company and adoption of their values, a belief eschewed in the more adversarial approach implied by the proposals from the southern states. Undoubtedly, the upper midwestern perspective on children and adolescents is characterized by a degree, perhaps a large degree, of romanticism of the sort disdained by Kevin Ryan, Thomas Lickona, and others who profoundly influenced the tenets of the Aspen Declaration and are explicitly consulted for their character education services by the southern states whose proposals we have analyzed.

Student Agency

The American education system is currently being challenged from within and without to examine its policies and practices and to implement strategies that will result in students who are prepared to take an active and positive role in a life-long learning process, which has at its core, demonstration of positive character.

This statement, taken from one of the proposals from the Upper Midwest, illustrates the discourse of student agency. This discourse is implicated in the various ways that the proposal authors argue for empowering young people with tools for navigating the pitfalls of childhood, adolescence, and adulthood. On the whole this emphasis is part of a greater effort to view young people in a positive way:

Focusing on assets development rather than a deficits model for conceptualizing what young people need, and focusing on specific strategies to promote resiliency in youth through provision of a caring adult consistently in their lives, meaningful opportunities to participate, skills for academic, social and emotional success, and high expectations will sustain positive character development over time.

This statement suggests some of the conflicts seemingly inherent to the project of articulating and operationalizing a conception of character. The discourse of family first exhibited elsewhere in this proposal is compromised by the *in loco parentis* role of the school in providing surrogate parents in the form of caring adults.

The proposals specifically identified two aspects of student agency that a character curriculum could foster, engagement and critical thinking.

> *I have a dream that my four little children will one day live in a nation where they will not be judged by the color of their skin but by the content of their character.*
>
> —*Dr. Martin Luther King, Jr.*

Engagement.   The notion of engagement was evident in proposals' efforts to create an affiliation among youngsters with school and its activities. This initiative was designed to make school more relevant for young people and their interests and to promote active learning about citizenship and democracy. Student surveys, argue the authors of one proposal, indicate that students do not feel ownership, pride, or respect for school or adults. It is imperative, then, to make a commitment to taking students' views and experiences seriously:

> Schools use many strategies and approaches to make learning relevant for students. Classrooms are interactive places that often take learning beyond the schoolroom door. Engaging students' minds keeps them connected to school and makes them responsible for their own learning. Students who are connected to school have the greatest opportunities for becoming caring, contributing, productive, and responsible citizens. Involve students beyond the classroom in meaningful participation in other activities such as school plays, clubs, sports, music, etc. Create an environment in which students feel free to express their thoughts and feelings or to make mistakes without ridicule; develop thoughtful challenging tasks and learning experiences. Students, staff, and family/community share equal responsibility for meeting citizenship goals.

The purpose of these efforts is to empower students by helping "children develop the knowledge, attitudes, and skills they need to make responsible decisions about these behaviors." Attention to student agency, then, will equip them with the tools they need to perform up to their potential in school, tying agency to academic achievement.

This belief in the value of engagement with school is the sort of progressive thinking that has drawn the derision of critics of the Deweyan tradition. Recall Sykes's (1995) criticism of whole language approaches to teaching reading, which he and Jeanne Chall dismiss as attending more to students' immediate good feelings than to the hard labor required for the difficult and long-term project of learning. Again, a degree of romanticism runs throughout the conception of young people in the proposals from the Upper Midwest. Children and adolescents are noble and sincere about learning and growing into contributing members of a peaceable community, rather than swinish as envisioned by Headmaster Jarvis and in need of a harshly disciplined upbringing. The states from the Upper Midwest implore educators to change the school climate to make education a more engaging experience and to increase students' respect for adults. In contrast,

> *The glory of a nation rests upon the character of her men.*
>
> —*Herbert Hoover*

the southern states assume that respect for adults is a responsibility of each individual child to adopt as part of character development; an absence of such respect indicates a lack of character.

Resiliency. One proposal states that "Resiliency researchers David Hawkins and Richard Catalano have identified several risk factors in youth. In their work, they advocate giving young people 'opportunities, skills and recognition' opportunities to contribute to their family, schools, and community; skills that enable them to participate, and recognition for their capabilities and participation (Communities that Care, 1992)."

Resiliency is described in the documents as follows:

> Research says that kids can develop incredible abilities to bounce back (be resilient) if four things are consistently present in their lives: (1) meaningful opportunities to participate in something adults value; (2) a caring adult consistently [available] through their growing up years; (3) skills in interpersonal relationships and critical thinking; and (4) high expectations for their behavior and performance. There are ways to involve community service organizations, churches, community service projects, city councils, clubs, and other entities to promote resiliency.

Student agency is thus tied to other discourses, particularly that of relationships but also of academic achievements and community. Student engagement and resiliency incorporate the following factors:

> *Engagement:* a psychological investment in and effort toward understanding and mastering knowledge and skills taught in the school—a personal intellectual investment in learning that enhances scholarly competence and confidence.

> *Membership:* a sense of attachment and *commitment* to the social group, involvement and participation in the activities of the group, and a belief in and commitment to the goals or purposes of the group.

> *Authentic Work:* work that is perceived as meaningful, valuable, significant, and worthy of effort—work that has a "real world" connection and is extrinsically rewarding while appealing to intrinsic interests.

> *Ownership:* a sense of some control and influence over the work in the school from its conception, through execution, and ending with evaluation of performance.

> *Future Orientation:* a belief that the work of the school is important to success in the future as well as in the present.

Peer Support: while related to a sense of belonging, includes a perception that peers help each other and treat each other with dignity and respect.

Efficacy: a sense that "I" do make a difference both now and in the future—that working hard will have a positive result.

The goal of developing student agency appears to run counter to the southern states' assumptions about the authoritarian society. One proposal from the Upper Midwest, for instance, identified the principle that they should "Create an environment in which students feel free to express their thoughts and feelings or to make mistakes without ridicule." Our first observation is that this statement reveals the sort of communitarian approach advocated throughout these proposals: The emphasis is on changing the environment, not the individual child in need of character improvement. Second, freedom of expression is not always compatible with authoritarian social structures. We assume that this freedom extends to the privilege of criticizing the school administration, an act that might be viewed as a sign of low character in the southern states. We see the possibility that in the southern states, free expression might be repressed because respect for adults is a premium virtue. The discourse of student agency, in contrast, would appear to empower students to speak up as a way to make the school a more congenial environment to all who make up its community. Whether the adults in the upper midwestern schools indeed appreciate students' agency to speak their minds is not substantiated in the proposals.

Local Control

Both states from the Upper Midwest emphasized the local nature of decision-making. One state included "Site-Managed Schools" as among the features of their program, arguing that

> Site management attempts to increase individual autonomy of stakeholders through shared information and expanded involvement in decision making.... The neighborhood school may be the best place to reconcile competing claims with local conditions and preferences. "One shoe does not fit all,"

so what may work in one building in a district may not be the perfect fit for another building in the district ... site management attempts to strike a balance between school autonomy and central office, or district, goals and initiatives.... The site-managed school, by its nature, involves all stakeholders in decision-making.

This view is quite different from the authoritarian conception of school management implied in the southern states' proposals, in which decisions are centralized and results replicated in other districts. It also embraces a certain degree of relativism, suggesting that what works for one group and setting might not for another.

In a telephone conversation with an official from one upper midwestern state, she said that her state's history of grassroots politics would make it nearly impossible to centralize decision making in any statewide effort, including a character education initiative. This observation fits well with the cultural context we provided at the beginning of this chapter, in which the historical practices of these states have established bottom-up decision making in local arenas that invite a broad range of voices, particularly those who do not control economic resources. This practice is evidenced in such institutions as the Iowa political caucuses for identifying presidential candidates, in which candidates have an opportunity to visit many of Iowa's small towns, discuss important issues face-to-face with ordinary citizens, and develop their platforms based on these conversations. This practice suggests a different approach to decision making, one based on local control, than that found in the historically authoritarian social structure of the Deep South.

Reproduction of the Social Division of Labor

This discourse was concerned with preparing young people for the workplace, particularly those presumed not to be bound for higher education. Character education is "situated within a global economy and workplace transformation that demands a new set of knowledges, skills, and attributes, some of which have not yet been discovered or defined," according to one proposal. The character education proposals from the Upper Midwest stressed the need to prepare students for this emerging economy and the jobs it provides. One proposal termed this effort "Lifework education ... designed to work with students in planning for personal, posthigh school goals" through "the linking of the Perkins and School-to-Work requirements of workplace readiness skills with the character education qualities."

> *I hope I shall possess firmness and virtue enough to maintain what I consider the most enviable of all titles, the character of an honest man.*
>
> *—George Washington*

To assist with this transformation, one proposal listed U.S. Department of Labor statistics regarding the characteristics that employers look for in teens:

- Learning-to-learn skills,
- Listening and communication,
- Adaptability: creative thinking and problem solving, especially in response to barriers/obstacles,
- Personal management: self-esteem, goal-setting/self-motivation, personal career development/goals, pride in work accomplished,
- Group effectiveness: interpersonal skills, negotiation, teamwork, and
- Organizational effectiveness and leadership; making a contribution.

Presumably, this attention to employee characteristics contributes to a more effective character curriculum. Benjamin Franklin, author of many maxims that contributed to the development of the U.S. character, believed that engagement in work would elevate the nation's moral quality: "The almost general mediocrity of fortune that prevails in America, obliging its people to follow some business for subsistence, those vices that arise usually from idleness are in a great measure prevented. Industry and constant employment are great preservatives of morals and virtue" (quoted in Isaacson, 2003, p. 424). We see productive work as fitting the discourse of the Protestant work ethic, to be instilled in young people so that they may advance through the employment ranks regardless of where they begin on the salary scale. And, given that these statistics refer to teen employment, we assume that this initiative will serve students who enter the workforce as teens rather than going on to tertiary education. As such this discourse is palpably at odds with the discourses of citizenship and community that are so central to the upper midwestern conception of character education.

SUMMARY

The states from the Upper Midwest conceive of character education generally as a community-based, relational, constructive process, driven by Jeffersonian and Deweyan conceptions of citizenship and democracy. This broad view is undermined by the discourses of class-based morality and the

---

Women's Club in Sioux Society

Members solicited but must be of good character. The husband's position not taken into account, the character of the woman, the point. No matter how high her position, she can't be a member if not of good character.

—Alice Cunningham Fletcher—field work diary

reproduction of the social division of labor, which target low-SES youth for both character improvement and placement in blue-collar jobs and therefore contradict the general value on diversity and equity. Furthermore, the effort to secure OERI funding required compromising the general emphasis on local control and the inclusion of diverse voices with the RFP's requirement to endorse the notion of core universal values. Like the proposals from the Deep South, then, the states from the Upper Midwest produced a vision of character education that is more pseudoconcept than concept. We next look at the content of the curriculum itself and the ways in which these states assessed students' development of character.

I wish the bald eagle had not been chosen as the representative of our country; he is a bird of bad moral character, he does not get his living honestly; you may have seen him perched on some dead tree, near the river where, too lazy to fish for himself, he watches the labors of the fishing-hawk.... The turkey is, in comparison, a much more respectable bird, and a true original native of America.... He is (though a little vain and silly, it is true, but not the worse emblem for that) a bird of courage, and would not hesitate to attack a grenadier of the British guards.

—Benjamin Franklin

Chapter 17

The Upper Midwest's Character Curriculum and Assessment of Character Growth

CURRICULUM

To help students become caring, contributing, productive, and responsible citizens, the entire school program must reflect a clear commitment to helping students acquire the skills, attitudes, values, and knowledge to achieve the ideal. Citizenship development includes in-class instructional opportunities woven throughout the curriculum. For example, social studies classes may concentrate on the development of knowledge about and the history of our democratic institutions and principles and on the critical thinking skills necessary for competent participation in the democratic process. In family and consumer education, health education, and developmental guidance, a focus on individual and family health helps students develop the skills they need to enhance interpersonal relationships and social/emotional development. A renewed emphasis on the attitudes and commitments required to practice and live the core citizenship values is needed in all of our school curriculums and programs. The basis for all of these forms of citizenship education is the Declaration of Independence and the United States Constitution. These documents guide our constitutional democracy and will be realized if we take seriously our obligation to be good citizens.

> *If you will think about what you ought to do for other people, your character will take care of itself. Character is a by-product, and any man who devotes himself to its cultivation in his own case will become a selfish prig.*
>
> *—Woodrow Wilson*

This statement of general philosophy embodies many of the discourses we have reviewed thus far as central to an upper midwestern conception of character education. Similar to the southern states, the states from the Upper Midwest provided little in terms of concrete pedagogical ideas about how to teach character. Rather, the effort was to provide a conception, presumably adopted and operationalized at the local level. The state official with whom we spoke again stressed the need for local control in decision making, saying that the people of her state would not tolerate a centrally developed character curriculum. Indeed, citizens and educators throughout the state had vigorously resisted the imposition of any external standards on their curriculum. Curricula would need to be developed in each community in concert with the general vision articulated in the proposal.

The other state from the Upper Midwest viewed its character education program to be a *citizenship initiative* designed to help students become productive, responsible, caring, and contributing citizens. The state's program was designed to assist a process for incorporating character and citizenship education into the academic curriculum. This effort to integrate the character curriculum into the existing curriculum was described by one state as follows:

> By the year 2001, the [State] Department of Education will have developed an approach to school improvement, consistent with the goals of the national Goals 2000 program, which integrates the Character Education Learning Community Model (CELCM) as an integral part of systemic school improvement processes, products and evaluation methods of LEAs and the intermediate service units (AEAs) which serve them.

The other state recommended the development of a "Citizenship Team" composed of teachers, support staff, administrators, and families and other community members "including those not normally involved" to implement and monitor its character intervention. These teams should identify

> key opinion leaders or communicators within parent circles. These are not necessarily individuals who hold high or very recognizable employment positions within the community (e.g., bank president, executive director of chamber of commerce, etc.) They are people who are opinion leaders by the work they do, the many contacts they may have, and, most importantly, the influence they may have on groups of people.... Representation should include working parents, single-parent families, and traditional two-parent families where one parent works and the other stays at home.

This Citizenship Team should meet regularly, at a variety of locations amenable to the team's various members, to identify and carry out an agenda for assisting schools with their character curricula. The pace of the effort ought to be slow, deliberate, and open, focusing on small rather

> *The beautiful person has more than just physical characteristics. He or she has good character. This encoded in the Akan maxim: Ahoofe ntua ka, suban pa na hia—physical beauty does not count much, it is good character that counts.*
>
> *—Akan Cultural Symbols Project*

than radical changes. The "micro view, while at times confusing and frustratingly slow-paced, ensures continuous progress toward stated goals and consistency in all efforts." As we hope is clear by now, this effort was designed to involve citizens from across the socioeconomic, racial, cultural, and linguistic spectrum. Like that of the southern states, the initiative was designed to be incorporated throughout the existing curriculum rather than being a separate character intervention. And, as with the southern states, the proposal provided few details as to what that curriculum would look like in practice.

ASSESSING THE EFFECTS OF CHARACTER EDUCATION

The two states from the Upper Midwest approached assessment in quite different ways. Rather than summarizing them together, we will review their efforts to assess the effects of their character interventions separately.

State #1

The key goals of the character education initiative were listed as objectives and accompanied by evaluation measures. These objectives included not only anticipated effects of the character pedagogy but goals for publicizing and administrating the program. For instance, one objective was to develop an "Imaging campaign to promote 'Kids Matter Most' theme and importance of adult modeling of desired character traits," with the evaluation being a "Record of actual airing of PSAs on various media." In other words, when the program listed the goal of erecting billboards to promote the initiative, someone would make sure that the billboards were up. Rather than reviewing the many bureaucratic and promotional facets of this state's effort, we will confine our summary of the assessment of the character curriculum to those evaluating the educational aspects of the program.

> *When wealth is lost, nothing is lost; when health is lost, something is lost; when character is lost, all is lost.*
>
> *—Billy Graham*

> *Watch your thoughts; they become words. Watch your words; they become actions.*
> *Watch your actions; they become habits. Watch your habits; they become character.*
> *Watch your character; it becomes your destiny.*
>
> *—Frank Outlaw*

Quantitative Data

Academic Achievement.   This state planned to collect reports on student achievement in terms of their acquisition of character traits, also known as *essential learnings* in this state's jargon. How these traits or essential learnings were to be identified as achieved was not elaborated in the proposal.

A second measure of academic achievement came in a report on student achievement toward content standards and benchmarks in literacy acquisition and mathematics. Although these achievement measures were not elaborated, we assume that they included routine measures such as grades and standardized test scores.

Behavioral Data.   The document described a set of behavioral data that presumably would indicate something about improvements in character:

> We are and will continue to submit to the Secretary a comprehensive evaluation of the program including impact on students, teachers, administrators, parents, and others every six months and at the end of the granting period utilizing the Factors in #3: discipline problems, students' grades, participation in extracurricular activities, parental and community involvement, faculty and administration involvement, and student and staff morale along with the Student Engagement/Resiliency Survey given every year, [State] Youth Survey—asset development, teacher evaluation of student performance on content standards, and Essential Learnings (Character Education Traits).

We would raise here the same concerns we described previously: that reduction in discipline problems could be a consequence of compliance rather than character; that extracurricular and parental participation could be a function

> *The adoption of character development programs in our country's schools must become a national priority. As Miss America, I am encouraging educators, parents and students to make character education an integral element of their school's culture and curriculum. I am specifically challenging educators to join me, while speaking out as their peer and advocate for better compensation and treatment. Educators must be recognized for the significant role they play in developing values and ethics among youth.*
>
> *—Angela Perez Baraquio, Miss America 2001*

of socioeconomic class and raise the possibility that working-class students and families could be judged of low character because of their rates of participation in school sponsored activities, and that with such a complex intervention coming in the midst of an overall conceptual change, it is questionable to correlate improvements in grades with improvements in character.

Student Surveys. Students were surveyed in fifth, eighth, and eleventh grades regarding their levels of engagement, ownership, membership and spirit in the context of their connection to increased academic achievement as measured by district essential learning goals and district content standards and benchmark goals. The survey was a 45-item student-completed measure rated on a 5-point Likert scale (A = Strongly agree; E = Strongly disagree). The instrument measured the following areas (see Appendix 17.1 for the complete survey):

- Engagement—five items (e.g., "I do my best to learn in school")
- Membership—14 items (e.g., "The purpose of this school is to help students learn")
- Authentic work—12 items (e.g., "Teachers reward you for giving your best effort")
- Ownership—two items (e.g., "I have enough say in deciding what I should learn")
- Future Orientation—three items (e.g., "What I am learning in school is important to me")
- Peer Support and Esprit—five items (e.g., "Students help each other succeed in school")
- Efficacy—two items (e.g., "If I study and work hard, I will be successful in school")
- Other—two items (e.g., "Teachers give the right amount of homework")

Findings were reported in terms of percent of agreement–disagreement for each scale. The survey data would be compiled and distributed to program participants for feedback on the effectiveness of the program. We have the same reservation with these measures that we have with the survey data from the southern states: We do not share the assessors' confidence

---

While parents have the ultimate responsibility, it is time for our schools to reassert their role in character development. We want our children to be prepared for their future with a conscience and an understanding of ethics to accompany intelligence and knowledge.

—Jim McGreevey

that students always respond honestly to surveys of their attitudes toward school and adherence to adult expectations.

Qualitative Data

Teacher Reflection.   One objective of this state's program was to

> Assess the level of implementation of curriculum units previously written by character education funds into the school curriculum, and their resulting impact on essential learning standards of effective communicator, collaborative worker, and effective problem solver, and the resulting impact on the curriculum units on content standards and benchmarks in literacy attainment and mathematics.

The means of evaluation were through what the documents called "teacher reflection" on students' engagement with their instruction and on student interviews conducted by program administrators. The manner of reflection was not described in the documents, nor the uses to which these reflections would be put.

Interviews.   Among this state's objectives was to

> Develop a school culture/climate cadre composed of a principal/teacher from each building who will act as local facilitators for educator study groups (in collaboration with building school improvement "design" teams) which will 1) examine the resiliency data and design appropriate interventions using an assets model; 2) study the findings of the cognitive sciences and brain research and implications for classroom practice; 3) examine alternative approaches to developing responsible student behavior in the context of (self) discipline and behavior expectations; 4) facilitate the implementation of conflict resolution strategies, facilitator trainings, and other skills-based initiatives that promote positive school culture and climate for both students and adults.

To assess these various goals, the state included interviews with the school culture and climate cadre, parents, students, and trainees. How these interview data were analyzed was not explained in the proposal.

For the past 23 years, when people have called the main telephone number at the district offices of Orangeburg Consolidated School District 5, they have heard the voice of one of the most pleasant and polite people on staff in the county's largest school district. So it is very appropriate that District 5 switchboard operator Sharon Howell is the latest person to be recognized through the Orangeburg County Community of Character initiative.

—Greg Carson, Orangeburg (SC) Consolidated School District 5

> *When voting, women should first consider the most important ingredient in a candidate: Character. If "character" were important to today's voters, then President Clinton, New Jersey Senators Robert Torricelli and Frank Lautenberg, and Governors Florio and McGreevey would never have won their elections. As long as "character" is not an issue (but abortion is), then New Jersey and America are destined to become a dysfunctional society. Sadly, we are swiftly evolving into a dysfunctional nation where the "rule of law" is being replaced by liberal "mob rule."*
>
> *—Gordon Bishop*

Action Research. This state included an action research component to provide "ongoing evaluation and feedback about progress towards achievement of character education goals and their connection of academic achievement, through analysis of resiliency surveys, rubrics for essential learnings, and achievement data regarding content standards and benchmarks in literacy acquisition and mathematics." The action research was to be conducted under the supervision of a faculty member from a state university.

The proposal defined action research as

> a process where an area of improvement is identified, a plan of action is designed, and data is [sic] collected as the change is implemented. This process meets the needs for schools wishing to work toward continuous improvement where decisions are based on facts, not hunches.... [Action research is] inquiry or research in the context of focused efforts to improve the quality of an organization and its performance. It typically is designed and conducted by practitioners who analyze the data to improve their own practice. Action research can be done by individuals or by teams of colleagues. The team approach is called collaborative inquiry.

The proposal did not provide details on which members of the school community would conduct the action research, how they would be trained, or how the data would be treated.

The proposal authors appeared to be ambivalent toward the value of action research. At one point the proposal authors stated that "It is our belief that action research in each school/community validates the need for improving the program for character qualities and improving the quality of education." Elsewhere they retreated from action research as a valid and reliable method of inquiry:

> there is no single "method" to be found in doing "action research," nor any clearly agreed upon definition. Concepts that emerge in the literature include the emphasis on using data for improvement, on reflection on practice, and on collaboration. One does not find an emphasis on adhering to specific kinds of research methodology, the use of statistics, or other similar things that would be emphasized in "traditional" research. There is much in

common with program evaluation, which might be conducted for purposes that are similar to those of a practitioner engaging in action research.... Because the assumptions and purposes for "action research" differ from those of classical research, it may be unfortunate that they both include the word "research." This can be confusing to both traditional researchers and practitioners engaging in gathering data to make more informed decisions. Traditional researchers may view action research as sloppy research (which it is, if it is being used for the purposes of traditional research), and the danger for practitioners is to think that because they have engaged in reflective data gathering and use, their conclusions are as valid (using definitions from classical research) as they might have been with a carefully designed research study. There may be a tendency to over generalize the conclusions, and then it does becomes nothing more than sloppy research. We need to keep in mind that the fundamental purpose for action research is to gather useful data to make educational decisions in a specific context.

Despite these reservations, this state included action research as part of its assessment process, though apparently of lesser value to the program administrators than traditional measurements such as numeric indicators more familiar and congenial to assessment specialists and federal policymakers. We should note that these assumptions have been contested by those who advocate action research as reliable and valid on its own terms (e.g., Fecho, 2003; MacLean & Mohr, 1999). More relevant to our discussion, teacher research is endorsed by those who believe that character education initiatives are most fruitfully assessed through teacher inquiry that provides a "cycle of inquiry that offers constructivist professional development for both prospective and practicing teachers leading to improved character education for children" (Silva & Gimbert, 2001, p. 29) as long as it is "supported and complemented by a whole school commitment to character education" (p. 30).

State #2

Rather than assessing the effects of the character curriculum following the intervention, the second state from the Upper Midwest—the one featuring citizenship—included a single assessment vehicle to be used during the process of its ongoing character program. They developed "An Inventory

---

At Camp Cherokee, values are acquired, self-reliance and sportsmanship learned, ideals formed, interpersonal skills developed, and character and confidence built. These ideals along with the YMCA's four character building traits: responsibility, honesty, caring, and respect, devise the values taught and learned at Camp Cherokee and help make up the Cherokee Philosophy.

http://www.campcherokee.org/

for Schools Fostering Citizenship" to be filled out by administrators, parents, teachers, students, pupil service personnel, and other stakeholders. This survey asked respondents to rate 9-11 statements on a Likert scale for each of the seven characteristics of the program: core values, safe and orderly places, family and community involvement, positive relationships, address societal issues, engage students' minds, and high expectations. These items included such statements as "Students and staff model the core values daily," "Student discipline policies promote student responsibility," "All students and staff feel safe and respected at school," "Students say they believe their teachers care about them personally," and so on.

The instructions for completing this inventory emphasize in boldface font that **"The dialogue about these issues is more important than the score."** Participants identify data on their cohort group, race, and gender so that perceptions among different demographic groups may be compared to see how various populations are experiencing the initiative. The instructions say that, in particular, the district's Citizenship Team should compare their consensus rating—that is, the rating that emerges from a discussion among Citizenship Team members—"to the rating given by the student, family, and community representatives. You may find certain groups have very different perceptions of the current status than those of your team. The differences may warrant further investigation and discussion, and can help to pinpoint areas of strength and areas for further effort." Given the document's assertion that "it will realistically take your building several years" to "build caring, contributing, productive, and responsible citizens," this in-process assessment provides important feedback as schools engage in "a cyclical process that repeats itself over time."

Assessment issues emerge, according to the documents, during the course of the deliberation inherent to the slow, open process. The program recommends that a series of questions be continually posed as part of the in-process assessment of the initiative:

- Which characteristics are currently evident in our school? Which are weak?
- Are our current efforts connected and coordinated, or fragmented?
- Are all students impacted positively by our efforts? Are some excluded from citizenship development efforts due to scheduling, ability, or other factors?
- Are families and community members aware of, involved in, and supportive of the citizenship initiative?
- Are all teachers and staff aware of, involved in, and supportive of the citizenship initiative?
- How do we want our school to be different three years from now in relation to citizenship development?

- How are our students succeeding on measures of achievement attitudes, attendance, and participation? How might targeting one or
  more of the characteristics improve student success?
- What costs are involved with our citizenship efforts? Are more resources needed? What are possible sources?
- How will school and community residents be recognized for their work?
- What have been the results of our current work? How will we assess the
  results of future efforts?

This approach was designed to have a completely local focus, with problems, strategies, and agendas identified by members of the school and community. In contrast to the southern states that purchased all-purpose
assessments with predetermined correct answers, this state viewed assessment as ongoing, formative, open-ended, inquiry-based, strategic, and sensitive to local conditions. The schools in this state were advised to develop a
"Citizenship Action Plan" to be used following assessment to "help the citizenship team select the characteristic(s) it would like to strengthen in your
school. Once a focus has been selected, the team can identify citizenship activities that will help strengthen the characteristics and results that identify
for the team that the goal is being achieved." The team was advised to consider which of the seven characteristics (core values, safe and orderly places,
high expectations, family and community involvement, positive relationships, address societal issues, engage students' minds) it wished to focus on,
identify goals for those characteristics selected, and identify "measurable
results—we will know we've achieved our goal when: _____."

The program recommends "using multiple strategies that are connected and focused" to "promote the development of caring, contributing, productive, and responsible citizens." These strategies were often
extracurricular, including youth service opportunities (e.g., service learning), peer mediation to help students to resolve differences nonviolently
and respectfully, mentor programs that match students with an adult from
the community for extended time together, character education to "help
students understand, develop, and model core values" adopted by the
school and community, and vocational school organizations that help
schools "develop citizenship in their student members by *engaging student
minds and keeping them connected to school* through provision of a variety of
co-curricular activities designed to increase student motivation and provide a framework for authentic learning experiences centering on *family
and community involvement.*"

The year-end assessment again came in terms of reflection on the process and product of the character intervention. The recommended evaluation form

poses critical questions to help your citizenship team document the accomplishments made during the school year in implementing one or more of the characteristics. Completion of this evaluation form and the discussion it generates with the citizenship team will help identify priorities for further efforts. These priorities can then be recorded as tasks on the action plan guide for the next school year. In this way, planning, implementation, and evaluation become a continual improvement process.

Typical of these evaluations was the one for the first characteristic, core values:

Characteristic 1—Core Values

These activities help identify core values for our school community and promote student, staff, and community modeling and recognition.

1. List all core values activities the citizenship team implemented or improved during the school year.

2. Overall, how would you rate the quality of all the core values activities the school conducts?

3. Select the core value activity that best describes efforts this year and answer the following questions:

Activity_____

How many were involved (approximately)? Families, Teachers, Students, Others

Which grade levels were involved?

What was the main goal of this activity?

How well was the activity implemented this year? Was it a new initiative or an improvement of an existing practice?

What result(s) did this activity produce for students, teachers, parents, and/or the community? How were the results measured?

What might be done to make this activity even more successful next year? Were there parents, teachers, or students who were *not* involved? How might they be involved in the future? Could other aspects of the practice be improved? Explain.

We place ourselves in bad company and our culture in bad company, it can undermine our Christian world view that under girds good character. We ought not completely isolate ourselves from the culture, but there is a price to pay. It changes the way we do things. And unless we are not aggressively retooling our minds, our perspectives, our worldview, it is very easy to start thinking like our culture, and then pretty soon bad stuff doesn't seem so bad.

—Gregory Koukl

Assessment for this state, then, came through the identification of what ought to be assessed and how it should be assessed by participants in the program. Consistent with the discourse of local control, no specific measurements were imposed, only a process through which measurements might be identified.

SUMMARY

As did the southern states, the states from the Upper Midwest produced proposals for character education funding that reflected the heritage and worldview of the dominant ethnic and cultural groups of the region. The labor organizations and populist political traditions created the conditions for proposing a character education program built on the foundation of local control, diversity, relationships, citizenship, and community, all values that can be traced to the region's European immigrants' communitarian roots.

This perspective is compromised by the proposal authors' presumably pragmatic approach to grantsmanship. They incorporated attention to moral absoluteness, as required by the Request for Proposals, while modifying it as local rather than universal, creating an internal contradiction in their conception of character education. Efforts to place working-class youth in employment programs as a way to make them productive contributors to the community suggest a conflict between the democratic ideals generally espoused and the reproduction of the social division of labor likely to follow from such a plan. Links between character development and academic achievement were claimed but not substantiated.

We see in these proposals the possibility that these states' commitment to diversity has created a conundrum that invites contradiction. The character education initiatives proposed by these states are perhaps undermined by the very values that make them democratic. By inviting pluralism they invite contradiction. The proposals from the Deep South appear to have been developed by more homogeneous committees better aligned to the ideology of the OERI RFP, thus producing less internally contradictory proposals. The proposals from the Upper Midwest involved Procrustean contortions to meet the RFP requirements and accommodated different perspectives that were not always in accord. The resulting conception of character education thus becomes problematic because of its fidelity to too many stakeholders—both a virtue and a detriment to the ultimate shape of the proposal.

We have termed this approach *reflective*, in contrast to the didactic approach taken by southern states. Both states relied on local communities to discuss and formulate their particular notion of character and character education. The authoritarian nature of the southern states centralized an official notion of character, normalizing it through hieratic positioning of different community members whose social standing typically predicted their likelihood of being considered people of virtue. This authoritarian approach is more in line with the ideology of the individuals who formulated the Aspen Declaration incorporated into the OERI RFP. States from the Upper Midwest relied on different assumptions and therefore produced a less conceptually coherent notion of character education, beholden to contrary philosophies and thus compromised in its outline of both character and the program designed to promote it.

"Don't Laugh at Me" is a project begun by Peter Yarrow of Peter, Paul, and Mary. It consists of the song "Don't Laugh at Me," a video, and activities designed to nurture children's emotional, social, and ethical development. The program is designed to be an introduction to, or enrichment of, the ongoing efforts of character education, conflict resolution, caring, and teaching tolerance that are already underway within the schools and the community.

The curriculum guide provides activities in four areas:

- *Expressing Feelings*—helping children recognize their own feelings, as well as those of others, and being able to express oneself in a non-threatening way
- *Caring, Compassion, and Cooperation*—working together toward a shared goal by taking responsibility for one's own actions, helping others, and making group agreements, such as a Constitution of Caring and a Ridicule Free Zone
- *Resolving Conflict Creatively*—teaching skills need to resolve conflict and disagreements respectively, creatively, and non-violently
- *Celebrating Diversity*—helping children to acknowledge differences without judgment and helping them to create an environment where everyone can feel comfortable about their own personal differences

APPENDIX 17.1: PARTNERS IN EDUCATION SURVEY

A	B	C	D	E
Strongly				Strongly
agree	Agree	Neutral	Disagree	disagree

ENGAGEMENT

1. 1 do my best to learn in school. A B C D E
2. 1 concentrate on what is being taught during class. A B C D E
3. 1 complete school assignments on time. A B C D E
4. 1 do my school work to learn. A B C D E
5. 1 take pride in doing my school work. A B C D E

MEMBERSHIP

6. The purpose of this school is to help students learn. A B C D E
7. Teachers treat students fairly. A B C D E
8. The school principal(s) treat students fairly. A B C D E
9. Adults in this school listen to the student's side of the story. A B C D E
10. The school provides enough opportunities for me to participate in clubs, sports, music, etc. A B C D E
11. Teachers will help me when I am having problems in class or with an assignment. A B C D E
12. Teachers and other adults in this school will help me deal with home or personal problems. A B C D E
13. The counselors in this school are helpful. A B C D E
14. I understand the school rules. A B C D E
15. The rules in the school are fair. A B C D E
16. Rules are enforced fairly in this school. A B C D E
17. Teachers treat me with respect. A B C D E
18. My teachers care about me. A B C D E
19. In this school I am treated like I am important. A B C D E

AUTHENTIC WORK

20. Teachers reward me for giving my best effort. A B C D E
21. I am praised in class when I do something well. A B C D E
22. This school recognizes and rewards student accomplishments. A B C D E
23. In this school the grades students receive are based on how well they perform. A B C D E
24. What I am learning in school is interesting. A B C D E

25. Teachers make learning interesting. A B C D E
26. There are enough opportunities for students to work together in this school. A B C D E
27. Teachers let me know how well I am doing. A B C D E
28. Teachers return my work with written comments and ways to improve. A B C D E
29. Teachers do their best to help me be responsible for my work. A B C D E
30. This school provides opportunities for students to have fun. A B C D E
31. Teachers try to make learning enjoyable. A B C D E

OWNERSHIP

32. 1 have enough say in deciding what I should learn. A B C D E
33. 1 have enough say in deciding how I should learn. A B C D E

FUTURE ORIENTATION

34. What I am learning in school is important to me. A B C D E
35. Things that I learn in school are useful to me now. A B C D E
36. 1 believe this school prepares students to be successful in the future. A B C D E

PEER SUPPORT AND ESPRIT

37. Students help each other succeed in school. A B C D E
38. Students in this school treat other students with respect. A B C D E
39. I look forward to coming to school each day. A B C D E
40. I am proud of this school. A B C D E
41. I feel safe in this school. A B C D E

EFFICACY

42. If I study and work hard, I will be successful in school. A B C D E
43. If I study and work hard, it will make a difference in my life. A B C D E

OTHER

44. Teachers give the right amount of homework. A B C D E
45. I have friends in this school. A B C D E
46. I am a (A) Male (B) Female
47. I am eligible for free or reduced lunch. (A) Yes (B) No

We would like to know a little about you. Please complete the following items. Your answers will be kept private.

MARK "A" IF YES, LEAVE BLANK IF NO

School activities you participate in:

51. Sports
52. Vocal Music
53. Instrumental Music
54. Other Club

Special school programs you attend:

55. Title I
56. Special Education
57. At Risk Program
58. Talented and Gifted

Source. Partners in Education Survey.

PART V

INTRODUCTION TO CONCLUSION

In this final section we conclude our consideration of the discourse of character education in two chapters. First, we review what we believe are the major discussion points emerging from our review of the character education proposals from these two regions. Here no doubt our progressive bias enters into our reflections on character education and the Culture Wars. Although we have attempted to reserve judgment during our analysis, we undoubtedly lean toward the progressive vision in our final consideration on this complex topic. We hope that in doing so we treat other worldviews with the respect that they deserve.

We then reconsider the character curriculum. Our analysis has provided little opportunity to say what character education looks like in practice. Although the OERI proposals outlined a general vision and method of assessment, they provided very little information on what classroom practice would look like in service of that vision. Although we believe that our analysis stands on its own merits—that is, an effort to document the notion of character as a cultural construct with an ideological basis—we also think, as educators, that it's important to consider how to teach character. Although this project does not provide the space to detail actual lessons, we do feel an obligation to outline the principles of what we believe ought to be included in a character curriculum, with references to sources that outline more specifically what teachers can do to implement the principles.

> With all their faults, trade unions have done more for humanity than any other organization of men that ever existed. They have done more for decency, for honesty, for education, for the betterment of the race, for the developing of character in men, than any other association of men.
>
> —*Clarence Darrow*

311

Chapter 18

Discussion

In this study we have identified the two clearest expositions of philosophy found in OERI-funded proposals and provided profiles of these distinct conceptions of character and character education. The other states whose materials we analyzed provided more hybrid conceptions of character and character education. Our goal has not been to report the frequency of various positions but to establish that these perspectives exist, to outline each in detail, and to

---

I do not so much object to the name, or word, but I should certainly insist, for the purposes of these States, on a radical change of category, in the distribution of precedence. I should demand a program of culture, drawn out, not for a single class alone, or for the parlors or lecture rooms, but with an eye to practical life, the west, the workingmen, the facts of farms and jackplanes and engineers, and of the broad range of the women also of the middle and working strata, and with reference to the perfect equality of women, and of a grand and powerful motherhood. I should demand of this program or theory a scope generous enough to include the widest human area. It must have for its spinal meaning the formation of a typical personality of character, eligible to the uses of the high average of men—and not restricted by conditions ineligible to the masses. The best culture will always be that of the manly and courageous instincts, and loving perceptions, and of self-respect—aiming to form, over this continent, an idiocrasy of universalism, which, true child of America, will bring joy to its mother, returning to her in her own spirit, recruiting myriads of offspring, able, natural, perceptive, tolerant, devout believers in her, America, and with some definite instinct why and for what she has arisen, most vast, most formidable of historic births, and is, now and here, with wonderful step, journeying through Time.

—Walt Whitman

---

trace, as evidence permits, their development in relation to the OERI RFP and its own history, to the regional cultures that provide the context in which character education is conceived and put into practice, and to the broader streams of discourse in U.S. society, particularly those employed in the Culture Wars.

Although we are not able to completely set aside our own beliefs, biases, and values, we should reiterate that our goal has not been to criticize one region or conception at the expense of the other, but to contrast the discourse of character education as we find it emerging from distinct regional cultures and discourses. We should emphasize that the discourses themselves are not exclusive to the regions—we give many examples of how they are employed well beyond the boundaries of the Deep South and Upper Midwest—but rather congenial to the ideologies of the dominant cultures of these regions and therefore familiar, sensible, accessible, and amenable to the authors of the character education proposals we have reviewed.

We also do not intend to represent these two views as a binary. We recall the old adage: There are two types of people in the world, those who think that there are two types of people in the world, and those who don't. We fall in the second category because we see binaries as overly simplistic, reductive, and unproductive except heuristically to establish points on a continuum. We hope that our own effort to contrast the conceptions of character education that we found in the Deep South and Upper Midwest to be less of a binary and more of a distinction between two positions, with many hybrids available in between. Our description of Jacobs and Jacobs-Spencer's (2001) Native American perspective, although not evident in any of the proposals that we reviewed, suggests that there is at least a trinary, and likely much more as the notion of character is explored through broad and inclusive studies of cultures.

We see character education as one among many educational strategies through which each generation seeks to socialize its young people. Children's literature scholars have argued that children's literature comprises a conversation between adults and children about values that shape the world (e.g., Kelly, 1974; Taxel, 1984). Given its historical role as a socializing medium, children's literature represents what adults want children to know and believe about the world and how to act appropriately in it. These adults include not only the authors who write children's literature, but the increasingly rationalized (i.e., following principles of scientific management) efforts of multinational publishing companies to market, advertise, and synergize these books as commodities in the global marketplace (Taxel, 2002); for example, including the didactic Berenstain Bears book series as "Happy Meal" items or tying book sales to the release of a film.

The character education curricula that we have analyzed reflect the concerns of the adults in these states in relation to the worldviews that they aspire to inculcate in their children and the social futures that they hope to suggest for them. By studying character education, then, we are outlining fundamental beliefs about how society works and how people contribute to its effective functioning. Booth (1998) considers this sort of socialization as essential to an ethical aim for educators:

> [W]hat kind of person pursuing what kind of ideas and practices and social improve-
> ments do we hope to see emerging from our labors [as teachers]? ... [W]hat ethical
> improvements *in ourselves* should we seek ... that will help our students create
> selves most useful to them—useful not just in the utilitarian sense but in the
> sense of yielding and ultimately rewarding life, working for an ultimately re-
> warding and defensible society? (p. 45)

Undoubtedly, such values as the Protestant work ethic are critical to the successful operation of an industrialized society. We imagine that most people who know us would say that we've internalized this ethic pretty well ourselves. The goals of industrialized societies are best achieved when people are punctual, hard working, and so on. Such values might not contribute so well, however, to a society in which the fluid time conception and less materialistic values inherent to a Native American perspective obtain, given this culture's more cyclical understanding of time and greater orientation to being in balance with nature than to competing with other people for goods. Our study has outlined these different cultural constructs and attempted to analyze how they are products of particular cultural activity. Rather than transcending cultures, then, as argued by Lickona (1991) and others, we see conceptions of good character as being ideological and idiocultural.

We next review what we see as the major conclusions available from our study.

CONCEPT, PSEUDOCONCEPT, COMPLEX
OF CHARACTER EDUCATION

In chapter 5 we reviewed Vygotsky's (1987) notions of concept, pseudo-concept, and complex. These terms refer to the degree of unity that may be attributed to the elements included within a generalization such as a conception of good character. As we have noted elsewhere in our work (e.g., Smagorinsky, Cook, & Johnson, 2003), the degree of unity among these elements is a matter of judgment rather than absolute certainty. In our judgment, neither version of character or character education that we profile constitutes a concept. Rather, we see both efforts producing a pseudo-concept in which the programs give the appearance of unity but include in-

---

Truth gains character from the soul she inhabits. In arid souls she is rigorous and harsh, in loving souls she is tempered and gentle.

—*Joseph Joubert*

ternal contradictions that work against one another in the character conception. We should note that as we understand Vygotsky's use of the word, *pseudoconcept* is not a pejorative term but refers rather to the appearance of a coherent idea that masks internal contradictions. Our characterization is thus not intended to criticize the proposal authors as inept or phony, but to point out the inevitable contradictions that emerge from complex group decisions, particularly those produced in dialogue with externally produced documents.

Both sets of proposals are contradictory in terms of the discourses they include. The upper midwestern proposals appear to include a greater range of contradictions, including democratic communities vs. reproduction of the social division of labor, diversity versus moral absoluteness, and class-based morality versus diversity and democratic communities. The primary contradiction in the proposals from the southern states is the concurrent beliefs in the primacy of the family, the degeneracy of youth, and the class-based nature of morality.

We infer that the proposals are internally contradictory for different reasons. The makeup of the committees charged with articulating each state's conception of character education appears to have been constructed quite differently. One southern state, for instance, appears to have assembled a homogeneous committee, as suggested by their goal of including minority representation in the second year of implementation. In contrast, one of the upper midwestern states listed its task force members, including representatives from industry, the American Jewish Committee, a Christian denomination, the state Senate, the state Taxpayers Alliance, a Teen Single Parents organization, the Safe and Drug-Free Schools Programs, the Bright Beginnings/Family-School-Community Partnerships, Family and Consumer Education groups, the AFL-CIO, United Way Charities, the state Congress of Parents and Teachers, a Family and Consumer Education group, the state's namesake research university, the police force, a newspaper, and various representatives from schools: students, teachers, administrators, psychologists, counselors, and student services and prevention and wellness staff. Given this state's commitment to diversity, we must assume that a range of racial, ethnic, sexual, economic, and other categories of people were represented among these task force members, although we could not identify with certainty the categories exhibited by the participants listed in the proposal.

This diversity, while meeting the democratic goals of the proposal itself, also invites contradiction. If we accept the aphorism that a camel is a horse designed by a committee, the greater diversity of the upper midwestern panelists risks a final product that represents pluralistic perspectives on character education, not all of which are congruent with one another. We can see, then, how some on the committee might press for a school-to-work program to benefit working-class students and assure their employment, perhaps with the belief that hard work and responsibility and thus good character will follow from steady employment. At the same time, others on the task force might express a vision of education as just and equitable. By accommodating both perspectives, the committee as a whole adopts both the discourse of the reproduction of the social division of labor and the discourses of diversity, citizenship, and community.

A second reason for internal contradictions is that the OERI RFP is not consistent with the Upper Midwest's vision of character education. As we have argued, the RFP requires a commitment to moral absoluteness, a value that emerges from the Aspen Declaration in which Thomas Lickona and Kevin Ryan, whose authoritarian conception of character education is clear from their many publications and proclamations, were key players. The states from the Upper Midwest had to acknowledge this view while also arguing for a relativistic conception of character due to their emphasis on democratic decision-making and local control. The dialogic nature of the proposal process, then, required a compromise between the orthodox tradition written into the RFP and the progressive tradition upheld in the Upper Midwest and the socialistic influence on its history.

Given one southern state's apparent homogeneity among its formative committee members, we see fewer contradictions built into the process of articulating a conception of character for OERI funding. Some contradictions appeared, however, such as the inability to resolve the simultaneous claims that families are a child's first and most important moral teachers, that youth are increasingly degenerate, that some kinds of families are lax in their instruction in virtue, and that schools need to act *in loco parentis* in moral matters. Given our admitted partiality to a progressive perspective, we see here a good reason to make diversity an issue in education. Diversity is often a rallying cry in the Culture Wars, with conservatives such as D'Souza (1991) and Stotsky (1999) arguing that attending to minority concerns and other issues of inclusion results in an overly sensitive (i.e., politically correct) climate and watered down curriculum in which worthy historical icons are displaced by less accomplished people who come from historically underrepresented groups.

The lack of diversity in the southern proposals, however, has led to what strikes us as clear oversights in their conception. Given our attention to the experiences of people of color in the United States, it is incomprehensible to us to consider previous eras in the Deep South as "saner and simpler" than today. We see, then, diversity of perspective as being key to providing critique so as to continually refine and develop our thinking. If, as John-Steiner and Meehan (2000) have argued, creativity is a product of the juxtaposition of ideas, then we see diversity of representation as an important vehicle for promoting dynamic new ideas. At the same time, we recognize that our acknowledged progressive orientation leads us to believe that new ideas and change are beneficial, which positions us in opposition to those conservatives who revere particular versions of traditions and wish to maintain things as they are.

This apparent homogeneity among the curriculum developers in the Deep South leaves the southern conception with few conflicting viewpoints, thus making the proposals issuing from such committees unidimensional and therefore more open to critique. The perspective that the good old days were saner and simpler, for instance, is unlikely to be offered by a committee that includes descendants of slaves or senior members of a community who have personally experienced a society that vigorously and violently enforced Jim Crow laws and, later, instituted informal means of perpetuating segregation.

The very authoritarian nature of the southern states, then, likely produced character education proponents from the privileged tier of upper and middle-class Whites who instituted a conception of character that reinforced their own class authority and denied other voices that could contest that vision. Controlling the process, however, does not eliminate the contradictions; rather, it simply denies voice to those who might articulate contradictory beliefs. We see the implementation of character education, then, as subject to internal contradictions due to the different perspectives on culture and character at large in society, whether they are acknowledged or represented in the proposals or not.

We should also repeat that these two regions produced what we considered to be the clearest and most consistent versions of the two conceptions of character education that we found throughout the proposals that we read, and still produced what we would consider to be pseudoconcepts for their central construct. The other proposals that we reviewed represented hybrid versions of these two notions, thus making them even less consistent conceptually. We interpret these variations not as shortcomings of the individual proposal developers but rather indicative of the contested nature of U.S. culture, of education in general, and of character education in particular.

INTELLECTUAL TRADITIONS
AND THEIR POLARIZING POTENTIAL

As many have argued, people living in complex societies with easy access to communication often develop their worldviews through engagement with

---

Grandeur of character lies wholly in force of soul—that is, in the force of thought, moral principle, and love; and this may be found in the humblest condition of life.

—William Ellery Channing

multiple traditions (Applebee, 1996; Taylor, 1985; Wertsch, 2000). These traditions are frequently incorporated into worldviews without resolution of their differences; rather, they produce a compromise that Taylor finds, while effective politically, "is a rotten one intellectually" (p. 247). We take a somewhat more sympathetic view of the compromises made in the development of these proposals. We see them as emerging at a time of heightened politicization of education, what we have referred to as the Culture Wars. We see them as well as products of efforts not only to accommodate the requirements of the OERI RFP, but also to operationalize a complex notion in the political arena of public education, a site in which ideologies have clashed since the earliest efforts at formal instruction. We next look more specifically at some of the competing traditions that have helped to shape the different ideologies that we found in the proposals submitted to OERI for character education funding.

Taylor (1985) argues that few people in industrialized nations can escape the influence of what he calls the designative and expressivist traditions in human thought. The designative tradition refers to ideas originating in the European Enlightenment (e.g., Augustine, and later Hobbes and Locke). Thinking in this tradition features rational (and now technological) approaches to understanding and controlling the world. Taylor's term *designative* arises from the representational role of language, which allows words to become "indispensable instruments ... for they allow us to deal with whole classes of ideas at a time" (p. 250). For the Enlightenment rationalist, the world may be parsed through discursive divisions into an abstract, organized whole through such devices as taxonomies, typologies, and other categorical schematics. Meaning is located in these abstractions and in the language that represents them. In perhaps its most extreme version, rationalist thinkers use observable facts to infer what is real, as in the positivist tradition. For a positivist, observing and measuring phenomena are the purposes of inquiry. What can't be observed and measured can't be known.

The expressivist tradition is grounded in Romanticism, which views people as intrinsically valuable and worthy, as living in harmony with nature, and as works in progress. Meaning and reality are not fixed but are emerging and interpretable. Taylor (1985) sees Herder, Humboldt, Heidegger, and Wittgenstein writing in this tradition and emphasizing action in the world rather than cognitive abstraction of the world. In terms of language, people formulate their ideas through the process of speaking or thinking through verbal means. From the standpoint of character education, we see this tradition at work in the upper midwestern state whose assessment came through discussion in which "The dialogue about these issues is more important than the score." We cannot imagine this approach being widely viable in the southern states whose proposals we have reviewed.

Taylor (1985) believes that these traditions both have deep roots in Western cultures, so much so that it is nearly impossible to formulate a position on meaning and human nature in today's complex world without drawing on them despite the fact that they are, he believes, contradictory. As a result, he argues, hybrid beliefs are both inevitable and unsatisfying. We have found both of the traditions he describes simultaneously at work in the proposals we have analyzed, particularly those from the Upper Midwest. Here, the generally romantic, idealistic view of young people as inherently worthy and in need of help in warding off the corruptive influence of the social world coexists with the rationalistic discourse of logical positivism, a primary instrument for ordering the world in the Enlightenment tradition. Rousseau's Emile, then, while living an emergent existence unadulterated by society's influence, would need to have his progress measured against standards and benchmarks as determined by external auditors—just the sort of rotten compromise described by Taylor.

As we make these distinctions, we should address a problem that we found in some opinions about character education, that being a misunderstanding and misrepresentation of the sources and traditions that particular authors attempt to critique. Sommers (2002), for instance, dismisses the romantic tradition in order to assert a more authoritarian conception of character education. In doing so she includes both Rousseau and Dewey as being nearly identical in their beliefs. We cannot imagine that she has read either Rousseau or Dewey very carefully. If she had, she would have difficulty conflating them into a shared ideology. Rousseau is perhaps history's most passionate author on the topic of the individual's right to live phenomenologically, that is, through reflection on the content of the mind to the exclusion of everything else (see Husserl, 1931). Dewey, in contrast, wrote extensively on the individual in relation to society, on the ways in which all human conduct is joint activity to some degree, and on the inherent interdependent relationship among people in social life. Rousseau and Dewey are fundamentally different on this key foundational idea, yet Sommers dismisses them both as sharing a similar romantic perspective in order to construct a binary so that she can reject all opposing viewpoints wholesale. We feel that if people are to critique whole schools of thought as a way of dismissing them, they at least ought to read them respectfully so as to characterize them properly.

We believe that binaries such as the one that Sommers (2002) constructs gloss over the great complexity of the world and of the world of ideas. All Enlightenment rationalism is not positivism, and positivism was asserted in reaction to metaphysics (which sought to know both the observable and unobservable worlds), not romanticism. The romanticism that Sommers hopes to dismiss is itself quite broad, encompassing conceptions that developed in a variety of nations and on different continents and thus, we would argue, are differentiated according to the cultures in which they emerged.

In another instance of what we believe is a caricature of opposing views, Schwartz (2002) reads progressive educators as rejecting any concessions to authority, saying,

> I glean from the writings of progressive educators that students should be honest and caring *only* when these values constitute their moral identity. This conception of moral identity focuses primarily on the authenticity of moral feelings and self-expression ("what feels good is good"). In addition, these educators repeatedly assert that something is terribly, terribly wrong if a student is honest or caring because these are the values that his or her parent, teachers, mentor, rabbi, or minister think important. The transmission of values from one generation to the next is dismissed by progressive educators as traditional or hegemonic or patriarchal in nature. In short, the moral umbilical cord must be severed cleanly and completely. Mikhael Bakhtin, a favorite theorist for many educational progressives, sums up this point of view when he writes: "[O]ne's own voice, although born of another or dynamically stimulated by another, will sooner or later begin to *liberate* itself from the authority of the other discourses" (emphasis added). (pp. 3–4)

We feel that Schwartz (2002) has engaged in the same kind of conflation and distortion that Sommers (2002) produced in her effort to lump together Dewey and Rousseau. Both authors of this book are political progressives in the tradition of John Dewey, Franklin D. Roosevelt, and others of their persuasion. We are also parents who believe we have transmitted our values to our children, though likely not intact. A telling example: Coauthor Peter Smagorinsky's ninth-grade son David recently took a web-based matching test (http://www.presidentmatch.com/) to see which of the contenders in the 2004 presidential race (at the time, including George W. Bush, Wesley Clark, Howard Dean, John Edwards, John Kerry, Dennis Kucinich, and Al Sharpton) best matched his beliefs and values. The vast majority of David's classmates matched up best with George W. Bush. David's match was Dennis Kucinich, also the best match for David's mother. Kucinich was the quintessential progressive Democrat with the smallest constituency among the electorate, as determined by votes in primaries, and to the left of John Kerry, his father's closest match. Given his great exposure to conservative ideology at school, we can only conclude that he has internalized the values he has learned at home.

Similarly, Joel's daughter Elizabeth has worked with homeless children in Nicaragua and currently is engaged in social work in a low-income Latino/a community. Not only is the moral umbilical cord still intact, we find Schwartz's (2002) statement that "these educators repeatedly assert that something is terribly, terribly wrong if a student is honest or caring because these are the values that his or her parent, teachers, mentor, rabbi, or minister think important" (p. 3) to be downright silly, not to mention a gross mis-representation of the beliefs of progressive educators. Surely there must be a better way to critique someone else's ideas than to reduce them to absurdities that can easily be refuted.

Schwartz (2002) further muddles the picture with his efforts to portray Mikhail Bakhtin as some kind of ahistorical modern progressive. Bakhtin is indeed a common citation in the work of progressive educators, though not because he wishes to discard the past. Quite to the contrary, Bakhtin (1981) emphasizes what he calls the "great historical destinies of genres" in repro-ducing discourse, including its ideology (p. 259). Bakhtin is fundamentally concerned with how the present is infused with history, and how the future is predicated on the past. Rather than believing that the past ought to be discarded, Bakhtin argues consistently that people embody the past in ev-erything they say and do, whether they recognize it or not. To Schwartz,

> Maxims constitute civilization's "memory bank." ... Indeed, maxims un-cover the voice of a second party—the commanding voice of one's elders, sages, or sacred ancestors. Consequently, whether maxims are seen as em-bodying universal truths or the norms of a society, they undeniably distill ex-pressions of wisdom, or what Meider and colleagues [Meider, Kingsbury, & Harder, 1992] call "apparent truths that have common currency" within a particular culture or society. (p. 6)

Bakhtin would agree and could have written this observation himself. He speaks of what Wertsch (1991) calls *voices of the mind* that people inter-nalize through engagement with culture. Again, we find it unfortunate that in producing critiques, people give superficial readings to those with whom they assume themselves to be in disagreement. It is possible, we be-lieve, to argue a position without trivializing opposing perspectives to the point of absurdity.

Once again, we wish to reject the binaries that typically pervade discus-sions about character education. Among these binaries is that the notions of cultural transmission of values and reflection on and reformulation of val-ues can't coexist. We disagree with Schwartz's (2000) effort to make these possibilities mutually exclusive. Our own experiences tell us that they can and do coexist. We find ourselves agreeing with Schwartz when he advo-cates using "maxims and wise sayings that have motivational and moral sig-nificance" and school-based honor codes to "transmit the values of honesty, trust, and integrity" (p. 5). As children long ago and currently as parents, we have relied on maxims to instill values, and have passed along some of our parents' wisdom to our children through these vehicles. The Jewish maxim, "Cheap is cheap," a likely saying for a frugal people who wandered the desert for 40 years in exile and learned to value durable materials, still works for us and our children. The problem is that we do not feel that maxims are sufficient, but rather ought to be part of a program of values education that invites reflection on maxims and other forms of wisdom and is tied to a community in which values are lived, not just invoked. When circumstances allow or dictate, we will buy a less expensive, lower quality good. These exceptions do not mean that we reject the maxim that "cheap is cheap," only that we find that on occasions other wisdom is appropriate.

One of the great problems with relying on binaries is that it eliminates productive disagreement and discussion. If we take the perspectives of people with whom we disagree and trivialize them into silly, easily dismissed opposing viewpoints, then we are not engaging with our antagonists. We are thus arguing to win, rather than arguing to learn (Smagorinsky, 2002c), an approach to debate that we find coming from not only orthodox critics but likely to follow from the authoritarian conception of teaching that they promote. But arguing to win leads to hollow victories; we have not engaged our adversaries, we have only spuriously diminished them. We find that through a genuine and respectful exchange of ideas—that is, by arguing to learn—we can sharpen and develop our own thinking. If the object is not to win but to grow, then we relish the opportunity to engage with others in discussion. But if we find our discussants incapable of listening and interested only in reducing us to absurdities and dismissing us, then we lose respect for their scholarship and their ideas.

We see a related problem in what we see as binary thinking in the tendency among character educators such as William Bennett to offer only exemplary people for young people to emulate. We see this inclination as producing a polarity of sorts—the "This is Good versus Evil" characterization by President George W. Bush of his battle against terrorists and those believed to be terrorists, those who comprised the "Axis of Evil." The oversimplification of such thinking has been revealed with the disclosure in 2004 of the prison abuses committed by U.S. soldiers in the Abu Ghraib prison in Iraq.

Yet as William Bennett's own life dramatically reveals, people are not wholly good or evil, just as nations are not simply right or wrong. One can be a generally good person and gamble away millions of dollars. One can be a good husband and invade another nation under false pretenses. Most people and communities of people are similarly somewhere between Good and Evil. Indeed, we see great advantages when a curriculum includes such morally ambiguous characters as the much-banned Holden Caulfield of J. D. Salinger's *The Catcher in the Rye:* He is the same kind of complex person that all students find themselves to be. But from the perspective of the Good vs. Evil binary, he lacks the uncompromised Goodness that allows for emulation by young people, and might even contribute to the use of profanity by those who find him to be a role model.

We see the proposals from the Upper Midwest reflecting the discourses of both Rousseauian Romanticism and Deweyan Progressivism, similar in some regards but different in others. The Romantic aspects might have to do with what we have called the discourse of grantsmanship. That is, in order for the proposal authors to write a fundable grant, they needed to make their conception of character education sound likely to be successful, if not downright flawless. And so young people are represented as the sort of youthful innocents who themselves will become beacons of hope for society if they can be nurtured for morality through character education. The kind of loutishness presumed by Headmaster Jarvis—who viewed children as "mean, nasty, brutish, selfish, and capable of great cruelty and meanness" (cited in Herbert, 1996, p. 58; cf. Sommers, 2002)—is not part of this happy image, nor are other references to infelicities in young people's makeup. Children are seen in this conception to be the solution to society's problems, rather than the problem as believed by the authors of the southern proposals.

A more truly Deweyan perspective might see people as more complex. Although undoubtedly child centered in his approach, Dewey also understood that collaboration is not necessarily easy. Rather, as Sumara and Luce-Kapler (1993) have argued, the notion of collaboration has its roots in the terms co-labor, which is a much more difficult and contested process than is typically found in notions of collaborative learning in educational writing (see, e.g., Tchudi & Tchudi, 1991). Educational discourse in the romantic tradition, however, tends to depict teaching and learning in the relatively painless manner criticized by Sykes (1992, 1995) and others. Our point is that traditions of thought are not so easily reduced. Indeed, when approached dialectically, they can serve as vehicles for reflecting deeply on belief systems and the consistency people display in their social actions, including their exhibition of good character.

THE IDEOLOGICAL NATURE OF CHARACTER EDUCATION

In a column raising concerns about President George W. Bush's justification for invading Iraq, conservative syndicated columnist George F. Will (2004) argued that

> After the war, in May, on Polish television, President Bush said, "We found the weapons of mass destruction. You know, we found biological laboratories." No, we did not. "So what's the difference?" said the president in December about the failure to find WMDs, because "if [Saddam Hussein] were to acquire weapons, he would be the danger." Such casualness, which would

Society's demands for moral authority and character increase as the importance of the position increases.

—John Adams

be alarming in any president, is especially so in one whose vaulting foreign policy ambitions have [been] devoted to planting democracy and "universal values" in hitherto inhospitable places.

Will's remarks suggest the difficulties of inserting one society's notion of universal values into another culture's practices. Viewed in such relief, the value system appears out of place and thus less universal than presumed when normalized in the culture of origin's daily life. Will—a self-described conservative who has influenced Republican public discourse through speech-writing, his syndicated columns, and his television commentaries—thus questions one of the conservative character education proposals' central claims, that a prescribed set of core values is universal and transcends cultures and nationalities. If Will is right, then character education is ideological at heart, a view that we endorse.

Goody (1997), in looking at the historical pattern of male domination over females in diverse societies, argues that

In looking at the relationship between domination and ideology it is useful to distinguish [among]:

- the current function of ideology in relation to existing patterns of domination.
- how an ideology comes to be formulated ...
- how an ideology comes to be institutionalized—made "official" (i.e., encapsulated in myth, or made the basis for public justification of action). (p. 450)

Among our central goals in this study has been to document the development of the discourse of character education and its attendant ideologies in the dominant cultures of two regions. As Goody would recommend, we have tried to document how these ideologies came to become dominant in these two distinct cultures and how they have become institutionalized, first in the OERI RFP and then in the states' proposals for character education funding and resultant character curricula.

We recall Cole's (1996) observation that "It has long been recognized that culture is very difficult for humans to think about. Like fish in water, we fail to 'see' culture because it is the medium within which we exist. Encounters with other cultures make it easier to grasp our own as an object of thought" (p. 8)." In this study we have tried, metaphorically, to take the fish out of the water and contrast not just the fish but the water itself and how it achieved its particular composition. Our goal with this project has been to infer how these different environments have produced different conceptions of what morality is and how to promote it through an educational intervention.

Both our opening review and our analysis of these four states' character education initiatives suggest that character is a concept that may be formulated differently depending on the culture in which it is conceived and the overall social goals and attendant ideology of those who advocate particular notions of character. To Lickona (1993) homosexuals, those who engage in premarital sex, those who masturbate, and others who do not share his vision of society are excluded from the possibility of being people of character. Whether these acts violate objective criteria of virtue, as he claims, is open to question. One might argue instead that Lickona, Ryan, Kilpatrick, and others who share an authoritarian conception of character have broad political and social goals that require a certain obedience to institutionalized standards and their guardians. Although these standards may have become normalized to the point that they become part of the dominant, commonsense ideology of society, they take on this status primarily among those who participate in an intertext of ideas and discourse in which their conception of appropriate thought and conduct has lost its subjectivity.

Our analysis has included what we see as a relation between the regional cultures of these four states and the notions of character that permeate their proposals to OERI for character education funding. As we have noted, the regional cultures from these states are far more diverse than the singular cultures we have outlined allow for, and the foundational ideas of the southern states' proposals have been best articulated by northeasterners such as William Bennett, William Kilpatrick, Thomas Lickona, and Kevin Ryan. Yet dominant cultures are dominant for a reason. They insinuate themselves into public institutions, public discourse, public assumptions, civil law, popular culture, and other deep-seated aspects of society that have lasting impact on regional beliefs.

Although the Civil Rights movement in the South eliminated most vestiges of legal segregation in the 1960s, segregation persists nonetheless in a variety of forms (Bell, 2000). Though perhaps most commonly associated with the South, segregation exists throughout the United States. More broadly, beliefs about the inferiority of races relative to Whites continue to have currency in both the lay imagination and in the published work of scholars (e.g., Herrnstein & Murray, 1994) who have access to power and those media that inform and shape public opinion. This belief is reflected in a letter to the *Atlanta Journal-Constitution* dated February 14, 2004, in response to an article lauding a minority job fair to encourage the hiring of faculty of color in the Cobb County, Georgia public schools—a county that elected conservative warhorses Newt Gingrich and Bob Barr to Congress and includes the city of Kennesaw, which in 1982 passed an ordinance that required heads of households to maintain a firearm and ammunition in their homes:

Teachers Stupidly "Dumbed Down"

One of the reasons our house in Cobb County sold quickly was the outstanding school system. All of that is about to change if the system implements its recruiting of minority teachers. [One teacher], who is being recruited with 11 years' [sic] of experience, said, "If they want us that bad, they must be willing to treat us good." One would hope that she will not be teaching English. Not only do we have to worry about the "dumbing down" of students. It seems that a bigger problem is the "dumbing down" of teachers.

The woman who wrote the letter believes that by encouraging minority teachers, the entire school system will suffer a drop in intelligence and the community's homeowners will no longer enjoy high real estate values. The evidence that she provides is a single sentence that includes two variations from standard usage. We should also point out that the letter's author's use of the apostrophe following *years* is incorrect. The apostrophe would only be appropriate if *years* directly modified *experience*. Our goal is not to pick nits with her language usage and punctuation, but to point out that she is just as guilty as the teacher of using the language in ways that violate the rules prescribed in grammar textbooks. We can only interpret her opprobrium as grounded in a deeper belief about inequality in the races, with deviations from her own normalized beliefs and ways of being in the world regarded as inferior.

As cultural psychologists (e.g., Cole, 1996) have argued, once a motive for a society is established, proleptic social forces—those so heavily embedded into cultural practice that they seem natural and normative—contribute to the persistence of those beliefs and practices and their perpetuation in subsequent generations who have been socialized into this motive and the beliefs it suggests. They shape the beliefs not only of the dominant privileged class but of society's less advantaged as well. Clark and Clark (1947/1958), for instance, demonstrated the tragic consequences of institutionalized beliefs in young Black children who had internalized White society's view of their inferiority. We see good reason to believe, then, that the regional cultures we have outlined do indeed contribute to the conceptions of character and character education that these states have produced.

Beliefs, however, are not simply regional. Jacobs and Jacobs-Spencer (2001) tie their Native-American conception of character more explicitly to an indigenous people's worldview. They acknowledge that their perspective is distinct from Western beliefs and outline clearly the consequences of these different beliefs on one's sense of harmony with the earth's creatures and elements. Character and character education are extensions of this worldview. Culture provides them with their beliefs about character and how one's character is defined by relationships, not only with people but with the whole of the natural world.

The community-based perspective emerging from Jeffersonian democracy and Deweyan progressivism also follows a clear ideology, one particularly at home in the Upper Midwest with its longstanding communitarian values. While culturally at odds with many in the United States who might regard its cooperative, socialistic, nurturing approach dissonant with their beliefs about the United States as a competitive, capitalistic nation of hard knocks, this approach is welcome among educators who favor democratic, caring approaches to community. Although this discourse stream is traceable to Dewey and his many publications beginning at the end of the nineteenth century, our cultural analysis suggests that the ideology of the German and Scandinavian settlements of the Upper Midwest in the mid-1800s provides an antecedent to Dewey's conception and itself emerges from ideas circulating in Europe prior to their immigration.

We see no reason to accord greater credibility to any one of these conceptions of character and character education than to others. We see them as representing competing ideologies not just about character education but about the organization and process of U.S. society. Perhaps commentators such as Kilpatrick (1992) might regard us as products of the process-oriented education movement that he believes has become so relativistic that people can no longer think critically or make moral judgments or, in this case, make judgments about which moral perspective best facilitates virtuous conduct. We would argue instead that we are open to the possibilities of different perspectives and that, after talking intensively about character education for several years now, still cannot separate our preference for the sort of vision we found in the Upper Midwest from our own cultural histories and ideologies.

CAPITALISM, COMMUNITY, AND CHARACTER EDUCATION

> Adam Smith, the eighteenth-century economist and intellectual father of capitalism, warned that without some sort of check, "the mean rapacity, the monopolizing spirit of merchants and manufacturers" would allow them to become "the rulers of mankind." ... Shed of restraint, market values have begun to intrude ever more rudely on human, moral, spiritual and community values. All of us recognize the problem, though we call it different things. When conservatives bewail the loss of family values, at root they are describing the intrusion of market forces into places where they don't belong. The same is true when liberals wring their hands over the loss of community. Some things ought to remain impervious to the Al-

---

The crown and glory of life is character. It is the noblest possession of a man, constituting a rank in itself, and an estate in the general good-will; dignifying every station, and exalting every position in society. It exercises a greater power than wealth, and secures all the honor without the jealousies of fame. It carries with it an influence which always tells; for it is the result of proved honor, rectitude, and consistency—qualities which, perhaps more than any other, command the general confidence and respect of mankind.

—Samuel Smiles

mighty Dollar. Otherwise, our drive to make ourselves richer will instead make us poorer. (Bookman, 2004)

Jay Bookman, the liberal deputy editorial page editor for the *Atlanta Journal-Constitution*, reached this conclusion when considering a capitalist economy's ability to serve people well without constraints on industry. His concern for the effects of capitalist self-interest echo longstanding beliefs grounded in Marxist thought regarding capitalism's tendency to fragment communities. To Marx, community is the goal toward which human social evolution is moving. Influenced by Darwin, to whom he dedicated *Das Kapital,* he argued indeed that society begins when capitalism is eclipsed by communism, given that capitalism requires people to compete like animals for the resources available for survival.

In this vision capitalism fragments communities because of its inherent competitiveness that emphasizes finance over family, places profit and personal acquisition above human needs, and encourages rivalry over the cooperation that leads to the development of a sense of community. Alperovitz (1996) discusses the communitarian values of Martin Buber (1949), who was influenced by Marx's critique of bourgeois society while rejecting his stance against religion (Tillich, 1948):

> Even as he excoriated the tyrannical centralized socialism he called "Moscow," Buber also judged capitalist society "as a society" to be "inherently poor in structure and growing visibly poorer every day...." In *Paths in Utopia,* he observed: "Under capitalist economy and the state peculiar to it, the constitution of society has been continually hollowed out, so that the modern individualizing process finished up as a process of atomization." ... [Buber] judged that "the structure of a society is to be understood by its social content or community-content." ... The central question for Buber was how to rebuild the social and, above all, economic institutions needed to restore, sustain, and nurture stable and cooperative human relationships. A nation could be a "community," he held, only "to the degree that it is a community of communities...." His radically decentralist socialist-communitarian vision stressed what he termed the "Full Cooperative"—i.e., consumer and worker cooperatives operating together in the same locality in such a manner as to alter the local culture.

Perhaps it is not surprising that Buber, Marx, and many early European settlers of the U.S. Upper Midwest came from Austria or Germany. Nor is it surprising that, considering the Upper Midwest's historical practice of communal social organization, their character education efforts are geared toward the preservation of cooperative communities of the sort idealized by Buber. A tension for life in this region is the attempt to preserve these values in a society that on the whole is dedicated to capitalist principles. We see the character education proposals working to preserve their communitarian heritage in the public institution of the schools, serving to some degree to forestall the inevitable advance of capitalism and its effects on communities. Meanwhile, the states from the Deep South, whose modern notion of capitalism emerged from a semifeudal slave economy, have sought to institute character education programs that approximate the hierarchical business model in which authority proceeds from the top down.

We again see the character education movement as situated in the broader, highly ideological Culture Wars. Many in the United States have a reflexive antipathy toward anything socialistic or communitarian. We date this opposition to the many iterations of the Red Scare, beginning with fear of Bolshevism in the wake of World War I. The Bolshevik leaders instigated the coup that overthrew the Russian revolutionary government that was about to ratify a national constitution based on American principles of private ownership, instituting instead the communist system whereby wealth was redistributed to the working class. This regime and its priorities were viewed as a threat not just to the United States but to most of the victorious nations during and following World War I (MacMillan, 2002). The specter of communism has continued to menace many in the United States, recurring during the McCarthy Era of the 1950s (see, e. g., Skousen, 1958/2003), present through much of our lifetime in Cold War politics (Haynes, 1996), and alive today in such organizations as the Anti-Communitarian League (http://nord.twu.net/acl/index.html).

We do not intend to overplay the Marxist hand with these observations. After all, Marx predicted that capitalism would be inexorably surpassed by communism (Marx & Engel, 1848), a forecast that has not been borne out by history. Furthermore, Marx himself found his own principles difficult to live by, supported as he was for much of his life by Friedrich Engel's family's wealth. Marx (e.g., 1867) has proven to be an insightful social analyst but, at least thus far, a poor architect of social orders, or at least an architect of social orders that have suffered from the greed, ambition, and totalitarianism of those who have ruled in his name. Although clearly flawed in his consistency and vision, Marx nonetheless has been a durable thinker with respect to his critique of the effects of capitalism on efforts to establish a humane cooperative society.

We also do not wish to position ourselves as socialists or communists. We appreciate much that capitalism affords us: the computers with which we write this book, the comfortable homes we have acquired through hard work, the absence of food lines at the grocery store, the abundance of choices the market provides us in virtually every line of products, and much more. Although we recognize the unfortunate consequences of capitalism, we regretfully accept Winston Churchill's observation that "Capitalism is the worst economic system, except for all the others."

At the same time we embrace the progressive vision of a world in which there is greater equality in sharing society's resources, a world in which even with dramatic differences in possessions, a nation marshals its resources so that families have homes, rudimentary health care, and other assets. We do not expect that everyone be wealthy, only that they have a certain level of sustenance. This vision represents a modified version of capitalism, one that includes the competitive balance that generates quality goods and services, creativity, advances in science and technology, exploration of new frontiers, and other consequences of free ideas but also ensures basic needs for even the most indigent of its members.

We recognize the failures of communism as applied to national politics and economies and reject it as a political system. Yet we also wonder why a nation that generates as much wealth as the United States has millions of children living in poverty, on the streets, and without health care. We wonder how our laws can permit industries to abandon communities that have supported them for decades. We are appalled by a tax code that permits the wealthiest individuals and corporations to pay few if any taxes while the government provides subsidies and tax breaks that amount to billions of dollars in a stressed economy. We are troubled that our economic system adheres to the monetarist assumptions of Nobel Laureate Milton Friedman (1977), who argues that full employment decreases productivity and efficiency and helps cause inflation, and thus is bad for the economy.

Yet, such conditions obtain under free market capitalism. Despite utopian conceptions of the American Dream in which young ghetto children can grow up to presidents and CEOs, many people who are born into poverty have difficulty escaping. We do not view these unfortunate people as *les miserables* who are responsible for their own misfortune. Rather, we see them as members of a "community of communities" who might make important contributions if this land of opportunity would extend a helping hand to help them get started.

COMMUNITIES AND INDIVIDUALS

In 1769, [Daniel Boone] set out with five others to explore the border region of Kentucky. They halted on Red River, a branch of the Kentucky, where they hunted for several months. In December, 1769, Boone and a companion named Stewart were captured by the Indians, but escaped, and Boone was soon after joined by his brother. They were captured again, and Stewart was killed; but Boone escaped, and his brother going shortly after to North

---

Character is not the enemy of self-expression and personal freedom, it is their necessary precondition.

—James Q. Wilson

Carolina, he was left alone for several weeks in the wilderness, with only his rifle for means of support. (*History of Boone County, Missouri*, 1882)

Daniel Boone captures well the spirit of rugged American individualism, going out beyond the frontier and into the wilderness to subdue the natives and carve out territory for himself and his family. Well before Ralph Waldo Emerson wrote *Self-Reliance* in 1841, Boone personified Emerson's "great man ... who in the midst of the crowd keeps with perfect sweetness the independence of solitude." Although the U.S. frontiers have shifted radically, the individualist, nonconformist, and pioneer remains an icon throughout the culture.

Indeed, the values distilled in Emerson's famous essay—required reading for just about any student in any American Literature class throughout the country—are viewed by many as distinctively American. Such bootstrapping individualists as Benjamin Franklin are still held as exemplary, in spite of their other human weaknesses (e.g., Franklin's decision to live as a celebrity in Europe while his wife languished in Philadelphia; see Isaacson, 2003). This value on the individual lies at the heart of the character education proposals from the Deep South, where character is regarded as a trait possessed by individuals regardless of cultural variation or social relationships. Yet, the beliefs exhibited in the character curricula require the sort of conformity that Emerson advised against, that is, unquestioning acceptance of value systems.

The Rev. Paul L'Herrou (1998), a Unitarian minister, tried to reconcile Emerson's celebration of individuality with what he feels is a concurrent human need for community:

> Rugged individualism is the go-it-alone, I am right and I will not be influenced by you, I don't need anyone else approach to life. Too often, our veneration of rugged individualism results in ragged and rent community. People feel compelled to defend one side or the other. The pursuit of rugged individualism suppresses true self-reliance.... Even though Emerson is cited as the justification of so-called rugged individualism, of unbridled freedom, of doing your own thing, he is really saying something very different. He is saying neither—be so convinced of your rightness that you march off in one direction no matter who or what gets in your way, nor allow the crowd, popular opinion, pop culture to determine your direction.... We can support each other in the quest for truth and meaning, and through our differing understandings and the respectful dialogue of strongly-held ideas and commitments, we can draw closer to what has ultimate meaning and satisfaction for us all.

> This is the meaning of community. It is not conformity, nor is it separateness. Community is the ability to be with one another in all of our uniqueness, with all of our differences, without losing our selfhood and to so respect our own understandings and perceptions that we also respect the sincere perceptions of others, while being vulnerable enough to allow our self to be influenced and changed by the very different viewpoint of another.

Self-reliance is the pre-condition for true community. True community is the nurturing environment for strong and healthy individualism. Maturity, individuation, is the ability to be self-reliant and intimate at the same time.

Self-reliance is the quality of respecting your own inner search for what seems most true and meaningful for you and contributing your resulting unique viewpoint to enrich the community through diversity.... The gist of the problem seems to be that we understand Emerson to be saying that it is noble not only to be an individual, but to be independent. But, every human being needs other human beings in order to survive. Total independence, the independence which much in our culture glorifies, is an illusion, an illusion which blinds us to the realities and the deficiencies of our dependencies and the dependencies of others upon us. (http://www.uucava.org/sermons/Emerson0.htm)

Through these remarks, Rev. L'Herrou attempts to reconcile a fundamental tension in U.S. society, one that is epitomized in the character education proposals from the Upper Midwest and Deep South, that between a value on individualism and a value on community. The inability to reconcile these two positions results in inconsistencies in the minds of many. Conservatives, for instance, often accuse liberals of being both narcissistic and self-centered (e.g., Auster, 1996) and of having socialist or communist tendencies (e.g., Dittohead Deb, n.d.). Meanwhile, liberals typically find conservatives to be selfishly individualistic (e.g., Franken, 2003) and overly concerned with conformity (e.g., Moore, 2003). As these contradictory claims suggest, people are more complex than simple characterizations allow for.

The conflict between individuality and community has been resolved in neither the character education debate nor the broader Culture Wars. Bellah, Madsen, Sullivan, Swidler, and Tipton (1996) argue that "individualism is eating away at the social and moral fabric which Tocqueville saw as taming capitalist America's destructive tendencies" (Atlas, n. d.). To Bellah et al., most people in the United States believe that economic success or misfortune is the individual's responsibility alone, a belief that sustains free-market principles. This perspective is evident in what Ryan (1971) calls *blaming the victim*, that is, assuming that, like *Les Miserables*, poor people in the United States are the agents of their own misfortune. Bellah et al. take a liberal perspective on the balance between individualism and community, arguing that the tradition of civic participation, evident not only in 1960s radicalism but older Biblical and republican traditions, can mitigate the free market's encouragement of personal greed.

Undoubtedly, this vision is at the heart of the upper midwestern conception of character education and is deeply engrained in upper midwestern culture, as suggested by the nineteenth century immigrant who knew to be wary of "a cunning businessman [who] knows how to get the better of you in a bargain" (Wefald, 1971, p. 12). A modern incarnation of this sort of Yankee capitalist might be Reagan advisor Justin Dart, whom Bellah et al. quote as saying, "I never looked for a business that's going to render a service to

> *Because it is the most character-building activity a child can engage in, children have the right to share significantly in the doing of household chores.*
>
> —*John Rosemond*

mankind.... Greed is involved in everything we do. I find no fault in that." Dart himself might have served as the model for Gordon Gekko, memorably played by Michael Douglas in the film *Wall Street* (Stone, 1987), who told his company's stockholders,

> The point is, ladies and gentleman, is that greed—for lack of a better word—is good. Greed is right. Greed works. Greed clarifies, cuts through, and captures the essence of the evolutionary spirit. Greed, in all of its forms—greed for life, for money, for love, knowledge—has marked the upward surge of mankind. And greed—you mark my words—will not only save Teldar Paper, but that other malfunctioning corporation called the USA.

This belief that greed is good, without any consideration for the greater good, cannot, we believe, serve as the basis of a strong character education program.

CHILDREN'S LITERATURE AND CHARACTER EDUCATION

> You know that the beginning is the most important part of any work, especially in the case of a young and tender thing; for that is the time at which the character is being formed and the desired impression is more readily taken.... Shall we just carelessly allow children to hear any casual tales which may be devised by casual persons, and to receive into their minds ideas for the most part the very opposite of those which we should wish them to have when they are grown up?
>
> We cannot.... Anything received into the mind at that age is likely to become indelible and unalterable; and therefore it is most important that the tales which the young first hear should be models of virtuous thoughts....
>
> Then will our youth dwell in a land of health, amid fair sights and sounds, and receive the good in everything; and beauty, the effluence of fair works, shall flow into the eye and ear, like a health-giving breeze from a purer region, and insensibly draw the soul from the earliest years into likeness and sympathy with the beauty of reason.
>
> There can be no nobler training than that. (Plato; quoted in Bennett, 1993, p. 17)

William Bennett quotes this passage from Plato's *The Republic* to open *The Book of Virtues: A Treasury of Great Moral Stories*. Bennett's volume, according to the testimonials on the back cover, "belongs in every home" (Rush Limbaugh) and "ought to be distributed, like an owner's manual, to new parents leaving the hospital" (*Time* magazine). Bennett is well-established as an important voice for the orthodox perspective in the Culture Wars, as evidenced in the titles of other books he has published: *Our Children and Our Country: Improving America's Schools and Affirming the Common Culture* and *The De-Valuing of America: The Fight for Our Culture and Our Children*. The purpose of *The Book of Virtues*, he states in the introduction, is "to aid in the time-honored task of the moral education of the young. Moral education ... involves rules and precepts—the *dos* and *don'ts* of life with others—as well as explicit instruction, exhortation, and training" (p. 11). He continues, "these stories, unlike courses in 'moral reasoning,' give children some specific reference points. ... Children must have at their disposal a stock of examples illustrating what we see to be right and wrong, good and bad—examples illustrating that, in many instances, what is morally right and wrong can indeed be known and promoted" (p. 12).

Molding the character through what he calls "moral literacy" is an especially critical task of teaching young children: "the formation of character and the teaching of moral literacy come first, in the early years; the tough issues come later, in senior high school or after" (p. 13). Hearkening back to the good old days, he says, "This book reminds the reader of a time— not so long ago—when the verities were the moral verities. It is thus a kind of antidote to some of the distortions of the age in which we now live" (p. 14). To Bennett, young children must be inculcated with a sense of morality so that they feel it in their bones. The internalization of these values does not come about through discussion or reasoning, but through steadfast exposure to moral adults and the texts through which they impress timeless virtues.

Bennett's (1993) views are disputed by many historians of children's literature. Although virtually all would agree that didacticism has been a central element of the genre from its beginnings, Segel (1986) and others view the genre's complexity as beginning much earlier than does Bennett. She asserts, for instance, that "children's literature until the mid-nineteenth century had, without exception, depicted obedience as the most important childhood virtue" (p. 172). The role of literary characters as moral exemplars, however, changed with the advent of the books containing the "good bad boys," characters who signaled a "radical change in what adults expected of children" or what adults defined as the *ideal child:*

> Jim Hawkins, Tom Sawyer, and many other rascals disobey adults and get away with it. In fact, their defiance of adult authority constitutes a major part of their charm.... The reason for this cultural redefinition of the ideal boy is not difficult to deduce. When the man's role will take him into the great world to engage in fierce battles of commerce and empire, pluck and enterprise are virtues to cultivate in male children.... The docile obedience required of adolescent girls in the girls' books stands as a marked contrast to the boys' book protagonist. (pp. 173–174)

Rather, then, than being an "antidote to some of the distortions of the age in which we now live," as claimed by Bennett, young people's literature began depicting human complexity—"distortions" in Bennett's view—over a century and a half ago.

Ironically, then, the rigors of the capitalist world—the world defended, preserved, and idealized by such corporate icons as William Bennett—contributed to the development of protagonists who, rather than serving as moral exemplars, behaved much in the manner of a cunning entrepreneur. Tom Sawyer might easily serve as the prototype for the captain of industry with his clever deceptions and ability to seduce others into working for him, as financiers such as Donald Trump (Trump & Schwartz, 1988) have boasted of doing. Yet at the same time, young Tom provides what many would consider to be a questionable moral exemplar for impressionistic children during their formative years.

The portrayal of the complexity of human experience in young people's literature took another turn between 1950 and 1990, described by Murray (1998) as a period of child liberation that coincided with the Civil Rights movement, Women's Rights movement, and other efforts to topple longstanding hegemonic social structures in the United States. She argues that during this period, writers of young adult literature had to choose "between creating stories mirroring traditional values and showing the consequences of antisocial behavior" (p. 184). Writers also were being challenged to "produce stories that accepted the teen subculture at face value and challenged adult prohibitions and mores" (p. 184). These shifts in content and behavior were evidenced by the presence of violence, drug abuse, and sexuality of all kinds in books for children and young adults.

The genre known as *New Realism*—typified by S. E. Hinton's *The Outsiders*, Paul Zindel's *The Pigman*, and other novels depicting social dilemmas faced by young teens—epitomized this turn in young people's literature. Many have argued (e.g., Smagorinsky, 2000; Tighe, 1998) that the morally complex characters found in such works of literature are potentially the richest source for discussions about human behavior and character. These books dramatize violent social class confrontations, the temptations of drugs and alcohol, explorations in sexuality, and other behaviors that most character education programs would hope to dissuade children from experiencing. Root (1977) describes the genre as

> fiction for young readers which addresses itself to personal problems and social issues heretofore considered taboo for fictional treatment by the general public, as enunciated by its traditional spokesmen: librarians, teachers, ministers, and others. The new realism is often graphic in its language and always explicit in its treatment. (p. 19)

Taxel (1999), in reviewing Murray's (1998) *American Children's Literature and the Construction of Childhood,* observes that in the New Realism the fictional worlds of S.E. Hinton, M.E. Kerr, Louise Fitzhugh, Norma Klein, Judy Blume, and others no longer have unambiguously defined rules. The family no longer is a haven and, indeed, "adults do not make the world better or safer for children; children themselves shoulder the responsibility for learning how the world works and finding a way to adapt to it" ([Murray,] p. 191). In short, the construction of childhood posited by the new realism sees children as "neither innocent nor sinful." They need no protection from reality because they can develop "the ego strength to overcome alienation and pain. Experiencing life is the best preparation for adulthood" ([Murray,] p. 194).

Taxel (1997) views these changes in the presentation of children's lives as violating previously taboo subjects and themes that emerged in children's and young people's literature through the New Realism. New Realism erased the previously safe and sanitized world of unambiguous right and wrong where all dilemmas were clearly defined and had readily available solutions. Lancto (n. d.) argues that in the work of Robert Cormier, whose young adult novels have appeared on numerous banned book lists,

> The language and sexuality are probably more disconcerting to adults because we would like to think that our thirteen- or fourteen-year-old children never use profanity or think about sex, but Cormier said that his books have credibility with young readers because he uses language and scenes that reflect how kids talk and what they think about. Young readers are more likely to take the language and sexuality in stride; seeing them in books assures them that they are not abnormal. Among themselves, preteen children often use language that would make their parents blush. Pubescent children might even entertain occasional thoughts about sex—their teen years being the occasion. (http://www.worldandi.com/newhome/public/2003/september/mt2publasp)

The changes found in this genre not only are specific to the books themselves but are indicative of broader shifts in the culture: the sexual revolution of the 1960s and 1970s, the increased access to greater varieties of recreational drugs, the cynicism and willingness to challenge authority engendered by the Vietnam War and Watergate scandal, and other developments that we have amply described as contributing to the current character education movement. As Hunt (1992) notes, not even the "most apparently simple book for children can be innocent of ideological freight" (p. 18).

Critics such as William Bennett regard these shifts in values as part of a general "slouching towards Gomorrah" (Bork, 1996), a trend that requires the reinstitution of moral education in which "what is morally right and wrong can indeed be known and promoted." Whether these changes in literature for young people represent "distortions," as believed by cultural conservatives such as Bennett, or an effort to more accurately depict "reality," as argued by progressive children's literature critics, is a question that lies at the heart of the Culture Wars of which the character education debate is a part.

> *Learning and knowledge—and even wisdom—are not enough.... At the risk of sounding a bit uncool, I say to the graduating class that your success in life, and the success of our country, is going to depend on the integrity and other qualities of character that you and your contemporaries will continue to develop and demonstrate over the years ahead. A generation from now, as you watch your children graduate, you will want to be able to say that whatever success you achieved was the result of honest and productive work, and that you dealt with people the way you would want them to have dealt with you.*
>
> *—Alan Greenspan*

THE GENDERING OF CHARACTER EDUCATION

We must draw attention to the fact that most of the commentators on character education are men. Most of our references are to men, most of the people involved with character education organizations and centers are men, and so are we. Why, we wonder, is character education an issue on which men are much more likely than women to have published their opinions? We recall the work of Lawrence Kohlberg on morality (e.g., 1976) and its critique by Carol Gilligan (1983) for its reliance on an exclusively male sample. To Gilligan, Kohlberg framed moral issues in ways that corresponded better to men's mental makeup than to women's. By using a male sample to test beliefs that Gilligan found to be distinctly masculine, Kohlberg confirmed his perspective regarding moral development without the disconfirming evidence that Gilligan later provided in her replications of Kohlberg's work with samples consisting of women. With the benefit of hindsight, we can wonder in astonishment how and why Kohlberg's work survived the external review process, given that his sample violated a key axiom of psychological research by representing only half the population under study (cf. Perry's, 1968, research on ethical development, conducted with students at Harvard, which was not fully coeducational until 1972). Yet in the 1970s, the field of educational psychology was dominated by men, whose own perspectives were likely normalized to the point where an all-male sample represented populations as they understood them. Like Cole's (1996) fish, they could not step outside their culture to see its composition and limitations.

We are puzzled by the paucity of perspectives from women in the public discourse on issues such as virtue, morality, and character. The predominance of male views is especially odd given that women have often been perveived as society's paragons; witness, for instance, the doctrine of separate spheres, a Victorian-era middle-class belief in the moral superiority of women that contributed to the growth of the many women's club movements of the late 1800s (Price, 1999). With attention now available to women's views through the positions they have achieved in academia, politics, business, and other platforms for expressing opinions, the superabundance of male perspectives in the current debate is quite remarkable. We must assume these issues to be central to women's concerns about the future, as evidenced by Noddings's (2002) emphasis on issues such as care and moral conduct. We are tempted to interpret the issue as one of authoritarianism—that is, in the view of Gilligan (1983) and others, men are more likely to establish hierarchies and rules in the rationalist tradition that, we believe, map well onto the approaches to character education institutionalized in the OERI RFP and central to the proposals submitted by states from the Deep South. Yet most published critics of this perspective are men as well.

We asked Nell Noddings if she could explain why most high-profile character educator proponents are men, and she replied:

> Well, this is hard to answer. Two things come to mind. First, men just don't read material written by women. My stuff is read, but I have written a lot, formed the right connections, etc. However, I looked at my shelf on moral education, and I note the following: Mary Brabeck, Ruth Charney, Sharon Lamb, Betty Sichel, Marilyn Watson, Sara Ruddick, Virginia Held, Joan Goodman & Howard Lesnick, Katherine Simon, Robin Berson, Lisa Kuhmerker, Kim Hays, and Mary Ann Glendon. That's for starters! I have cited all of these in one place or another. Several of them are directly relevant to character education, e.g, Charney, Sichel, Goodman, Simon, Berson, and Hayes.
>
> Second, women scholars are more likely than men (I guess) to work across disciplinary lines. Our work may appear in nursing, law, feminist philosophy, peace studies, environmental studies, religion, etc. If male scholars don't read across fields, they will miss relevant work. The basic reason, however, seems to be a continuing prejudice against women. I can't explain it, but I'm weary of it. (N. Noddings, personal communication, July 4, 2004)

We do not have a clear answer to this question either, but feel that the observation is worth making and worthy of further consideration by those concerned with character education.

MENTAL HEALTH AND CHARACTER EDUCATION

We have briefly expressed our concern that the issue of mental health is virtually absent from discussions about character education. Yet many students who come to school with non-normative mental health makeups are treated as discipline problems of the sort measured as indexes of low character in the pro-

---

There is no greater wonder than the way the face and character of a woman fit so perfectly in a man's mind, and stay there, and he could never tell you why. It just seems it was the thing he most wanted.

—Robert Louis Stevenson

posals we have studied. We believe that it is important for any character education initiative to recognize and account for mental health in its conception of good character, both for those with nonnormative makeups and those with whom they interact.

Mental health is the elephant in the character education closet. The World Health Organization (2001) reports that about 7.5 million children in the United States—12% of all children under 18—have mental disorders, nearly half of which lead to serious disability. Jamison (1997) found that 20% of high school students had seriously considered committing suicide during the year prior to his study, with most having drawn up a suicide plan; suicide is the third leading cause of death of teenagers between 15 and 19 years of age, often following from a depressive disorder. Yet most parents and teachers feel that mental health issues are poorly addressed in schools (Dowling & Pound, 1994; Rappaport & Carolla, 1999), many teachers have little understanding of how to recognize or respond to students with mental health problems (Madison, 1996), and only recently has mental health been identified as a reason to develop an Individual Education Plan (IEP) for students.

These widespread misunderstandings have resulted in many such students being regarded as troublesome or lacking character in schools. Yet, as reporter Anne Imse (1999) wrote following the Columbine school shooting tragedy,

Even teens as dangerously troubled as Eric Harris stand a good chance of slipping through the cracks in Jefferson County and across Colorado, failing to get badly needed mental health care. There are serious roadblocks to getting treatment for sick kids [including]

- State prohibitions against law enforcement agencies telling schools about a problem kid unless there's a conviction;
- Schools worrying about being saddled with psychiatric bills if they recommend treatment, or even being sued;
- Not enough money earmarked for counselors and counseling for the state's youth.

So, even though Jefferson County school officials have become more sensitive to kids' mental states ... they remain hamstrung about arranging treatment. "We have no place to go with them," said Clark Bencomo, a counselor at Green Mountain High School. "All we can do is suspend or expel." "We are oftentimes reduced to putting a kid in a place where they're safe, but it's not the right program," added Kay Cessna, intervention services director for Jefferson County schools. "There are not enough places." [One parent of a child with disabilities complained], "They don't have the time, the manpower, and they don't get it."

Cook (2004) finds this problem occurring in other states as well, reporting that students with mental health problems are often put in special education programs or disciplined when they act out, either as a consequence of their makeup (e.g., a child with Tourette's syndrome's involuntary profanity) or in response to the taunting they face from their peers.

Yet a mental health professional would surely argue that the problem is not a lack of character and the solution is not to punish students with mental health problems. Rather, a broader understanding of mental health among students and faculty—the sort of attention to climate we found in the states from the Upper Midwest—would contribute to a more sympathetic and less punitive environment for such students in school. Indeed, Damasio (1994) argues in his somatic-marker theory against the classic Cartesian mind/body binary, instead positing that brain and body are integrally related not just to one another but to the environment. A change in the environment, he finds, may contribute to changes in how a person processes new information (cf. Luria, 1979; Pert, 1997); that is, in response to developments in the surroundings, the brain will encode perceptions in new kinds of ways.

Conceivably, then, changes in school climate can contribute to the emotional well-being of students whose mental makeup falls outside the normal range. The therapy for such students is still widely debated. While medication and counseling have benefited many with nonnormative makeups in their relationships with others, the medical model has been criticized because it assumes that a normative mental state is best for all. This criticism frequently comes up in debates about whether medications for Attention Deficit Disorder are prescribed too often for any students who have difficulty focusing in school. Some argue that prescribing such medications is designed more to increase the comfort levels of those around such students than to help those students themselves.

The jury is still out concerning the question of whether people with such diagnoses are sick and in need of medicine. Cook (2004) argues that relying simply on medication and counseling is inadequate, that a broader environmental change that enables an understanding and tolerance of difference, and gives young people tools for managing their difference, is essential to helping young people construct positive lives for themselves and in turn

---

T. S. Eliot once observed that some of his contemporaries were in the habit of "dreaming of systems so perfect that no one will need to be good." The dream of finding a substitute for character is still, of course, very much alive.... The dream of a society "so perfect that no one will need to be good" is really a child's dream.... We need to stop dreaming. The truth is, there is no substitute for personal character and there never will be.

—William Kilpatrick

contribute to a more humane society. Taking a punitive approach to difference, she argues, is regressive and only makes life more fragile for those characterized as different and more emotionally and cognitively unhealthy for those who surround them.

FINAL THOUGHTS

We do not expect our study of the character education proposals to find that any approach is better than any other; indeed, we have no basis for making such an argument. Rather, we have attempted to regard the proposals we have analyzed as the distillation of many years of debate about the purpose of U.S. society and how that debate is framed and elaborated. The notions of character that we have outlined are essential mediators in moving a society toward its goals. Even with such disparate overall conceptions of character, a number of values are shared, in part because of the need for grantsmanship and in part because U.S. culture—at least that part of the culture that derives from its European base of immigrants—in spite of its differences, appears to have some common values.

Our study provides somewhat of a snapshot, given its reliance on proposals submitted within a limited time frame and in response to a particular request. Yet this snapshot, like any good photograph, reveals much that is outside the frame: It distills the essence of the subject so that one can infer a great deal about its antecedent cultural history and its position relative to other images from the same period. Character is, as the many quotations we have sprinkled throughout the text suggest, a value central to any belief system. Yet while conceiving of good character seems to be a human disposition, the essence of that notion varies from culture to culture. We argue that references to character reveal the human values that produce a particular kind of person and society, rather than describing what is universally true about humanity. Instead of being transcendent, character traits and the values they promote are particular to specific cultural goals and practices, producing the behaviors and dispositions that afford the most prosperous journey on the path toward a society's teleological ends. At the same time, by reproducing those values and reaching that destination, each traveler reifies that pathway and endpoint, making it more likely that fellow and future travelers will find it a worthwhile way to go within the confines of that culture's purpose and practices.

Americanism is a question of principles, of idealism, of character: it is not a matter of birthplace or creed or line of descent.

—Theodore Roosevelt

Toward a Reconsideration
of the Character Curriculum

We close by outlining our views of what we see as possible in a character curriculum. We recognize that the approach we advocate follows from our progressive values and that people with orthodox views might find them
dubious. We hope that even those who disagree with the approach that we
advocate will regard it as an earnest effort to promote character development in young people that is grounded in a long and respectable tradition
of Western thought, if not the only tradition that has contributed to the development of a U.S. perspective.

THE RECONSTRUCTION AND INTERPRETATION
OF CURRICULA

Researchers of teaching and learning have consistently found that any text,
including a curriculum, may be constructed, interpreted, and acted on
quite differently depending on the values, mental frameworks, goals, and
other factors that particular readers and teachers bring to them in given
times and places. Transactional theories of reading (Beach, 1993) are
grounded in the finding that readers construct meaning from literary texts
on the basis of a constellation of textual, contextual, intertextual, and per-

> *Character is formed by doing the thing we are supposed to do, when it should be
> done, whether we feel like doing it or not.*
>
> *—Father Edward Flanagan*

> *Character isn't inherited. One builds it daily by the way one thinks and acts, thought by thought, action by action.*
>
> —*Helen Gahagan Douglas*

sonal factors. For instance, the ways in which readers reliant on principles of New Criticism read, discuss, and write about literature in educational settings is quite different from the ways in which lay readers read and respond to literature either individually (Beach, 1993) or in voluntary book clubs (Marshall, Smagorinsky, & Smith, 1995). Even among more seemingly homogenous groups of readers, different reading cultures develop. In university departments of English and English Education, for instance, readers are encouraged to emphasize different aspects of the reading transaction, with English faculty foregrounding the text and English Education faculty foregrounding the reader and the potential classroom applications of the text (Addington, 2001; Marshall & Smith, 1997).

If one accepts that individuals within communities of practice read texts through particular cultural filters, and that within these communities of practice there is individual variation in the ways in which texts are read, then one must, along with Nystrand (1986), reject the notion that a text has a singular autonomous meaning. If a curriculum may be understood as a text, then it is likely that teachers and their students bring different interpretations to their reading of it (Smagorinsky, 1995b). Furthermore, Sarason (1971) has argued that teachers subvert, transform, or modify curricula to fit with their own worldviews and the contingencies of their classrooms. The likelihood of curricular interpretation is predicted by researchers of schema theory, whose have consistently found that people reorganize new information so that is consistent with prior mental frameworks, even to the point of distorting the new information (e.g., Bransford, 1979). The character curriculum issued by the state, then, regardless of its inscribed ideology, may be interpreted and implemented in ways that incorporate a different ideology.

Our study includes no empirical basis for knowing how the curricula are implemented by the teachers in these states or the meanings that young people construct from the curricula in relation to the ways in which they are taught. The required means of assessment will undoubtedly have a great influence on how the curriculum is interpreted. Presumably, as follows from almost any assessment vehicle, the means of evaluation will influence how a curriculum is taught (Hillocks, 2002). Smagorinsky, Lakly, and Johnson (2002) have found that teachers will teach to assessment measures even when they disagree philosophically with a prescribed curriculum and its mandated evaluation. Our study has focused on the ways in which character education is discussed primarily at the policy level. How individual teachers and groups of teachers interpret and implement those policy decisions is a question for another study.

We should also acknowledge our own constructive and social processes in reading and analyzing the proposals submitted to OERI. As we have outlined, the cultural filter of our progressive ideology framed our reading of the curricula. Even within this shared perspective, we disagreed on a number of points, including how to position ourselves relative to the ideologies we are delineating. Much of the time we spent in our weekly research meetings was dedicated to airing, discussing, and reconciling our occasionally different interpretations of the documents. Teachers who are charged with teaching for character undoubtedly have a more difficult and complex task in interpreting and implementing the curriculum. They work in diverse settings and are often under intense pressure from mandates to teach an extraordinary range of content, skills, and dispositions. We feel certain that these contextual factors in combination with idiosyncratic personalities and experiences would lead teachers to have widely varying interpretations of the curricula that they are required to teach.

THE TRIVIALIZATION OF CHARACTER EDUCATION

We believe that character education ought to be substantive. Yet many efforts at character education that teachers have reported to us appear to trivialize the notion of character. Many schools, for instance, have a character word of the day or week, which is announced over the school public address system with the expectation that students will then begin to demonstrate the appropriate behaviors. Both of us have taught in public schools and know how seriously people treat the daily announcements: Typically, teachers update their records, grade papers, fill out paperwork, and so forth, while students doze, chat, do homework, and only peripher-

> *The most authentic witnesses of any man's character are those who know him in his own family, and see him without any restraint or rule of conduct, but such as he voluntarily prescribes to himself. If a man carries virtue with him into his private apartments, and takes no advantage of unlimited power or probable secrecy; if we trace him through the round of time, and find that his character, with those allowances which mortal frailty must always want, is uniform and regular, we have all the evidence of his sincerity that one man can have with regard to another; and, indeed, as hypocrisy cannot be its own reward, we may, without hesitation, determine that his heart is pure.*
>
> *—Samuel Johnson*

> *Ethics is a matter of being good (character) and doing right (action).*
>
> *—Russell Gough*

ally attend to the voice over the loudspeaker. We see this approach as having little if any impact on student behavior or moral development, even while it might satisfy some administrators that they have incorporated character education into the curriculum or allow school officials to claim that they have done so in their annual reports.

The idea of teaching students complex moral behavior through announcements and signposts has been expanded by some districts. One of our colleagues, for instance, visited an elementary school in which every hallway had been renamed as a street: Diligence Drive, Punctuality Place, Respect Road, Honesty Highway, Loyalty Lane, and so on. The effort, we assume, is to saturate the environment with attention to character issues. We have serious doubts about whether walking these hallways enables students to absorb these traits into their moral makeup and believe that such efforts take an important construct and trivialize it in the minds of students. Surely a character curriculum ought to do more than exhort students to do good; rather, it should engage them with real questions about how to live the most emotionally satisfying and socially responsible lives in relation to others.

INCORPORATING THE NATIVE AMERICAN PERSPECTIVE

Our views prior to conducting this study have not remained entirely intact. We see great merit, for instance, in the Native American perspective's emphasis on living in harmony with the natural world (Jacobs & Jacobs-Spencer, 2001). Both of us are serious gardeners who spend a great deal of time outside, creating a natural environment not only for plants but for the abundant wildlife that they support: birds, mammals, insects, reptiles, and amphibians in great abundance. Like Beatrix Potter's Mr. McGreggor, we are not always pleased by the balance of this relationship but accept our losses to the local fauna as part of our effort to live amidst natural surroundings.

We experience something deeper than simple visceral pleasure in maintaining gardens, finding them to be places of deep spiritual knowledge and inspiration. Prior to our study of character education, we had not conceived of this avocation as having potential for character development. However, our reading of this perspective has opened our eyes to the environmental benefits that might follow from the sorts of activities recommended by Jacobs and Jacobs-Spencer (2001) as part of a character curriculum. Although not all students might benefit from talking to trees, as they recommend, they might see themselves as part of a greater natural system with which they may live in balance. Given the deteriorating state of our world's fragile ecosystems, we believe that this feeling of interrelatedness would be a good thing for us and a critical disposition for the generations that follow us.

On the other hand, we understand that people from some cultural backgrounds might find this approach to be somewhere between silly and sacrilegious. Native American beliefs about the human relationship with nature have much in common with some aspects of Wiccanism, which is associated with witchcraft and other forms of mysticism that are threatening to many orthodox Christians. Furthermore, some interpretations of the Christian Bible stress the subservience of nature to humanity, a perspective that has justified extensive real estate development, heavy foresting of wooded areas, aggressive development of oil fields, and other utilitarian uses of nature, even to the point where "act of God" has successfully been used in court to account for environmental disasters brought about by industry (Williams, 2004).

Both parents and students who adhere to such beliefs might find an approach to education that accords the natural world the same respect as the human world to be a violation of the Biblical imperative, a profanation of humanity's primacy among earthly creatures and elements, and a romantic value on cuddly creatures rather than a sober understanding of the need for economic development. Dr. Seuss's environmentally friendly *The Lorax*, for instance, was banned in the Laytonville, California, school district because, in their words, it "criminalizes the forestry industry" by representing clear-cutting in a negative way—well illustrating our point that any text is open to a range of interpretations. We assume that not all would agree with our embrace of the Native American perspective as part of a character education. Rather, we see its incorporation as a matter of local culture and its influence on curricular choices.

REFLECTING ON CHARACTER EDUCATION

In previous work (Smagorinsky, 1999, 2000, 2001b, 2002a, 2002b, 2004; Smagorinsky & Taxel, 2002a, 2002b) we have advocated a reflective approach to character education. In this method students consider situations

> *Coaches are, first and foremost, teachers; they are among the most influential people in a young athlete's life. Because coaches are such powerful role models, young athletes learn more from them about character than about athletic performance.*
>
> *—Dr. Mike*

and moral codes, a process through which they develop and live by standards that they generate from careful and considerate contemplation of problematic situations. In the English curriculum these situations can be organized according to themes, including the very traits identified by the Aspen Declaration and institutionalized in the OERI RFP. These themes would not be offered didactically, however; rather, they would serve as the basis for reflection on what moral action is.

Although the particular activities and assessments of reflective approaches might vary, what they share is a focus on a more constructivist approach to developing a code of ethics. In most cases, we imagine, students would settle on the same codes of behavior impressed on them through didactic approaches; that is, we assume that most students would come to the conclusion that responsibility and honesty are desirable traits. In a reflective approach, however, the process of teaching and learning would emphasize the students' engagement with the issues and the resolutions they come up with for considering moral dilemmas.

Our assumption is that students will have greater investment in rules that they develop themselves than rules that others try to instill in or impose on them. Furthermore, a reflective approach is more responsive to complex moral situations. Consider, for instance, the situation faced by our grandparents as they endured the pogroms in Eastern Europe nearly 100 years ago. In resisting and escaping from government-supported death squads, they exhibited the courage that often appears on lists of desirable character traits. Yet they also displayed traits that violated the character qualities enumerated in the proposals we studied: They were unpatriotic toward their government, disloyal to government officials and policies, resistant to authority, and likely discourteous, uncheerful, and unkind toward their oppressors.

A complex situation such as the ones faced by our grandparents requires a consideration of the potentially conflicting elements that comprise character. This less certain stance is not available through the strict emulation of the great and good, as recommended by Bennett (1993). Rather, a definition of morality is required that takes conditions into account and demands extensive reflection on which traits are called for, possibly at the expense of others. We see our grandparents as being quite similar to those who escaped from slavery through the Underground Railroad, which is heralded in history books as a courageous act of defiance, in keeping with traditional U.S. value on resistance to oppression and active efforts to attain personal liberty and freedom. Like our grandparents, however, the runaway slaves were disloyal to their owners, disrespectful toward authority figures, and deceptive in their efforts to conceal the truth. Their actions illustrate how any consideration of the quality of a person's character needs to take into account the circumstances that surround his or her decisions.

A novel through which students can discuss similar issues of ethical conduct is Mildred Taylor's *Roll of Thunder, Hear My Cry*. In this novel the members of the Logan family oppose the oppressive strictures of the Jim Crow South in the 1930s through a range of behaviors and actions, including their organization of a boycott of a store owned by the ruthless Wallace family. They also seek to inculcate in their children the values of resistance to unjust laws and social structures. In virtually all literature that focuses on the fight against injustice, simple lists of simplified traits are inadequate to the task of making moral judgments. Rather, an understanding of moral complexity and the context in which decisions are made, we believe, should be at the heart of the character education curriculum.

Like many who have thought about character education, and in particular as educators with backgrounds in literature, we see the English curriculum as having great potential for consideration of these issues. Thematic units on such topics as success, progress, peer group allegiance, and other topics enable students to consider questions of character in the context of the moral dilemmas of literary characters (see Smagorinsky, 2002c). Texts might come from classic or contemporary works. Arthur Miller's *Death of a Salesman,* for instance, includes characters who define success in different ways: starkly materialistic, widely popular, largely relational, and so on. A consideration of their various ways of seeking success contributes to compelling discussions and writing. Similarly, T. J. in *Roll of Thunder, Hear My Cry* is a fascinatingly complex character who has evinced dramatically variable responses from readers. This ambivalence follows from the fact that he betrays the trust of the sympathetic Logan family, yet he lives in such desperate circumstances and is so cruelly manipulated by racist Whites that he evokes sympathy among some readers. Others, however, loathe him and feel that he is the architect of his own unfortunate ending. Such opportunities for attention to moral questions are widely available through reading, discussing, and writing in relation to complex literary works.

Characters of this sort defy the one-dimensional moral exemplars called for by William Bennett and others; rather, each is morally complex. Teaching and learning in relation to such texts can provide opportunities for students to consider what makes for a moral person in relation to a theme (success, loyalty, etc.) and what kind of character they need to develop in order to promote that trajectory. Doing so requires reflection on who they are, how they relate to others, what they believe to be important in life, and what must be sacrificed when goals compete.

This relational, reflective approach to character education would surely be considered relativistic by orthodox character educators. By having students approach themes, values, and ideas on their own terms, instead of through the inculcation of definitions by adults—the indoctrination favored by Ryan (1996)—teachers will encourage students to ar-

> *Character building begins in our infancy and continues until death.*
>
> *—Eleanor Roosevelt*

rive at personal formulations that will undoubtedly diverge on some points, thus defying the moral absolutism presumed by Lickona, Kilpatrick, and others. In our view this relativism is supported by substantial research that finds cultures to construct different goals, codes for behavior, and cultural practices depending on the environments that their inhabitants must negotiate to survive and thrive (e.g., Cole, 1996; Scribner & Tobach, 1997; Tulviste, 1991).

ON THE VALUE OF CONFLICT
AND QUESTIONING AUTHORITY

Implicit in the views of orthodox character educators is the belief that adherence to the values they promote will lead to the sort of social harmony that is the basis of a good society, or at least the society that they envision. Further, obedience within a social system—a nation, a corporation, a team—is believed to contribute to the achievement of the group goals, at least as defined by the group leaders. During the current debates over the Iraq War, for instance, the Bush administration has consistently sought to command unwavering support for the president's policies by equating agreement with President George W. Bush's decisions with patriotism and good citizenship. Attorney General John Ashcroft testified to the Senate that "those who are challenging Bush's policies are giving aid and comfort to the enemy." Tom Daschle (D-S. Dakota) expressed concern with this formulation, telling NBC's *Meet the Press*, "I think that there is an implication here, as they've done throughout this debate on Iraq, that if you oppose the president, your patriotism ought to be questioned." Ultimately, we agree with Theodore Roosevelt, who said, "To announce that there must be no more criticism of the president, or that we are to stand by the president right or wrong, is not only unpatriotic and servile, but is morally treasonable to the American public."

The question of whether to blindly or at least uncritically support a leader's policies, or instead to critique them, is an old dilemma. Henry David Thoreau, for instance, in *On the Duty of Civil Disobedience* (originally titled *Resistance to Civil Government*), argues for what he calls a "majority of one": a person whose conscience dictates his or her position on critical issues, rather than following the lead of others, including elected officials. On this issue, Thoreau chastised *Self-Reliance* author Ralph Waldo Emerson from his jail cell, where he had been confined for refusing to pay a tax that supported the Mexican War of 1846–1848. When Emerson asked Thoreau why he was locked in jail, Thoreau is said to have answered, "The question is, Mr. Emerson, what are you doing out there?"

Many people using Thoreau as their inspiration have argued that conscience-driven dissent not only is a central right in a democracy but is necessary to maintain its vitality. Twentieth-century dissidents Mahatma Gandhi and Dr. Martin Luther King, Jr. among others explicitly drew on Thoreau to mount their challenges to oppressive conditions for their people. Although we are not arguing that respect for authority, obedience for law, and other values associated with moral absolutism are inherently bad—we find it hard to imagine any society functioning in the absence of adherence to laws—we have also provided examples throughout our study of situations when moral action requires that authority be defied and laws be contravened. We wonder where U.S. society would be today had Colonial revolutionaries not opposed the dictates of the British, abolitionists not opposed the various fugitive slave laws, women not fought for the right to vote, Civil Rights advocates not violated segregation laws, workers not united against unsafe factory conditions, and countless other U.S. citizens, in both small and great ways, not acted against what they saw as unjust laws and policies.

Similar questions can be posed about the military chain of command, surely a requirement for a strong and efficient military and among the most universally acknowledged requisites of maintaining an effective fighting force. However, the Nuremburg trials clearly established that while the Nazi soldiers who slaughtered millions were acting on the orders of their superior officers, they were simultaneously obligated to disobey those orders because of their horrific nature. This principle was followed in the trial of Lt. William Calley after the 1968 My Lai massacre in Vietnam in which more than 300 unarmed villagers were murdered by Calley's Charlie Company. Calley unsuccessfully argued that he was ordered by his commanding officer to kill everyone in the village. The need for absolute adherence to the chain of command, then, can be problematic, no matter how well entrenched in a culture.

At the time we are writing, U.S. soldiers implicated in the heinous abuses in Iraq's Abu Ghraib prison are similarly saying that they were following orders to "soften up" detainees for interrogation, a claim substantiated by the investigative journalism of Seymour Hersh (2004). We wonder whether the trials that await these soldiers will find that if they were following orders, they had a higher obligation to defy them. Yet if they had refused, they stood the likelihood of being court-martialed. Catch-22.

We imagine that soldiers who had experienced a character education curriculum based on principles of unambiguous moral absolutism—even those who had successfully internalized the lessons of didactic instruction—would have a hard time deciding where to place their loyalties when ordered to commit acts that they find morally questionable. We also fear that people in the United States will abandon their honored tradition of dissent if orthodox character educators continue to institute a moral chain of command that is not open to question, critique, and resistance when warranted. We believe that such abandonment may have a disastrous impact on the health of our democracy, silencing the alternative voices that have historically introduced innovation and revitalization into our society and its operations.

In addition to the U.S. tradition of conscionable dissent articulated by Patrick Henry, Sojourner Truth, Frederick Douglass, Ida B. Wells, Susan B. Anthony, Dr. Martin Luther King, Jr., Cesar Chavez, Russell Means, Harvey Milk, and many others, a number of psychologists and social theorists believe that there is great value in the process of engaging in conflict. Piaget (1950) found that when a child experiences cognitive conflict, he or she achieves adaptation through assimilation or accommodation. Kuhn (1963) argues that scientific disciplines advance when existing theories are challenged by newer theories, with the resulting debate leading to a new formulation—a new paradigm—that, if accepted by members of the community, advances thinking in the field. Without such conflict, Kuhn believes, the rate of scientific advancement would be slowed considerably if not arrested altogether.

Dahrendorf (1959) argues that conflict fosters creativity, saying that "The clash of values and interests, the tension between what is and what some groups feel ought to be, the conflict between vested interests and new strata and groups demanding their share of power, have been productive of vitality" (p. 27). Coser (1956) argues for the productive, indeed generative benefits of conflict:

> No group can be entirely harmonious for it would then be devoid of process and structure. Groups require disharmony as well as harmony, disassociation as well as association; and conflicts within them are by no means disruptive factors.... Far from being necessarily dysfunctional, a certain degree of conflict is an essential element in group formation and the persistence of group life. (p. 31)

These positive aspects of conflict suggest that educators should be cautious in reducing the values and dispositions taught to young people in schools to a set of absolute truths to be unquestioningly internalized. Rather, we would argue that this reduction flattens students' social reality by oversimplifying the complexity of the world in which these values operate to a set of axioms. It is no doubt reassuring to many educators, parents, and politicians to believe that the solution to social discord and disruption is to impose a set of absolute values that are believed to have governed the good old days of a more peaceable past. We have argued that the vision of

> *The right time to show your good character is when you are pestered by somebody weaker than you.*
>
> —*Buddha*

such a bygone era is a nostalgic fiction poorly informed by a well-rounded study of U.S. history and ill-suited as the basis for negotiating the frightening complexities of the twenty-first century.

ERRORS, EXPECTATIONS, AND GROWTH IN CHARACTER

Mina Shaughnessy was among the pioneers in the field of composition studies. She was a teacher in the City College of New York system when it adopted an open admissions policy that suddenly placed thousands of academically underprepared students in college classes. Shaughnessy (1977) and other teachers had to find effective ways of teaching these students to write at the college level. In *Errors and Expectations* she describes the approach she and her colleagues adopted, one predicated on an understanding that errors are part of human development and ought not be treated as mistakes simply to be corrected. Rather, errors can be used diagnostically to identify areas of growth, especially in new learning experiences. In particular, she argues, errors often occur when learners are trying something new and risky. In her case, these new experiences involved trying new syntactic structures, vocabulary, and other efforts to develop new writing capabilities. Errors, in other words, should be expected in the context of new learning. The task of a good teacher, she argues, is to recognize how errors function in students' growth trajectories and build on their knowledge to help them learn new ways of communicating clearly.

If, as Alexander Pope wrote in *An Essay on Criticism,* "to err is human; to forgive, divine," we find this forgiving approach to have great merit. We profoundly disagree with the view of Headmaster Jarvis that young people are categorically wanting in character. His vision illustrates Pope's observation that "all looks yellow to the jaundic'd eye." We see character education as having an important developmental dimension, one that subordinates the rightness and wrongness of particular immediate behaviors to the long-term growth to which any individual action contributes. The *growth* approach is consistent with the Deweyian vision that informs our own conception of education. This focus foregrounds the situated psychological development of the child, whose growth in the setting of school occurs in relation to the curricula of academic disciplines. Focusing on the development of the student departs from the well-entrenched educational approach of foregrounding the academic disciplines and their conventions, with students evaluated on their mastery of these bodies of knowledge.

When taking a growth perspective, character education is concerned with the moral development of the student. Rather than using punitive measures such as disciplinary referrals to determine the success of teaching character, this approach would attempt to teach moral concepts over time, with the understanding that they are complex and difficult to learn, internalize, and act upon. We have previously referred to the trivialization of character education. A developmental approach to character and morality would not assume that one's ability to recite definitions of terms indicates moral soundness; cognitively, memorization and recall are among the least critical cognitive faculties (Bloom, 1956). Rather, character education would focus more on concept development through a consideration of moral themes and problems of the sort not amenable to easy reduction to hortatory slogans.

During this extended process students might indeed commit acts that they later regret, perhaps as ways of trying out new ideas. To return to our analogy from Shaughessy (1977): Orthodoxies exist in both the world of composition and the realm of morality. Many people refer to "standard" English and correct composition form, even while theorists such as Ball (1999), Lee (1993), and Smitherman (2000) have argued persuasively that African-American discourse constitutes a separate rule-governed genre that is legitimate in its own right and indeed serves the communication needs of its speakers and writers far better than does "standard" English in intracultural settings. This is not to argue against the importance of learning the standard dialect, but to recognize the richness and possibilities to other forms of expression (Delpit, 1995). Similarly, the orthodox character education movement claims that it relies on invariant, culture-free universals— "standard" morality, if you will—while others identify moral systems that rely on different principles that serve other communities of practice well. Rather than learning to adhere strictly and solely to the "standard"—in either composition or morality—students ought, we believe, to have opportunities to try out new ways of thinking.

A didactic approach assumes that impressing character qualities on young people is sufficient for them to internalize and act on them. We have disagreed with this belief throughout our presentation. In taking this perspective we are not endorsing Values Clarification, whose greatest flaw, we believe, was not in its relativism but in its belief that values could be clarified independent of meaningful content. Rather, we agree with such cognitive researchers as Craik and Lockhart (1972) that depth of processing—that is, learning by associating new information with existing information in meaningful ways—enables greater understanding of the material learned. Craik and Lockhart argue that by being an active participant in their own learning, with that learning grounded in events with clear reference points for learners, students will develop a greater understanding of the material and be able to recall it more clearly later.

The reflective approach that we endorse relies on depth of processing. Students can engage with moral issues through a variety of activities: discussion of characters in history or literature, role playing or other perspective taking to consider how people experience situations requiring moral thinking, essay writing or other composition that requires the synthesis and articulation of complex ideas related to ethics, and other active consideration of moral questions in terms of people who are real or who are presented with verisimilitude. We see the social studies and literature curricula as being particularly ripe areas of the curriculum for the inclusion of character education, although ethics can be incorporated across the curriculum—in considering the ethics of the conduct of science, the morality of different artistic expressions, the ethical uses of statistics (see Huff's, 1954, *How to Lie with Statistics*), the moral implications of different approaches to homemaking, ethical conduct in sports and at sporting events, and attention to issues of character in other areas of the curriculum.

As they engage with these questions across the curriculum, students would no doubt begin to stretch the envelope of their thinking and actions, perhaps even to the point of taking risks and crossing boundaries. Students who read Thoreau's *On the Duty of Civil Disobedience*, for instance, often begin to assert their consciences in newly principled ways. They engage in defiance and resistance in ways that their parents, teachers, coaches, and other adult authorities can find to be disrespectful and inappropriate. Ultimately, these students might decide that in stretching the boundaries of their thinking, some of their actions might have crossed other moral lines. Yet without putting their evolving principles into action, they can never refine their understanding of how they can inform their engagement with the world. Like Shaughnessy's writing students, they learn by taking risks and making errors that lead to new growth.

By taking a developmental approach, we are not advocating a strict stage theory of moral development, such as that proposed by Kohlberg (1977). As Gilligan argued, Kohlberg's work was flawed by his sampling error of choosing only privileged White male participants. If anything, his research substantiates our cultural argument: He capably outlined a developmental path taken by elite young men, who are socialized to experience Western culture in particular ways. Accepting a strict stage progression such as Kohlberg's commits the error of normalizing one cultural group's experiences and generalizing them to the broad population, which we have argued is irresponsible. Our sense of human development subscribes more to

---

All leaders must face some crisis where their own strength of character is the enemy.

—Richard Reeves

the principles of cultural psychology (e.g., Cole, 1996), in which developmental stages are not universal but rather emerge as a function of engagement with cultural practice.

REDEFINING CHARACTER

Lickona (1991) and others argue that character consists of a set of invariant, culture-free, universal traits or dispositions. Based on our study, we must conclude that this view is parochial and myopic. Rather, notions of character are cultural constructions that are fundamentally tied to a society's idealized notion of its past, present, and possible futures. As Loewen (1996, 1999) has argued, that perceived past often has a mythical basis that is overlooked when people pine for the good old days—which were surely experienced differently by people from various vantage points within the society—and project their social futures based on the trajectory they provide. People who become dissidents and advocates for the oppressed often emerge from social groups who do not share this vision. The perspective they develop from society's margins gives them an experience of the past that often leads them to agitate for social change and a future that departs from, rather than conserves, the past as constructed by society's advantaged. Such change may involve a questioning, rethinking, and reformulation of values and dispositions believed to be sacrosanct among those with the greatest cultural capital and power—those whose advantages prevent them from seeing the perspectives that produce such critique. In this way a single nation or social group may include more than one cultural outlook with respect to a society's past and its consequential ideal destination and pathways for achieving it.

In industrialized societies such as the United States, many of the traits emphasized by orthodox character commentators are undoubtedly quite useful. Any capitalist nation benefits when its workers are punctual, productive, loyal, and have other qualities that contribute to a smoothly running unit within a competitive economy. This sort of general disposition further produces citizens who are obedient to authority, a quality that is suggested in the idea of measuring character improvement through such data as declines in disciplinary referrals. A corporation, organization, or polity likely runs most efficiently when all of its cogs are working together toward the assigned destination. The key for any social group is to agree that this destination is the best place to go and that this method of transport is the most effectual. However, we have argued that organizations of any kind might also be served by encouraging the creation of environments in which dissenting ideas or beliefs interrogate and problematize long-accepted orthodoxies. In this mix of old and new, orthodox and unorthodox, breakthroughs often occur.

After having studied a variety of conceptions of character, however, we see the human qualities that serve capitalist economies—those normalized in the discourses central to an orthodox conception of character—as being especially useful for particular cultural ideals and worldviews, but not necessarily all. The perspective outlined by Jacobs and Jacobs-Spencer (2001), for instance, values balance with the natural world over exploitation of the natural world for economic advancement. Punctuality might not be a key quality in this culture unless timeliness serves the purpose of achieving this balance. Efficiency is not necessarily the highest value in all aspects of life. For instance, the ability to experience visions, as Jacobs did leading him to change his name to Four Arrows, is more in tune with the goals of a Native-American perspective.

This differentiation in cultural constructions of character suggests that a new definition of character is called for, one that is responsive to cultural variation. We see character consisting of those dispositions, traits, attitudes, and practices that advance a society toward its consensual ideal outcome, its perceived teleological destination. For a capitalist society, these dispositions and so forth, are generally consistent with the values of the Protestant work ethic. Even this general set of traits, however, is not necessarily understood and practiced in the same way by all within a broad culture's many subcultures. As we have shown, the states from the Upper Midwest tempered this value with attention to how a competitive society ought to deliberately strive to provide an equitable structure (through, e.g., unions and other worker alliances) and social practices (e.g., voluntary efforts at inclusion) so as to enable all citizens to have access to opportunity. A person of good character in this region, then, values diversity, community, and other virtues that are too often out of sync with the more competitive and paternalistic world envisioned not only in the Deep South but by all who articulate an orthodox perspective on character education.

We are arguing, then, for a form of cultural relativism of the sort disdained by orthodox character commentators. In endorsing relativism we do not mean that anything goes. We are quite comfortable judging Hitler's Nazis to be immoral, guilty of behavior so abhorrent that it could never withstand moral scrutiny. Most character conflicts are not as clear cut as those involving the genocide, torture, medical and scientific experimentation on prisoners, construction and operation of crematoria, and other well-documented atrocities practiced by the German Nazis of the 1940s. Rather, cherished values and the traits, actions, and dispositions believed to comprise character can conflict with other dearly held virtues.

The study of history and literature—both of which are rife with a vast array of characters involved in complex, often profoundly ambiguous situations—provides ripe contexts in which to explore the way that the development of character is informed, and often shaped, by the particulars of time, place, and circumstance. Rather than advocating an absolute set of invariant values said to be apply at all times, in all places, regardless of circumstances, we believe in an approach that suggests that even those values we generally agree on sometimes must be superseded by a value more appropriate to the situation. Responsibility, for instance, is generally defined as being accountable or answerable, particularly in moral matters. A sense of responsibility suggests the obligation to comply with authorities, to answer honestly to questions aimed at determining the truth of the matter in times of dispute. Yet in some circumstances, one might jettison this value on moral grounds in deference to other virtues. If, for instance, one were asked or ordered to name names during an inquisition, and if one felt that doing so would result in a disloyal betrayal of people and their principles, the value on responsibility might give way to the value on loyalty, and the courage it would take to practice it, or, put differently, one would have to decide to whom to be responsible. Such difficult decisions require an understanding that simple lists of virtues can be of little value under duress, that greater thought and reflection are required to resolve difficult situations.

From an educational standpoint, adopting these assumptions assumes a belief that young people, with proper guidance, can learn to navigate their way among the ambiguities and confusions that inevitably result when values come into conflict. We are convinced, following Dewey and his modern interpreters (e.g., West, Weaver, & Rowland, 1992), that schooling should be regarded as an exploration, as a voyage of discovery, as an invitation, rather than as a tool of didacticism or moralizing. Conservative critics of education (e.g., D'Souza, 1991) often maintain that today's students are being socialized into a liberal perspective through their teachers' "politically correct" content and methods, which the critics believe to comprise a radical departure from traditional U.S. values. We see their own desire for a didactic education in what they believe to be traditional values to be just as politically motivated and ideological, substituting a conservative worldview for a liberal one, albeit an orthodox perspective normalized in their thinking so as to mask its political agenda.

Indeed, we see an ideologically conservative education as far more limiting than a liberal or progressive approach, especially when accomplished through what orthodox character education Kevin Ryan (1996) endorses as "indoctrination" (p. 1) which leaves little room for question and discussion. Rather, we hope that young people can have educational experiences that prepare them for the ambiguity, ideological differences, competing worldviews, conflict, and complexity that await them in the contested world beyond school. Included in this more open-ended education is attention to character, not through *inculcation*—a term rooted in the Latin term for *to tread on* or *to trample*—in a specific ideology but through recognition that different conceptions of character serve different cultural, economic, and political ends. To shut down such thinking is to shut off the world's possibilities and narrow students' vision of the potential of their lives and the lives of those with whom they inhabit society.

Unlike President George W. Bush, who famously stated "I don't do nuance," we believe that recognizing and sorting out nuance is a critical faculty in our increasingly complex world. Indeed, we think that as cultures more and more come into contact and conflict, "doing nuance" might serve as a good character trait as our culture evolves to take globalization into account. We see efforts to oversimplify the world and turn back the clock to a mythical past as being misinformed, misguided, and mystifying. The twenty-first century presents us with complex challenges, and it will take people of character to navigate them successfully. An education that contributes to the development of people capable of such nuanced transactions cannot reduce the world to pieties that reify the dominant culture's values. Rather, it should interrogate the value system itself to reveal its ideological basis and equip students to conduct such inquiries into the worldview underpinning any society's outlook. Such an approach should provide them with a better understanding of cultural difference and help them generate more visionary insights into constructing sensitive resolutions to cultural conflicts.

The struggle for your own character is the struggle for the nation's character.

—Bill Clinton

References

> *You cannot dream yourself into a character; you must hammer and forge yourself one.*
> —*James A. Froude*

Abu-Lughod, L. (1991). Writing against culture. In R. E. Fox (Ed.), *Recapturing anthropology: Working in the present* (pp. 137–162). Santa Fe, NM: School of American Research Press.

Ackerman, J. M. (1993). The promise of writing to learn. *Written Communication, 10*, 334–370.

Addington, A. H. (2001). Talking about literature in university book club and seminar settings. *Research in the Teaching of English, 36*, 212–248.

Allington, R. L. (2002). *Big brother and the national reading curriculum: How ideology trumped evidence.* Portsmouth, NH: Heinemann.

Alperovitz, G. (1996). The reconstruction of community meaning. *Tikkun, 11*(3), 13–16, 19. Retrieved June 1, 2003, from http://www.ncesa.org/html/commeaning.html

Apple, M. W. (1979). *Ideology and curriculum.* New York: Routledge & Kegan Paul.

Apple, M. W. (1982). *Education and Power.* Boston: Ark Paperbacks.

Apple, M. W. (1986). *Teachers and texts: A political economy of class and gender relations in education.* New York: Routledge and Kegan Paul.

Apple, M. W. (1993). *Official knowledge: Democratic education in a conservative age.* New York: Routledge.

Apple, M. W., & Wexler, P. (1978). Cultural capital and educational transmissions. *Educational Theory, 28*, 34–43.

Applebee, A. N. (1974). *Tradition and reform in the teaching of English: A history.* Urbana, IL: National Council of Teachers of English.

Applebee, A. N. (1996). *Curriculum as conversation: Transforming traditions of teaching and learning.* Chicago: University of Chicago Press.

Aristotle (350 B.C.E.). *Nicomachean ethics*. (W. D. Ross, Trans.). Retrieved June 1, 2003, from http://classics.mit.edu/Aristotle/nicomachaen.html

Aronowitz, S., & Giroux, H. (1988). Schooling, culture, and literacy in the age of broken dreams: A review of Bloom and Hirsch. *Harvard Educational Review 58*, 173–194.

Aspen Conference Participants (www.charactercounts.org/aspen.htm)

Atlas, J. (n.d.). Review of *Habits of the Heart* by Robert Bellah, Richard Madsen, William M. Sullivan, Ann Swidler, and Steven M. Tipton. 1986. Berkeley, CA: University of California Press. Retrieved June 4, 2003, from http://www.montclair.edu/Pages/ICS/HabitsJA.html.

Auster, L. (1996, October). *The political religion of modernity; Or, from Corpus Christi to the Macarena*. Catholic Renaissance, New York City. Retrieved May 20, 2003, from http://www.amnation.com/vfr/archives/001644.html

Bahmueller, C. F. (1998 Summer). A framework for teaching democratic citizenship: An international projects. *International Journal of Social Education*. Retrieved February 14, 2005 from http://www.civiced.org/cbframe.html

Bakhtin, M. M. (1981). *The dialogic imagination: Four essays by M. M. Bakhtin*. M. Holquist (Ed.); C. Emerson & M. Holquist (Trans.). Austin, TX: University of Texas Press.

Bakhtin, M. M. (1984). *Problems of Dostoevsky's poetics*. C. Emerson (Ed. & Trans.). Minneapolis: University of Minnesota Press.

Bakhtin, M. M. (1986). *Speech genres and other late essays*. C. Emerson & M. Holquist (Ed.); V. W. McGee (Trans.). Austin, TX: University of Texas Press.

Balfour, C., Aiken, T-C. T., & Jones, S. (Eds.) (1986). *African Americans, the butterfly tree: An anthology of Black writing from the upper Midwest (Many Minnesotas Project, #2)*. St. Paul, MN: New Rivers Press.

Ball, A. F. (1999). Evaluating the writing of culturally and linguistically diverse students: The case of the African American vernacular English speaker. In C. R. Cooper & L. Odell (Eds.), *Evaluating writing: The role of teachers' knowledge about text, learning, and culture* (pp. 225–248). Urbana, IL: National Council of Teachers of English.

Barnes, D. R. (1992). *From communication to curriculum* (2nd ed.). Portsmouth, NH: Heinemann.

Bates, D. (1989). *William the Conqueror*. Gloucestershire, UK: Tempus.

Batson, A. B. (1993). *Having it y'all*. Nashville, TN: Rutledge Hill Press.

Beach, R. W. (1993). *A teacher's introduction to reader-response theories*. Urbana, IL: National Council of Teachers of English.

Beinart, P. (2001, August 13). Mittel America. *The New Republic Online*. Retrieved January 10, 2003, from http://www.thenewrepublic.com/punditry/beinart081301.html

Belenky, M. F., Clinchy, B., Goldberger, N., & Tarule, J. M. (1986). *Women's ways of knowing: The development of self, voice, and mind*. New York: Basic Books.

Snarling at other folks is not the best way of showing the superior quality of your own character. He is blind who thinks he sees everything. The observant man recognizes many mysteries into which he can not pretend to see, and he remembers that the world is too wide for the eye of one man. But the modern sophists are sure of everything, especially if it contradicts the Bible.

—Charles Haddon Spurgeon

> *Moral cowardice that keeps us from speaking our minds is as dangerous to this country as irresponsible talk. The right way is not always the popular and easy way. Standing for right when it is unpopular is a true test of moral character.*
>
> *—Margaret Chase Smith*

Bell, D. A. (2000). *Race, racism, and American law*. Gaithersburg, MD: Aspen Law and Business.

Bellah, R. N., Madsen, R., Sullivan, W. M., Swidler, A., & Tipton, S. M. (1996). *Habits of the heart: Individualism and commitment in American life. Updated edition with a new introduction*. Berkeley: University of California Press.

Bennett, W. J. (1980). The teacher, the curriculum, and values education development. In M. L. McBee (Ed.), *Rethinking college responsibilities for values* (pp. 27–34). San Francisco: Jossey-Bass.

Bennett, W. J. (1989). *Our children and our country: Improving America's schools and affirming the common culture*. New York: Simon and Schuster.

Bennett, W. J. (1992). *The de-valuing of America: The fight for our culture and our children*. New York: Summit Books.

Bennett, W. J. (Ed.). (1993). *The book of virtues: A treasury of great moral stories*. New York: Simon and Schuster.

Bennett, W. J. (2000, September 20). Statement of William J. Bennett on Senator Lieberman's recent comments about Hollywood. Retrieved October 24, 2002, from http://www.unspun.org/bennett-lieberman.html

Benninga, J. S. (1997). Schools, character development, and citizenship. In A. Molnar (Ed.), *The construction of children's character: Ninety-sixth yearbook of the National Society for the Study of Education* (pp. 77–96). Chicago: University of Chicago Press.

Berger, P. L., & Luckmann, T. (1966). *The social construction of reality: A treatise in the sociology of knowledge*. New York: Doubleday.

Berkowitz, M. W. (2002). The science of character education. In W. Damon (Ed.), *Bringing in a new era in character education* (pp. 43–63). Stanford, CA: Hoover Press.

Berliner, D. C., & Biddle, B. J. (1995). *The manufactured crisis: Myths, fraud, and the attack on America's public schools*. New York: Longman.

Bernstein, R. (1994). *Dictatorship of virtue: Multiculturalism and the battle for America's future*. New York: Knopf.

Bloom, A. D. (1987). *The closing of the American mind*. New York: Simon and Schuster.

Bloom, B. S. (1956). *Taxonomy of educational objectives: The classification of educational goals*. New York: Longmans Green.

Bogenschneider, K., Small, S., & Riley, D. (1993). *An ecological, risk-focused approach for addressing youth-at-risk*. Chevy Chase, MD: National 4-H Center.

Bookman, J. (2004, March 3). Market lacks a conscience, but we don't. *The Atlanta Journal-Constitution*. Accessed February 16, 2005 at www.ajc.com/opinion/content/bookman/2004/032204.html

Booth, W. C. (1998). The ethics of teaching literature. *College English, 61,* 41–55.

Bork, R. H. (1996). *Slouching towards Gomorrah: Modern liberalism and American decline*. New York: Regan Books.

> *The world needs men and women … who put character above wealth.*
>
> *—Dr. Larry M. Groves*

Bowles, S. (1972). Unequal education and the reproduction of the social division of labor. In M. Carnoy (Ed.), *Schooling in a corporate society* (pp. 36–64). New York: David McKay.

Bowles, S., & Gintis, H. (1976). *Schooling in capitalist America: Educational reform and the contradictions of economic life*. New York: Basic Books.

Boyle, C. C. (1996). *Rise of the Georgetown rice culture*. Retrieved August 16, 2003, from http://www.ego.net/us/sc/myr/history/rise.htm

Bransford, J. (1979). *Human cognition: Learning, understanding, and remembering*. Belmont, CA: Wadsworth.

Branson, M. (2000, June). *Critical issues in civic education*. Paper presented at the We the People ... National Conference for State and District Coordinators, Washington, DC. Retrieved from http://www.civiced.org/articles mb june00.html

Buber, M. (1949). *Paths in Utopia*. London: Routledge & Kegan Paul.

Bunting, E. (1991). *Fly away home*. New York: Clarion Books.

Burke, K. (1941). *The philosophy of literary form: Studies in symbolic action*. Baton Rouge: Louisiana State University Press.

Bush, G. W. (1999, October 26). Campaign speech in Gorham, NH. Retrieved November 11, 2004, from http://nytimes.com/library/politics/camp/110399wh~gop~bush~text.html

Bush, G. W. (1999, November 18). *The true goal of education*. Retrieved February 21, 2001, from http://thomas.loc.gov/cgi-bin/query/D?r106:4:./temp/~r106GNrTjP::

Butler, J. (1997). *The psychic life of power: Theories in subjection*. Stanford, CA: Stanford University Press.

Butts, R. F. (1995). *Civitas@UWMadison.1995*. Presentation at the 10th Annual Convocation of the Meiklejohn Education Association, Madison, WI. Retrieved November 1, 2004, from http://www.civiced.org/civitas-butts.html

Byrne, J. H. (1974). *Mrs. Byrne's dictionary of unusual, obscure, and preposterous words*. Secaucus, NJ: Citadel Press and University Books.

Callahan, D. (2004a). *The cheating culture: Why more Americans are doing wrong to get ahead*. New York: Harcourt.

Callahan, D. (2004b). Take back values: Democrats need to offer a compelling vision of a morally based social contract. *The Nation, 278*(5), 14–20.

Censorship News Online (1999, Summer). *Issue #74: Media scholar warns Senate: Listen to our children. Don't fear them*. National Coalition Against Censorship. Retrieved January 30, 2002, from http://www.ncac.org/cen news/cn74 jenkins.html

Center for the Fourth and Fifth Rs. (n.d.). *Eleven Principle Survey (EPS) of character education effectiveness*. Cortland, NY: Author.

Centers for Disease Control and Prevention. (2000). *Youth risk behavior surveillance—United States, 1999*. Retrieved March 11, 2001, from http://www.cdc.gov/mmwr/preview/mmwrhtml/ss4905a1.htm

Charen, M. (2001, March 9). *Overreacting?* Retrieved March 11, 2001, from http://www.creators.com/opinion/charen/

Clark, K. B., & Clark, M. (1947/1958). Racial identity and racial preference in Negro children. In E. E. Maccoby, T. M. Newcomb, & E. L. Hartley (Eds.), *Readings in social psychology* (pp. 602–611). New York: Holt.

Your character will be what you yourself choose to make it.

—*Sir John Lubbock*

Scientists readily accept that animals and humans share a similar anatomy and physiology, says [Sam] Gosling, but many are reluctant to say that they share the traits of emotion and personality too. "Some see it as one more blow against the special status of humans," he says. Instead, many people believe that pet owners project their own personality onto their animals, and that true character is lacking. But personality traits are just as likely to have evolved in animals as physical traits, argues Gosling. What was needed was a test to prove that canine character exists.... In total, 78 dogs of all shapes and sizes were tested. In general, owners and strangers agreed on an individual dog's personality. This suggests that the dog personalities are real, says Gosling.

Clarke, C. (2002). Keynote speech at the Social Market Foundation, Westminster, UK, 12 December, 2002. Retrieved February 16, 2005 from http://www.dfes. gov.uk/pns/displayPN.cgi?pn_id=2002_0239

Clifton, J. (1990). *The invented Indian: Cultural fictions and government policies*. New Brunswick, NJ: Transaction Books.

Clinton, H. R. (1996). *It takes a village and other lessons children teach us*. New York: Simon and Schuster.

Clinton, W. J. (1996). *1996 State of the Union Address*. Retrieved October 22, 1999, from http://www.washingtonpost.com/wp-srv/politics/special/states/docs/sou96.htm

Cobb, J. C. (1997). *Georgia odyssey*. Athens, GA: The University of Georgia Press.

Cobb, J. C. (2002, June). *"Beyond the y'all wall": The American South goes global*. Paper presented at the conference on The South and Globalization, Athens, GA.

Cole, M. (1996). *Cultural psychology: A once and future discipline*. Cambridge, MA: Harvard University Press.

Coleman, K. (1978). *Georgia history in outline* (rev. ed.). Athens, GA: The University of Georgia Press.

Commission on Presidential Debates Transcripts (2000, October). *Third presidential debate*. Retrieved October 10, 2001, from http://www.debates.org/transcripts/ textfiles/CPD Debate 4 Final Transcript (English).txt

Conason, J. (2003). *Big lies: The right-wing propaganda machine and how it distorts the truth*. New York: Thomas Dunne Books/St. Martin's Press.

Cook, L. S. (2004). *Authoring self: Framing identities of young women diagnosed with mood disorders*. Unpublished doctoral dissertation, The University of Georgia.

The 7 Modern Sins:
Politics without principles
Pleasures without conscience
Wealth without work
Knowledge without character
Industry without morality
Science without humanity
Worship without sacrifice.

—Canon Frederic Donaldson

Cope, B., & Kalantzis, M. (1993). Contradictions in the canon: Nationalism and the cultural literacy debate. In A. Luke & P. Gilbert (Eds.), *Literacy in contexts: Australian perspectives and issues* (pp. 85–177). St. Leonards, AU: Allen and Unwin.

Coser, L. (1956). *The functions of social conflict*. Chicago: Free Press.

Cotton, R. (1996). *The morality of the West: From bad to worse*. Retrieved September 3, 2000 from http://www.leaderu.com/org/probe/docs/morality.html

Covey, S. R. (1990). *The 7 habits of highly effective people: Restoring the character ethic.* New York: Simon and Schuster.

Craik, F., & Lockhart, R. (1972). Levels of processing: A framework for memory research. *Journal of Verbal Learning & Verbal Behavior, 11,* 671–684.

Curti, M. (1959). *The social ideas of American educators*. New York: Pageant.

Cummins, J. (1996). Foreword. In S. Nieto, *Affirming diversity: The sociopolitical context of multicultural education* (2nd ed., pp. xv–xvii). New York: Longman.

Dahrendorf, R. (1959). *Class and class conflict in industrial societies*. Stanford, CA: Stanford University Press.

Damasio, A. R. (1994). *Descartes' error: Emotion, reason, and the human brain*. New York: Putnam.

Damon, W. (2002). Introduction. In W. Damon (Ed.), *Bringing in a new era in character education* (pp. vii–xxii). Stanford, CA: Hoover Press.

Davis, K. S. (1986). *FDR, the New Deal years, 1933–1937: A history*. New York: Random House.

Deloria, V. (1995). *Red earth, white lies: Native Americans and the myth of scientific fact*. New York: Scribner.

Delpit, L. (1995). *Other people's children: Cultural conflict in the classroom*. New York: The New Press.

DeVries, R., & Zan, B. (1994). *Moral classrooms, moral children: Creating a constructivist atmosphere in early education*. New York: Teachers College Press.

Dewey, J. (1900). *The school and society*. Chicago: University of Chicago Press.

Dewey, J. (1902). The school as social center. In *National Education Association Proceedings* (pp. 373–83). Chicago: University of Chicago Press. Retrieved January 15, 2004, from http://www.uic.edu/jaddams/hull/urbanexp/documents/Dewey SchoolAsSocialCenter.htm

Dittohead, Deb (n.d.). *60 hard truths about Liberals*. Retrieved November 1, 2003 from http://www.dittohead.org/liberals.html

Donald, D. (1960). *Why the North won the Civil War*. Baton Rouge: Louisiana State University Press.

Doris, J. M. (2002). *Lack of character: Personality and moral behavior*. New York: Cambridge University Press.

Doudna, E. G. (1948). *The making of our Wisconsin schools, 1848–1948*. Madison, WI: State Centennial Executive Committee, 1948. Retrieved August 16, 2002, from http://www.weac.org/Resource/1997-98/March98/wil.htm

Dowling, J., & Pound, A. (1994). Joint interventions with teachers, children and parents in the school setting. In E. Dowling & E. Osborne (Eds.), *The family and the school: A joint systems approach to problems with children* (pp. 69–87). New York: Routledge.

Good character is like a rubber ball—thrown down hard—it bounces right back. Good reputation is like a crystal ball—thrown for gain—shattered and cracked.

—*A. L. Linall Jr.*

D'Souza, D. (1991). *Illiberal education: The politics of race and sex on campus.* New York: Free Press.

Eckert, P. (1989). *Jocks and burnouts: Social categories and identity in the high school.* New York: Teachers College Press.

Ehle, J. (1988). *Trail of tears: The rise and fall of the Cherokee Nation.* New York: Anchor Books.

Elazar, D. J. (1994). *The new north.* Retrieved March 17, 2002, from http://www.jcpa.org/dje/articles/newnorth.htm

Ellington, L., & Rutledge, V. C. (2001). Core knowledge: A content foundation for civic virtue? *International Journal of Social Education, 16*(1), 34–44.

Ellis, J. (1997). *American sphinx: The character of Thomas Jefferson.* New York: Knopf.

Emerson, R. W. (1841). Self-reliance. In *Essays.* Boston: J. Munro & Company.

Employment of 16- and 17-year-old students. Retrieved November 5, 2004, from http://www.nces.ed.gov/pubs/yi/y9642a.html

Espelage, D. L., & Swearer, S. M. (2004). *Bullying in American schools: A social-ecological perspective on prevention and intervention.* Mahwah, NJ: Lawrence Erlbaum Associates.

Fahnestock, J., & Secor, M. (1991). The rhetoric of literary criticism. In C. Bazerman & J. Paradis (Eds.), *Textual dynamics of the professions: Historical and contemporary studies of writing in professional communities* (pp. 76–96). Madison: University of Wisconsin Press.

Fairclough, N. (1995). *Critical discourse analysis.* New York: Longman.

Fecho, B. (2003). Yeki bood/Yeki na bood: Writing and publishing as a teacher researcher. *Research in the Teaching of English, 37,* 281–294.

Field, S. L. (1996). Character education: A historical perspective. *The Educational Forum, 60*(2), 118–123.

Finn, C. (2000). Education and the election. *Commentary, 100*(3). Retrieved July 17, 2001, from http://www.commentary.org/0010/finn.html

Foner, E., & Weiner, J. (1991, July 29/August 5). Fighting for the West. *The Nation,* 163–166.

Foote, S. (1958). *The Civil War: A narrative.* New York: Random House.

Franken, A. (2003). *Lies and the lying liars who tell them: A fair and balanced look at the right.* New York: E. P. Dutton.

Fregier, H. A. (1840). *Desclasses dangereuses de la population dans les grandes villes et des moyens de les rendor meilleures.* Bruxelles: Meline Caus et Compagnie.

Freidel, F. B. (1990). *Franklin D. Roosevelt: A rendezvous with destiny.* Boston: Little Brown.

Freire, P. (2000). *Pedagogy of the oppressed.* New York: Continuum.

Friedman, M., & Friedman, R. D. (2002). *Capitalism and freedom.* Chicago: University of Chicago Press.

Gallagher, M. (2001, March 9). School shootings: Moral tribalism overtakes what used to be absolutes. *Atlanta Constitution.* Retrieved March 11, 2001, from http://www.accessatlanta.com/partners/ajc/epaper/editions/friday/opinion a38ae 780d004f18f0094.html

> *Character is not built by battling and excitement alone. The harvest is not ripened by the thunderous forces of nature, but by the secret silent invisible forces. So the best qualities of our spiritual lives are matured by quietness, silence and commonplace.*
>
> —A. P. Gouthey

> *Character is much easier kept than recovered.*
>
> *—Thomas Paine*

Gay, G. (1997). Connections between character education and multicultural education. In A. Molnar (Ed.), *The construction of children's character: Ninety-sixth yearbook of the National Society for the Study of Education* (pp. 97–109). Chicago: University of Chicago Press.

Gee, J. P. (1990). *Social linguistics and literacies: Ideology in discourse*. New York: Falmer.

Gee. J. P. (2003). *What video games have to teach us about learning and literacy*. New York: Palgrave Macmillan.

Gibson, S. R. (n.d.). Was the revelation received in response to pressure? Retrieved November 11, 2004, from www.lightplanet.com/answers/Pressure.htm

Gilbert, S. (2003, March 18). Scientists explore the molding of children's morals. *The New York Times* (Final, Section F, Page 5 , Column 2). Retrieved March 20, 2003, from http://www.nytimes.com/2003/03/18/health/children/18MORA.html?ex= 1056859200&en=df16c16e1385594d&ei=5070

Gilligan, C. (1983). *In a different voice: Psychological theory and women's development*. Cambridge, MA: Harvard University Press.

Giroux, H. A. (1981). *Ideology, culture and the process of schooling*. New York: Falmer.

Giroux, H. A. (1988). *Teachers as intellectuals: Toward a critical pedagogy of learning*. Westport, CT: Bergin and Garvey.

Glaser, B. G., & Strauss, A. L. (1967). *The discovery of grounded theory: Strategies for qualitative research*. Chicago: Aldine.

Goody, E. (1997). Why must might be right? Observations on sexual herrschaft. In M. Cole, Y. Engeström, & O. Vasquez (Eds.), *Mind, culture and activity: Seminal papers from the Laboratory of Comparative Human Cognition* (pp. 432–472). New York: Cambridge University Press.

Griffin, L. J., & Thompson, A. B. (2003). Enough about the disappearing South, what about the disappearing Southerner? *Southern Cultures, 9*, 51–65.

Gross, M. L. (1998). *The end of sanity: Social and cultural madness in America*. New York: Avon.

Hartshorne, H., & May, M. A. (1928). *Studies in the nature of character. I. Studies in deceit. Book I: General methods and results. Book II: Statistical methods and results* (Vol. 1). New York: Macmillan.

Hawkins, J. D., Catalano, R. F., & Associates. (1992). *Communities that care: Action for drug abuse prevention*. San Francisco: Jossey-Bass.

Haynes, J. E. (1996). *Red scare or red menace?: American communism and anticommunism in the cold war era*. Chicago: Ivan R. Dee.

Heath, S. B. (1983). *Ways with words: Language life, and work in communities and classrooms*. New York: Cambridge University Press.

Henry, W. (1994). *In defense of elitism*. New York: Doubleday.

Herbert, W. (1996). The moral child. *U.S. News & World Report, 3*, 58.

Herrnstein, R. J., & Murray, C. (1994). *The bell curve: Intelligence and class structure in American life*. New York: Free Press.

Hersh, S. M. (2004). The gray zone: How a secret Pentagon program came to Abu Ghraib. *The New Yorker,* May 24, 38–44.

Higham, J. (1988). *Strangers in the land: Patterns of American nativism, 1860–1925* (2nd ed.). New Brunswick, NJ: Rutgers University Press.

Hillocks, G. (2002). *The testing trap: How state writing assessments control learning*. New York: Teachers College Press.

Hirsch, E. D. (1987). *Cultural literacy: What every American needs to know*. Boston: Houghton Mifflin.

Hirsch, E. D. (1996). *The schools we need and why we don't have them*. New York: Doubleday.

Huff, D. (1954). *How to lie with statistics*. New York: W. W. Norton.

Hunt, P. (1992). *Literature for children: Contemporary criticism*. New York: Routledge.

Hunter, J. D. (1991). *Culture wars: The struggle to define America*. New York: Basic Books.

Hunter, J. D. (2000). *The death of character: Moral education in an age without good and evil*. New York: Basic Books.

Imse, A. (1999, May 16). Roadblocks keep mentally ill kids from getting treatment. *Rocky Mountain News*. Retrieved May 30, 2000, from http://denver.rocky mountainnews.com/shooting/0516ment2.shtml

Isaacson, W. (2003). *Benjamin Franklin: An American life*. New York: Simon & Schuster.

Jacobs, D. T. (1998). *Primal awareness: A true story of survival, transformation and awakening with the Raramuri Shamans of Mexico*. Rochester, VT: Inner Traditions International.

Jacobs, D. T., & Jacobs-Spencer, J. (2001). *Teaching virtues: Building character across the curriculum*. Lanham, MD: Scarecrow Press.

Jamison, K. R. (1999). *Night falls fast: Understanding suicide* (1st ed.). New York: Knopf.

John-Steiner, V. P., & Meehan, T. M. (2000). Creativity and collaboration in knowledge construction. In C. D. Lee & P. Smagorinsky (Eds.), *Vygotskian perspectives on literacy development: Constructing meaning through collaborative inquiry* (pp. 31–48). New York: Cambridge University Press.

Johnson, H. B. (1976). *Order upon the land: The U.S. rectangular land survey in the Upper Mississippi country*. New York: Oxford University Press.

Johnson, H. C. (1987). Society, culture, and character development. In K. Ryan & G. F. McLean (Eds.), Character development in schools and beyond New York: Praeger

Josephson Institute of Ethics (2000). Report card on the ethics of American youth. Retrieved June 19, 2001, from http://www.josephsoninstitute.org/Survey 2000/survey2000-pressrelease.htm

Jubera, D. (2004, February 21). Atlanta a hub for black gays. *Atlanta Journal-Constitution*. Retrieved February 22, 2004, from http://www.ajc.com/metro/content/metro/atlanta/0204/22mecca.html

Kaya. (n.d.). *Post-Columbine paranoia: A Goth speaks. Story tellers challenge*. Retrieved November 1, 2004, from http://www.storytellerschallenge.com/STTrush/ttf033.asp

Kelly, R. G. (1974). Literature and the historian. *American Quarterly, 26,* 141–159.

Kilpatrick, W. (1992). *Why Johnny can't tell right from wrong*. New York: Simon & Schuster.

Klee, M. B. (2000). *Core virtues: A literature-based program in character education*. Chicago: Link Institute.

Knoblauch, C. H. (1988). Rhetorical considerations: Dialogue and commitment. *College English, 50,* 125–140.

Koch, A., & Peden, W. J. (Eds.). (1972). *The life and selected writings of Thomas Jefferson*. New York: The Modern Library.

Kochman, T. (1981). *Black and white styles in conflict*. Chicago: University of Chicago Press.

Character is the impulse reined down into steady continuance.

—*Charles H Parkhurst*

Kohn, A. (1997, February). How not to teach values: A critical look at character education. *Phi Delta Kappan, 78,* 429–439. Retrieved April 22, 2000, from http://www.alfiekohn.org/teaching hnttv.htm

Kohlberg, L. (1958). *The development of moral thinking and choice in the years 10–16.* Unpublished doctoral dissertation, University of Chicago.

Kohlberg, L. (1976). Moral stages and moralization: The cognitive developmental approach. In T. Lickona (Ed.), *Moral development and behavior: Theory, research, and social issues* (pp. 34–35). New York: Holt, Rinehart, and Winston.

Kohlberg, L., & Turiel, E. (1971). Moral development and moral education. In G. Lesser (Ed.), *Psychology and educational practice* (pp. 402–424). Glenview, IL: Scott Foresman.

Kristeva, J. (1984). *Revolution in poetic language.* M. Waller (Trans.). New York: Columbia University Press.

Krueger, V. (1989). Reflections: Victoria Krueger. In B. Perrone, H. H. Stockel, & V. Krueger, *Medicine women,* curanderas, *and women doctors* (pp. 225–229). Norman, OK: University of Oklahoma Press.

Kuhn, T. S. (1963). *The structure of scientific revolutions.* Chicago: University of Chicago Press.

Lakoff, G. (2002). *Moral politics: How liberals and conservatives think.* Chicago: University of Chicago Press.

Lancto, C. (n.d.). Banned books: How schools restrict the reading of young people. *World & I.* Article # 23320. Retrieved January 4, 2004, from http://www.world andi.com/newhome/public/2003/september/mt2pub.asp

Lasch, C. (1969). *The agony of the American left.* New York: Knopf.

Lather, P. A. (1991). *Getting smart: Feminist research and pedagogy with/in the postmodern.* New York: Routledge.

Lee, A. (1996). *Gender, literacy, curriculum.* London: Taylor and Francis.

Lee, C. D. (1993). *Signifying as a scaffold for literary interpretation: The pedagogical implications of an African American discourse genre.* Urbana, IL: National Council of Teachers of English.

Leming, J. S. (1993). In search of effective character education. *Educational Leadership, 51*(3), 63–71.

Leming, J. S. (1994). Character education and multicultural education: Conflicts and prospects. *Educational Horizons, 72*(3), 122–130.

Leming, J. S. (1997). Research and practice in character education: A historical perspective. In A. Molnar (Ed.), *The construction of children's character: Ninety-sixth yearbook of the National Society for the Study of Education* (pp. 31–44). Chicago: University of Chicago Press.

Leming, J. S. (2001). Historical and ideological perspectives on teaching moral and civic virtue. *International Journal of Social Education, 16*(1), 62–76.

Leming, J. S., Henricks-Smith, A., & Antis, J. (1997, March). *An evaluation of the Heartwood Institute's "An Ethics Curriculum for Children."* Paper presented at the annual meeting of the American Educational Research Association, Chicago.

L'Herrou, P. (1998, January 11). *Self-reliance and Ralph Waldo Emerson.* Sermon given at The Unitarian Universalist Church of Arlington, VA. Retrieved December 3, 2000, from http://www.uucava.org/sermons/Emerson0.htm

Lickona, T. (1991). *Educating for character: How our schools can teach respect and responsibility.* New York: Bantam.

Lickona, T. (1993). The return of character education. *Educational Leadership, 51*(3). Retrieved from http://www.ascd.org/readingroom/edlead/9311/lickona.html

Lickona, T. (1997). Educating for character: A comprehensive approach. In A. Molnar (Ed.), *The construction of children's character: Ninety-sixth yearbook of the National Society for the Study of Education* (pp. 45–62). Chicago: University of Chicago Press.

Lickona, T., Schaps, E., & Lewis, C. (2003). *CEP's eleven principles of character education.* Washington, DC: Character Education Partnership. Retrieved from http://www. character.org/principles/files/ElevenPrinciples.pdf

Lieberman, J. (2000, August, 16). Speech to the Democratic Convention. Retrieved September 1, 2001, from http://www.aardvarknews.com/lieberman.htm

Lindblom, K., & Dunn, P. A. (2003). The roles of rhetoric in constructions and reconstructions of disability. *Rhetoric Review, 22*(2), 167–174.

Lindemans, M. F. (1997). Golden Age. *Encyclopedia Mythica.* Retrieved November 1, 2004, from http://www.pantheon.org/articles/g/golden-age.html

Litwack, L. F. (1961). *North of slavery: The Negro in the free states.* Chicago: University of Chicago Press.

Locke, E. A. (2001). Keep the SAT to promote fairness, objectivity and individualism. Retrieved August 20, 2002, from http://aynrand.org/medialink/sat.shtml

Lockwood, A. L. (1985/1986, December/January). Keeping them in the courtyard: A response to Wynne. *Educational Leadership, 10,* 9–10.

Lockwood, A. L. (1991). Character education: The ten percent solution. *Social Education, 55,* 246–48.

Lockwood, A. L. (1997). What is character education? In A. Molnar (Ed.), *The construction of children's character: Ninety-sixth yearbook of the National Society for the Study of Education* (pp. 174–185). Chicago: University of Chicago Press.

Lockwood, A. L. (2001). Blending civic decency and civic literacy. *International Journal of Social Education, 16*(1), 55–61.

Loewen, J. W. (1996). *Lies my teacher told me: Everything your American history textbook got wrong.* New York: Simon and Schuster.

Loewen, J. W. (1999). *Lies across America: What our historic sites get wrong.* New York: The New Press.

Luria, A. R. (1979). *The making of mind: A personal account of Soviet psychology.* M. Cole (Trans.). Cambridge, MA: Harvard University Press.

Luxemburg, R. (1918, December). The socialisation of society. D. Hollis (Trans.). Retrieved December 1, 2000, from http://www.marxists.org/archive/luxembur/works/1918/12 20.htm

Macherey, P. (1978). *A theory of literary production.* G. Wall (Trans.). London: Routledge.

MacLean, M. S., & Mohr, M. M. (1999). *Teacher-researchers at work.* Berkeley, CA: National Writing Project.

MacMillan, M. (2002). *Paris 1919: Six months that changed the world.* New York: Random House.

Madison, A. (1996). *Depression in school: A student's trial.* Bloomington, IN: Indiana University Center for Adolescent and Family Studies. Retrieved October 20, 2001, from http://education.indiana.edu/cas/tt/v3i2/v3i2toc.html

Males, M. (2001). Drug war scapegoats teens, overlooks boomers' abuse. *The Atlanta Constitution,* A21, February 9.

Malone, D. (1981). *The sage of Monticello*. Boston: Little, Brown and Company.

Mapp, A. J., Jr. (1991) *Thomas Jefferson: Passionate pilgrim*. Lanham, MD: Madison Books.

Marshall, J. D., Smagorinsky, P., & Smith, M. W. (1995). *The language of interpretation: Patterns of discourse in discussions of literature*. NCTE Research Report No. 27. Urbana, IL: National Council of Teachers of English.

Marshall, J. D., & Smith, J. (1997). Teaching as we're taught: The university's role in the education of English teachers. *English Education, 29*, 246–267.

Marx, K. (1867). *Das capital: Kritik der politischen oekonomie*. Hamburg, New York: O. Meissner; L. W. Schmidt.

Marx, K., & Engel, F. (1848/1998). *The Communist manifesto*. New York: Oxford University Press.

Maxwell, B. (2004). Southerners dwindling in the New South. *St. Petersburg Times* [online] p. 17A. Retrieved February 5, 2004 from http://www.sptimes.com/2004/02/04/columns/southerners_dwindling.shtml

McCarthy, C. (1991). Multicultural approaches to racial inequality in the United States. *Oxford Review of Education, 17*, 301–316. Retrieved September 1, 2004 from http://www.smh.com. au/articles/ 2004/03/07/1078594236177.html?from=storyrhs

McMahon, E. M., & Karamanski, T. J. (2002). *Time and the river: A history of the Saint Croix*. Omaha, NE: Midwest Regional Office, National Park Service, United States Department of the Interior. Retrieved January 15, 2003, from http://www.nps.gov/sacn/hrs/hrst.htm

McPherson, C. B. (1962). *The political theory of possesive individualism*. Oxford, U. K.: Clarendon Press.

Mosier, R. (1965). *Making the American mind: Social and Moral ideas in the McGuffy readers*. New York: Russell and Russell.

Meier, D., & Schwarz, P. (1995). Central Park East Secondary School. In M. W. Apple & J. A. Beane (Eds.), *Democratic schools* (pp. 29–30). Alexandria, VA: Association for Supervision and Curriculum Development.

Metress, S., & Rajner, R. A. (1996). *The great starvation: An Irish holocaust*. Stony Point, NY: American Ireland Education Foundation.

Miller, M. (1992). *Cultural diversity and conflict in American agriculture: Intergenerational responses of a Wisconsin farm family*. Unpublished master's thesis, University of Wisconsin-Madison Institute for Environmental Studies. Retrieved March 1, 2001 from http://www.uwex.edu/ces.susag/thesis/

Molnar, A. (1997). Editor's preface. In A. Molnar (Ed.), *The construction of children's character: Ninety-sixth yearbook of the National Society for the Study of Education* (pp. ix–x). Chicago: University of Chicago Press.

Mondale, C. (1998). *The history of the Upper Midwest: An overview*. Retrieved September 28, 2002, from http://memory.loc.gov/ammem/umhtml/umessay8.html

Moore, M. (2003). *Dude, where's my country?* New York: Warner Books.

Mosier, R. (1965). *Making the American mind: Social and moral ideas in the McGuffy Readers*. New York: Russell and Russell.

Murray, C. A. (2001, February 6). Prole models. *The Wall Street Journal,*. A18

Murray, G. S. (1998). *American children's literature and the construction of childhood*. New York: Twayne Publishers.

You can tell a man's character by what he turns up when offered a job, his nose or his sleeves.

—Unknown

Nash, G. B. (1974). *Red, white, and black: The peoples of early America*. Englewood Cliffs, NJ: Prentice-Hall.

Nash, R. J. (1997). *Answering the "virtuecrats": A moral conversation on character education*. New York: Teachers College Press.

National Center for Education Statistics. (1996, September). *Youth indicators 1996: Trends in the well-being of American youth* (NCES96-027). Retrieved July 20, 2004 from http://nces.ed.gov/pu6598/yi

National Commission on Excellence in Education. (1983, April). *A nation at risk: The imperative for educational reform*. Retrieved November 1, 2004, from http://www.ed.gov/pubs/NatAtRisk/

National Education Association. (1997). *Estimates of school statistics*. Washington, DC: Author. Retrieved November 3, 2002, from www.nea.org/publiced/edstats/estim97.pdf

National Reading Panel. (2000). *Report of the National Reading Panel: Teaching children to read*. Washington, DC: National Institute of Child Health and Human Development. Retrieved October 20, 2002, from http://www.nichd.nih.gov/publications/nrppubskey.cfm

Nickell, P., & Field, S. L. (2001). Elementary character education: Local perspectives, echoed voices. *The International Journal of Social Education, 16*(1), 1–17.

Noddings, N. (1984). *Caring: A feminine approach to ethics and moral education*. Los Angeles: University of California Press.

Noddings, N. (1992). *The challenge to care in schools: An alternative approach to education*. New York: Teachers College Press.

Noddings, N. (1997). Character education and community. In A. Molnar (Ed.), *The construction of children's character: Ninety-sixth yearbook of the National Society for the Study of Education* (pp. 1–16). Chicago: University of Chicago Press.

Noddings, N. (2002). *Educating moral people: A caring alternative to character education*. New York: Teachers College Press.

Nystrand, M. (1986). *The structure of written communication: Studies in reciprocity between writers and readers*. Orlando, FL: Academic Press.

Nystrand, M., Greene, S., & Wiemelt, J. (1993). Where did composition studies come from? An intellectual history. *Written Communication, 10*, 267–333.

Ostergren, R. (1987). Environment, culture and community. In S. E. Jørgensen, L. Scheving, & N. P. Stilling (Eds.), *From Scandinavia to America* (pp. 176–198). Odense, Denmark: Odense University Press.

Owens, B. (2000). *A year after Columbine: How do we heal a wounded culture?* Heritage Lecture #662. Washington, DC: The Heritage Foundation. Retrieved September 5, 2001, from http://www.heritage.org/Research/Family/hl662.cfm

Padover, S. K. (1952). *Jefferson: A great American's life and ideas*. New York: Harcourt, Brace & World.

Parents of Teenagers (1992, February/March). College a cheating haven. Author, 5.

Paul, R. (n.d.). *A draft statement of principles*. Dillon Beach, CA: The National Council for Excellence in Critical Thinking. Retrieved November 1, 2004, from http://www.criticalthinking.org/ncect.html

Peck, M. S. (1990). *The different drum*. New York: Arrow Books.

Perry, W. G. (1968). *Forms of intellectual and ethical development in the college years: A scheme*. New York: Holt, Rinehart and Winston.

Characters do not change. Opinions alter, but characters are only developed.

—Benjamin Disraeli

Pert, C. B. (1997). *Molecules of emotion: Why you feel the way you feel.* New York: Scribner.

Peterson, M. D. (1960). *The Jefferson image in the American mind.* New York: Oxford University Press.

Pfaff, T. (1993). *Paths of the people: The Ojibwe in the Chippewa Valley.* Eau Claire, WI: Chippewa Valley Museum Press.

Piaget, J. (1932). *The moral judgment of the child.* London: Routledge.

Piaget, J. (1950). *The psychology of intelligence.* London: Routledge.

Pinkerton, J. (2001, July). Happy birthday to America's air and space museum. New America Foundation. Retrieved August 15, 2001, from http://www.newamerica. net/index.cfm?pg=article&pubID=498

Pitts, L. (2001, March 10). Take aim at suburbia to address school assaults. *Miami Herald.* Retrieved March 11, 2001, from http://www.miami.com/herald/content/features/columnists/pitts/digdocs/050376.htm

Powell, J. (2003). *FDR's folly: How Roosevelt and his New Deal prolonged the Great Depression.* New York: Crown Forum.

Power, F. C. (2002). Building democratic community: A radical approach to moral education. In W. Damon (Ed.), *Bringing in a new era in character education* (pp. 129–148). Stanford, CA: Hoover Press.

Power, F. C., Higgins A., & Kohlberg, L. (1989). *Lawrence Kohlberg's approach to moral education.* New York: Columbia University Press.

Price, J. (1999). *Flight maps: Adventures with nature in modern America.* New York: Basic Books.

Purpel, D. E. (1997). The politics of character education. In A. Molnar (Ed.), *The construction of children's character: Ninety-sixth yearbook of the National Society for the Study of Education* (pp. 140–153). Chicago: University of Chicago Press.

Rappaport, M., & Carolla, B. (1999). *Hellish lives for children with severe mental illness and their families: Landmark national survey finds families forced to relinquish custody, lose children to juvenile jails due to pervasive lack of basic treatments, services, educational programs.* Chicago, IL: National Alliance for the Mentally Ill.

Ravitch, D. (2000). *Left back: A century of failed school reforms.* New York, Simon & Schuster.

Reasoner, R. (n.d.). *The true meaning of self-esteem.* Retrieved February 14, 2005 from http://www.self-esteem-ndse.org/whatisselfesteem.shtml

Ricoeur, P. (1983). *Time and narrative* (Vol. 1), K. McLaughlin & D. Pellauer (Trans.). Chicago: University of Chicago Press.

Robertson, P. (2003, July 17). Pat Robertson on the Supreme Court: "Time for a change." The Christian Broadcast Network. Retrieved November 1, 2004, from http://chr.org/about/pressrelease.030717.asp

Rogers, A. (2002, November 28). From the chairman of the committee on the Baptist faith and message. Retrieved from www.sbc.net/bfm/bfmchairman.asp

Root, S. L. (1977, January). The New Realism—Some personal reflections. *Language Arts, 54,* 19–24.

Rothstein, M. (1988). Farmer movements and organization: Numbers, gains, and losses. *Agricultural History, 12*(3), 161–181.

Rousmaniere, K. (n.d.) Education section statement. In R. Sisson & C. Zacher (Eds.), *The encyclopedia of the Midwest.* Retrieved February 11, 2003, from http://www.allmidwest.org/encyclo/education/statement.html

Rousseau, J.-J. (1979). *Emile: Or, on education.* A. Bloom (Trans.). New York: Basic Books.

Ryan, F. J., Sweeder, J. J., & Bednar, M. R. (2001). *Drowning in a clear pool: Cultural narcissism, technology, and character education.* New York: Peter Lang.

Ryan, K. (1993). Mining the values in the curriculum. *Educational Leadership, 51*(3), 16–18.

Ryan, K. (1996). Character education in the United States. *Journal for a Just and Caring Education, 2*(1), 75–84.

Ryan, K. (2003). Character education: Our high schools' missing link. *Education Week.* Retrieved February 5, 2003, from http://www.edweek.org/ew/ewstory. cfm?slug=20ryan.h22&keywords=Kevin%20Ryan

Ryan, K., Bohlin, K. E., & Thayer, J. D. (1996). *Character education manifesto.* Boston: The Center for the Advancement of Ethics and Character. Retrieved January 20, 2005 from http://www.bu.edu/education/caec/files/manifesto.htm

Ryan, K., & McLean, G. F. (Eds.) (1987). Character development in schools and beyond. New York: Praeger.

Ryan, W. (1971). *Blaming the victim.* New York: Pantheon Books.

Sackett, H. (1997). Chemistry or character? In A. Molnar (Ed.), *The construction of children's character: Ninety-sixth yearbook of the National Society for the Study of Education* (pp. 110–119). Chicago: University of Chicago Press.

Sarason, S. B. (1971). *The culture of the school and the problem of change.* Boston: Allyn and Bacon.

Schaps, E., Battistich, V., & Solomon, D. (1997). School as a caring community: A key to character education. In A. Molnar (Ed.), *The construction of children's character: Ninety-sixth yearbook of the National Society for the Study of Education* (pp. 127–139). Chicago: University of Chicago Press.

Schlesinger, A. M. (1992). *The disuniting of America.* New York: W. W. Norton.

Schloffand, L. M. (1996). *"And prairie dogs weren't kosher": Jewish women in the upper Midwest since 1855.* St. Paul, MN: Minnesota Historical Society.

Schubert, W. H. (1997). Character education from four perspectives on curriculum. In A. Molnar (Ed.), *The construction of children's character: Ninety-sixth yearbook of the National Society for the Study of Education* (pp. 17–30). Chicago: University of Chicago Press.

Schwartz, A. J. (2002). Transmitting moral wisdom in an age of the autonomous self. In W. Damon (Ed.), *Bringing in a new era in character education* (pp. 1–21). Stanford, CA: Hoover Press.

Scribner, S., & Tobach, E. (1997). *Mind and social practice: Selected writings of Sylvia Scribner.* New York: Cambridge University Press.

Segel, E. (1986). "As the twig is bent ...": Gender and childhood. In E. Flynn & P. Schweickert (Eds.), *Gender and reading* (pp. 165–186). Baltimore, MD: Johns Hopkins University Press.

Character Education in 4-H Livestock Projects

Cutting corners to win is not the right way. Everyone involved in youth livestock projects (members, parents, leaders, agents) should be aware of the damage that can be done to these programs by unethical behavior. Here is a list of materials available that deals with this important topic.

A Question of Ethics (20 minutes)

A Step Beyond a Question of Ethics (23 minutes)

The Line in the Sand (16 minutes)

—Virginia 4-H

Senate Resolution 176—Proclaiming "National Character Counts Week." Retrieved June 10, 2002 from www.charactercounts.org/senate_proclaim_cc!week 1998./htm

Sense of Congress Regarding Good Character. Retrieved November 5, 2004, from www.ed.gov/policy/highered/leg/heu98/

Shannon, C. E., & Weaver, W. (1949). *A mathematical model of communication.* Urbana, IL: University of Illinois Press.

Shaughnessy, M. P. (1977). *Errors and expectations: A guide for the teacher of basic writing.* New York: Oxford University Press.

Silva, D. Y., & Gimbert, B. G. (2001). Character education and teacher inquiry: A promising partnership for enhancing children's classrooms. *The International Journal of Social Education, 16*(1), 18–33.

Six Pillars of Character, The. Retrieved January 20, 2005 from www.character counts.org/defsix.htm

Skertic, M., & Dedman, B. (2001, March 18). Chicago clinging to color lines. *Chicago Sun-Times.* Retrieved March 20, 2001, from http://mumford1.dyndns.org/cen2000/newspdf/suntimes1.pdf

Skousen, W. C. (1958/2003). *The naked communist.* New York: Buccaneer Books.

Smagorinsky, P. (1992). Towards a civic education in a multicultural society: Ethical problems in teaching literpature. *English Education, 24,* 212–228.

Smagorinsky, P. (1995a). The social construction of data: Methodological problems of investigating learning in the zone of proximal development. *Review of Educational Research, 65,* 191–212.

Smagorinsky, P. (1995b). New canons, new problems: Promoting a sense of kinship among students of diversity. In B. A. Goebel & J. Hall (Eds.), *Teaching a "new canon"?: Students, teachers, and texts in the college literature classroom* (pp. 48–64). Urbana, IL: National Council of Teachers of English.

Smagorinsky, P. (1999, June). *The character of character education.* Invited talk presented at The English Teacher as Curriculum Maker in the Face of Reform Conference, Chicago.

Smagorinsky, P. (2000). Reflecting on character education through literary themes. *English Journal, 89*(5), 64–69.

Smagorinsky, P. (2001a). If meaning is constructed, what is it made from? Toward a cultural theory of reading. *Review of Educational Research, 71,* 133–169.

Smagorinsky, P. (2001b, November). *Character as relationship.* Presentation made at the annual fall meeting of the National Council of Teachers of English, Baltimore.

Smagorinsky, P. (2002a). Rethinking character education. In P. Smagorinsky, *Teaching English through principled practice* (pp. 302–317). Upper Saddle River, NJ: Merrill/Prentice Hall.

Smagorinsky, P. (2002b, October). *The American character: The story of the modern character education movement and how you can rewrite its sequel.* Keynote address presented at the 22nd annual Indiana Teachers of Writing fall conference, Indianapolis.

Smagorinsky, P. (2002c). *Teaching English through principled practice.* Upper Saddle River, NJ: Merrill/Prentice Hall.

> *The four cornerstones of character on which the structure of this nation was built are: Initiative, Imagination, Individuality and Independence.*
>
> *—Edward Rickenbacker*

Smagorinsky, P. (2004, May). *The discourse of character education*. Keynote address presented at the annual conference of the American Association for Applied Linguistics, Portland, OR.

Smagorinsky, P., Cook, L. S., & Johnson, T. S. (2003). The twisting path of concept development in learning to teach. *Teachers College Record, 105,* 1399–1436.

Smagorinsky, P., Cook, L. S., & Reed, P . (2005). The construction of meaning and identity in the composition and reading of an architectural text. *Reading Research Quarterly. 40*(1), 70–88.

Smagorinsky, P., Lakly, A., & Johnson, T. S. (2002). Acquiescence, accommodation, and resistance in learning to teach within a prescribed curriculum. *English Education, 34,* 187–213.

Smagorinsky, P., & Taxel, J. (2002a, April). *Questions about character: An analysis of OERI-funded character education initiatives*. Paper presented at the annual meeting of the American Educational Research Association, New Orleans.

Smagorinsky, P., & Taxel, J. (2002b, November). *Character education: Why it's happening, where it comes from, what it is, and how it's implemented in U.S. schools*. Invited address presented at the annual fall meeting of the National Council of Teachers of English, Atlanta.

Smith, M. W., & Wilhelm, J. (2002). *"Reading don't fix no Chevys": Literacy in the lives of young men*. Portsmouth, NH: Heinemann.

Smitherman, G. (2000). *Talkin that talk: Language, culture, and education in African America*. New York: Routledge.

Sommers, C. H. (2002). How moral education is finding its way back into America's schools. In W. Damon (Ed.), *Bringing in a new era in character education* (pp. 23–41). Stanford, CA: Hoover Press.

Spears, A. K. (1998). African-American language use: Ideology and so-called obscenity. In S. S. Mufwene (Ed.), *African-American English: Structure, history, and use* (pp. 226–250). New York: Routledge.

Starr, L. (2000). The diversity bus: On the road to understanding. *Education World*. Retrieved June 26, 2001, from http://www.education-world.com/a curr/ curr227.shtml

State Historical Society of Iowa. (n.d.) *Prairie voices Iowa heritage curriculum: Annotated Iowa history timeline*. Retrieved April 2, 2003, from http://www.iowa history.org/education/heritagecurriculum/timeline/iowatimelinepage3.html

Stone, O. (Director). (1987). *Wall Street*. Hollywood, CA: Warner Studios.

Stotsky, S. (1999). *Losing our language: How multicultural classroom instruction is undermining our children's ability to read, write, and reason*. New York: The Free Press.

Suggs, E. (2001, March 11). Moore's Ford lynching. *Atlanta Journal-Constitution*, Section C, pp. 1, 4.

Sullivan, J. (2000, April 12). *Schoolhouse hype: Two years later*. Center on Juvenile and Criminal Justice. Retrieved November 1, 2004, from http://www.cjcj.org/pubs/ schoolhouse/shh2pr.html

Sumara, D., & Luce-Kapler, R. (1993). Action research as a writerly text: Locating co-labouring in collaboration. *International Journal of Educational Action Research, 1,* 387–396.

Every man has three characters—that which he exhibits, that which he has, and that which he thinks he has.

—*Alphonse Karr*

Sykes, C. J. (1992). *A nation of victims: The decay of the American character*. New York: St. Martin's Press.

Sykes, C. J. (1995). The reading wars. In C. J. Sykes, *Dumbing down our kids: Why America's children feel good about themselves but can't read, write, or add*. New York: St. Martin's Press. Retrieved July 15, 2002, from http://www.sntp.net/education/The Reading Wars.htm

Taxel, J. (1981). The outsiders of the American revolution: The selective tradition in children's fiction. *Interchange, 12*, 206–228.

Taxel, J. (1984). The American revolution in children's fiction: An analysis of historical meaning and narrative structure. *Curriculum Inquiry, 14*(1), 7–55.

Taxel, J. (1993). The politics of children's literature: Reflections on multiculturalism and Christopher Columbus. In V. J. Harris (Ed.), *Teaching multicultural literature in grades K–8* (pp. 1–36). Norwood, MA: Christopher-Gordon.

Taxel, J. (1997). Multicultural literature and the politics of reaction. *Teachers College Record, 98*, 417–448.

Taxel, J. (1999, November). American children's literature and the construction of childhood: A book review. *Reading Online*. Retrieved December 10, 2002, from http://www.readingonline.org/reviews/books/USchildlit.html

Taxel, J. (2002). Children's literature at the turn of the century: Toward a political economy of the publishing industry. *Research in the Teaching of English, 37*, 145–197.

Taylor, C. (1985). *Human agency and language: Philosophical papers 1*. New York: Cambridge University Press.

Taylor, J. M., Gilligan, C., & Sullivan, A. M. (1995). *Between voice and silence: Women and girls, race and relationship*. Cambridge, MA: Harvard University Press.

Tchudi, S. N., & Tchudi, S. J. (1991). *The English/language arts handbook: Classroom strategies for teachers*. Portsmouth, NH: Heinemann.

Tiberius, R. G. (n.d.). The why of teacher/student relationships. Retrieved November 7, 2003, from http://www.cte.umd.edu/library/podresourcepackets/ studentteacher/why.html

Tiberius, R. G., & Billson, J. M. (1991). The social context of teaching and learning. In R. J. Menges & M. D. Svinicki, (Eds.), *College teaching: From theory to practice*. San Francisco: Jossey-Bass.

Tighe, M. A. (1998). Character education + young adult literature = critical thinking skills. *ALAN Review, 26*(1). Retrieved May 3, 2001, from http://scholar.lib.vt.edu/ejournals/ALAN/fall98/tighe.html

Tillich, P. (1948). Martin Buber and Christian thought. *Commentary, 5*(6), 515–521.

Townsend, B. L. (2000). The disproportionate discipline of African American learners: Reducing school suspensions and expulsions. *Exceptional Children, 66*, 381–391.

Toynbee, A. J., & Royal Institute of International Affairs. (1934). *A study of history*. London: Oxford University Press.

Instead of saying that man is the creature of circumstance, it would be nearer the mark to say that man is the architect of circumstance. It is character which builds an existence out of circumstance. From the same materials one man builds palaces, another hovels; one warehouses, another villas; bricks and mortar are mortar and bricks until the architect can make them something else.

—Thomas Carlyle

> *There is no such thing as a "self-made" man. We are made up of thousands of others. Everyone who has ever done a kind deed for us, or spoken one word of encouragement to us, has entered into the make-up of our character and of our thoughts, as well as our success.*
>
> —George Matthew Adams

Truesdale, C. W. (1988). Introduction. In J. Agee, R. Blakely, & S. Welch (Eds.), *Stiller's pond: New fiction from the Upper Midwest* (pp. ix–xi). St. Paul, MN: New Rivers Press.

Truettner, W. (Ed.). (1991). *The West as America: Reinterpreting images of the frontier, 1820–1920.* Washington, DC: Smithsonian Institution Press.

Trump, D., & T. Schwartz (1988). *Trump: The art of the deal.* New York: Random House.

Tulviste, P. (1991). *The cultural-historical development of verbal thinking.* Commack, NY: Nova Science Publishers.

Turiel, E. (1983). *The development of social knowledge.* New York: Cambridge University Press.

Turiel, E. (2002). *The culture of morality: Social development, context, and conflict.* New York: Cambridge University Press.

Tyack, D. B. (1974). *The one best system: A history of American urban education.* Cambridge, MA: Harvard University Press.

Tyack, D. B., & Hansot, E. (1982). *Managers of virtue: Public school leadership in America 1820–1980.* New York: Basic Books.

Tyler, R. (1949). *Basic principles of curriculum and instruction.* Chicago: University of Chicago Press.

United Methodist Church. (2000). *The Book of Discipline.* Nashville, TN: The United Methodist Publishing House.

U.S. Census Bureau (2000). *Poverty in the United States 1999.* Washington, DC: Author. Retrieved September 17, 2001, from http://www.census.gov/ftp/pub/hhes/www/povty99.html

Vidal, G. (2003). *Inventing a nation: Washington, Adams, Jefferson.* New Haven, CT: Yale University Press.

USA Study Guide. (2002). *Life in the USA.* Author. Retrieved November 1, 2004, from http://www.usastudyguide.com/lifeinusa.htm

Vygotsky, L. S. (1987). Thinking and speech. In L. S. Vygotsky, *Collected works* (vol. 1, pp. 39–285). R. Rieber & A. Carton (Eds.), N. Minick (Trans.). New York: Plenum.

Wagner, R. E. (2001). In praise of capitalist morality. Retrieved February 23, 2002, from http://mason.gmu.edu/~rwagner/capitalist.pdf

Walker, L. J. (2002). Moral exemplarity. In W. Damon (Ed.), *Bringing in a new era in character education* (pp. 65–83). Stanford, CA: Hoover Press.

Weber, M., T. (1930). *The Protestant ethic and the spirit of capitalism.* London: G. Allen & Unwin.

> *The little troubles and worries of life may be as stumbling blocks in our way, or we may make them stepping-stones to a nobler character and to Heaven. Troubles are often the tools by which God fashions us for better things.*
>
> —Henry Ward Beecher

Weedon, C. (1987). *Feminist practice and poststructural theory*. Oxford, UK: Blackwell.

Wefald, J. (1971). *A voice of protest: Norwegian-Americans in American politics*. Northfield, MN: Norwegian-American Historical Society.

Werner, E. E., & Smith, R. S. (1992). *Overcoming the odds*. Ithaca, NY: Cornell University Press.

Wertsch, J. V. (1991). *Voices of the mind: A sociocultural approach to mediated action*. Cambridge, MA: Harvard University Press.

Wertsch, J. V. (1999). Revising Russian history. *Written Communication, 16*, 267–295.

Wertsch, J. V. (2000). Vygotsky's two minds on the nature of meaning. In C. D. Lee & P. Smagorinsky (Eds.), *Vygotskian perspectives on literacy research: Constructing meaning through collaborative inquiry* (pp. 19–30). New York: Cambridge University Press.

West, J., Weaver, D., & Rowland, R. (1992). Expectations and evocations: Encountering Columbus through Literature. *The New Advocate, 5*, 247–263.

Wexler, P. (1982). Structure, text, and subject: A critical sociology of school knowledge. In M. Apple (Ed.), *Cultural and economic reproduction in education: Essays on class, ideology, and the state* (pp. 275–303). New York: Routledge.

White, B. (2002). Caring and the teaching of English. *Research in the Teaching of English, 37*, 295–328

Wilke, G., & Wagner, K. (1981). Family and household: Social structures in a German village between the two World Wars. In R. J. Evans & W. R. Lee (Eds.), *The German family: Essays on the social history of the family in nineteenth and twentieth-century Germany* (pp. 120–147). Totowa, NJ: Croom Helm.

Will, G. F. (2004). For Bush, it's game time. *The Washington Post*. Sunday, February 8, p. B07. Retrieved February 10, 2004, from http://www.washingtonpost.com/wp-dyn/articles/A20482-2004Feb6.html

Williams, R. (1977). *Marxism and literature*. New York: Oxford University Press.

Williams, T. (2004). Sludge slinging. *Audubon, 106*(2), 22–31. Retrieved October 24, 2004, from http://magazine.audubon.org/incite/incite0405.html

World Health Organization (2001). *The world health report 2001: Mental health: New understanding, new hope*. Geneva, Switzerland: Author.

Wynne, E. A. (1979). The declining character of American youth. *American Educator, 3*, 6–9.

Wynne, E. A. (1985/1986, December/January). The great tradition in education: Transmitting moral values. *Educational Leadership, 43*, 4–9.

Wynne, E. A. (1989). Transmitting traditional values in contemporary schools. In L. B. Nucci (Ed.), *Moral development and character education: A dialogue* (pp. 19–36). Berkeley, CA: McCutchan.

Wynne, E. A. (1997). For-character education. In A. Molnar (Ed.), *The construction of children's character: Ninety-sixth yearbook of the National Society for the Study of Education* (pp. 63–76). Chicago: University of Chicago Press.

Author Index

A

Abu-Lughod, L., 150
Ackerman, J. M., 190
Adair, J. G.
Addington, A. H., 344
Aiken, T.-C. T., 246
Allington, R. L., 74
Alperovitz, G., 329
Antis, J., 210
Apple, M. W., 13, 35, 83, 119, 215
Applebee, A. N., 74, 319
Aristotle, 117, 196
Aronowitz, S., 90
Atlas, J., 333
Auster, L., 333

B

Bahlmueller, C. F., 109
Bakhtin, M. M., 61, 63, 64, 322
Balfour, C., 246
Ball, A. F., 78, 354
Barnes, D. R., 48
Bates, D., 98
Batson, A. B., 166
Battistich, V., 50
Beach, R. W., 49, 343, 344
Bednar, M. R., 19, 20, 23, 24, 25, 41
Beinart, P., 249
Belenky, M. F., 52, 80
Bell, D. A., 326

Bellah, R. N., 333
Bennett, W. J., 44, 46, 49, 75, 334, 335, 348
Benninga, J. S., 44
Berger, P. L., 215
Berkowitz, M. W., 52, 53, 58
Berliner, D. C., 74, 90
Bernstein, R., 34, 35, 95, 110
Biddle, B. J., 74, 90
Billson, J. M., 112
Bloom, A. D., 74, 111
Bloom, B. S., 354
Bogenschneider, K., 115
Bohlin, K. E., 39
Bookman, J., 329
Booth, W. C., 315
Bork, R. H., 34, 337
Bowles, S., 25, 83, 120
Boyle, C. C., 156
Bransford, J., 344
Branson, M., 267
Buber, M., 329
Bunting, E., 209
Burke, K., 63, 64
Bush, G. W., 130
Butler, J., 62
Butts, R. F., 106
Byrne, J. H., 97

C

Callahan, D., 79, 94

Carolla, B., 340
Catalano, R. F., 289
Charen, M., 98
Clark, K. B., 327
Clark, M., 327
Clarke, C., 95
Clifton, J., 56
Clinchy, B., 52, 80
Clinton, H. R., 108
Clinton, W. J., 11
Cobb, J. C., 153
Cole, M., 149, 194, 213, 325, 327, 338, 350,
Coleman, K., 152, 153
Conason, J., 34
Cook, L. S., 174, 269, 315, 340, 341
Cope, B., 35
Coser, L., 352
Cotton, R., 90
Covey, S. R., 193, 206
Craik, F., 354
Cummins, J., 55
Curti, M., 44

D

Dahrendorf, R., 352
Damasio, A. R., 341
Damon, W., 42
Davis, K. S., 4
Dedman, B., 246
Deloria, V., 56
Delpit, V., 80, 214,
DeVries, R., 48
Dewey, J., 279
Dittohead Deb, 333
Donald, D., 159
Doris, J. M., 21
Doudna, E. G., 256
Dowling, J., 340
D'Souza, D., 35, 74, 110, 317,
Dunn, P. A., 26

E

Eckert, P., 83, 119, 121, 133, 214, 216, 277
Ehle, J., 153
Elazar, D. J., 245
Ellington, L., 38
Ellis, J., 129
Emerson, R. W., 332

Engel, F., 330
Espelage, D. L., 41

F

Fahnestock, J., 65
Fairclough, N., 62
Fecho, B., 302
Field, S. L., 24, 58, 256
Finn, C., 198
Foner, E., 36
Foote, S., 71
Franken, A., 34, 333
Fregier, H. A., 82
Freidel, F. B., 4
Freire, P., 48
Friedman, M., 100, 331
Friedman, R. D., 100

G

Gallagher, M., 76
Gay, G., 51, 54, 55
Gee, J. P., 13, 61, 62, 63, 94, 213, 215
Gibson, S. R., 157
Gilbert, S., 22
Gilligan, C., 29, 52, 338
Gimbert, B. G., 302
Gintis, H., 25, 83
Giroux, H., 90
Giroux, H. A., 83, 272
Glaser, B. G., 14
Goldberger, N., 52
Goody, E., 325
Green, S., 18
Griffin, L. J., 151
Gross, M. L., 74

H

Hansot, E., 25
Hartshorne, H., 46, 48, 49, 58, 132
Hawkins, J. D., 289
Haynes, J. E., 330
Heath, S. B., 214
Henricks-Smith, A., 210
Henry, W., 95
Herbert, W., 40, 324
Herrnstein, R. J., 326
Hersh, S. M., 351
Higgins, A., 29
Higham, J., 26

Hillocks, G., 344
Hirsch, E. D., 38, 48, 95, 104, 111
Huff, D., 355
Hunt, P., 337
Hunter, J. D., 19, 22, 23, 24, 25, 27, 28, 30, 31, 33, 34, 38, 116
Huynh, C.,

I

Imse, A., 340
Isaacson, W., 78

J

Jacobs, D. T., 55, 56, 57, 59, 314, 327, 346,
Jacobs-Spencer, J., 55, 56, 57, 59, 314, 327, 346,
Jamison, K. R., 340
Johnson, H. B., 246
Johnson, H. C., 55
Johnson, T. S., 315, 344
John-Steiner, V. P., 317
Jones, S., 246
Jubera, D., 151

K

Kalantzis, M., 35
Karamanski, T. J., 248
Kaya, 84
Kelly, R. G., 314
Kilpatrick, W., 40, 328
Klee, M. B., 38
Knoblauch, C. H., 18
Koch, A., 104
Kochman, T., 214
Kohn, A., 37, 44, 45, 48, 50, 51, 53
Kohlberg, L., 28, 29, 338,
Kristeva, J., 61
Krueger, V., 80
Kuhn, T. S., 352

L

Lakly, A., 344
Lakoff, G., 34, 38, 116
Lancto, C., 337
Lasch, C., 251

Lather, P. A., 80
Lee, A., 62
Lee, C. D., 354
Leming, J. S., 23, 24, 25, 27, 30, 37, 38, 41, 48, 49, 54, 58, 59, 210
Lewis, C., 183, 193
L'Herrou, P., 332
Lickona, T., 20, 21, 28, 37, 39, 40, 41, 42, 44, 46, 47, 65, 66, 155, 170, 183, 193, 315, 326,
Lieberman, J., 93
Lindblom, K., 26
Lindemans, M. F., 97
Litwack, L. F., 101
Locke, E. A., 99
Lockhart, R., 354
Lockwood, A. L., 45, 46, 58, 66
Loewen, J. W., 64, 71, 76,
Luce-Kapler, R., 324
Luckman, T., 215
Luria, A. R., 341
Luxemburg, R., 26

M

Macherey, P., 71
MacLean, M. S., 302
MacMillan, M., 330
Madison, A., 340
Madsen, R., 333
Males, M., 38, 91
Malone, D., 103
Mapp, A. J., Jr., 103
Marshall, J. D., 344
Marx, K., 330
Maxwell, B., 151
May, M. A., 46, 48, 49, 58, 132
McCarthy, C., 111
McLean, G. F., 21
McMahon, E. M., 246
McPherson, C. B., 99
Meehan, T. M., 317
Meier, D., 52
Metress, S., 3
Miller, M., 254
Mohr, M. M., 302
Molnar, A., 45
Mondale, C., 256
Moore, M., 302, 333
Mosier, R., 24
Murray, C., 326
Murray, C. A., 220

Murray, G. S., 336, 337

N

Nash, G. B., 152, 153
Nash, R. J., 20, 22, 24
Nickell, P., 58, 256
Noddings, N., 22, 46, 50, 52, 54, 112, 339
Nystrand, M., 18, 344

O

Ostergren, R., 243
Owens, B., 97, 99

P

Padover, S. K., 104
Paul, R., 115
Peden, W. J., 104
Perry, W. G., 338
Pert, C. B., 341
Peterson, M. D., 113
Pfaff, T., 246
Piaget, J., 29, 352
Pinkerton, J., 36
Pitts, L., 19, 84
Pound, A., 340
Powell, J., 5
Power, F. C., 29, 54
Price, J., 338
Purpel, D. E., 21, 23, 25, 41, 42, 50, 59, 61

R

Rajner, R. A., 3
Rappaport, M., 340
Ravitch, D., 74, 95, 104
Reasoner, R., 114
Reed, P., 174, 269
Ricoeur, P., 64
Riley, D., 115
Robertson, P., 35
Rogers, A., 155
Root, S. L., 336
Rothstein, M., 251
Rousmaniere, K., 256
Rousseau, J. -J., 41

Rowland, R., 358
Rutledge, V. C., 38
Ryan, F. J., 19, 20, 23, 24, 25, 41
Ryan, K., 21, 39, 40, 42, 43, 46, 51, 77, 116, 349,
Ryan, W., 100, 333

S

Sackett, H., 92
Sarason, S. B., 344
Schaps, E., 50, 183, 193
Schlesinger, A. M., 95, 111
Schloffand, L. M., 245
Schubert, W. H., 51
Schwartz, A. J., 39, 321, 322
Schwarz, P., 53, 336
Scribner, S., 350
Secor, M., 65
Segel, E., 335
Shannon, C. E., 48
Sharpe, D.,
Shaughnessy, M. P., 353, 354
Shor, I.,
Silva, D. Y., 302
Skertic, M., 246
Skousen, W. C., 330
Smagorinsky, P., 6, 14, 21, 45, 47, 48, 49, 53, 92, 111, 174, 215, 269, 315, 323, 336, 344, 347, 349
Small, S., 115
Smith, J., 344
Smith, M. W., 94, 344
Smith, R. S., 115
Smitherman, G., 354
Solomon, D., 50
Sommers, C. H., 41, 320, 321, 324
Spears, A. K., 78
Starr, L., 110
Stone, O., 334
Stotsky, S., 74, 110, 317
Strauss, A. L., 14
Suggs, E., 199
Sullivan, A. M., 29
Sullivan, J., 91
Sullivan, W. M., 333
Sumara, D., 324
Swearer, S. M., 41
Sweeder, J. J., 19, 20, 23, 24, 25, 41
Swidler, A., 333

Sykes, C. J., 79, 193, 288, 324

T

Tarule, J. M., 52, 80
Taxel, J., 6, 14, 35, 37, 92, 215, 314, 336, 337, 347
Taylor, C., 319, 320
Taylor, J. M., 29
Tchudi, S. J., 324
Tchudi, S. N., 324
Thayer, J. D., 39
Thompson, A. B., 151
Tiberius, R. G., 112
Tighe, M. A., 336
Tillich, P., 329
Tipton, S. M., 333
Tobach, E., 350
Townsend, B. L., 214
Toynbee, A. J., 82
Truesdale, C. W., 246
Truettner, W., 36
Trump, D., 336
Tulviste, P., 350
Turiel, E., 20, 29, 45, 47, 48, 92, 98, 150
Tyack, D. B., 25, 73, 74
Tyler, R., 273

V

Vidal, G., 129

Vygotsky, L. S., 61, 66, 67, 315

W

Wagner, K., 254
Wagner, R. E., 27
Walker, L. J., 47
Weaver, D., 358
Weaver, W., 48
Weber, M. T., 25, 78
Weedon, C., 62
Wefald, J., 249, 333
Weiner, J., 36
Werner, E. E., 115
Wertsch, J. V., 64, 322
West, J., 358
Wexler, P., 134
White, B., 112
Wiemelt, J., 18
Wilhelm, J., 94
Wilke, G., 254
Will, G. F., 324
Williams, R., 120, 215
Williams, T., 347
Wynne, E. A., 22, 40, 43, 44, 46, 92

Z

Zan, B., 48

Subject Index

A

Abortion, 33–34, 119, 155, 163, 195
Academic achievement, 73–75, 132,
    190–191, 271–273
Academics
    improving, 259–262
African American(s), 98, 150
    community, 83, 85, 214–215
    discourse, 354
    discrimination against, 157–158, 199
    gay, 151
    English, 78
    families, 83
    oppressing, 47
    students, 91, 214
Agency (*see also* Student agency), 17, 106,
    114–115, 243, 249, 252
Aspen conference, 18, 126, 168,
    171–172, 177, 210
    participants, 141–142
At-risk behavior, 14, 123, 262–263, 275
Authoritarian
    approach to character education, 31,
        37, 43, 45, 89, 104, 279,
        317, 320, 323, 326
    relationships, 122
    roles, 42
    schools, 54
    social hierarchies, 282
    society, 89, 95–96, 116, 129, 132–133,
        145, 147, 160, 169–172,
        174, 198, 212–213, 216,
        219, 286, 290
Authority, 14, 43, 111, 213
    biblical, 161
    decentering of, 74, 95
    deference to, 25
    divine, 27
    lack of respect for, 92, 170, 248
    moral, 40–41, 155, 171, 184–185, 277
    questioning, 17, 65, 116–117, 337,
        350–353
    respect for, 96, 151, 218, 238, 351

B

Bill of Rights, 1
Boaz, David, 117–118
Bolshevism, 26–27
Book of Virtues, 75
B-ROW (Basic Right Over Wrong), Inc.,
    173–175
Burnouts, 83, 119, 133, 277
Bush, George, W., 11, 72, 75, 82, 98, 129,
    323–324, 350, 359
Butts, R. Freeman, 105–106

C

Capitalism, 4, 26, 52, 78–79, 100, 106,
    109, 193, 251, 328–331
Catcher in the Rye, The, 323

Center for the Advancement of Ethics
and Character, 171
Center for the 4th and 5th Rs, 169–171
Character
conception of, 8, 18, 38–44
deficiencies, 21
institutions addressing, 21–22
definition of, 17
good, 3, 17, 24, 27, 39–42, 51, 54,
57–58, 80, 84, 87, 94, 122,
133–134, 139, 144, 147,
168–169, 179–180,
194–196, 198, 202,
212–219, 232–237, 251,
261–267, 270, 280, 283,
315, 317, 324, 340, 342,
357, 359
national, 21
poor, 44, 49, 147
redefining, 356–359
six pillars of, 42, 67, 127, 143, 167,
274
strength of, 24
universally valid notion of, 42–43
Character Development Group, 175–176
Character education
among ancient Greeks, 22
assessing the effects of, 210–214,
297–306
complexes, 67–68, 315–318
concepts, 66–68, 315–318
in the curriculum, 202–204, 207–208
decline of, 28
didactic, 43–44, 46, 49
the gendering of, 338–339
history of, 8, 22–31
ideological nature of, 324–328
manifesto, 184–185
and mental health, 339–342
Native-American perspective of, 55
pilot project program, 137–138
process of, 208–210
pseudoconcepts, 67–68, 315–318
rationale for, 14
research on, 58–59
trivialization of, 345–346
Character Counts Week, 12, 126–127,
139–140
Charity, 22, 25, 49, 105, 253
Cheating, 22, 226
on exams, 11–12, 89–90, 237
rises in, 170

student, 182–183
as a way to get ahead, 54
website for, 290
Cherokee
language, 16
people, 152–154
philosophy, 302
Child
abuse, 16, 81
abusers, 117
development, 262
liberation, 336
rearing, 31, 107–110
Child-centered
approach, 324
classroom, 79
teaching, 95, 104
Children's literature, 334–337
Christians, 23, 64, 347
Church and state
separation of, 7, 35
Citizenship, 11, 42, 103–107, 279–280,
288, 292, 295–296, 302
Civic partnerships, 266–267
Civility, 17, 19–20, 23, 73, 96, 151,
159–160, 176, 264
Civil Rights, 5, 77, 96, 118, 154, 156,
326, 336, 351
CIVITAS project, 106
Class hierarchy, 83
Class-based morality (see Morality,
class-based)
Classroom(s)
child-centered, 79
democratic, 39
productivity, 210, 213
rules of behavior for, 43
security in, 112
strategies, 170–171
Clinton, Bill, 11, 40, 43, 77, 82, 96, 184,
215, 301, 359
Clinton, Hillary Rodham, 108, 276
Collectivism, 99, 109
Columbine tragedy, 41, 84, 99, 340
Commitment(s), 263, 332
to diversity, 306
to goals, 112, 119
inability to make, 20
to moral integrity, 115, 179–183, 234,
317
to social group, 289
to well-being, 112

Communitarianism, 106–107
Community, 103, 105, 107–109, 122,
    280–283, 328–331
  discourse of, 276–278, 280–292
  involvement, 137, 174, 189, 250, 270,
    277, 303–304
  leaders, 139
  of learners, 50
  service, 182, 237, 266–267
  values, 85
Community-based perspective, 45–46,
    243, 251–252, 327–328
Community of practice, 49–51
Compathy, 53
Conservative orientation, 5–6, 8, 31,
    34–38, 66–67, 100–101, 122,
    151–152, 317, 333, 358
Constructivist perspectives, 48–49, 302,
    348
Conventions, 45–46
Cooperative communities, 254–255
Core knowledge curriculum, 38
Core virtues program, 38
Corruption, 19, 44, 82
Courtesy, 20, 26, 96, 174, 189, 232–233
Creator, 66
  respect for, 61–62
Crisis in society, 37
Critical thinking, 115–116, 287, 289, 295
Cultural
  critics, 110–111
  decline, 82–83
  diversity, 26, 109
  identity, 104
  literacy, 267
  phenomena, 13
  preservation, 23
  traditionalists, 30
  transmission of values, 322
  values, 8, 37, 54, 105, 174
Culture(s), 5, 13, 66, 78, 85, 110–111,
    198, 254, 305, 342, 344,
    350–351, 359
  agrarian, 248, 255
  American Indian, 57
  corrupt, 147
  diverse, 25, 172, 283
  dominant, 120, 152, 155, 160, 220,
    246, 257, 313–315, 325
  Euro-American, 95
  national, 54
  nihilistic, 41

  peer, 42, 236
  postmodern, 155, 161
  preliterate, 22
  regional, 7, 18, 118, 150, 220, 249,
    313, 326
  role of, 40
  southern, 151
Culture wars, 8, 33–37, 311, 314, 317,
    319, 330, 333, 335, 337
Curricula, 15, 295–297
  reconstruction and interpretation of,
    343–345

D

Das Kapital, 329
Declaration of Independence, 4
Deep South,
  character education in, 8, 34
  conception of character in, 12
  cultural context of, 17–18
  discourses found in, 190–197
Democratic
  communities, 105
  personality, 24
  perspective, 38
  society, 51–52
Democracy, 105
Deviant behavior, 50
Dewey, John, 27, 48, 104–105, 320
Dialectic inquiry, 18
Dialogism, 61–65
Didactic, 147
  conception of character education, 40,
    43–44, 57, 67, 96, 122, 147,
    173, 195, 220
  instruction, 14–17, 29, 303, 335,
    351–354
Discipline, 35, 79, 96
  improving, 190, 211
  problems, 90, 94, 97, 132, 137, 189,
    270, 277–278, 339
  records, 219
Discourse, 13–16, 26, 33, 37, 59–66, 68,
    71–73
  of academic achievement, 73–75
  of authoritarian society, 95–96
  of citizenship, 106
  of class-based morality, 82–85
  of the good old days, 96–98
  of logical positivism, 85–87
  of moral absoluteness, 75–78

of Protestant work ethic, 78–82
of the virtuous individual, 99–101
of youth depravity, 90–94
Diversity, 26, 54, 109–111, 220, 245,
    283–285, 293, 306–307,
    316–317, 333, 357
Dole, Bob, 107–108
Domestic policy, 4
Dominant minority, 220
Dredd Scott vs. Sanford, 47
Drinking
    and driving, 85
    in school, 12
Drug abuse, 19

E

Economic
    democracy, 251
    distress, 16
    incentives, 108
    inequality, 50
    limitations, 121
Economics, 6
Economy, 13
    agrarian, 246
    capitalist, 5, 79, 329, 357
    free market, 50
    global, 151, 191
    modern, 150
    political, 31
    slave-based, 158–159, 330
    socialist, 26
Education, 255–256
Education World, 110
Empathy, 52–53, 177
Employment, 292, 317, 331
    of 16-and 17-year olds, 145–146
    abetting, 259, 264–265
    networks for, 266–267
    programs, 306
    of women, 253
English proficiency
    limited, 16–17
Entitlement, 20
Errors and Expectations, 353
Ethical
    aim for educators, 315
    attributes, 209
    awareness, 126

behavior, 46–48, 172–173
development, 307, 338
illiteracy, 170
values, 126, 139, 168–169, 179
Ethics, 64–65, 184–189
    code of, 57, 348
    egalitarian, 51
    traditional view of, 20
    universal, 76

F

Fairness, 29, 42, 75, 115, 126–127,
    131–132, 137–139, 144,
    179–180, 182, 189, 234–235,
    274, 283
Family
    breakdown of, 20
    decline of, 37
    first, 73, 80–81, 107, 128, 130–131,
        155, 168, 171, 194–195,
        215, 219, 276–277, 287
    involvement, 291, 303–304
FDR New Dealers, 4
Fight for the Water Hole, The, 36
Foreign policy, 4
Forrest, Nathan Bedford, 71
Franklin, Benjamin, 78, 293, 332
Fugitive Slave Act of 1850, 47
Fundamental traits, 76

G

Good old days, 74, 76, 83, 89, 95–99,
    115, 151, 155, 160, 199, 220,
    318, 335, 352, 356
Government, 81, 104, 183
    conception of character adopted by,
        168
    funding by, 21
    German notion of, 249
    programs for employment, 264–265
    requirements for character education
        funding, 40
    Russian revolutionary, 330
    student, 183, 236
Grandparents, 81, 348
Gratification, 28, 63
    immediate, 20
Gun(s), 97

control laws, 85, 118
obtaining, 12

H

Heartwood Books, 186–187
Heartwood Institute, 172–173
Heritage, 4, 150–151, 306
   Baptist, 161–163
   civic, 64
   communitarian, 330
   Confederate, 156
   cultural, 51
   Southern, 72, 160
   United States, 59, 64
Hesternopothia, 97
Honesty, 25, 46, 64, 75, 90, 172, 174,
   179, 189, 202, 208–209, 218,
   273, 322, 346, 348
Hollywood
   perceived immorality of, 11
   vulgar images presented by, 93
Homosexuality, 33–34, 81, 155, 162, 213,
   252, 326
Human nature, 22, 40–42, 57, 59, 76,
   203, 320
Hypocrisy, 52, 345

I

Ideology, 14, 35, 62–63, 87, 220, 283,
   325–328
   communist, 26
   conservative, 100, 321
   of OERI RFP, 306
   progressive, 345
   of southern states, 134
   of a text, 71
   of the United States, 123
   of Upper Midwest, 106
Ideologies
   of character education movement, 61
   as represented through discourse,
      12–13
   of social action, 13
   through which character education is
      proposed, 1
Immigrants, 24–26, 105, 247–248
Immorality, 11, 19, 44

Individualism, 20, 56, 82, 99–100,
   332–333
Industrialisti, 250
Infant mortality, 16
   high, 15
Infanticide, 19
Integrity, 28, 58, 83, 90, 109, 114–116,
   123, 134, 172, 185, 218, 248,
   264, 322, 338
Intellectual traditions, 318–324
Interpretive wars, 36–37, 80
Intertextuality, 61–62, 65–66
Iowa Test of Basic Skills, 16

J

Jackson, Andrew, 77, 150, 153, 156, 251
Jackson, Janet, 19
Jefferson, Thomas, 24, 43, 77, 96,
   103–104, 113–114, 121, 151,
   264, 279
Jocks, 83–84, 119
Josephson Institute of Ethics, 11–12, 18
Journal of Character Education, 21
Journal of College and Character, 21
Journal of Research in Character Education,
   21
Juvenile
   delinquency, 197
   homicides, 91
   offenders, 16
Just Communities, 29

K

Kohlberg, Lawrence, 28–30, 47
Ku Klux Klan (KKK), 71, 154

L

La Follett, Robert, 5, 106, 250
Language, 110, 247
   of character, 43–44, 51
   derogatory, 110
   deterioration of, 170
   discourse as, 12
   obscene, 78
   role of, 319
   of therapy, 51, 116, 186
   whole, 79

Language Arts and Literature, 202
Les Misérables, 82
Liberal, 34
  approach, 122
  judges, 35
  political exiles, 249
  political orientation, 25–26, 119, 333, 358
  view of morals, 19
Liberalism, 52, 90, 109, 251
Libertarian view, 64, 100, 118
Lickona, Thomas, 20–21, 47, 75, 179–183
Loco parentis, 67, 108, 195, 287, 317
Logical positivism, 28, 73, 85–87, 196–197, 219, 278, 320
Low-income status, 16
Luxemborg, Rosa, 26–27

M

Males
  Black, 197
  domination, 325
  White, 30, 36, 76, 104, 355
Manners, 17, 24, 143
  Southern, 159–160, 164–165
McGuffy Readers, 25, 38
McREL's Dimensions model, 260–261
Media
  characterizations depicted in, 247
  corrupting influence of, 160
  derogatory imagery in, 110
  influence on students, 93
  multi-cultural influences through, 150
  public opinion expressed in, 71
  self-serving, 147
  sex in, 19
  sleaze in, 20
  violence in, 19
Mental health, 92, 262, 339–341
Minority, 278, 284–285
  children, 194
  cultural, 195, 215
  concerns, 317
  exclusion of (from judicial system), 157–158
  groups, 65
  involvement, 158
  population, 195, 220
  racial, 98
  representation, 157, 316

struggle of in U.S., 37
students, 16, 284
teachers, 326–327
youths, 90
Moral
  absoluteness, 29, 73, 75–78, 97, 128–132, 169, 173–174, 191–197, 273–279, 350–351
  behavior, 17, 27, 46, 346
  character, 7
  codes 45, 47, 76, 348
  crisis, 19, 59, 82
  decline, 19, 41, 50, 79–80
  development, 23, 30, 43, 113–114, 346
  dilemmas, 40, 47–49, 184, 192, 202, 348–349
  education, 19, 23, 26, 41, 44, 56, 75–76, 111, 335
  excellence, 28, 123
  theology, 28
  thinking, 6
Morality, 28–34, 51, 64–65, 73, 76, 194–195
  Christian, 25, 35
  class-based, 16, 81–85, 119, 132–133, 157, 159, 195–196, 212, 217, 277–278, 283–285, 316
  declining, 40, 64
  new, 76
  principles of, 6
  sexual, 20
  six stages of, 28–29
  traditional view of, 20
Morals
  declining, 92
  deterioration of, 21
  Southern, 165–166
  ultraliberal view of, 19–20
Mulitculturalism, 35–36, 39, 65, 95, 110–111

N

Narcissism, 20
Native American perspective, 38–39, 55, 80
Native Americans, 246, 284, 314–315, 327, 346–347, 357
Nature, 56
New Deal, 4–5
No Child Left Behind, 117–118

Northern Trails Area Education Agency, 260–261

O

OERI
character education curricula, 65, 68
funding proposals, 9, 68
Request for Proposals (RFP), 8, 18, 64, 67, 71–72, 75, 86–87, 102, 104, 112, 167–169, 173, 189, 220, 243, 269, 273–274, 281, 306–307, 325, 339, 348
congressional discussions surrounding, 128–131
discourses embedded in, 131–133
discourse stream that produced, 125–127
ideology of, 306
requirements of, 319
statutory origin of, 127–128
On the Duty of Civil Disobedience, 355
Orthodoxy, 8, 34, 37–38, 58, 93, 101, 317, 323, 335, 343, 349–358

P

Pan-Protestantism, 25
Parent involvement, 137, 189, 260, 267, 270, 276–278
Parental
instruction in virtue, 81
satisfaction, 212
Parents
absentee, 16
drug-addicted, 91
gay, 81
as moral educators of their children, 168, 171, 184–185, 194, 215
nurturing, 45
strict, 38–40, 116–117
Patriotism, 24, 174, 198, 350
Personalism, 41, 50
Pluralism, 109, 111, 155, 163, 306
Political
agendas, 4
correctness, 35, 74, 160, 165, 317, 358
exiles, 259
movements, 61, 248–252, 255
society, 100

stability, 120
Poor Richard's Almanac, 78
Popular culture, 90, 93–94, 130, 197–198, 326
Populism, 251
Poverty, 19, 50, 82, 85, 121, 131, 151, 156, 158–160, 220, 267, 331
guidelines, 16
Producer values, 25
Progressive, 5
Progressive period, 28
Progressivism, 34, 45, 95, 279, 323, 327
Prolepsis, 194
Protestant
civilization, 26
view, 252
work ethic, 25, 73, 78–80, 192–193, 269, 274–276, 283, 285, 292, 315, 357
Protestant Ethic and Spirit of Capitalism, The, 78
Public memorials, 71
Public schooling, 11, 20, 23, 35, 97, 189, 256, 326, 345
Puritan
schools, 23
traditions, 25
Puritanical notion, 79

R

Race, 24, 80, 110, 133, 156–159, 214, 216, 246, 274, 283, 303
Racism, 6, 77, 99, 101, 151, 157, 253
Reflective approach, 49
Relational analysis of schooling and culture, 13
Relationships, 111–113, 285–287
Relativism, 17, 19, 29, 46, 90, 155, 161, 171, 281, 350, 354, 357
Religion, 23, 57, 110, 154–157, 202, 252–253
rejection of, 27, 35
Resiliency, 115, 263–264, 287, 289, 298, 300–301
Resolutions, 18, 348, 359
Respect, 14, 37, 42–43, 47, 56, 58, 75, 96, 98, 104, 114, 126, 132, 143, 169, 172, 179–185, 189, 219, 356
for the creator, 61–62
declining, 20

for established institutions, 41
for parents, 23
Revisionism, 43
Revisionist wall texts, 36
Richter, Jean Paul., 24, 30
Roll of Thunder, Hear My Cry, 349
Romanticism, 100, 113, 287–288,
    319–320, 323–324
Roosevelt, Franklin, Delano,4–5, 321
Roosevelt, Theodore, 13, 132, 184, 342,
    350

S

Schooling, (*see also* Public schooling) 83
    authoritarian conceptions of, 198
    business-oriented approach to,
        198–199
    central goal of, 112
    comprehensive approach to, 180
    modern interpretation of, 358
    origins of US, 125
    political nature of, 13
    history of public (in US), 23–24
    role of, 64
Self-esteem, 31, 40, 43, 113–114,
    116–117, 134, 171, 184, 262,
    267, 292
Self-government, 54
Self-reliance, 332–333
Self-Reliance, 332, 350
Sex, 14, 34–35, 89, 114, 262, 337
    education, 180, 233
    extramarital, 123
    in the media, 19
    premarital, 275, 326
Six pillars of character (*see* Character, six
    pillars of)
Slaves, 47–48
Social construction of reality, 14
Social division of labor, 103, 119–121,
    132–133, 265, 291–293, 306,
    316–317
Socialism, 5, 27, 105, 109, 251, 329
Socio-economic status (SES), 183
    lower, 82, 84, 133, 265, 293
Southern
    Baptist Church, 81, 151, 154–158,
        161–163, 203
    heritage groups, 72
Spirituality, 23, 39, 57–58, 263–264
Stereotypes, 24, 150, 187, 253

Student agency, 103, 113–117, 264, 269,
    272, 275, 280, 282, 287–292
Student behavior, 219, 262, 271, 274,
    286, 300, 346
Study of History, A., 82
Substance abuse, 67, 91, 123, 130, 144,
    170
    preventing, 177, 259, 262–264
Supreme Court, 34–35
Sympathy, 27, 53, 222

T

Teacher-centered, 49
Teachers
    as caregivers, 170
    leaving the profession, 90, 96
    portrayed as inept, 43
    promoting good character, 39
Teaching Virtues: Building Character Across
    the Curriculum, 55
Teen
    birth rates (high), 16
    crime, 90
    drug use, 14
    pregnancy, 14, 130, 171, 174–175,
        194, 275–276
    violence, 14
Telos, 194
Ten Commandments, 7, 35, 43
Textbooks, 24, 327
Thoreau, Henry David, 19
Thug code, 82
Title I funding, 16, 261
Topoi, 65
Trust, 20, 52, 64, 182, 322
Trustworthiness, 42, 114, 126–127,
    131–132, 136–139, 143–144,
    169, 189, 193, 273–274
Truth, 34–35, 96, 155–156, 161–162,
    168–169, 173, 279, 315, 322,
    332
Truth, 250
Truthfulness, 26, 28, 51, 162, 185
Twain, Mark, 14
Työmies, 250

U

Upper Midwest
    character education in, 9, 34,
    conception of character in, 12

cultural context of, 17–18, 245–247
discourses found in 190–197
U.S. Constitution, 4, 35

V

Values, (*see also* Producer values) 14, 220,
    246, 264, 272–274, 281–282,
    287, 293, 295, 303–306, 315,
    321, 335–337, 342–343,
    349–358
  deterioration of, 21
  diverse, 273
  survey, 240
  traditional, 43–44
  of White Western males, 30
Violence, 11, 14, 20, 71, 92, 114,
    129–130, 139, 144, 174–175,
    336
  in the media, 19
  preventing, 167, 177, 259, 262–263
  in school, 84–85, 90, 99, 190
  students with records of, 16
  in the workplace, 94
Virtues, 42–43, 80–81, 90, 101, 112, 123,
    274, 281, 290, 292, 306–307,
    357–358
  civic, 127, 132, 137–138, 185
  development of, 144, 185
  industrial, 25
  of the Puritan commonwealth, 23
  religious, 28
  teaching, 55–56
  universal, 57–58
Virtues, The Book of, 75–76, 335
Virtuous individual, 200–201
Voices of the mind, 322

W

West as America: Reinterpreting Images
    of the Frontier, 1820–1920, 36
Why Johnny Can't Tell Right From Wrong,
    90
Wisconsin Idea, The, 106
Women
  Catholic, 252–253
  Jewish, 245
  moral superiority of, 338
  radical subjugation of, 111
  struggle of in U.S., 37
White middle-class, 29
Women's Rights Movement, 336
Work ethic, 121, 170, 215, 275
World War I
  character education following, 46
  United States' nativist response to, 26
  Western value structure following, 27

Y

Youth
  character deficiencies of, 21, 65
  depravity, 14, 81, 89–94, 101,
      128–130, 155, 170–171,
      194, 197–198, 275, 277
  drug culture, 65, 91
  errant, 39–44, 64, 89
  leaders, 126, 139
  low SES, 293
  moral decline of, 33, 67, 92
  uncivilized nature of, 40
  violence, 93, 169